Robert Nothhelfer
Financial Accounting

Robert Nothhelfer

Financial Accounting

Introduction to German GAAP with exercises

2nd Edition

DE GRUYTER

Sponsored by

EY Building a better
working world

ISBN 978-3-11-074412-5
e-ISBN (PDF) 978-3-11-074417-0
e-ISBN (EPUB) 978-3-11-074424-8

Library of Congress Control Number: 2022933834

Bibliographic information published by the Deutsche Nationalbibliothek
The Deutsche Nationalbibliothek lists this publication in the Deutsche Nationalbibliografie;
detailed bibliographic data are available on the internet at http://dnb.dnb.de.

© 2022 Walter de Gruyter GmbH, Berlin/Boston
Cover image: Gettyimages/AlexSecret
Typesetting: Integra Software Services Pvt. Ltd.
Printing and binding: CPI books GmbH, Leck

www.degruyter.com

Preface to the First Edition

Accounting is one of the core topics of any business administration study program. For most German companies German Generally Accepted Accounting Principles (GAAP) based on the Commercial Code are the relevant accounting standard, even if in times of globalization international accounting has become more frequent.

Thus, any German student of business administration needs to have a basic understanding of accounting according to German GAAP. But globalization pays its toll here as well: At Pforzheim University (and probably at other universities in Germany as well) we offer courses about German accounting in English to improve the language skills of our students. So far, we have done that without a textbook covering lecture topics in detail.

Globalization pays its toll in another way as well: Many German companies have subsidiaries in other countries. If these German parent companies must prepare consolidated financial statements according to the Commercial Code, the subsidiaries need to apply German GAAP. Typically, this is done by a detailed accounting guideline, which not only explains German GAAP to the extent necessary but also clarifies the specific recognition and measurement methods that must be applied. Nevertheless, for new employees in these foreign subsidiaries, a textbook explaining the basic concepts without going into too much detail might be helpful.

I tried to write a book that would appeal to both audiences: students learning about German GAAP in English and professionals looking for explanations when preparing data for consolidated financial statements. I hope I was able to strike the right balance between too much and too little detail so as not to overload the students while still being helpful for professionals.

With great diligence I have tried my best to eliminate any errors. If, despite my best efforts, you find any mistakes, inaccuracies, or omissions, or if you have suggestions for improvements, please let me know: robert.nothhelfer@hs-pforzheim.de

Robert Nothhelfer
Pforzheim, October 2017

https://doi.org/10.1515/9783110744170-202

Preface to the Second Edition

The positive reception of the first edition of this book gave me the opportunity to prepare a second edition. While references and some minor parts of the text have been updated, and some remaining errors eliminated, the big change is a complete translation of the parts of the German Commercial Code that are directly relevant for accounting.

In the "Additional Information" section you will find a synopsis of the German legal text and my translation of it. Thus, any student or professional can now go back to the original source when working out accounting problems.

Robert Nothhelfer
Pforzheim, July 2022

https://doi.org/10.1515/9783110744170-203

Contents

Part I: Financial statements according to German GAAP

Abbreviations

AktG	Aktiengesetz	Stock Corporation Act
AG	Aktiengesellschaft	Stock corporation
AO	Abgabenordnung	General Tax Code
Art.	Artikel	Article
DCGK	Deutscher Corporate Governance Kodex	German Corporate Governance Code
DRS	Deutscher Rechnungslegungs Standard	German Accounting Standard
DRSC	Deutsches Rechnungslegungs Standard Committee	German Accounting Standards Committee
EG/EC	Europäische Gemeinschaft	European Community
eK	eingetragener Kaufmann/-frau	registered merchant/businessperson
EStG	Einkommensteuergesetz	Income Tax Act
EU	Europäische Union	European Union
FIFO		First in, first out
GAAP	Grundsätze ordnungsmäßiger Buchführung	Generally Accepted Accounting Principles
GbR	Gesellschaft bürgerlichen Rechts	Civil Code company
GmbH	Gesellschaft mit beschränkter Haftung	Limited liability company
GmbHG	GmbH-Gesetz	Limited Liability Company Act
HGB	Handelsgesetzbuch	Commercial Code
IAS		International Accounting Standards
IASB		International Accounting Standards Board
IDW	Institut der deutschen Wirtschaftsprüfer	Institute of Chartered Public Accountants in Germany
IDW ERS	Entwurf einer Stellungnahme zur Rechnungslegung durch das Institut der deutschen Wirtschaftsprüfer	Draft version of an accounting statement of the Institute of Chartered Public Accountants in Germany
IDW RH	Rechnungslegungshinweis des Institut der deutschen Wirtschaftsprüfer	Accounting note of the Institute of Chartered Public Accountants in Germany
IDW RS	Stellungnahme zur Rechnungslegung durch das Institut der deutschen Wirtschaftsprüfer	Accounting statement of the Institute of Chartered Public Accountants in Germany
IFRS		International Financial Reporting Standards
IT	Vorsteuer	Input tax (paid VAT)
KG	Kommanditgesellschaft	Limited partnership
KGaA	Kommanditgesellschaft auf Aktien	Limited partnership with shares
LIFO		Last in, first out
oHG	Offene Handelsgesellschaft	General partnership
OCI		Other comprehensive income
PublG	Publizitätsgesetz	Disclosure Act
SE	Societas Europea	European stock company
sect.	Absatz	Section
sent.	Satz	Sentence
T€	Tausend Euro	Thousands of Euros
UG	Unternehmergesellschaft	Entrepreneurial company
UStG	Umsatzsteuergesetz	Value-Added Tax Act
VAT	Umsatzsteuer	Value-added tax

https://doi.org/10.1515/9783110744170-205

List of tables

https://doi.org/10.1515/9783110744170-206

List of figures

https://doi.org/10.1515/9783110744170-207

How to use this book

This book aims to provide an introduction to financial accounting based on German Generally Accepted Accounting Principles (GAAP). This is not a new topic; in fact, there are many good textbooks for students and even more advanced literature for scholars and professionals. Not surprisingly, since the topic is German GAAP, all such works are in German. To reach a larger community, this book was written in English.

Apart from Chapter 1, which presents a general overview, all other chapters focus on the specifics of German GAAP. General questions of financing or financial analysis that are closely related to some topics but not specific to German GAAP have been omitted.

Even if the book touches on many topics and explains many concepts, it represents a first introduction to the topic; it is impossible to sum up thousands of pages of commentary, notes, interpretations, and so forth in a short book. If deeper insights are required, a reference to the German literature is necessary. To allow for that, all legal texts and basic standard literature are referenced. All legal references refer to the Commercial Code (Handelsgesetzbuch HGB) unless stated otherwise.

Because the International Financial Reporting Standards (IFRS) are widely adopted across the world, the important differences between German GAAP and IFRS are highlighted at each topic.

There is a long-standing tradition in Germany whereby the commercial balance sheet (based on the Commercial Code) should be – at least to a large extent – identical to (or congruent with) the tax balance sheet. In recent years, conformity to this tradition has been relaxed, though it remains relevant. German tax law will be mentioned only insofar as it is necessary to understand commercial financial statements or common practices used in their preparation; the book does not provide a systematic overview of German corporate taxes.

Legislation referred to in this book is as of June 2021.

There are large three parts:
Part I explains the theory, starting with very basic concepts and concluding with consolidated financial statements. Students should start at the beginning and work through the different topics. Examples, but no specific exercises, are given.

Chapter 1 gives a brief introduction to financial accounting in general; readers with sufficient prior knowledge may skip this chapter.

Chapter 2 highlights the general approach to German GAAP, focusing on basic principles and methods used in the different specific regulations.

Chapter 3 provides a detailed explanation of individual financial statements, including their various elements, for example the balance sheet and income statement, and their contents, for example non-current assets and equity.

https://doi.org/10.1515/9783110744170-208

Chapter 4 continues the explanations with consolidated financial statements, focusing on consolidation procedures.

Part II is composed of exercises with solutions to the different topics explained in Part I. All exercises are categorized according to the complexity of the exercise:

– Knowledge: a reproduction of knowledge is necessary to complete this exercise.
– Knowledge/Application: a mere reproduction is not sufficient; the knowledge must be applied in a specific situation.
– Knowledge/Application/Transfer: not only does the knowledge need to be applied in a specific situation, but either different topics are combined or further analysis of the results or the concepts used is necessary.

The approximate amount of time necessary to complete each exercise is given; note that the assumption here is that the reader is ready to take the test; initially you will probably not be able to do the exercises in the indicated amount of time, but you should train to do so.

Chapter 5 provides exercises sorted by topics to get started or work through in parallel to the theoretical explanations. Solutions immediately follow the exercises.

Chapters 6 and 7 provide more complex case studies that combine different topics. To allow for a more exam-like training, Chapter 6 presents the exercises and Chapter 7 the solutions.

In **Part III**, Chapter 8 provides the legal texts in a two-column format. The left column shows the original (and binding) German text; the right column the translation to English.

Chapter 9 provides a glossary of the most important terms and their explanations.

Chapter 10 provides an English-to-German vocabulary of the most important terms. For many terms there is no single, clear translation from German to English; often British English and American English or British accounting and US accounting use different terms. I kept the translations as close as possible to the terms used in the International Financial Reporting Standards (IFRS).

Part I: **Financial statements according to German GAAP**

1 Introduction to accounting

Why is accounting necessary? Many students and professionals consider it boring, tedious, complex, or worse. So many laws and regulations, so many principles and methods – all sound similar, but are different. Why bother?

Imagine a businessman running a small business. He has no employees; he just works on his own. In a market economy, a business provides goods or services for other people, typically customers who pay for them. On the other hand, the businessman runs the business to provide a cash flow to cover his living expenses. When the businessman looks for new customers, an important question arises: What price should he charge for his goods or services? There are two perspectives on this question. The first is the marketing perspective and asks the question: How much are customers willing to pay? This is an important issue, but it is not the focus here. The other perspective is connected to the issue of how much does he need to charge to cover his business costs and to earn a decent living? Put another way: What living standard can he afford with this business?

The core intention of accounting is to answer these questions, to provide information about the financial performance of a business to its owners (or to management, if they are not the same). Other intentions have evolved over time.[1]

1.1 Purpose of accounting

1.1.1 The fundamental question and the fundamental equation

As mentioned earlier, the original purpose of accounting was to inform business owners about their financial performance. But what does financial performance mean? Financial performance means the value of the business that is available to the owner, which is usually money that can be spent by the owner, but it can also be in other forms of goods or rights.

But our businessman has more than just a bank account with a positive balance. Let us assume he provides consulting services for companies. For that he needs some equipment, so he buys some assets for example a computer, a mobile phone, and some software. He rents office space and buys some office furniture. Thus, he spends money and acquires other assets that have value. Perhaps one of his suppliers does not ask for cash payment but offers credit, which the businessman takes advantage of. Then he acquires some asset; he does not lose money (at least for now) but he does have a liability: He will eventually have to pay a certain amount of money to settle his purchase.

---

[1] Coenenberg et al., 2021 (1), p. 3.

https://doi.org/10.1515/9783110744170-001

This leads to the following fundamental accounting equation:[2]

$$\text{Net Assets} = \text{Assets} - \text{Liabilities}$$

The value that is available for the businessman are the net assets, that is all valuable items the business owns minus all obligations for future payments the business incurs. In accounting, net assets are also called (owner's) equity:

$$\text{Equity} = \text{Assets} - \text{Liabilities} \quad \text{or} \quad \text{Assets} = \text{Equity} + \text{Liabilities}$$

This fundamental equation gives the first important information to the owner of the business, and it must be satisfied all the time at a specific point in time; we return to this point later on.

Another important piece of information is change in equity. To analyze a change in equity, we need to look at a specific time period: At the beginning of this period there is a starting value, and at the end there is an ending value. If the ending value is higher than the starting value, equity increased; this is called *profit* because the value of the business increased. If the ending value is lower than the starting value, then equity decreased; this is called a *loss*.[3]

Example

The aforementioned businessman starts his business with €10,000 in cash. He purchases office equipment for a total of €6,000. Part of it, €4,000, he pays in cash; part of it, €2,000, he buys on credit. He provides services for €24,000, which is paid in cash, and has current expenses for rent and other items of €8,000, which he pays for in cash as well.

What is his financial position at the end of this period?

At the beginning, his equity stake in the business comes to €10,000.

Thus, we sum up his assets as follows (all figures in Euros):

Cash at the beginning	10,000
– purchases in cash	– 4,000
– current expenses	– 8,000
+ cash from services	24,000
= cash at end	22,000
+ purchased assets	6,000
= total assets	28,000

Applying the fundamental accounting equation

$$\text{Equity} = \text{Assets} - \text{Liabilities} = 28,000 - 2,000 = 26,000$$

---

2 Coenenberg et al., 2021 (1), p. 6.
    Weygandt et al., 2015, p. 12.
3 Neglecting the possibility of external changes of equity (capital increases or decreases) here for the moment.

we see that his equity (the value of his business) increased from €10,000 to €26,000, i.e. he made a profit of €16,000.

For simplicity, taxes on profit and depreciation are neglected in the example.

1.1.2 Financial and managerial accounting

The original idea of accounting was to inform the owner of a business about the business's financial situation. In 1494, Luca Pacioli, a Franciscan monk, made the first comprehensive presentation of double-entry bookkeeping. This is the method still used today in the vast majority of companies. In the following sixteenth and seventeenth centuries, it became common practice for businessmen to account for their transactions and to prepare financial statements, usually at the end of the year.[4]

The wider use and better understanding of accounting and, as a consequence, one's own financial position allowed people to develop more complex business models: Selling and purchasing on credit, the use of different forms of credit and insurance and, in consequence, the development of a financial sector with banks and insurance companies all occurred in parallel.

With these more complex business transactions, interdependencies grew: If a customer who purchased on credit becomes insolvent and can no longer fulfil his obligations, this may be not only his own problem, because he will remain impoverished and may face penalties for bankruptcy; it may become a problem for his supplier as well because he will lose part of his assets – the receivables of sales made on credit. In consequence – depending on the importance of the insolvent customer – the supplier may incur a loss as well or – even worse – become insolvent himself. Thus, creditworthiness and the ability to judge the creditworthiness of one's customers became more and more important. To reduce this risk and give creditors access to the necessary information, accounting procedures were made legally mandatory and financial statements had to be published for certain companies. King Louis XIV in 1674 issued the first French accounting law, the "Ordonnance de Commerce", and in 1861 the first German accounting law, "Allgemeines Deutsches Handelsgesetzbuch", was issued.[5]

Other parties wanted to use financial statements: the tax authorities to calculate income taxes, employees to be informed about their employers, and many other parties. All these different users have at least partially different interests in financial statements and focus on different information. Tab. 1.1 gives an overview as an example.

Because of the different interests of the various users (stakeholders), different forms of accounting were developed, described in what follows.[6]

---

4 Coenenberg et al., 2021 (1), p. 10.
5 Coenenberg et al., 2021 (1), p. 11.
6 Coenenberg et al., 2021 (2), p. 7.
  Weygandt et al., 2013, p. 5.

Tab. 1.1: Users of financial statements and their interests.[7]

User	Interest in financial statements
Management	– Show a high profit or growing business – Show a positive business in general – Earn a high bonus/variable payment
Employees	– Have a safe job – Earn a higher salary or bonus
Shareholders/owners	– Increase wealth – Earn higher dividends
Suppliers	– Receive payments on time/creditworthiness – Continue or expand business – Negotiate higher prices if profits of customers are high
Customers	– Receive reliable services, i.e. continuing business in the future – Negotiate lower prices if supplier profits are high
Competitors	– Know financial situation of competing companies – Draw conclusions for own company (financing, cost situation)
Banks	– Obtain repayment of all loans and credits, i.e. creditworthiness of customers – Increase business if creditworthiness is good
Government/tax authorities	– Increase tax basis – Establish a reliable basis for tax calculations
General public	– Create new jobs, pay existing jobs well – Know large employers and their importance

Financial accounting

Financial accounting is based on legal requirements and typically focuses on fulfilling the requirements of users that are outside of the company, which is why this type of accounting is also called external or statutory accounting or reporting. Typically, the financial statements that are the output of financial accounting are prepared once a year (for companies listed on a stock exchange, often quarterly) and then published so that every interested party can acquire the information.

Managerial accounting

Managerial accounting is not a legal requirement but an operational necessity that focuses on fulfilling the information needs of management and, partially, employees. Typically, this information is produced much more often than financial statements,

---

7 Bacher, p. 2.
   Coenenberg et al., 2021 (2), p. 6.

i.e. weekly or monthly (some key data even daily), to support the operational decisions of management. Usually, it not only incorporates actual data (that has occurred) but is supplemented or accompanied by budgeted or planned data. This information is in most cases treated as confidential and not published.

This book focuses on financial accounting and the preparation of financial statements.

1.1.3 Content of accounting/basic terms

So far the terms we have used have been more colloquial and not very precise. In what follows, we will distinguish and define important terms that will be used throughout the subsequent chapters.

Cash inflow and cash outflow

In its typical accounting meaning, cash comprises not only cash on hand but also bank accounts with a positive balance that represent short-term assets (often called cash and cash equivalents). A cash inflow is an increase in cash and cash equivalents, for example a customer pays for a delivery by cash or bank transfer. A cash outflow is a decrease in cash and cash equivalents, for example the company pays a supplier by cash or bank transfer.

Proceeds and expenditures

Whereas cash in- or outflows cause a change of the cash available, proceeds or expenditures represent a change in the net financial assets. Net financial assets are defined as cash (and cash equivalents)[8] plus receivables minus debt:[9]

   Cash
+ Receivables
− Debt
= **Net financial assets**

An increase in net financial assets is called *proceeds*, a decrease is called an *expenditure*.

---

8 To make it easier to read, *cash* denotes *cash and cash equivalents*.
9 Jung, p. 1028; Wöhe/Döring, p. 633.

Example

A company sells products to a customer. If the transaction is in cash, this is a cash inflow and represents proceeds because cash increases and receivables and debt are unchanged. If the company sells on credit, there are only proceeds: Receivables increase, but there is (so far) no change in the cash position.

Income and expense

A further distinction focuses on changes in net assets, i.e. all assets minus all liabilities:[10]

    All assets (cash, receivables, other current assets, non – current assets)

– All liabilities (debt and provisions)

= **Net assets (equity)**

An increase in net assets is called *income*, whereas a decrease is called an *expense*. This means there can be income or an expense that is not cash flow, proceeds or expenditures.

    Income and expense are the basis of financial accounting.

Example

A typical example is the depreciation of non-current assets: Cash flow and expenditures occur when assets are acquired (typically at the beginning). As the assets are used, usually their value decreases. This decrease in value is reflected in the depreciation of the assets, and a value adjustment is made, but there is no payment (for more details see Chapter 3.1.3.2.1).

Output/operating income and cost

Whereas income and expense reflect any change in net assets, output and cost focus on the operating processes of the company. Output/operating income is the value of goods produced and services performed in the course of normal operations. Costs are the measured use of goods and services for the normal operating procedures. Output and costs are the basis of cost accounting or managerial accounting.

    Some costs are identical to expenses: These are called *basic costs* or *operating expenses*. Expenses that are not costs are called *neutral expenses*. Costs that are not expenses are called *imputed costs*. Fig. 1.1 shows the differences in more detail.[11]

    The same logic can be applied to income and output.

---

10 Jung, p. 1028.
    Wöhe/Döring, p. 645.
11 Jung, p. 1028.
    Wöhe/Döring, p. 634.

TOTAL EXPENSES					
Neutral expenses			Operating expenses		
Non-operating	Non-period-related	(Extraordinary)	Basic costs	Measurement differences	Additional costs
				Imputed costs	
			TOTAL COSTS		

Fig. 1.1: Total expenses vs. total costs.

Neutral expenses can be further classified as follows:

-   **Non-operating expenses** do not focus on the purpose of the business but are nevertheless an expense (a decrease in net assets). For example, a company may donate money to a church or a political party. This is a cash outflow, an expenditure and an expense. It is not a cost, because the purpose of the company is not to donate to charity or for politics.
-   **Non-period-related** expenses result from events in prior periods, for example an additional tax payment for prior years due to a tax review.
-   **Extraordinary** expenses are rare (do not occur regularly or often) and extraordinary in amount, for example as a result of natural disasters or catastrophic fire damage. Since such expenses are rare and very high, they occur very seldom. They are put in brackets because, following the latest changes to German GAAP, extraordinary items are no longer reported in the income statement, only in notes.[12]

Imputed costs can be distinguished as follows:

-   **Measurement differences**: These costs are included in financial accounting, but with a different value.

---

[12] Note that the definition of *extraordinary* depends on the size and kind of business being reported. Imagine a large retail group with several thousand stores but only 100 central warehouses. If one of the stores burns down – even if damages are high – this will hardly be an extraordinary item because with several thousand stores something like this will happen now and then and the losses will not be extraordinarily high. In contrast, if one of the central warehouses burns down, damages will be much higher, and this is much more likely to be an extraordinary item.

Example

A typical example is depreciation: In financial accounting depreciation must be based on acquisition or production costs. This is the maximum amount possible according to German GAAP (acquisition or production cost as ceiling for the depreciation). For cost accounting, another approach would be reasonable: If increases in replacement costs are expected, i.e. prices on a replacement investment rise, it is reasonable to base the cost accounting on replacement costs because the costs may be used as a basis for price negotiations, and a commercially reasonable price should include expected price increases on one's own end (if acceptable to the counterparty).

- **Additional costs**: These are costs that are not included at all in financial accounting.

Example

An example is imputed salary: According to German law, the owner of a sole proprietorship or partnership receives no salary but a share of the profits. Nevertheless, he/she wants to earn a living from the business, so an imputed salary is included in the cost accounting to make sure these costs will be earned (if a profit is made).

1.2 Elements of financial statements

1.2.1 Balance sheet

After clarifying the basic accounting terms, let us return to the basic accounting equation:

$$Assets = Equity + Liabilities$$

As mentioned earlier, this equation must be fulfilled all the time at a specific point in time, i.e. it is balanced (a change in assets is reflected by a change in equity or liabilities). Furthermore, assets and liabilities are split into different categories, and the split is presented in two columns. This is called a balance sheet. The date for which the balance sheet is prepared is called the balance sheet date (also: closing date).[13]

The equity and liability side shows the future financial obligations (i.e. liabilities) and what is left for the owners of the business (i.e. equity). Usually, a company has future financial obligations if it has received financial funds or resources, for example if the company takes on a loan, it receives money today with the obligation

---

[13] Coenenberg et al., 2021 (2), p. 64.
    Weygandt et al., 2013, p. 24.

to repay the loan (and additional interest) in the future. Thus, the equity and liability side shows the source of financial funds and resources.

On the other hand, the asset side shows what the financial funds were used for, i.e. which assets were acquired. If some of the raised financial funds were not used, they are reported on the asset side as cash and cash equivalents.

Balance sheet (§ 247)

Use of funds		Source of funds	
	A. Non-current assets	A. Shareholder's equity (net assets)	
	B. Current assets	B. Provisions	
	C. Deferred expenses	C. Debt/payables	
		D. Deferred income	
	Total assets	**Total equity and liabilities**	

Fig. 1.2: Balance sheet.

This is the basic structure; the more detailed legal requirements are explained later (Chapter 3.1.1), as is the content of deferred items (Chapter 3.1.10.1).

1.2.2 Income statement and changes-in-equity statement

As explained earlier, an increase in equity is called a profit, whereas a decrease in equity is called a loss if it is not due to external changes such as additionally paid-in money or withdrawal of money. Being able to analyze the sources of profits or losses is very important for management. This is not possible with the balance sheet because there changes in equity are simply reported, i.e. you can see that you made a profit, but not why.

To make this analysis possible, all income and expense items are reported separately in the income statement (recall that we defined income as an increase in equity and expense as a decrease in equity). Line by line, different categories of income and expense are summed up to obtain the profit or loss in the reporting period, which then changes the equity.[14] Thus, the income statement is a subcategory (later we will call it a *subaccount* or *subledger*) of equity that is reported separately for clarity. Whereas the balance sheet is prepared for a specific point in time, i.e.

---

14 The different formats of an income statement will be explained later (Chapter 3.2).

the balance sheet date, the income statement covers a period of time. Typically, for financial accounting a year is used – the business year (also: financial year).[15]

The balance sheet and income statement are the mandatory parts of financial statements. Depending on the company's size, structure, legal forms or financing forms, other elements may be required.

The changes-in-equity statement explains all changes in equity, which includes the profit or loss in the period as well as any external changes or reclassifications within equity. The changes-in-equity statement is not mandatory for all companies according to German GAAP.[16]

1.2.3 Cash flow statement

Like the income statement, which explains internal changes in equity, the cash flow statement explains changes in cash and cash equivalents. Whereas the income statement is based on income and expenses, the cash flow statement is based on cash inflows and outflows. It makes it possible to analyze where cash is generated or used by calculating cash flow from operating activities, investing activities and financing activities.[17]

A cash flow statement is not mandatory for all companies under German GAAP.

1.2.4 Notes and management report

To be able to understand, interpret and analyze the balance sheet and income statement beyond the raw figures, additional information about the content of the financial statements and the way they are prepared is necessary. This information is given in the notes. Notes are not mandatory for all companies under German GAAP.[18]

Apart from the quantitative information in the balance sheet and income statement, a verbal description of the course of business during the reporting period and the situation at the closing date, as well as a forecast for the near future, might be helpful in terms of evaluating the situation of a company. This information is given

---

15 Coenenberg et al., 2021 (2), p. 71 and p. 106.
Weygandt et al., 2013, p. 22.
16 For further details see Chapter 4.3.
17 For further details see Chapter 3.4.
Coenenberg et al., 2021 (1), p. 817.
Weygandt et al., 2013, p. 25.
18 For further details see Chapter 3.3.

in a management report. A management report is not mandatory for all companies under German GAAP.[19]

1.3 Accounting procedures

1.3.1 Accounts, debiting, crediting

The financial statements as described earlier consist of summarized, aggregated information. Even small companies usually have several hundreds or thousands of transactions that need to be recorded. A direct entry in a balance sheet or income statement would be very confusing and time consuming. Therefore, accounts are used. An account is a summary of similar transactions. It has – as the balance sheet – two columns; the left column is the debit side, the right column is the credit side. This naming applies to the balance sheet as well.[20]

Debit		Account X	Credit
Transaction 1	A €	Transaction 3	X €
Transaction 2	B €	Transaction 4	Y €
...		...	
If the sum of all debit entries is larger than the sum of all credit entries		If the sum of all credit entries is larger than the sum of all debit entries	
→ **debit balance**		→ **credit balance**	

Fig. 1.3: Accounts and balances.

In the balance sheet in Fig. 1.2 the assets are recorded in the left column, i.e. on the debit side. Thus, an increase (or a first recognition) of an asset is always recorded as a debit entry in the left column of an account. A decrease or disposal of an asset is then recorded on the right side, i.e. as a credit entry.

---

19 For further details see Chapter 3.5.
20 Coenenberg et al., 2021 (2), p. 95.
   Weygandt et al., 2013, p. 54.

Example

A company buys a new machine for €10,000 cash. This results in a debit entry of €10,000 in the account "machinery" because the value of the available machinery increases by the purchase amount. On the other hand, cash – also an asset – decreases because €10,000 are spent. Thus, a credit entry in the "cash" account must be made.

An entry on the debit side of an account is called *debiting*, and an entry on the credit side is called *crediting*.

As shown in Fig. 1.2, equity and liabilities are recorded in the right column, the credit side. Therefore, an increase in equity or liabilities is a credit entry, whereas a decrease is a debit entry.

If the sum of all debit entries is larger than all credit entries at a specific point in time, this account is said to have a *debit balance*; if the opposite is true, it is called a *credit balance* (Fig. 1.3). Therefore, asset accounts (e.g. "machinery" or "raw materials") typically have a debit balance at year end, whereas equity and liability accounts (e.g. "bank loans" or "trade payables") typically have a credit balance.

Recall the definition of income as an increase in equity. As increases in equity are recorded as a credit entry, any income is recorded as a credit entry on an account. In consequence, an expense is recorded as a debit entry because it reduces equity. Therefore, income accounts typically have a credit balance at year end and expense accounts have typically a debit balance (Tab. 1.2).[21]

Tab. 1.2: Accounting rules.

Debit	Account X	Credit
Increase in assets	Decrease in assets	
Decrease in equity or liabilities	Increase in equity or liabilities	
Expenses	Income	

1.3.2 Journalizing and posting

The basic accounting equation

$$\text{Assets} = \text{Equity} + \text{Liabilities}$$

21 Coenenberg et al., 2021 (2), p. 97.
    Weygandt et al., 2013, p. 55.

must be satisfied at all times.[22] That is why any transaction that is recorded in an accounting system has at least one debit entry and one credit entry, and the sum of all debit entries must equal the sum of all credit entries. This procedure is called **journalizing** and is the reason why this form of accounting is called double-entry bookkeeping: A journal entry always has (at least) one debit and (at least) one credit entry, and they must balance.

All transactions are first recorded in chronological order; the documentation of all transactions is called a **journal**. If all journal entries are correct (i.e. balanced), then the system of double-entry bookkeeping is retained. The journal itself helps to detect errors because it allows for searches by transaction or date.[23]

Example[24]

Transaction 1

A company purchases new raw materials for €10,000 on credit; the delivery and the invoice are received on 15 May 15 20X1.

Journal entry

Debit raw materials	10,000	Increase in asset account
Credit trade payables	10,000	Increase in liability account

Transaction 2

The same day, the company sells products for €15,000 in cash.[25]

Journal entry

Debit cash	15,000	Increase in asset account
Credit sales revenue	15,000	Increase in income account

Transaction 3

The same day, the company receives an invoice from its tax consultant in the amount of €2,500.

Journal entry

Debit consulting expenses	2,500	Increase in expense account
Credit trade payables	2,500	Increase in liability account

The journal entries for this day (assuming no other transactions) look as follows (Tab. 1.3):

---

22 The reason is that any asset that is recognized by a company gives rise to claims on the company by either the shareholders (equity) or a third party (liabilities), and vice versa.
23 Jung, p. 1095.
    Weygandt et al., 2013, p. 60.
24 The examples neglect VAT for simplicity.
25 The cost of goods sold is neglected here.

Tab. 1.3: Example of a journal.

Date	Account	Transaction	Debit	Credit
15/5/20X1	Raw materials	Purchase of . . .	10,000	
15/5/20X1	Trade payables			10,000
15/5/20X1	Cash	Sale of . . .	15,000	
15/5/20X1	Sales revenue			15,000
15/5/20X1	Consulting expenses	Invoice . . .	2,500	
15/5/20X1	Trade payables			2,500

For analyzing the financial situation of a company, the journal is not really helpful because many different kinds of transactions are mixed in, just as they occurred. To allow for an analysis, organization by kind of transaction is needed, i.e. identical or similar transactions are grouped together. This is done by transferring the individual entries of the journal to accounts. This is called **posting**. All accounts of the balance sheet and income statement together are called the **general ledger**.[26]

Example

The general ledger accounts of the earlier journal entries look as follows (Tabs. 1.4 to 1.8):

Tab. 1.4: General ledger accounts (1).

Debit (€)	Raw materials	Credit (€)
Transaction 1	10,000	

Tab. 1.5: General ledger accounts (2).

Debit (€)	Cash	Credit (€)
Transaction 2	15,000	

Tab. 1.6: General ledger accounts (3).

Debit (€)	Consulting expenses	Credit (€)
Transaction 3	2,500	

---

26 There are special ledgers as well which give further detail on general ledger accounts, e.g. for non-current assets there exists typically a special ledger in which each asset is reported on a separate account; the general ledger account trade receivables has a special ledger in which each debtor is reported on a separate account, etc.; Coenenberg et al., 2021 (2), p. 121; Weygandt et al., 2013, p. 60.

Tab. 1.7: General ledger accounts (4).

Debit (€)	Trade payables		Credit (€)
	Transaction 1		10,000
	Transaction 3		2,500

Tab. 1.8: General ledger accounts (5).

Debit (€)	Sales revenue		Credit (€)
	Transaction 2		15,000

As can be seen, the sorting by accounts gives a much better overview for analytical purposes than the journal does; for example you can easily see that the company must pay a total of €12,500 (balance of the account "trade payables").

A modern information-technology-based accounting system does the posting automatically together with the journal entry; journal and accounts/ledgers represent just two different perspectives on the same transactions. In earlier times, companies kept two large books, which had to be kept manually. First, all transactions were entered in the journal to make sure that all transactions were recorded. Then, in a second step, the journal entries had to be copied to the second book, the general ledger. This basic logic still works today, even if it is no longer technically necessary.

1.3.3 Opening and closing of accounts

We have already looked at two accounting procedures, journalizing and posting, but to complete an accounting cycle others are necessary:

1. Opening of accounts
   Unless a company was just founded and therefore has no history, it has done business in the past and recorded transactions in its financial statements. The first step in a new reporting period is to transfer the closing values of the prior period to the new period. This called the *opening of accounts*.[27]

---

[27] Technically, these are journal entries as well, i.e. the opening balance sheet has a 1:1 relation to the closing balance sheet of the prior period. Then each opening balance sheet item is transferred with a journal entry to the corresponding account: the account is opened. The result is a completely empty opening balance if and when all items are transferred to the accounts.

Income and expense accounts do not have an opening balance because they are used to report changes in the reporting period, so that the profit of the previous year is not redistributed to the income and expense accounts but remains in equity.

2. Journalizing and posting

   As described earlier, individual transactions are journalized and then posted to the accounts.

3. Closing of accounts

   At the end of the reporting period, all accounts must be closed. Closing an account means that the balance of the account is transferred to the closing balance sheet or the account that is used for closing (see subsequent discussion). In consequence, the account that was closed is balanced and its balance is an additional item in the closing balance sheet.[28]

   Not all accounts are closed directly to the closing balance sheet; there is a hierarchy of accounts (Tab. 1.9):

Tab. 1.9: Closing accounts.

Account to be closed	Closing account
Income	Income statement
Expense	Income statement
Income statement	Equity
Asset accounts	Balance sheet
Equity accounts	Balance sheet
Liability accounts	Balance sheet
Subledger accounts	Corresponding general ledger account

Thus, the closing balance sheet is the final summary of all transactions that had to be recorded during the reporting period, even if the reporting was done by a hierarchy of accounts and, thus, multiple closing entries.

A **trial balance** is a preparatory balance that is produced during the reporting period, typically for control purposes.

The total procedures in overview are as follows:

---

28 Coenenberg et al., 2021 (2), p. 101.
   Weygandt et al., 2013, p. 170.

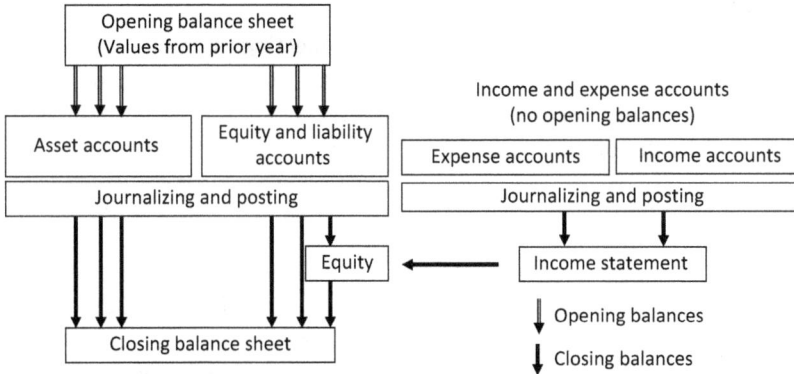

Fig. 1.4: Overview of accounting procedures.

1.3.4 Specific topics of double-entry accounting

1.3.4.1 Taxes

Taxes are reported in financial statements in several ways.[29]

Taxes as part of operating transactions

Depending on the national tax laws, some transactions may result in tax payments by the company; these taxes are then reported as "other taxes", as operating expenses,[30] or as asset acquisition costs (Chapter 2.4.2.1). Examples in Germany are a land acquisition tax, if a piece of land is acquired (part of acquisition cost), or an insurance tax (operating expense).

Taxes based on profit

Some taxes are typically based on company profits, i.e. the higher the profit, the higher the tax bill. These also represent a company expense; however, they are reported not as operating expenses but in a separate line, "income taxes". In Germany, there is a trade tax for all companies and a corporate tax for corporations that are reported as income taxes.[31]

---

29 Coenenberg et al., 2021 (2), p. 273.
30 The legal structure of the income statement requires a separate reporting, whereas a widespread practice is a reporting as other operating expenses; see *Beck'scher Bilanzkommentar*, § 275, no. 167.
31 In Germany, the income tax that must be paid on the profit of a partnership must be paid (and borne) by the partner, not by the partnership.

Taxes as transitory item

For some taxes, a company may be responsible for collecting the money and transferring it to the tax authorities, but tax law intends that somebody else should bear the payment in the end (e.g. customers, employees).

Two typical examples of this in Germany are described in what follows.

Payroll tax[32]

Salaries and wages of employees are taxed under a payroll tax: Employees pay the tax, i.e. it represents a reduction of the gross salary to the net salary. But the employer is responsible for the payment, meaning the employer pays only the net salary to the employee, withholds the payroll tax and pays it to the tax authorities. The expense of the employer is the gross salary, but a part of it is transferred directly to the tax authorities. As a consequence, the payroll tax is not an expense of the employer but of the employee and the employer reports only a payroll tax liability (if it is not paid yet).

Value-added tax[33]

Whereas a payroll tax occurs only in the context of salary payments, a value-added tax (VAT) is much more pervasive, and the way it is handled is a bit more complex. The following refers to the VAT in Germany.

In general, all business transactions are liable to a VAT; the general rate is 19%. There are exceptions that are not subject to a VAT, for example medical services, interest payments, wages and salaries, and there is a reduced rate of 7% for some goods or services like books and newspapers, (basic) food and flowers.[34]

The VAT is borne by the purchaser (at least in a legal sense), i.e. the VAT is added to the net sales price, but the seller is responsible for transferring it to the tax authorities. To make sure multiple production stages do not influence the tax burden of the VAT paid, an input tax (IT) is deductible from the VAT charged, i.e. the company transfers VAT only on the value added by its own operations, not on acquired values (e.g. purchased raw materials or services).

---

32 Coenenberg et al., 2021 (2), p. 176.
33 Coenenberg et al., 2021 (2), p. 144.
34 This can be only exemplary here. All exceptions and reduced rates are a highly complex matter of definitions and distinctions. The legal basis is § 4 and § 12 UStG.

Example 1

Sale of goods on credit for €10,000 net:

Debit trade receivables	11,900	
Credit sales revenue		10,000
VAT		1,900

Customers must pay the full (gross) amount of €11,900, but the seller can keep only €10,000 as sales revenue (income) and must transfer €1,900 to the tax authorities; that is why the VAT account is a liability account.

Example 2

Purchase of raw materials on credit for €10,000 net:

debit raw materials	10,000	
IT	1,900	
Credit trade payables		11,900

The purchaser must pay the seller €11,900 but can deduct the paid VAT (i.e. the input tax, or IT); the acquisition cost of the materials are only the net value of €10,000 because the €1,900 can be collected from the tax authorities again. That is why the IT account is a receivable account.

At the end of each month, (charged) VAT and (paid) IT are netted to determine whether there is a net payable or receivable to or from the tax authorities.

Any advance payments for transactions that are subject to VAT are themselves subject to the VAT.

Example

A supplier must charge the regular VAT of 19%. Say a company wants to order products and the supplier asks for an advance payment. Then the advance payment (not only the final invoiced amount) is also subject to the VAT.

1.3.4.2 Received price reductions[35]

Often prices change following an initial transaction. There are various reasons for this: cash discounts, additional bonus payments or rebates because of complaints, for example.

From an accounting perspective, any received price reduction is a correction of the initial transaction. If the initial transaction includes IT, the IT must be corrected as well.

---

35 Coenenberg et al., 2021 (2), p. 148.

Example

Let us continue with the earlier example: a purchase of raw materials on credit for €10,000 net; payment is made by deducting a cash discount of 2%:

Journal entry of purchase (as earlier)

Debit raw materials	10,000	
IT	1,900	
Credit trade payables		11,900

Journal entry of payment with 2% cash discount:

Debit trade payables	11,900	
Credit bank		11,662
Raw materials		200
IT		38

The trade payable is completely settled by the payment and, thus, debited. However, in effect, the full amount was not paid: the bank is credited with only €11,662. The difference of €238 in gross value must be split into two components, acquisition cost of raw materials (to be reduced because less is paid) and IT (to be reduced as well because less is paid)[36].

1.3.4.3 Granted price reductions[37]

The same logic applies to the sales side, just the converse. Price changes may occur basically for the same reasons: trade or cash discounts, additional bonus payments or rebates.

If this occurs, the initial transaction must be corrected, meaning the sales revenue or another income entry is reduced and the (charged) VAT is reduced.

Example

To continue with the example from earlier, goods are sold on credit for €10,000 net, and the customer pays with a cash discount of 1%.

Journal entry of sale (as earlier):

Debit trade receivables	11,900	
Credit sales revenue		10,000
VAT		1,900

Journal entry of payment with a cash discount of 1%:

---

36 For a general definition of acquisition costs see Chapter 2.4.2.1.
37 Coenenberg et al., 2021 (2), p. 154.

Debit bank	11,781	
Sales revenue	100	
VAT	19	
Credit trade receivables		11,900

The trade receivables are settled by the payment and thus completely credited (reversed). Because the whole amount is not collected, the initial transaction must be adjusted for the difference, i.e. the cash discount. Again, it must be split (like the initial transaction) into a correction of the sales revenue (net value) and a correction of the (charged) VAT.

2 Introduction to German accounting

2.1 Legal framework

2.1.1 Legal regulations

Because Germany is a member of the European Union (EU), German accounting is harmonized with European accounting rules, meaning the EU sets up a framework that must be applied by the member states but leaves certain decisions up to the member states. EU directives are not directly applicable law but must be transferred and enacted by the member states. Thus, German accounting will be explained, not the EU framework, keeping in mind that German accounting complies with the EU framework.

Starting with the transferral of the fourth, seventh and eighth directives of the council of the European Communities (EC) directives into German law, the "Accounting Directive Act" (Bilanzrichtliniengesetz) was enacted in 1985. It included a summary of accounting rules in one law, the "Commercial Code" (Handelsgesetzbuch HGB); until then the accounting rules for companies were spread out over many laws with partially different content.

The third book of the Commercial Code comprises all accounting rules that are applicable to all kinds of commercial businesses as long as the business itself requires, because of its nature or size, a commercial organization (§ 1 sect. 2).

In addition, additional laws specify accounting requirements for the following issues:
- specific large companies: sole proprietorships and partnerships considered "large" must satisfy the more detailed requirements of corporations regarding preparation and publication of financial statements ("Disclosure Act", Publizitätsgesetz PublG; for details see Chapter 2.1.2.2);
- specific legal forms, for example limited liability companies (GmbH-Gesetz) or stock companies (Aktiengesetz);
- specific industries, for example banks and financial institutions (Kreditwesengesetz) or insurance companies (Versicherungsaufsichtsgesetz).

For consolidated financial statements, the application of the International Financial Reporting Standards (IFRS) can be mandatory (see Chapter 4.2). Whereas the IFRS are prepared by a private organization, the International Accounting Standards Board (IASB), they are adopted by the EU and transferred directly to applicable law by a specific procedure called a *comitology procedure* (or endorsement).[1]

Apart from the formally codified law, there exist soft laws, which are formally accepted but usually include recommendations or interpretations of legal rules.

---

[1] Coenenberg et al., 2021 (1), p. 58.

https://doi.org/10.1515/9783110744170-002

Relevant for accounting are the "German Accounting Standards" (Deutsche Rechnungslegungsstandards DRS), which are issued by the German Accounting Standards Committee (Deutsches Rechnungslegungs Standards Committee DRSC) and interpret the requirements for consolidated financial statements. The "German Corporate Governance Code" (Deutscher Corporate Governance Kodex DCGK) focuses on the governance of listed stock companies.

In addition, the decisions of supreme courts should be taken into account because they can give guidance on specific situations.

Finally, if the application of a specific rule is unclear, the GAAP[2] (Grundsätze ordnungsmäßiger Buchführung) as underlying principles and other legal commentaries and best practices can be used. Of particular importance are statements of the "Institute of Chartered Public Accountants in Germany" (Institut der deutschen Wirtschaftsprüfer IDW) because chartered accountants need to follow these statements.

Here is an overview:

	Not directly applicable: Directives of the European Union
code law	Directly applicable: **Commercial Code (Handelsgesetzbuch HGB)** For large proprietorships and partnerships: Publicity Act (Publizitätsgesetz PublG) For specific legal forms: e.g. Aktiengesetz (AktG), GmbH-Gesetz (GmbHG) For specific industries: e.g. Kreditwesengesetz, Versicherungsaufsichtsgesetz For consolidated financial statements: International Financial Reporting Standards
soft law	German Accounting Standards (DRS) German Corporate Governance Code (DCGK)
court decisions	Decisions of a supreme court in Germany
best practices & interpretations	Generally Accepted Accounting Principles (GoB) Statements of Institute of Chartered Public Accountants in Germany (IDW) Legal commentaries and other interpretations (research, expertise)

Fig. 2.1: Applicable rules.

---

2 The notion of Generally Accepted Accounting Principles (GAAP) is used with at least two meanings: In a very general meaning, this refers to all applicable rules, i.e. code law, soft law, court decisions and commentaries interpretations. In a narrower meaning, it refers only to the underlying principles of accounting. In subsequent text, "German GAAP" refers to all rules applicable in Germany, whereas "GAAP" refers to the underlying principles.

In what follows, this book focuses on the parts of the Commercial Code applicable to all companies (proprietorships, partnerships and corporations), the additional rules for corporations, and necessary commentaries/best practices where relevant. References will be given to the relevant DRS and IDW statements as well as to the IFRS. There will be no treatment of topics related to specific industries.

2.1.2 Applicability and simplifications

As mentioned earlier, the rules of the Commercial Code are applicable to any commercial business that requires, because of its nature or size, a commercial organization. That includes most businesses or companies. The term *commercial business* does not include all kinds of business activities. Management of one's own assets (not for others) and professionals such as lawyers and architects are excluded. Apart from that, only very small businesses with no or few employees or business transactions that are run on a part-time basis are excluded.[3]

For all other businesses, the Commercial Code is applicable; but there are differences regarding the extent to which the rules must be applied. First, the rules to be applied depend on the legal form; second, they depend on company size.

2.1.2.1 Applicability of commercial code depending on legal form

The Commercial Code distinguishes between proprietorships and partnerships on the one hand and corporations on the other. For proprietorships and partnerships, only §§ 238–263 must be applied, whereas for corporations §§ 264–335b must be applied as well.

According to German company law the most important legal forms are listed in Tab. 2.1.

There are many other legal forms, for example for professionals, public companies and insurance companies. These will not be treated here.

The general partners of a partnership or the owner of a proprietorship are fully liable for the obligations of the partnership, i.e. they are not only liable with their contribution, but with all their possessions, meaning they have unlimited liability. Thus, the motivation to conduct business in a proper way is assumed to be high, because any failure and in particular insolvency will harm the general partners or owner personally. In contrast to that, a corporation is at risk only for its own assets, meaning it has limited liability. Therefore, the motivation to avoid insolvency can be smaller, or higher risks may be taken by the managers, because they will not be affected personally (at least not their private assets). In consequence, the Commercial Code has basic rules to be applied by all companies and additional rules for

---

3 *Beck'scher Bilanzkommentar*, § 238 nos. 6–16.

Tab. 2.1: Classification of common legal forms.

Proprietorship/partnerships	Corporations
Sole proprietorship (Einzelkaufmann eK)	**Limited liability company** (Gesellschaft mit beschränkter Haftung GmbH)
General partnership (Offene Handelsgesellschaft oHG)	**Entrepreneurial company** (Unternehmergesellschaft UG; this is a specific subcategory of the limited liability company)
Limited partnership (Kommanditgesellschaft KG)	**Stock company** (Aktiengesellschaft AG)
Civil-law partnership (Gesellschaft bürgerlichen Rechts GbR)	**European stock company** (Socieatas Europea SE)
	Limited partnership with shares (Kommanditgesellschaft auf Aktien KGaA)

corporations. Tab. 2.2 presents a simple overview; details will be discussed in subsequent chapters.

Tab. 2.2: Accounting rules for partnerships and corporations.

	Partnerships[a]	Corporations
Content of financial statements		
– Balance sheet	Yes, but only aggregated structure (non-current assets, current assets, equity, liabilities, deferred items; § 247 sect 1.); details according to GAAP	Yes, detailed structure in § 266
– Income statement	Yes, but only aggregated structure (income and expense; § 242 sect. 2); details according to GAAP	Yes, detailed structure in § 275
– Use of profit	No	Only for stock companies § 158 AktG
– Notes	No	Yes, detailed rules, in particular §§ 284 and 285
– Management report	No	Yes, § 289
Audit	No	Yes, §§ 316–324a
Publication	No	Yes, §§ 325–329

[a] For more information about financial statements of partnerships, see IDW RS HFA 7 "Handelsrechtliche Rechnungslegung bei Personengesellschaften" – Accounting of partnerships according to the Commercial Code.

If a partnership has only legal persons (corporations, trusts or foundations) as general partners, i.e. there is no physical person who is general partner, then the partnership is treated like a corporation for accounting purposes (§ 264a).[4] In subsequent chapters, the term *corporation* should be understood to include these specific partnerships that are treated like corporations.

Excursus: Combination of legal forms

Under German company law, it is possible to combine several legal forms. A very common form of combination is the GmbH & Co. KG, which is a limited partnership (KG) with a limited liability company as general partner. A common case of this is where the limited partners of a limited partnership are also the shareholders of the limited liability company that serves as the general partner (see below).

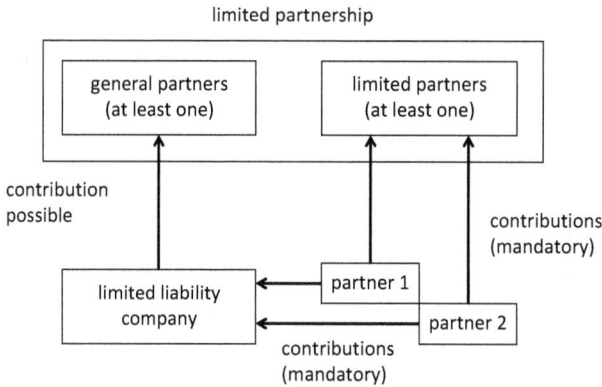

Fig. 2.2: Limited partnership with no physical person as general partner.

Partners 1 and 2 founded a limited partnership and act as limited partners with a certain contribution to the company. To avoid the unlimited liability of a general partner, they additionally founded a limited liability company that serves as general partner. By this two-step combination, a limited partnership can be set up and the full liability of a general partner can be avoided. If there is only one general partner, and it is a corporation (or if there are several of them, all corporations), the effect is identical to founding a corporation but using a partnership, i.e. having the limited liability of a corporation and the flexibility of a partnership (which may have advantages in company law, accounting or taxation). In 1999, this was considered an unfair advantage, so § 264a was implemented, and such companies are treated like corporations.

---

4 *Beck'scher Bilanzkommentar*, § 264a.

2.1.2.2 Applicability of commercial code depending on size class

As described earlier, the legal requirements for corporations are much more comprehensive than for sole proprietorships and partnerships. Fulfilling these requirements is time consuming and expensive. For smaller companies, the trade-off can be disproportionate: The advantage of better information for stakeholders is smaller than the additional expense and effort necessary to prepare the information. For this reason, the Commercial Code defines size classes; if a corporation fits in one of these classes, it can use simplifications.

The size classes use three criteria: total assets, sales revenue and average number of employees (Tab. 2.3).[5]

Tab. 2.3: Size classes in Commercial Code.

Size class	Total assets (€)	Sales revenue (€)	Average number of employees
Very small (§ 267a)	< 350,000	< 700,000	< 10
Small (§ 267 sect. 1)	< 6,000,000	< 12,000,000	< 50
Medium (§ 267 sect. 2)	< 20,000,000	< 40,000,000	< 250
Large	≥ 20,000,000	≥ 40,000,000	≥ 250

To be classified in a larger size class (e.g. large instead of medium), two of the three criteria must be fulfilled for two consecutive years. For an example, see exercise 3 in Chapter 5.2.

If a corporation is capital market oriented, it is always treated as large (independently of its size class; § 264d). *Capital market oriented* means that the company has issued securities that are traded in an organized market; this can be shares, but also bonds or other debt or equity instruments. Even if the company has not issued the securities yet, but is in the process of application for issuance, it is already treated as capital market oriented.[6]

Sole proprietorships or partnerships have much less stringent accounting requirements than corporations because there is at least one general partner who has unlimited liability. If proprietorships or partnerships become large, the need for additional information for stakeholders will increase as the importance of the company as employer, supplier or customer increases. Therefore, the Disclosure Act imposes additional requirements for large proprietorships or partnerships: they are basically treated like large corporations, must be audited and must publish their financial statements. For individual financial statements, there exist some simplifications (§ 5 PublG).

---

5 *Beck'scher Bilanzkommentar*, §§ 267 and 267a.
6 *Beck'scher Bilanzkommentar*, § 264d.

The size classes are as follows. The categorization works the same way as in the Commercial Code (Tab. 2.4).

Tab. 2.4: Size classes, Disclosure Act.

Size class	Total assets (€)	Sales revenue (€)	Average number of employees
Large (§ 1 PublG)	> 65,000,000	> 130,000,000	> 5,000

2.1.3 Consequences of legal form and size classes

Tab. 2.5 shows the possible simplifications of legal form and size classes.

Note that there are no simplifications for recognition and measurement, only for the amount of detail to be provided, audited and published.

If a company is capital market oriented (§ 264d) and does not prepare consolidated financial statements (see subsequent discussion), it must prepare in addition a cash flow statement as part of its individual financial statements.

2.1.4 Consolidated financial statements

If a **corporation** controls at least one other company, it must prepare consolidated financial statements (§ 290).

According to § 297, the consolidated financial statements consist of
- a consolidated balance sheet,
- a consolidated income statement,
- a consolidated cash flow statement,
- a consolidated changes-in-equity statement and
- consolidated notes.

In addition, a consolidated or group management report must be prepared (§ 315).

For further details on consolidated financial statements, see Chapter 4.

2.2 Reporting conception

Three questions must be answered to decide upon the accounting for a specific transaction:
1. Recognition
   Does this transaction have to be included in the financial statements or in the balance sheet, i.e. does it result in an asset or a liability? That is the question of whether or not.

Tab. 2.5: Accounting rules for partnerships and corporations including size classes.

	Partnerships Not large	Large	Corporations Very small	Small	Medium	Large
Content of financial statements:						
– Balance sheet	Yes, aggregated (§ 247 sect 1.); details according to GAAP	Yes, detailed (§ 266)	Yes, but very reduced (§ 266 sect. 1)	Yes, but reduced (§ 266 sect. 1)	Yes, detailed (§ 266)	Yes, detailed (§ 266)
– Income statement	Yes, aggregated (§ 242 sect. 2); details according to GAAP	Yes, § 275 possible	Yes, but very reduced (§ 275 sect. 5)	Yes, but reduced (§ 276)	Yes, but reduced (§ 276)	Yes, detailed (§ 275)
– Use of profit	No	No	Only for stock companies (§ 158 AktG)	Only for stock companies (§ 158 AktG)	Only for stock companies (§ 158 AktG)	Only for stock companies (§ 158 AktG)
– Notes	No	Yes, similar to §§ 284 and 285	Not mandatory (§ 264 sect. 1)	Yes, but reduced (§ 288 sect. 1)	Yes, but partially reduced (§ 288 sect. 2)	Yes, detailed rules, in particular §§ 284 and 285
– Management report	No	Yes, § 289	No, § 264 sect. 1	No, § 264 sect. 1	Yes, § 289	Yes, § 289
Time for preparation	Not specified	3 months	Not specified	6 months	3 months	3 months

(continued)

Tab. 2.5 (continued)

	Partnerships Not large	Large	Corporations Very small	Small	Medium	Large
Audit	No	Yes, §§ 316–324a	No	No	Yes, §§ 316–324a	Yes, §§ 316–324a
Publication	No	Yes, §§ 325–329; complete income statement not necessary (§ 5 sect. 5 PublG)	Only deposition (not publication; § 326 sect. 2)	Only balance sheet and notes (§ 326 sect. 1)	Yes, but reduced content for balance sheet and notes (§ 327)	Yes, §§ 325–329
Time for publication	Not necessary	12 months	12 months	12 months	12 months	12 months

2. Measurement

    If a transaction must be recognized, i.e. if it must be included in the financial statements, the next question that arises is: What is the correct value? Or: How do we measure this transaction?

    In this context, initial and subsequent measurement can be distinguished: Initial measurement refers to the value at which the transaction is recognized the first time in the financial statements. Subsequent measurement refers to the value that is attached to the transaction at a later point in time, typically at the closing date.

3. Presentation

    When recognition and measurement are clarified, the final question arises: How do we need to present this information? Do we have to provide details? Where are the details given, in the balance sheet or in the income statement or in the notes?

All three questions must be answered for all transactions at the beginning and at each closing date – at the beginning the focus is more on recognition, initial measurement and presentation, whereas at subsequent closing dates typically the focus is on subsequent measurement and, eventually, derecognition or presentation.

These three questions will guide the discussion in Chapters 2, 3 and 4.

2.3 Generally accepted accounting principles

2.3.1 Overview

As mentioned earlier, the notion of Generally Accepted Accounting Principles is used in two ways: The first meaning comprises all rules and guidelines that constitute German accounting (referred to as "German GAAP"), whereas the second focuses on the underlying principles that need to be applied in the accounting and that are used for transactions that lack specific rules. In this section, we focus on this second meaning, the underlying principles, and will refer to them as "GAAP".

The term Generally Accepted Accounting Principles means that these principles represent best practices in accounting. Some of them are codified by law, some are just common practice. Originally, the GAAP were derived by induction from the behavior of honorable businessmen. This method is limited to observable behavior and leads to a discussion about what is honorable. Thus, using deduction, principles are derived from the goals of the accounting. Today, typically the method of hermeneutics is used, i.e. not only the goals of accounting but all relevant influences are taken into account to argue for or against a principle.[7]

---

7 Coenenberg et al., 2021 (1), p. 39.
  Beck'scher Bilanzkommentar, § 243 nos. 11–23.

The GAAP must be applied to the current bookkeeping (§ 238 sect. 1), to financial statements according to the Commercial Code (§ 243 sect. 2) and to the tax balance sheet (§ 5 sect. 1 EStG).

The GAAP can be distinguished in

- principles of documentation focusing on how information is recorded and
- principles of accounting focusing on the content of this information.

2.3.2 Principles of documentation

One part of the principles of documentation focuses on clarity and transparency, i.e. the formal side of documentation. The other part focuses on completeness and correctness, i.e. the substantial side of documentation.[8]

In overview:[9]

Tab. 2.6: Principles of documentation.

Formal Principle of clarity and transparency	Substantial Principle of completeness and correctness
– **Use of a systematic order;** § 239 sect. 2 This is typically done by a chart of accounts, i.e. a structured system of accounts. This implies a systematic numbering and naming of accounts.	– **Completeness of transactions,** § 239 sect. 2 This means that all transactions must be recorded without gaps and without double entries. The transactions need to be reported separately (unless simplifications exist). To guarantee completeness, typically a chronologically ordered journal is kept.
– **Use of a living language,** § 239 sect. 1 For bookkeeping any living language is acceptable (i.e. not Latin); the financial statements must be in German (see below).	– **Correctness of transactions,** § 239 sect. 2 This means that transactions must be recorded according to their content. In particular, no fictitious accounts or arbitrary values are acceptable.
– **Voucher principle** This is not codified by law. It states that for any journal entry or posting, documentation about the transaction must be available; this can be electronic or in hard copy.	

---

8 Wöhe/Döring, p. 668.
9 Wöhe/Döring, p. 669.
   For more details: *Beck'scher Bilanzkommentar*, §§ 239 and 257.

Tab. 2.6 (continued)

Formal Principle of clarity and transparency	Substantial Principle of completeness and correctness
– **Clear recognition of subsequent changes,** § 239 sect. 3 It must be possible to trace changes, meaning changes or mistakes may not be deleted but must be openly corrected by a correcting entry.	
– **Timeliness of bookkeeping,** § 239 sect. 2 A transaction must be attributed to the correct reporting period and the bookkeeping should not take too long (typically not more than a month).	
– **Keeping of retention periods,** § 238 sect. 2 and § 257 All required documentation is to be stored for 6 or 10 years; storage can be done electronically, as long as the IT systems are accessible for that time.	

2.3.3 Principles of accounting

The principles of accounting are relevant for the preparation of the financial statements. Because this information is retrieved from current books, they influence the organization of the bookkeeping as well.

In overview:[10]

---

10 Wöhe/Döring, p. 669.

Principles of accounting

General principles	Recognition principles	Measurement principles

• Compliance with GAAP
• True and fair view
• Clarity and transparency
• Preparation in German and in Euros
• Correctness
• Closing date principle
• Timely preparation
	• Balance sheet identity
	• Completeness
	• No offsetting
	• Formal comparability
		• Prudence principle
		  Realization principle
		  Imparity principle
		• Accrual basis
		• Going concern
		• Substantial comparability
		• Individual measurement
		• Paid cost

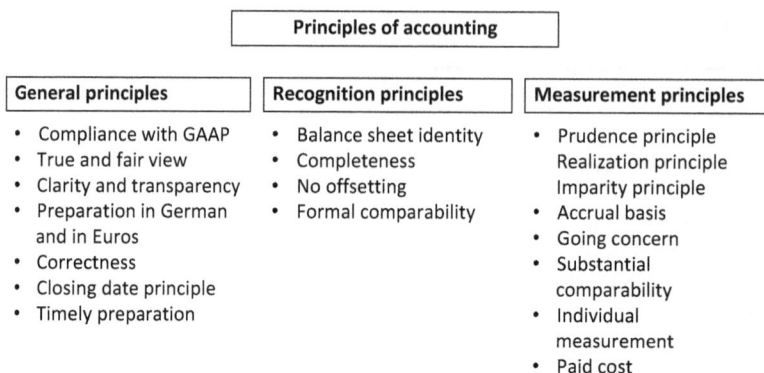

Fig. 2.3: Accounting principles.

2.3.3.1 General principles

Tab. 2.7: General principles of accounting.

Principle	Content	Codification
Compliance with GAAP	The financial statements need to be in compliance with all GAAP.	§ 243 sect. 1 § 264 sect. 2
True and fair view	For corporations:The financial statements must provide a true and fair view of the financial situation (assets and capital) and the performance situation of the company.[a]	§ 264 sect. 2
Clarity and transparency	Clarity and transparency refer to the presentation of the financial statements. The structure used for the balance sheet and income statement must be in compliance with legal requirements, i.e. naming of items and order of items must meet legal requirements. If applicable, notes and management reports need to be clearly structured as well.	§ 243 sect. 2
Preparation in German and in Euros	Whereas current bookkeeping can be done in any living language and currency (§ 239 sect. 1), for the financial statements preparation in German and Euros is required.	§ 244
Correctness	Correctness means that the values of transactions are reflected correctly in the financial statements; whereas it might be difficult to find a real (objective) true value, the values must be verifiable by a qualified third party. This means not using arbitrary values, i.e. necessary estimates must correspond to the professional judgment of the businessperson and must be verifiable.	Not codified[b]

Tab. 2.7 (continued)

Principle	Content	Codification
Closing date principle	The financial statements must include all assets and liabilities as of closing date. Any transaction that occurs after the closing date may not be recognized (corporations must report all material subsequent events in the management report). But a careful distinction must be made between subsequent events, i.e. a (new) transaction occurs after the closing date, and subsequent information (also called value clarifying), i.e. new information about a transaction that has already happened is available. This value-clarifying information must be used in the preparation of the financial statements.[c]	§ 242 sect. 1
Timely preparation	The financial statements should be prepared within the time needed for proper business conduct. This is commonly understood to be not longer than 12 months. This is only applicable for proprietorships and partnerships; for corporations there are precise deadlines (see earlier, Chapter 2.1.3): 3 months; simplification for (very) small corporations: 6 months (not specified).	§ 243 sect. 3 § 264 sect. 1

[a] According to the structure of the Commercial Code, this principle applies only to corporations and capital-market-oriented companies, meaning it does not apply to sole proprietorships and partnerships (*Beck'scher Bilanzkommentar*, § 264, nos. 235–238). In consequence, sole proprietorships and partnerships must be in compliance with all the other GAAP, but not legally with "true and fair view"; nevertheless, this legal difference will usually not result in important differences in accounting.

[b] Wöhe/Döring, p. 671.

[c] *Beck'scher Bilanzkommentar*, § 252, no. 38.

2.3.3.2 Recognition principles

Tab. 2.8: Recognition principles.

Principle	Content	Codification
Balance sheet identity	The values of the closing balance of the previous year must be the values of the opening balance of the current year. Nothing may be added or left out; the attribution of individual assets and liabilities to balance sheet items must remain constant.[a]	§ 252 sect. 1 no. 1
Completeness	All assets, liabilities and deferred items must be recognized in the balance sheet and all income and expenses must be recognized in the income statement. For assets economic ownership is the relevant criterion (see Chapter 2.4.1).	§ 246 sect. 1

Tab. 2.8 (continued)

Principle	Content	Codification
No offsetting	Assets and liabilities as well as income and expenses must be reported separately.[b]	§ 246 sect. 2
Formal comparability	This can be viewed as a subprinciple of the principle of clarity and transparency, but it is codified for corporations only: The form and structure of subsequent balance sheets and income statements must be retained; changes may be made only if necessary and unavoidable; any changes must be explained in the notes.[c]	§ 265 sect. 1
	Another element of formal comparability is to keep the recognition methods constant, meaning the approach to recognizing or derecognizing assets and liabilities must be used consistently from one year to the next. In particular, recognition options (e.g. internally generated non-current intangible assets) must be exercised identically for similar items.[d]	§ 246 sect. 3

[a] *Beck'scher Bilanzkommentar*, § 252, nos. 3–8.
[b] Offsetting of assets and liabilities is possible only if legally acceptable (§ 387 BGB); the criteria for legal offsetting are very strict, so it is seldom done (see *Beck'scher Bilanzkommentar*, § 246, nos. 100–115).
[c] *Beck'scher Bilanzkommentar*, § 265 nos. 2–4.
[d] *Beck'scher Bilanzkommentar*, § 246 nos. 125–132.

2.3.3.3 Measurement principles

2.3.3.3.1 Principle of prudence

The most important principle of GAAP is the principle of prudence – in its strictness it makes German accounting different from many other accounting standards. It stems from the idea of an honorable businessman: judging risks carefully – rather estimating a bit higher, judging chances also carefully – rather estimating a bit lower. In sum, it is a risk-averse approach to accounting that aims to protect creditors, i.e. to make sure that the net assets reported are really available and not just market-price fluctuations.[11]

The principle of prudence states that the measurement of assets and liabilities should be done cautiously taking into account all predictable risks and losses (§ 252 sect. 1 no. 4). It can be split into the following two subprinciples.

---

11 *Beck'scher Bilanzkommentar*, § 252 nos. 29 and 30.
Wöhe/Döring, p. 673.

Realization principle

Any income and gains may be recognized only if and when they are realized. Unrealized gains, for example pure market values, cannot be recognized, even if they exist at the closing date.

Income or gains are realized when the underlying transaction is completed, i.e. the company has fulfilled all its obligations by supplying products or rendering services and can now reliably expect the counterparty to fulfil its obligation, which means in most cases to pay the associated invoice. German accounting strictly follows the completed contract method, even if it is not codified by law.[12]

A completed contract typically means, for a sales agreement,[13]
- a contract or similar agreement exists;
- the products have been supplied or delivered or the services rendered;
- the transfer of risk has occurred, i.e. in particular the risk of accidental loss is borne by the buyer;
- additional conditions that have to be fulfilled for remuneration have been fulfilled.

Only if all of these conditions are met can a transaction be completed and the revenue, income or gain recognized in the income statement. Because detailed arrangements can vary from contract to contract, for international trade standardized terms of trade are often used, which are known as Incoterms, issued by the International Chamber of Commerce in Paris. These standardize several issues related to international deliveries, in particular when (and where) risk is transferred and who bears the costs of transport and insurance.[14]

Example 1

A company acquired a piece of land many years ago for €250,000. Meanwhile, prices on land have risen significantly. With good reason and backed by similar recent transactions, company management estimates the current fair value of the land at €1,000,000.

Owing to the realization principle, this gain cannot be realized, i.e. the land cannot be assessed at fair value, until the land is sold and the increase in value is confirmed by the sale.

Example 2

A producer of machines exports a machine to East Asia; in the sales contract, "free on board" is specified as the Incoterm. At the closing date, the machine is removed from the premises of the manufacturer and is stored at the harbor for shipping.

---

12 *Beck'scher Bilanzkommentar*, § 252 nos. 43–49.
13 Bacher, p. 32.

Further reading: IDW ERS HFA 13 "Einzelfragen zum Übergang von wirtschaftlichen Eigentum und zur Gewinnrealisierung nach HGB" – Specific questions about the transfer of economic ownership and revenue recognition according to the Commercial Code – draft version.
14 International Chamber of Commerce, Incoterms 2010.

"Free on board" implies that the risk is transferred when the machine is loaded onto the ship (more precise: when it crosses the railing). Because it is stored at the harbor on the closing date, delivery is not complete. In consequence, the machine is still a piece of inventory of the manufacturer (even if not in its warehouse), and no revenue may be recognized.

Imparity principle

Any expenses or losses must be recognized if and when they become probable, i.e. even before they are realized.

This results in an asymmetrical approach: Income and gains are recognized only when realized, expenses and losses when probable, even if not realized; this is why this principle is called the *imparity principle* because gains and losses are not treated in the same way.

The Commercial Code states explicitly that any risks that occurred before the closing date but that become known after the closing date must be recognized in the financial statements (see earlier discussion: closing date principle and value clarification).[15]

Example

A company has sold a machine to a customer on credit. When the payment is due, the customer does not pay and a dunning process is started. On the closing date, payment is still outstanding. The management comes to the conclusion that probably not all of the receivables can be collected and estimates the risk with good reason to be 15%.

Owing to the imparity principle, the receivables must be impaired: the loss is probable, even if it is not realized yet.

The combination of these two principles and their application to assets or liabilities results in two principles that can also be viewed as subprinciples of the principle of prudence.

Lower-of-cost-or-market principle (§ 253 sect. 3 and 4)

This principle is the basic approach to the subsequent measurement of assets. It means the upper limits are the acquisition or production costs of an asset (see Chapter 2.4.2). Because of the realization principle, any increases in value above the acquisition or production costs may not be recognized until they are realized (because they would result in an income/gain). On the other hand, any decreases in value must be recognized if they are probable because of the imparity principle (as they result in an expense/loss).

---

15 *Beck'scher Bilanzkommentar*, § 252, nos. 34–42.

Thus, on the closing date two values must always be compared for an asset: the (depreciated or amortized) acquisition or production costs and the fair value. The lower one must be chosen.[16]

Several specific versions of this principle will be explained, together with the relevant balance sheet items.

Higher-of-cost-or-market principle

This principle is the basic approach to the subsequent measurement of liabilities. It means the lower limit of a liability is the original settlement amount. Because of the realization principle, any decreases in value below the original settlement amount may not be recognized until they are realized (because they would result in an income/gain). On the other hand, any increases in value must be recognized if they are probable because of the imparity principle (as they result in an expense/loss).

Thus, on the closing date, two values must always be compared for a liability: the original settlement amount and the fair value or current settlement amount. The higher one must be chosen.[17]

2.3.3.3.2 Other measurement principles

Tab. 2.9: Other measurement principles.

Principle	Content	Codification
With focus on comparability of profit		
Accrual basis	Income and expense are recognized when they occur; occurrence refers to the economic effect a specific transaction may have: if and when a transaction has its economic effect, it is recognized as income or expense, independently of its legal occurrence (which can be earlier or later) or payments (which can be earlier or later as well).[a]	§ 252 sect. 1 no. 5
Going concern	For the measurement of assets and liabilities it is assumed that the business will continue unless there are actual or legal reasons not to.[b]Actual reasons can be, for example, – threat of insolvency, – substantial losses, – inability to take on necessary loans, – violation of financial covenants.	§ 252 sect. 1 no. 2

---

16 *Beck'scher Bilanzkommentar,* § 253 nos. 506–509.
17 *Beck'scher Bilanzkommentar,* § 253 no. 50.

Tab. 2.9 (continued)

Principle	Content	Codification
	Legal reasons can be, for example, – opening of insolvency proceedings, – legal or statutory requirements to liquidate the company.	
Substantial comparability	The methods of measurement must be consistent, i.e. they must be applied in the same way as in earlier financial statements. This is particularly relevant for any legal or actual measurement options (e.g. definition of production costs).[c] Corporations: If changes are unavoidable, they must be explained in notes.	§ 252 sect. 1 no. 6
With focus on verifiability of values		
Individual measurement	Any asset or liability must be measured individually unless simplifications are acceptable (e.g. constant value approach, group measurement, hedge accounting[d]).	§ 252 sect. 1 no. 3
Paid cost	Any income or expense must have resulted or will result in a payment. Imputed costs or income, i.e. costs/income that will never result in a payment, may not be included in financial statements.	§ 255 sect. 1 and 2

[a] *Beck'scher Bilanzkommentar*, § 252 nos. 51–54.
[b] *Beck'scher Bilanzkommentar*, § 252, nos. 9–16
Further reading: IDW RS HFA 17 "Auswirkungen einer Abkehr von der Going-concern-Prämisse auf den handelsrechtlichen Jahresabschluss" – Effects of a dismissal of the going concern principle on financial statements according to the Commercial Code.
[c] *Beck'scher Bilanzkommentar*, § 252, nos. 55–62.
[d] *Beck'scher Bilanzkommentar*, § 252, nos. 22–28.

Further reading

IDW RS HFA 17 "Auswirkungen einer Abkehr von der Going Concern-Prämisse auf den handelsrechtlichen Jahresabschluss" – Effects of a renunciation of the going-concern-premise on financial statements according to the Commercial Code.

IDW RS HFA 38 "Ansatz- und Bewertungsstetigkeit im handelsrechtlichen Jahresabschluss" – Formal and substantial comparability in financial statements according to the Commercial Code.

IDW RS HFA 39 "Vorjahreszahlen im handelsrechtlichen Jahresabschluss" – Prior year's figures in financial statements according to the Commercial Code.

IDW RH HFA 1.1011 "Insolvenzspezifische Rechnungslegung im Insolvenzverfahren" – Specific accounting for insolvency purposes during insolvency proceedings.

IDW RH HFA 1.1012 "Externe (handelsrechtliche) Rechnungslegung im Insolvenzverfahren" – External accounting (according to the Commercial Code) during insolvency proceedings.

Important differences to IFRS

The IFRS specify their underlying principles in a conceptual framework. Most GAAP of German accounting and the principles of IFRS are aligned. The most important difference is the principle of prudence and its dominance in German accounting. The conceptual framework has no corresponding principle and follows the overarching principles of a true and fair view or decision usefulness. This results in a (more) symmetrical approach to measurement, in contrast to the asymmetrical approach in the Commercial Code, and is detailed in many IAS/IFRS in which, for example, fair values above acquisition/production costs are possible.[18]

In addition, German accounting specifies (of course) the currency and language of financial statements and the timeline for their preparation. There is no need for the IFRS to do so.[19]

In German GAAP, the realization principle implies the application of the completed contract method for revenue recognition. In IFRS, the revenue recognition principles are specified in IFRS 15 "Revenue from contracts with customers". IFRS 15 must be applied to all contracts with customers, with only a few exceptions (leasing contracts, insurance contracts, financial instruments, non-monetary exchanges of companies within the same line of business).

It defines a general five-step approach to recognizing revenue (IFRS 15.IN7):

1. Identify the contract(s) with a customer. A contract is a mutual agreement that defines enforceable rights and obligations. In some cases, contracts must be aggregated and accounted for as one.
2. Identify the performance obligations in the contract. A contract includes a promise to transfer goods or services to the customer. If those goods or services are clearly distinct, performance obligations exist and are accounted for separately.
3. Determine the transaction price. The consideration the company expects to receive in exchange for the promised goods or services is the transaction price. It may be fixed or variable, cash or non-cash. If a substantial financing component is included, discounting is necessary.
4. Allocate the transaction price to the performance obligation in the contract. Typically, this is done on a stand-alone basis. If a stand-alone selling price is not given, the company needs to estimate it.
5. Recognize revenue when (or as) the company fulfils performance obligations. This can happen at a specific point in time (typically for goods) or over a period

---

18 IFRS conceptual framework, OB17.
19 For a more detailed comparison, see Hayn/Waldersee, p. 78.

of time (typically for services). If a performance obligation is fulfilled over a period of time, the company recognizes revenue over time. The transfer of goods is completed if the goods are under the control of the customer (IFRS 15.31).

A fulfillment over time occurs (IFRS 15.35) if

– the customer simultaneously receives and consumes the benefits as the company fulfils its obligation,
– the company creates or enhances an asset that is already controlled by the customer or
– there is no alternative use for the asset and the company has an enforceable right to be paid to date.

Depending on the business model of the reporting entity, the revenue recognition can differ substantially between German GAAP and IFRS due to the substantially different approach of IFRS 15.

2.4 Balance sheet: general recognition rules

§ 247 specifies that the balance sheet must include all non-current and current assets, equity and liabilities, as well as deferred items.

In what follows, we will briefly look at the general recognition and measurement rules for assets and liabilities.

2.4.1 Recognition of assets

There is no legal definition of the term *asset* in the Commercial Code.

The general (or abstract) criteria for the recognition of an asset are as follows:[20]

– **Economic benefit**

An asset must provide a concrete economic benefit in the future. If an asset is acquired, for example if raw materials are purchased, the purchaser must be able to use the raw materials for its own production or be able to resell them. But assets can also be intangible, like software, or financial, like a share or a bond. The requirement is the same: the asset must probably provide some economic benefit. Mere chances or options are not sufficient if the realization of a benefit is not concrete and probable.

---

20 *Beck'scher Bilanzkommentar*, § 247, nos. 10–17.
Coenenberg et al., 2021 (1), p. 84.

- **Separately measurable** It must be possible to measure the value of one asset separately from other assets. If no value can be assigned individually, it is not a separate asset.

Example

A company buys a new car. The different parts of the car, the engine, the transmission, the chassis and so forth, cannot be measured separately; one price is paid for the car, but not separate prices for the components (at least not for the standard components; for the extras separate prices may be available). Therefore, the standard components of the car (even if they could be sold separately – see subsequent discussion) are not separate assets.

- **Separately marketable**
  It must be possible to market (sell or use otherwise) an asset separately from other assets. If the asset cannot be marketed on its own, it is not a separate asset.

Example

The roof of a building provides economic benefit (it provides protection from weather); often it can be measured separately because the invoices of the carpenter allow a precise attribution of expenses. But it cannot be used separately from the building; the roof cannot be sold or leased without the rest of the building. Therefore, the roof is not a separate asset; it is part of the asset "building".

All three criteria must be fulfilled at the same time.

Apart from these general criteria defining an asset, additional criteria must be fulfilled whereby an asset can be recognized in a specific situation:

- **Economic ownership**
  All assets that are economically owned must be recognized (§ 246 sect. 1 sent. 2). Economic ownership means that the assets can be used and that the economic owner is responsible for the majority of risks and opportunities related to their use; the latter also includes sales proceeds or changes in value in which the company participates (§ 39 sect. 2 AO).[21] In many cases, legal and economic ownership are identical, but not necessarily. Typical examples are as follows:

---

[21] *Beck'scher Bilanzkommentar,* § 246 nos. 5–8.
   Coenenberg et al., 2021 (1), p. 86.

Tab. 2.10: Examples for differences between legal and economic ownership.

Transaction	Legal owner	Economic owner
Sale with retention of title	Seller	Buyer
Goods transferred as security/with transfer of title	Creditor/holder of security	Borrower/user of security
Use of goods as pledge	Original owner	Holder of pledge
Leasing[a]		
Operating leases	Lessor	Lessor
Finance leases	Lessor	Lessee

[a] There is no legal definition of leasing in the Commercial Code. The typical classification is based on tax rules; the classification here is a bit superficial – just to clarify the tendency. For details refer to Chapter 3.1.10.4.

- For proprietorships/partnerships:

  Distinction between business assets and private assets of owner(s):
  Some assets can be used for both commercial and private purposes, for example a car can be used to deliver goods to customers and for personal shopping. However, many assets are unambiguously either part of a business or held privately, though some assets are not so easily defined and may be owned both by a company and privately. Since only the assets of a company or business are to be included in financial statements, the owners must assign assets to either the business or private individuals (under the rebuttable presumption that an asset that was acquired by the owner must be included in the business).[22] More detailed rules on how this assignment must be made exist for tax purposes.[23] Such a distinction is necessary only for proprietorships and partnerships. A corporation has no private assets. Thus, no assignment is necessary.[24]

- **Specific legal recognition rules**
  The Commercial Code requires, prohibits or allows certain transactions to be recognized as an asset. These specific rules may deviate from the general rules. They will be explained in Chapter 3 in a detailed explanation of balance sheet items.

---

22 *Beck'scher Bilanzkommentar*, § 246 nos. 55–57 and 63.
　　Coenenberg et al., 2021 (1), p. 88.
23 *Beck'scher Bilanzkommentar*, § 246 nos. 58–62 and 64.
24 *Beck'scher Bilanzkommentar*, § 246 no. 66.

Important differences to IFRS
The conceptual framework defines assets in CF 4.8–4.14. The major difference is that the Commercial Code requires separate marketability of an asset and is thus stricter than IFRS.

2.4.2 Initial measurement of assets

The Commercial Code prescribes different measures for the initial measurement of assets; this depends on whether the assets were acquired or produced.

An acquisition against remuneration is assumed in the following cases:[25]
–   Purchase of asset against cash or on credit;
–   Barter trades, where assets are exchanged against other assets and no cash is used;
–   Capital increases of the company, i.e. a contribution to the equity independent of whether it is in cash or in kind/goods.

An acquisition without remuneration is assumed in cases of donations of assets; typically the acquisition costs are assumed to be zero; donations of money are measured at the nominal value. For tax purposes, specific rules must be applied.[26]

If other parties are used to produce the asset for the purposes of the company, the line between acquisition and production may not be completely clear. Whether an event is treated as an acquisition or production depends on the detailed contractual arrangements; in particular, it is important to know who bears the risk of the production process, meaning if the production fails, who covers the costs and any damages? If these risks are borne by the contractor, the produced asset is assumed to be acquired by the customer (in the easiest case the customer pays only if a fully functional asset is received). If these risks are borne by the customer, the produced asset is assumed to be produced by the customer (with the help of the contractor; in the most straightforward case, the customer must pay the contractor even if the asset does not work properly).[27]

This question can become important for outsourcing arrangements or other complex service agreements.

Example

A company (the customer) needs new software that must be programmed to its specific needs. Because it does not have sufficient programming capacity in its IT department, an external IT company (the contractor) is used.

---

25 *Beck'scher Bilanzkommentar* § 255.
26 *Beck'scher Bilanzkommentar* § 255 no. 100.
27 *Beck'scher Bilanzkommentar,* § 255 nos. 35–38.

Case A: Acquisition

The customer provides the contractor with a detailed description about the new software. The contract states that the customer must accept and pay the software only if it complies with the description. In this case, the software will be treated as acquired because the risk of failure (i.e. programming a software that does not fulfil the requirements) is borne by the contractor.

Case B: Production

The customer has an idea about the new software, but not yet a detailed plan. The project management is carried out by the customer and the specification of the software is produced on an ongoing basis (evolutionary development). The contractor makes available several people to do the programming according to the instructions of the customer. In consequence, the contractor is paid on the basis of working hours of its employees – independently of whether or not the programming was successful. In this case, the software is considered to be produced by the customer himself.

2.4.2.1 Acquisition costs

If an asset is acquired (against a remuneration, see earlier discussion), it is measured using acquisition costs. § 255 sect. 1 defines acquisition costs as follows: any expenses that are incurred to acquire an asset and make it ready for operation, meaning the acquisition process does not stop with the initial purchase but continues until the asset can be used; this does not imply that it is used, only that it can be used.[28]

Any expenses incurred must be directly attributable to the acquisition, i.e. only direct expenses can be recognized, no indirect expenses.[29] Imputed costs may not be included in the acquisition costs.

Tab. 2.11 shows this in more detail.[30]

Subsequent price reductions or acquisition costs change the acquisition costs when they are incurred, meaning there is no retrospective application.[31]

Important differences to IFRS

The conceptual framework provides a general definition of acquisitions costs that is detailed further in the specific standards. Any specific important differences are described there.

The Commercial Code does not provide legal rules for the accounting of the exchange of assets (barter trades). IAS 16 provides specific rules for that.

---

28 *Beck'scher Bilanzkommentar*, § 255 nos. 33 and 34.
29 *Beck'scher Bilanzkommentar*, § 255 no. 28.
30 Coenenberg et al., 2021 (1), p. 102.
31 *Beck'scher Bilanzkommentar*, § 255 no. 75.

Tab. 2.11: Components of acquisition costs (§ 255 sect. 1).

Component of acquisition costs	Examples
Purchase price/consideration	As typically specified in purchase agreement (net of VAT)
− Price reductions that can be attributed to specific transaction	Trade or cash discounts, rebates and any additional bonuses, if directly attributable
+ Incidental acquisition costs	Any costs incurred to make the asset ready for operation, for example: − purchaser transport expenses − customs duties on imported goods − transport insurance − installation expenses − prototypes or test runs − security checks − notary or broker fees (if necessary for acquisition) − land acquisition tax
= **Initial acquisition costs**	
− Subsequent price reductions	Any subsequent price reductions that are directly attributable
+ Subsequent acquisition costs	Expenses that are a direct consequence of the acquisition but charged at a later point in time (e.g. public fees for the development of roads and sewer systems are often charged years after the acquisition of the land) or expenses that improve the usability or extend the useful life of the asset (e.g. when a truck is upgraded with an air-conditioning/cooling system).
= **Final acquisition costs**	

2.4.2.2 Production costs

If an asset is not acquired, it has been produced by the company itself. When an asset is produced or has been produced, it is measured initially with its production costs. Production costs are defined in § 255 sect. 2, 2a and 3: Production costs are expenses incurred by the use of goods or services to produce an asset, enlarge it or improve it over its original condition.

This can be seen in more detail in Tab. 2.12.[32]

Imputed costs may not be included in production costs (the same as for acquisition costs).

Indirect costs may be included with an adequate portion that relates to the production process. This means, in particular, that any impairments of assets, idle

---

32 Coenenberg et al., 2021 (1), p. 104.

Tab. 2.12: Components of production costs (§ 255 sect. 2, 2a and 3).

Mandatory component of production costs	Examples
Direct material costs	Acquisition costs of raw materials, parts or services used for production
+ Direct manufacturing costs	Costs directly attributable to production process, such as wages of production workers, including all legal social security expenses
+ Special direct costs of manufacturing	Special direct costs are costs that can be directly attributed to the production process but are typically one-time items and not linked to the quantity produced, for example models or prototypes, specific molds or tools[a]
+ Indirect material costs	Costs of materials that cannot be directly attributed to the specific production process, for example procurement costs, transport costs within the company, storage costs, insurance costs, costs for quality management
+ Indirect manufacturing costs	Costs that cannot be directly attributed to the production process, for example energy costs (if not directly attributable), costs for production administration and planning, maintenance costs, costs for quality management
+ Depreciation/amortization of non-current assets	Depreciation for non-current assets used in production process
= **Mandatory components/ Minimum production costs Optional components**	
Adequate portion of + General administration costs	For example costs of human resource management, finance and accounting, information and communication technology
+ Voluntary social benefits	For example costs of a canteen, day care center, sports facilities, anniversary and other voluntary payments
+ Voluntary pension scheme/ retirement benefits	Costs for additional (not mandatory) payments for retired employees
+ Borrowing costs	In principle, borrowing costs are not included; only if the credit capital has been used for the specific production process and the interest corresponds to the period of production can they be included

Tab. 2.12 (continued)

Mandatory component of production costs	Examples
= **Maximum of production costs** **Prohibited is the inclusion of**	
Distribution costs	Any costs incurred after the production has finished, for example costs of storage of finished goods or merchandise, costs of transport to customers or sales facilities, salaries and wages and other costs of sales department, costs of marketing and advertising, costs to reach a sales agreement (see above on special direct costs of production)
Research costs	Research and development are defined in § 255 sect 2a: Research is the search for and creation of new knowledge; it is an open-ended process, and success is uncertain. In contrast, development is the application of existing knowledge to a new situation; this is also an open-ended process, but the degree of certainty that it will be successful is substantially higher

[a] A specific topic here are special direct costs of distribution, in particular costs incurred to reach a sales agreement. These may not be included in the production costs because they are distribution costs; see *Beck'scher Bilanzkommentar*, § 255 nos. 454–456.

time costs or extraordinary expenses may not be included.[33] In consequence, which costs may be included to what extent depends also on the methods of cost accounting that are used in the company.

Whether or not optional elements are included depends on the accounting policy of the company and the corresponding decisions of management. From 2017 onwards, options must be applied in the commercial balance sheet and the tax balance sheet in the same way, meaning the use of options not only is accounting policy in the commercial balance sheet but has a tax effect as well.[34]

The accounting effect of the definition of production costs is not completely intuitive. This definition is relevant for the measurement of assets, i.e. it defines which expenses that were incurred are recognized in the balance sheet and thus reduce the expenses in the income statement. This definition is not about cost management, i.e. a reduction of costs. In consequence, the higher the production costs are defined, the higher the profit (because more expenses are transferred as assets to the balance sheet) and vice versa.

---

33 *Beck'scher Bilanzkommentar*, § 255 nos. 436 and 437.

34 Until 31 December 2016, for tax purposes there was only the option of including interest expenses (see above). All other elements were mandatory or prohibited in the tax balance sheet. With the Gesetz zur Modernisierung des Besteuerungsverfahrens as of 22 July 2016, the use of the options for tax purposes was tied to the use of the options in the commercial balance.

Subsequent production costs occur, if an asset

- was completely worn out and is reproduced. This means that not just parts of the asset but the asset in total can no longer be used. This worn-out asset is reproduced so that a new asset exists (even if some parts that are still functional are reused);
- can be used for other functions/purposes after changes are made;
- is enlarged, for example when the usable space of a building is increased by adding an additional floor;
- is substantially improved over its initial condition, i.e. the usage potential has been enhanced.

Any expenses incurred that are not subsequent production costs are in consequence (maintenance) expenses of the period.[35]

Under German tax law, a more detailed simplification is relevant: Any expenses incurred within the first 3 years after acquisition or production that do not exceed 15% of the initial acquisition or production costs are assumed to be maintenance costs without any further documentation (§ 6 sect. 1 no. 1a EStG).

Further reading

IDW RS HFA 31 neue Fassung (new version) "Aktivierung von Herstellungskosten" – Recognition of production costs

Important differences to IFRS

There is no general definition of production costs in IFRS. IAS 2.12–18 specifies that general administration costs or voluntary social security are not to be included under production costs when measuring inventories (overhead costs are to be included only insofar as they relate directly to the production process).

Interest expenses for the production of qualifying assets must be included (IAS 23). A qualifying asset is an asset that takes a considerable period of time to be acquired or produced.[36]

2.4.3 Recognition of liabilities

There is no legal definition of *liabilities* in the Commercial Code. Liability is a more general term for provisions and debt or payables (for more details see chapters 3.1.7 and 3.1.8).

---

35 *Beck'scher Bilanzkommentar*, § 255 nos. 375–392.
36 Coenenberg et al., 2021 (1), p. 116.

The general (or abstract) criteria for the recognition of a liability are as follows:[37]

– **Obligation** There must be an obligation to a third party that needs to be fulfilled in the future. This can be a legal, contractual or constructive obligation. A constructive obligation is an obligation that cannot be avoided (even if not legally enforceable) because of common practice in the industry, past behavior of the company and so forth.

Example

A company sold its products. A customer is not satisfied with the product.

Case A: Legal obligation

The product is faulty and the company is legally required to fulfil its obligation to supply a proper model of the product, say, by repairing it or exchanging it. This is a legal obligation.

Case B: Constructive obligation

The customer does not like the color of the product; he has no legal right to exchange or return it. In the past, the policy of the company was driven by customer friendliness – all wishes to return or exchange products were honored. The customer knows that and expects the company to behave that way again. This can be a constructive obligation.

– **Economic burden** Economic burden means that the settlement of an obligation requires economic resources that can no longer be used, for example cash, goods, working time of employees. The economic burden must be probable, i.e. even if not certain it must be more likely than not that the economic resources will be used.

Example

A company gives a guarantee to a business partner, for example as collateral for a loan: The company guarantees to repay a loan instead of the business partner if the business partner fails to do so. This is typically a contractual obligation and is quantifiable (see below). As long as the business partner fulfils his duties, this obligation will probably not result in an economic burden; thus, it is not a liability (in this specific case it is what is known as a contingent liability) and is not recognized in the balance sheet of the company.

Only if the business partner fails to fulfil his duties (or it becomes probable that he will do so), the economic burden becomes probable and only then must a liability be recognized.

---

37 *Beck'scher Bilanzkommentar*, § 247 nos. 201–207.
  Coenenberg et al., 2021 (1), p. 84.

- **Quantifiable**

  The economic burden to settle the obligation must be quantifiable. If the quantity of economic resources that will be needed cannot be estimated with sufficient reliability, it is not a liability.

All three criteria must be fulfilled to establish that a liability exists. The liability must be recognized by the company (or person) who has the obligation to fulfil it.[38]

2.4.4 Measurement of liabilities

The basic measure of liabilities is the settlement amount, or the amount of economic resources required to meet an obligation (§ 253 sect. 1 sent. 2). The settlement amount includes any economic resources that will be used, such as cash, goods or services. For debt/payables the initial measurement is typically the nominal value of the contract. For provisions the settlement amount must be estimated based on commercial judgment (for further details see Chapters 3.1.7 and 3.1.8).[39]

Annuity charges are measured based on the present value of the expected future payments (§ 253 sect. 2; for further details see Chapter 3.1.7).[40]

2.5 Stock taking/inventory

The basis for any accounting is the regular verification and documentation of all assets and liabilities, which is legally required for the beginning of a business (opening balance) and then once a year (§ 240 sect. 1 and 2). Physical assets must be counted (or, if that is not possible, measured, weighed or estimated); this is the process of stock taking. Intangible assets, financial assets and liabilities must be verified by supporting documents, for example a receivable is verified by an invoice that was sent to the customer.[41]

The purpose of stock taking is to verify the amounts and to detect any errors, meaning missing or additional amounts. Detected errors can then be corrected in the financial accounting (missing amounts of an asset result in an expense, additional amounts in income).

---

38 *Beck'scher Bilanzkommentar*, § 246 nos. 50–54.
39 *Beck'scher Bilanzkommentar*, § 253 nos. 50–53 and 150–152.
40 Coenenberg et al., 2021 (1), p. 110.
41 In addition, balance confirmation can be used, that is, the company sends a list with all open items to its customer and asks for confirmation (vice versa for payables). This is often done by or requested by auditors.

Example Methods of stock taking

Tab. 2.13: Examples of Methods of stock taking.

Asset	Method
Large parts or components	Counting
Numerous small parts (e.g. small screws)	Weighing: weigh a sample of 10–20 screws and then estimate the total number by weighing all screws
Liquids (e.g. fuel)	Measuring: measure and eventually calculate volume of tank and measure filling level
Numerous, irregular parts (e.g. a heap of coal)	Estimating: measure and calculate volume of heap (approximately), estimate weight of a cubic meter of coal and then estimate total weight

The **annual stock taking at the closing date** is the applicable principle (§ 240 sect. 2): All assets and liabilities are verified at the closing date. Common practice is to allow for 10 days before and after the closing date, but this range should be kept as small as possible. The amounts must be adjusted for any changes (increases or decreases) between the date of the stock taking and the closing date.

Several simplifications are possible:
- **Stock taking before or after closing date** (pre- or post-terminated stock taking) (§ 241 sect. 3): The stock taking can be done 3 months before or 2 months after the closing date if the value of the assets at the closing date can be determined properly.[42]
- **Permanent stock taking** (§ 241 sect. 2): This can differ in two ways from the stock taking at the closing date:
  a) It can be done on any date (not only within the limits of the pre- or post-termination stock taking).
  b) Not all items must be counted on the same date; stock taking on multiple dates (theoretically every day) is possible. Nevertheless, all assets must be verified at least once a year. All amounts and values must be updated for the closing date values. Typically, this must be done by an IT system.[43]
- **Sample stock taking** (241 sect. 1): If statistical methods can be applied, it is sufficient to verify only a sample and then calculate a projection of the total

---

42 *Beck'scher Bilanzkommentar*, § 241 nos. 50–57; it is not necessary to determine the amounts at the closing date; the values are sufficient.
43 *Beck'scher Bilanzkommentar*, § 241 nos. 31–33.

amounts and values. Nevertheless, the GAAP must be applied, meaning completeness and correctness must be ensured and the process must be documented properly.[44]

– **Constant value approach** (§ 240 sect. 3): This is a simplification for both stock taking and measurement for tangible non-current assets and raw materials. This is explained in more detail in Chapter 3.1.3.5.

– **Group measurement** (§ 240 sect. 4): Similar inventories or other similar moveable assets or payables can be grouped and measured together. Similar means similar in kind/function or similar in value. This is explained in more detail in Chapter 3.1.5.1.[45]

Further reading

IDW RH HFA 1.1010 "Bestandsaufnahme im Insolvenzverfahren" – Stock taking during insolvency proceedings.

2.6 Definition of income and expense

There is no legal definition of income and expense in the Commercial Code.

The dominant opinion is that income and expense reflect changes in net assets (assets – liabilities), as long as these changes are not caused by changed relations with shareholders. Put another way, any increase in the value of an asset that is not offset by a decrease in the value of an asset or an increase in the value of a liability is income; any increase in the value of a liability that is not offset by a decrease in the value of a liability or an increase in the value of an asset is an expense (vice versa).[46]

There are no specific measurement rules for income or expense. Any income or expense that is incurred in one's own account is to be recognized in the financial statements; typically this coincides with economic ownership, i.e. changes in the recognized assets or liabilities must be reflected in the income statement.

---

44 *Beck'scher Bilanzkommentar*, § 241 nos. 5–27.
45 *Beck'scher Bilanzkommentar* § 240 nos. 130–140.
46 Jung, 2016, p. 1028.
   Coenenberg et al., 2021 (2), p. 69.

Tab. 2.14: Definition of income and expense.[47]

Income	**Increase in net assets =**
	Increase in assets – liabilities
	unless caused by contributions or withdrawals of shareholders
Expense	**Decrease in net assets =**
	Decrease in assets – liabilities
	unless caused by contributions or withdrawals of shareholders

Important differences to IFRS

The conceptual framework defines the terms *income* and *expense*. Income encompasses revenue and gains; whereas revenue results from ordinary operating activities, gains can also result from non-operating activities or from one-time items. Expenses are subdivided into expenses (ordinary operating) and losses (possibly non-operating or one-time). There is no consistent concept about how income and expense are linked to the balance sheet (IFRS CF4.29–35).[48]

Depending on specific standards, in some cases changes in the value of assets or liabilities are not recognized as income or expenses in the income statement, but only as other comprehensive income in equity. This possibility does not exist in the Commercial Code.

---

47 Own representation based on Jung, 2016, p. 1028.
48 IFRS, Conceptual framework, 4.29–4.35.

3 Financial statements according to commercial code

3.1 Balance sheet

First the legal structure of the balance sheet is explained; then the different balance sheet items are explained in detail focusing on recognition, measurement and presentation.

3.1.1 Structure

For proprietorships and partnerships, the Commercial Code prescribes only a very basic structure (§ 247):

Tab. 3.1: Basic structure of a balance sheet (§ 247).

Debit	Balance sheet	Credit
Non-current assets	Equity	
Current assets	Liabilities	
Deferred expenses	Deferred income	

Further detailing to fulfil the GAAP, in particular the principle of clarity and transparency, is up to the judgment of the reporting unit. Once a structure has been decided upon, it should be kept constant (principle of formal comparability).[1]

For corporations, § 266 prescribes a detailed structure.

For the debit side see Tab. 3.2.[2]

For the credit side see Tab. 3.3.[3]

The asset side is structured according to the common current/non-current distinction. Within the current and non-current assets, a further detailing is done according to the kind of asset. Advance payments are shown depending on what is paid for in advance, meaning each category of non-current items has a separate category of payments made in advance.

The credit side singles out equity and then according to differences in certainty provisions and debt, i.e. the current/non-current distinction is not used here, but

---

1 *Beck'scher Bilanzkommentar*, § 247, nos. 600–630.
2 *Beck'scher Bilanzkommentar*, § 266, nos. 59–162.
3 *Beck'scher Bilanzkommentar*, § 266, nos. 170–262.

https://doi.org/10.1515/9783110744170-003

Tab. 3.2: Debit side according to § 266 sect. 2.

A. **Non-current assets**
   I. **Intangible assets**
      1. Internally generated commercial property rights, and similar rights and assets
      2. Concessions, commercial property rights and similar assets as well as licenses of such rights and similar assets, acquired against remuneration
      3. Goodwill
      4. Payments made in advance
   II. **Tangible assets**
      1. Land, rights similar to land, and buildings including buildings on third-party land
      2. Technical facilities and machines
      3. Other facilities and office equipment
      4. Payments made in advance and assets under construction
   III. **Financial assets**
      1. Shares in affiliated companies
      2. Loans to affiliated companies
      3. Participations
      4. Loans to companies in which a participation exists
      5. Non-current securities
      6. Other loans
B. **Current assets**
   I. **Inventories**
      1. Raw materials and other materials
      2. Unfinished goods and services
      3. Finished goods and merchandise
      4. Payments made in advance
   II. **Receivables and other assets**
      1. Trade receivables
      2. Receivables from affiliated companies
      3. Receivables from companies in which a participation exists
      4. Other assets
   III. **Securities**
      1. Shares in affiliated companies
      2. Other securities
   IV. **Cash, positive deposits at central bank or other banks, checks**
C. **Deferred expenses**
D. **Deferred tax assets**
E. **Asset surplus from netting**

Tab. 3.3: Credit side according to § 266 sect. 3.

A. Equity
    I.   Subscribed capital
    II. Capital reserves
    III. Revenue reserves
        1. Legal reserves
        2. Reserves for shares of a controlling entity
        3. Statutory reserves
        4. Other revenue reserves
    IV. Profit/loss carry forward
    V. Net profit/loss of the year
B. Provisions
    1. Provisions for pensions and similar obligations
    2. Tax provisions
    3. Other provisions
C. Debt
    1. Bonds, thereof convertible
    2. Bank debt
    3. Received advance payments for orders
    4. Trade payables
    5. Payables from bills of exchange
    6. Payables to affiliated companies
    7. Payables to companies in which a participation exists
    8. Other payables, thereof tax payables and social security payables
D. Deferred income
E. Deferred tax liabilities

---

this information must be given in the notes. Further detailing is again based on the kind of liability.

For the application of this structure the following is to be considered:[4]

- This structure must be applied in this way. Small corporations can neglect items with Arabic numerals (§ 266 sect. 1).
- In the balance sheet, the figures of the current year and of the previous year must be reported. If previous year information is not comparable or was adjusted, this needs to be explained in the notes (§ 265 sect. 2).
- If an asset or a liability cannot be attributed unambiguously to one item, it is attributed to one item with reference to the other relevant items or with an explanation in the notes (§ 265 sect. 3).
- A further detailing of the structure is possible when the given structure is respected. Additional items and subtotals can be added if the content is not covered by existing items (§ 265 sect. 5).

---

4 *Beck'scher Bilanzkommentar*, § 265 and § 266, nos. 1–30.

- Structure and naming of the items with Arabic numerals can be changed if this improves clarity and transparency because of the particularities of the corporation (§ 265 sect. 6).
- Items with Arabic numerals may be aggregated if the amounts are not material for a true and fair view or if clarity and transparency are improved by doing so; in the latter case detailed information must be given in the notes (§ 265 sect. 7).
- Blank lines, i.e. items with a zero value in the current and the preceding period, can be neglected (§ 265 sect. 8).
- Once a structure and naming are decided, they must be kept according to the principle of formal comparability (see Chapter 2.3.3.2, § 265 sect. 1).

Further reading
IDW RS HFA 39 "Vorjahreszahlen im handelsrechtlichen Jahresabschluss" – Previous year's figures in the financial statements according to the Commercial Code.

Important differences to IFRS
The IFRS define the minimum requirements in IAS 1.54 and 1.60, usually using the current/non-current distinction. Further detailing depends on the judgment of the reporting entity and should be based on the underlying principles. Thus, the IFRS are more flexible than the Commercial Code.

3.1.2 Recognition prohibitions

§ 248 sect. 1 specifies several explicit recognition prohibitions. Not to be recognized as assets are
- **expenses incurred for the founding of a company**, such as consulting fees, notary and registration fees, expenses for a formation audit, fees for publication or travel expenses of the founders;
- **expenses incurred for the procurement of equity**, for example expenses for issuing shares, consulting fees or an initial public offering;
- **expenses for concluding an insurance contract**, such as broker fees.[5]

These transactions always result in expenses of the period.

Important differences to IFRS
Expenses related to the procurement of equity are deducted from the capital reserves (IAS 32.37).

---

5 *Beck'scher Bilanzkommentar*, § 248, nos. 1–9.

3.1.3 Non-current assets

3.1.3.1 Classification non-current–current

An asset is classified as non-current if it is intended to serve a business continuously (§ 247 sect. 2). There are objective indicators of this, such as the function of the asset (in relation to the business of the company) and useful life. On the other hand, the classification depends on the way the asset will be used in the business process, meaning it depends on the (subjective) judgment of management:[6]

- If the asset is to be sold to customers, it is current;
- If the asset will be used multiple times in business operations, it is typically non-current;
- A long-term production process does not require classifying the product as non-current if the intention is to sell the product after completion;
- Any asset that is not classified as non-current is current.

Examples

Tab. 3.4: Examples of the classification non-current–current.

Software	If acquired or produced/developed for the purpose of selling it to customers: → current assets (inventory)
	If acquired or produced/developed to be used within the company continuously → non-current assets (intangible assets)
Land	If acquired to be sold (e.g. real estate development) → current assets (inventory)
	If acquired to be used for example as the basis for a production or administration building → non-current assets (tangible assets)
Traded shares	If acquired to be sold again to realize a trading gain → current assets (current securities)
	If acquired to establish a permanent relationship with the issuing company or to control the issuing company → non-current assets (participations or shares in affiliated companies)

3.1.3.2 Subsequent measurement

These rules are relevant for all non-current assets. In the subsequent chapters only specifics for the different items will be explained.

---

6 *Beck'scher Bilanzkommentar*, § 247, nos. 350–357.

3.1.3.2.1 Depreciation/amortization

Because a non-current asset serves a company continuously, the decrease in its value should be reflected over the periods of usage according to the accrual principle. This is done by a depreciation or an amortization.[7]

§ 253 sect. 3 states that for non-current assets that have a definite useful life, the initial acquisition or production costs must be distributed over the useful life in a planned manner. This implies:[8]

- The useful life is definite, i.e. foreseeably limited. In consequence, there is no depreciation for assets with an unlimited or indefinite useful life such as land.
- The useful life is the time period for which the asset can be presumably used in an economically effective way, meaning what's important is the economic life, not the technical life. An asset's useful life ends if it brings no additional economic benefits when used (even if it is technically possible). Typically, the economic life is shorter than the technical life because of technical progress, obsolescence, changed market conditions or other factors.
- The initial acquisition or production costs must be distributed, meaning no more than the initial acquisition or production cost may be distributed. Higher replacement costs may not be recognized. If the asset is already completely depreciated but is still used (i.e. the useful life was estimated too short), there is no further depreciation.
- Costs must be distributed in a planned manner, i.e. a specific method must be used and this plan must be set up at the beginning.
- Depreciation is an expense (a reduction of net assets) but not an expenditure or cash outflow, because nothing is paid. The cash flow occurred in the past by paying the initial acquisition or production costs; depreciation is the expense effect of a prior payment. This distinction is important for the preparation of the cash flow statement (Chapter 3.4).

Basis for depreciation

The initial acquisition or production costs serve as the basis for depreciation. A residual value, i.e. sales proceeds at the end minus any costs for decommissioning or selling, must be recognized if it is substantial and can be estimated reliably; only rough guesses may not be deducted owing to the imparity principle.[9] Subsequent acquisition or pro-

---

7 Typically the notion of *depreciation* is used for tangible assets, whereas *amortization* is used for intangible or financial assets. Because the rules are the same for depreciation and amortization according to the Commercial Code, I use only depreciation for simplicity.

8 *Beck'scher Bilanzkommentar*, § 253, nos. 212–220.

9 *Beck'scher Bilanzkommentar*, § 253, no. 223.

duction costs increase the basis at the point in time when they are incurred, meaning the depreciation schedule must be changed prospectively (not retrospectively).[10]

Useful life

The useful life of an asset must be estimated based on the information available; this means a certain range is possible.

For tax purposes specific depreciation tables must be used. These tables attach to nearly all possible assets a specific useful life that must be used for tax purposes; a shorter useful life may be used only if there are good reasons for doing so.[11]

Because useful life is an estimate, changes may occur during the actual usage of the asset. If substantial changes in the estimates are necessary, the depreciation schedule must be revised from the point in time in which the estimates are changed (prospectively, not retrospectively). The estimates of the useful life should be reviewed regularly.[12]

Start and end of depreciation

In general, depreciation starts with the end of acquisition or the end of production, meaning when the asset is ready for operation. It ends with the end of usage. Thus, the first and eventually the last business years are depreciated on a pro rata basis. The common simplification is to start with the complete month in which the asset is ready for operation and to end with the complete month in which the asset is no longer used.[13]

Depreciation methods

The distribution of the initial acquisition or production costs must be done in a planned manner, meaning a specific method must be used. The Commercial Code does not require a specific method, but it must fulfil the GAAP, in particular it should reflect real decreases in value. The most common methods are as follows:[14]

- Linear (straight line)

  Acquisition or production costs are distributed equally over the useful life; this method assumes a continuous usage pattern. The annual depreciation is calculated as follows:

---

10 *Beck'scher Bilanzkommentar*, § 253, no. 260.
11 *Beck'scher Bilanzkommentar* § 253, nos. 224–236.
12 *Beck'scher Bilanzkommentar*, § 253, no. 260.
13 *Beck'scher Bilanzkommentar*, § 253, nos. 224–236.
   This is common practice as it is accepted for tax purposes. A daily depreciation/amortization schedule could be used as well, of course, but this is not common practice.
14 *Beck'scher Bilanzkommentar*, § 253, nos. 238–247.
   Coenenberg et al., 2021 (1), p. 164.

$$\text{Depreciation per year} = \frac{\text{Initial acquisition or production costs}}{\text{Useful life in years}}$$

This implies a constant rate of depreciation, meaning a certain percentage of the initial value is depreciated in each year.

- Declining balance (degressive)

A certain percentage is applied here as well, not to the initial value, but to the remaining book value. As the remaining book value decreases, depreciation decreases. This implies that the loss of value is higher at the beginning than at the end.

Because a certain percentage is applied to the remaining book value, the remaining book value would never reach zero. This would not comply with the legal requirement that the initial acquisition or production costs must be distributed over the useful life, i.e. the remaining value should be zero at the end. Therefore, when using the declining balance method, you necessarily switch to the linear method when the linear depreciation over the remaining useful life becomes higher than the corresponding depreciation according to the declining balance method.[15]

This is not considered a change in the measurement methods because it is planned from the beginning this way and it is necessary to fulfil the legal goal. The declining balance method is currently not acceptable for tax purposes.

- Performance oriented/units of activity

If the performance of an asset can be measured precisely, for example the mileage of a car or the flight hours of a plane, and if the total performance can be estimated, these values can be used as the basis for performance-oriented depreciation. Depending on the effective use of the asset, the depreciation rate will change each year:

$$\text{Depreciation rate for year } x = \frac{\text{Performance in year } x}{\text{Estimated total performance}}$$

This depreciation rate is applied to the initial acquisition or production costs.

- Progressive

This means that the depreciation amounts increase from year to year. In most cases, this will not be compliant with the GAAP; it is not acceptable for tax purposes.

---

[15] This is typically checked by a side calculation: for each year the linear depreciation over the remaining useful life is calculated and compared to the depreciation based on the declining balance method. Once the linear value is higher, only the linear depreciation is used for the remaining useful life.

Further reading

IDW RH HFA 1.015 "Zulässigkeit degressiver Abschreibungen in der Handelsbilanz vor dem Hintergrund der jüngsten Rechtsänderungen" – Acceptability of depreciation according to the declining balance method in financial statements according to the Commercial Code with regard to the latest legal changes.

IDW RH HFA 1.1016 "Handelsrechtliche Zulässigkeit einer komponentenweisen planmäßigen Abschreibung von Sachanlagen" – Acceptability of depreciation for components of tangible assets according to the Commercial Code.

Important differences to IFRS

According to IAS 16.51, the remaining useful life of an asset must be reviewed regularly, at least annually (no formal rule exists in the Commercial Code).

A residual value of tangible assets must reduce the depreciation basis if it is material – the reliability of estimates is not a reason to exclude a residual value (IAS 16.6 and 16.53). For intangible assets regularly a residual value of zero is assumed (IAS 38.100).

3.1.3.2.2 Impairment and reversal of impairment

Whereas depreciation/amortization reflects the regular decrease in value of an asset, an impairment reflects an additional, unscheduled decrease in value.

Non-current assets must be impaired to the lower fair value if this decrease in value is foreseeably permanent. This means, in consequence, that temporary decreases in value are not a reason for an impairment. This is known as the **moderate lower-of-cost-or-market principle**.

The fair value can be a market value if a procurement market exists (i.e. a replacement value). This refers to the acquisition costs of a comparable asset less necessary depreciation. If a replacement value is not available, a reproduction value can be used, i.e. the production costs if this asset were produced again. For non-current assets, a focus on the sales market is usually not acceptable because such assets are intended to serve the business continuously. A present value might be used if no other values are available.[16]

A common understanding of a permanent decrease in value for a depreciable asset is that the value at the closing date after impairment is, for a substantial part of the useful life or the next 5 years, lower than the future remaining book values without impairment. Put differently, if the impairment is caught up within 5 years by regular depreciation, the decrease in value is not considered permanent.[17]

---

16 *Beck'scher Bilanzkommentar*, § 253, nos. 306–310.
17 *Beck'scher Bilanzkommentar*, § 253, nos. 316–319.

Based on the principle of individual measurement, the need for impairment must usually be judged for each asset separately (unless simplifications can be used).

Like depreciation, an impairment is an expense, but not an expenditure or a cash flow. Typical reasons for an impairment may be, for example,

- substantial damage, destruction or loss of an asset;
- permanent decrease in the procurement market price or technical or economic obsolescence;
- substantial shifts in demand for products that lead to closure or continuous underutilization of facilities;
- for financial assets: substantial decrease in the market price (if listed) or earnings rate.

If the reasons for an impairment are no longer valid, the impairment must be reversed to the new fair value of the asset. In case of a non-depreciable asset, the maximum level is the initial acquisition or production cost. In the case of a depreciable asset, the maximum level of the reversal is the remaining book value that would have resulted without impairment.[18]

Presentation
Corporations must report impairments for non-current assets as a separate line item in the income statement or in the notes (§ 277 sect. 3).

Important differences to German tax law
German tax law uses a different logic:[19]

- There is no requirement for an impairment in the case of a permanent decrease in value, but it is an option.
- The remaining book value is compared with the partial value. The partial value is the fictitious value an acquirer of the whole company would be willing to pay for the specific asset as part of the whole. There are several assumptions about how this approach can be measured in real life.
- A permanent decrease in the value of a depreciable asset is assumed if the values at the closing date (after impairment) will be at least 50% of the remaining useful life below the remaining book values without impairment.

---

18 *Beck'scher Bilanzkommentar*, § 253, nos. 632–653.
19 *Beck'scher Bilanzkommentar*, § 253, nos. 313–314 and 320–326.

Because of these differences, the accounting for impairments will often be different in the commercial balance sheet and in the tax balance sheet and may result in deferred taxes.

Important differences to IFRS

Impairments of assets are specified in IAS 36 (with exceptions). It uses a different and more detailed concept than the Commercial Code:

–   Impairments must be assessed on the basis of cash-generating units to which cash inflows can be attributed.
–   The recoverable amount of a cash-generating unit is the higher value of its fair value (according to IFRS 13) less costs of disposal and the value in use. The value in use is the present value of the future cash in- and outflows of the cash-generating unit.
–   An impairment must be recognized if the recoverable amount is less than the book value of the cash-generating unit. There is no distinction between a temporary and a permanent decrease in value.
–   An impairment test must be conducted at least annually. It is a 2-step approach: first, indicators are checked as to whether or not an impairment is probable; then, the recoverable amount is calculated. Apart from goodwill and intangible assets with indefinite useful life, the recoverable amount has to be calculated only if there are indications for an impairment.
–   If the need for an impairment no longer exists, it must be reversed.

3.1.3.3 Presentation

Corporations must prepare in the notes for all non-current assets a development from the opening balance to the closing balance split into development of total acquisition and production costs and accumulated depreciation, amortization and impairment (§ 284 sect. 3). This needs to be prepared for all the different items according to § 266 (see Tab. 3.5).[20]

In addition, it must reported whether and to what extent interest on borrowings has been included in the production costs.[21]

3.1.3.4 Intangible assets

Intangible assets are assets without physical presence and that are not financial assets, i.e. they do not entail a claim to financial means. Typically, they are intellectual or commercial property rights, for example patents, software, licenses, brands.

---

20 *Beck'scher Bilanzkommentar*, § 284, nos. 220–305.
21 *Beck'scher Bilanzkommentar*, § 284, no. 310.

Tab. 3.5: Development of non-current assets (§ 284 sect. 3).

	Content	Line
	Total acquisition or production costs at beginning of reporting period	1
+	Additions to acquisition or production costs during period	2
−	Disposals from acquisition or production costs during period	3
±	Reclassifications of acquisition or production costs during period	4
=	**Total acquisition or production costs at end of reporting period**	$5 = 1 + 2 - 3 \pm 4$
	Accumulated depreciation, amortization and impairment at beginning of reporting period	6
+	Depreciation, amortization and impairment of the period	7
−	Reversal of depreciation, amortization and impairment of the period	8
+	Changes of accumulated depreciation, amortization and impairment in context of additions (without 7)	9
−	Changes of accumulated depreciation, amortization and impairment in context of disposals	10
±	Changes of accumulated depreciation, amortization and impairment in the context of reclassifications	11
=	**Accumulated depreciation, amortization and impairment at end of reporting period**	$12 = 6 + 7 - 8 - 10 \pm 11$
	Book value at beginning (opening balance)	$1 - 6$
	Book value at end (closing balance)	$5 - 12$

Intangible assets must be subdivided into three categories, which will be explained separately: acquired intangible assets, self-produced intangible assets and goodwill.

Acquired intangible assets

Recognition
Acquired intangible assets are recognized as any other asset if they fulfil the recognition criteria.[22]

Initial and subsequent measurement
Acquired intangible assets are measured at acquisition costs and amortized/impaired as any other asset.

Presentation
No additional requirements.

---

22 See the remarks about distinguishing acquisition against remuneration and production in Chapter 2.4.2.

Important differences to German tax law
See earlier remarks for all non-current assets.

Important differences to IFRS
IAS 38 allows the use of a revaluation model for measurement as alternative to the cost model, i.e. assets are regularly revalued to their fair value and amortized on that basis; this is only possible if an active market exists for the intangible asset (IAS 38.75–87). If the useful life of an asset cannot be estimated, meaning it has an indefinite useful life, it is not amortized (but only impaired if necessary; IAS 38.107 and 108). See the earlier remarks for all non-current assets.

Further reading
IDW RS HFA 11 neue Fassung (new version) "Bilanzierung entgeltlich erworbener Software beim Anwender" – Accounting for acquired software by the user.

Internally generated intangible assets

Recognition
Specific internally generated intangible assets are prohibited from recognition (§ 248 sect. 2): internally generated brands, mastheads, publishing titles, customer lists and similar items.[23]

For all other internally generated, non-current, intangible assets there exists a recognition option, meaning these assets can be recognized but need not be (§ 248 sect. 2). If this option is used, a profit distribution restriction exists for corporations (§ 268 sect. 8): The difference between the book value of the recognized asset and the corresponding deferred tax liability must be kept in the revenue reserves and may not be distributed as profit to shareholders.[24]

Initial measurement
If the aforementioned option is used, assets must be recognized with their production costs. Because these are non-current assets, production costs consist only of development costs (and the fair part of general administration and voluntary social security). Research costs are prohibited from recognition (see earlier, Chapter 2.4.2.2).[25] If research and development costs cannot be distinguished clearly, recognition is prohibited.

---

23 *Beck'scher Bilanzkommentar*, § 248, nos. 10–21.
24 *Beck'scher Bilanzkommentar*, § 268, nos. 65–76.
25 *Beck'scher Bilanzkommentar*, § 255, nos. 480–493.

Subsequent measurement

Internally generated intangible assets are amortized and/or impaired as any other asset. If – under rare circumstances – the useful life of an internally generated intangible asset cannot be estimated reliably, a useful life of 10 years must be assumed (§ 253 sect. 3 sent. 3).

Presentation

Corporations must furnish the following information in the notes:
- If the recognition option is used, the total amount of research and development costs and the part recognized as intangible assets (§ 285 no. 22).
- If the recognition option is used, the amount of revenue reserves that cannot be distributed as profit (§ 285 no. 28).

Important differences to German tax law

A recognition of internally generated intangible assets is prohibited in general, i.e. there is no recognition option. Therefore, the use of the option always results in a deferred tax liability.

Important differences to IFRS

According to IAS 38, internally generated intangible assets must be recognized (i.e. mandatory recognition, not optional) if certain recognition criteria are fulfilled (IAS 38.57). Research costs cannot be recognized. As in the Commercial Code, a recognition prohibition exists for brands, mastheads, publishing titles, customer lists and similar items (IAS 38.63). See the earlier comments on acquired intangible assets and for all non-current assets.

Goodwill

Recognition

Acquired goodwill is defined as the difference between the consideration for an acquired business and the net assets at time value. According to § 246 sect. 1 sent. 4, an acquired goodwill is treated as an asset with a definite useful life and therefore must be recognized. This has three implications: first, goodwill is not an asset, but only treated as one; goodwill does not fulfil the criterion of separate marketability because it cannot be sold separately from the business. Second, the generic goodwill, i.e. internally generated goodwill, of a company cannot be recognized. Third, goodwill is amortized.[26]

---

26 *Beck'scher Bilanzkommentar*, § 246, nos. 82 and 83.

Goodwill can arise in individual and consolidated financial statements depending on the form of the acquisition transaction. If a business is acquired in an *asset deal*, i.e. by acquiring all relevant assets and liabilities but not a specific legal entity, the goodwill arises in the individual financial statements. If a business is acquired in a *share deal*, i.e. the majority of shares of the legal entity that comprises the business is acquired, the goodwill arises in the consolidated financial statements (Chapter 4).

Initial measurement

Goodwill is measured as follows:

Tab. 3.6: Acquired goodwill (§ 246 sect. 1 sent. 4).

	Acquisition costs of the business: Purchase price or other form of consideration including all incidental acquisition costs
–	Net assets at time value, which are acquired assets at time value less acquired liabilities at time value
=	**Acquired goodwill**

It is important that net assets must be measured at time value, not at book value, i.e. any hidden reserves or hidden burdens must be uncovered; this process is called *purchase price allocation*. It includes not only a new measurement of the already recognized assets and liabilities but also the recognition of as yet unrecognized assets or liabilities.

Example

A company may have developed its own brand and therefore not be allowed to recognize this brand as an intangible asset. If the business of this company is acquired in an asset deal and the acquirer attributes value to this brand, he/she must recognize it, because for him/her it is an acquired brand (which must be recognized) and not an internally generated brand (which is not allowed to be recognized).

Subsequent measurement

Because goodwill is treated as an asset with a definite useful life, the useful life must be estimated and the goodwill is amortized over it. If – under rare circumstances – the useful life of goodwill cannot be estimated reliably, a useful life of 10 years must be assumed (§ 253 sect. 3 sent. 3 and 4).

In addition, goodwill must be impaired if its value decreases permanently (see earlier). The Commercial Code does not specify a method of testing goodwill impairment.

If goodwill has been impaired, the impairment will not be reversed, even if the reasons for the impairment are no longer valid (§ 253 sect. 5 sent. 2).[27]

Presentation
Corporations must describe for each occurrence of goodwill the useful life used for amortization (§ 285 no. 13).

Important differences to German tax law
Acquired goodwill must be amortized over 15 years independently of the useful life estimated for the commercial balance sheet (§ 7 sect. 1 sent. 3 EStG).

Important differences to IFRS
According to IFRS 3 and IAS 36, goodwill is not amortized, only impaired (impairment-only approach). The goodwill must be allocated to a cash-generating unit and is tested together with the cash-generating unit for impairment (IAS 36.80–99).

3.1.3.5 Tangible assets
Tangible assets are assets that have a physical presence, for example buildings, machines and vehicles.

Recognition
Tangible assets are recognized as any other asset if they fulfil the recognition criteria.

Initial measurement and subsequent measurement
Tangible assets are measured at acquisition or production costs and depreciated/impaired as any other asset.

Constant-value approach
As a simplification, tangible assets and raw materials can be recognized and measured using the constant-value approach (§ 240 sect. 3)[28]
-   if the total value of the assets is not material compared to total assets; a rule of thumb is that all constant values should not exceed 5% of total assets;

---

27 *Beck'scher Bilanzkommentar*, § 253, no. 676.
28 *Beck'scher Bilanzkommentar*, § 240, nos. 71–126.

- if the amount, value and composition of the assets fluctuate only slightly; this excludes, for example, assets with high market price fluctuations;
- if the used assets are replaced regularly.

If all three criteria are fulfilled, the assets can be recognized at a constant amount and value. They do not need to be included in annual stock taking. Any additions to these assets, i.e. replacement of used assets, are directly recognized as expenses.' Typically, after 3 years a physical stock taking is necessary. If this stock taking results in a higher or lower value, the value needs to be adjusted. Common practice is that an increase in value is only recognized if it is material (typically an increase of 10% or more), whereas decreases in value are always recognized owing to the prudence principle.

Example

A typical example of the use of the constant-value approach is the cutlery or tableware of a restaurant: Often, the value will be immaterial. Typically, the available amount, value and composition do not fluctuate: There is a fixed number of seats available and for each seat a defined amount of cutlery and tableware is necessary. The composition is constant, i.e. a missing knife cannot be replaced by an additional spoon or fork. Missing items will be replaced regularly because they are needed.

   If all this is true, the cutlery and tableware can be recognized using a constant value, meaning there is no depreciation, but all replaced items are directly expensed.

Low-value goods

For non-current assets there are no further simplifications included in the Commercial Code (apart from group measurement and constant value approach; see above). German tax law specifies the approach for low-value goods, which is typically applied for the commercial balance sheet as well (§ 6 sect. 2 and 2a EStG).[29]

   Low-value goods are defined as moveable assets that are tangible and noncurrent and whose value is not more than €1,000 net.

   The following simplifications exist:

Tab. 3.7: Low-value goods (§ 6 sect. 2 and 2a EStG).

Value of asset	Direct expense	Direct depreciation	Aggregated asset
Up to €250 net	Applicable	Applicable	Applicable
More than €250 net up to €800 net	Not applicable	Applicable	Applicable
Or: More than €250 net up to €1,000 net	Not applicable	Not applicable	Applicable

---

29 Coenenberg et al., 2021 (1), p. 171.
   Beck'scher Bilanzkommentar, § 253, nos. 275–277.

Direct expense

The asset is directly expensed, that is, it is not recognized as an asset. The kind of expense depends on the kind of asset or the context of the acquisition (it is not depreciation; see subsequent discussion).

Direct depreciation

The asset is recognized as a non-current asset, but then depreciated completely in the first year (i.e. a useful life of one year is assumed). A register must be kept that explains which assets were recognized and completely depreciated (this can be the usual asset ledger, but it can be a simplified register as well).

Aggregated asset

All assets of this category are aggregated together. Aggregated assets are no longer recognized and measured individually; this means that they are depreciated for 5 years independently of the individual useful life and that any subsequent changes (e.g. destruction, disposal) are not recognized. A register must be kept that explains which assets were recognized and aggregated (see above).

The method of simplification can be chosen freely for each of the three categories of assets but must be applied uniformly for all assets of that category.

Presentation

No additional requirements

Important differences to German tax law

See earlier remarks for all non-current assets.

Important differences to IFRS

IAS 16 requires including the future costs of dismantling, disposal and site restoration in the acquisition cost of an asset (IAS 16.16); the corresponding entry is a provision that will be used when the costs are incurred.

IAS 16 allows the use of a revaluation model for measurement as an alternative to the cost model, i.e. assets are regularly revalued to their fair value (revaluation model) and depreciated on that basis (IAS 16.31–42).

IFRS requires the component approach, meaning substantial parts of an asset that have a different useful life are depreciated separately according to that useful life (IAS 16.43–47).

Real estate held as a financial investment (investment property), must be accounted for according to IAS 40. For subsequent measurement, the company can choose between the cost model and the fair value model, but independently of other tangible assets (IAS 40.32A–33).

See the earlier remarks on all non-current assets.

3.1.3.6 Financial assets

Financial assets are assets that represent claims on financial means or are a part of the equity of another company.

§ 271 defines participations and affiliated companies:

- A participation consists of shares of another company with the intention of establishing a continuous connection with this company. This is assumed if the acquired shares comprise at least 20% of the total share capital of the company i.e. the acquirer has substantial influence, but no control.[30]
- Affiliated companies are companies that are included as parent company or subsidiary in the same consolidated financial statements. This means, typically, that the companies are controlled by the same parent company or that one company controls the others.[31]

Recognition

Financial assets are recognized as any other asset if they fulfil the recognition criteria.

Initial measurement

Financial assets are measured at acquisition cost.

Subsequent measurement

§ 253 sect. 3 sent. 6 provides an additional impairment option for financial assets: Financial assets not only must be impaired in the case of a permanent decrease in value but can also be impaired in the case of only temporary decreases in value.[32]

Presentation

If the option for an additional impairment is not used, a corporation needs to report the following items in notes (§ 285 no. 18):[33]

- the book value and the fair value of financial assets and

---

30 *Beck'scher Bilanzkommentar*, § 271, nos. 4–28.
31 *Beck'scher Bilanzkommentar*, § 271, nos. 30–35.
32 *Beck'scher Bilanzkommentar*, § 253, nos. 350–353.
33 *Beck'scher Bilanzkommentar*, § 285, nos. 530–545.
  § 285 no. 18 uses the term *financial instruments*, which is not legally defined. The common understanding is that it includes all financial assets.

– the reason for not impairing the assets, including arguments as to why the decrease in value is considered temporary.

A list of companies that classify as participations must be included in the notes; this list must include the name and location of the company, portion of capital of the participation, total equity and profit for the last year for which financial statements are available (§ 285 no. 11).[34]

Further reading
IDW RS HFA 8 "Zweifelsfragen in der Bilanzierung von asset backed securities-Gestaltungen und ähnlichen Transaktionen" – Specific questions about the accounting for transactions with asset backed securities and similar transactions.

IDW RS HFA 10 "Anwendung der Grundsätze des IDW S 1 bei der Bewertung von Beteiligungen und sonstigen Unternehmensanteilen für die Zwecke eines handelsrechtlichen Jahresabschlusses" – Application of company valuation principles according to IDW S 1 for the measurement of participations and other shares for the accounting according to the Commercial Code.

IDW RS HFA 18 "Bilanzierung von Anteilen an Personenhandelsgesellschaften im handelsrechtlichen Jahresabschluss" – Accounting for shares in partnerships according to the Commercial Code.

IDW RS HFA 22 "Zur einheitlichen oder getrennten handelsrechtlichen Bilanzierung strukturierter Finanzinstrumente" – Aggregated or separated accounting for structured financial instruments according to the Commercial Code.

IDW RH HFA 1.1014 "Umwidmung und Bewertung von Forderungen und Wertpapieren nach HGB" – Reclassification and measurement of receivables and securities according to the Commercial Code.

Important differences to German tax law
See earlier remarks for all non-current assets.

3.1.4 Excursus: accounting for financial instruments according to IFRS

The current standards for the accounting of financial instruments are IAS 32 "Financial Instruments: Presentation" and IFRS 9 "Financial Instruments". The approach is complex. In addition, IFRS 7 "Financial Instruments: Disclosures" requires extensive information in the notes.

---

34 *Beck'scher Bilanzkommentar*, § 285, nos. 360–406.

The IFRS do not follow the current/non-current distinction for assets and liabilities but require an additional classification that must be used for all financial assets and liabilities.

IAS 32.11 defines a financial instrument as "any contract that gives rise to a financial asset of one entity and a financial liability or equity instrument of another entity". It further details this as follows:[35]

Tab. 3.8: Financial assets and liabilities according to IAS 32.11.

Financial assets are	Financial liabilities are

– Cash
– An equity instrument of another entity
– A contractual right:
  a) to receive cash or another financial asset from another entity; or
  b) to exchange financial assets or financial liabilities with another entity under conditions that are potentially favorable to the entity;
– A contract that will or may be settled by the reception of the entity's own equity instruments, including further definitions that are beyond the scope of this discussion.
	– a contractual obligation:
	  a) to deliver cash or another financial asset to another entity; or
	  b) to exchange financial assets or financial liabilities with another entity under conditions that are potentially unfavorable to the entity;
	– a contract that will or may be settled by the delivery of the entity's own equity instruments, including further definitions that are beyond the scope of this discussion.

Financial assets and liabilities must be recognized and measured according to IFRS 9, unless their recognition and measurement are accounted for according to another standard (IFRS 9.2.1). IFRS 9.4 requires a further categorization:

Financial assets must be categorized as
- at amortized costs,
- at fair value through other comprehensive income or
- at fair value through profit or loss.

A financial asset can be designated as "at fair value through profit or loss" even if the criteria for another classification are fulfilled.

Financial liabilities must be categorized as
- at amortized costs or
- at fair value through profit or loss.

---

35 Coenenberg et al., 2021 (1), p. 273.

The initial categorization can be changed only in very limited cases.[36]

Depending on the classification, financial assets and liabilities are measured differently. In a simplified overview:

The fair value must be determined according to IFRS 13.

Category	Subsequent Measurement	Accounting for measurement changes
At amortised costs	At amortised costs in the meaning of IFRS 9; eventually additional impairments or their reversal (IFRS 9.5.4.3 and 5.4.4)	Through profit or loss to the extent that no hedge accounting is used (IFRS 9.5.4.1 and B5.4.1)
At fair value through profit or loss	At fair value (IFRS 9.5.2.1)	Through profit or loss (IFRS 9.5.2.1)
At fair value through other comprehensive income	At fair value (IFRS 9.5.2.1)	Measurement changes are accounted for in other comprehensive income apart from interest rate changes, dividends, impairments or effects of currency translation (IFRS 9.5.2.1 and 5.7.10)

Fig. 3.1: Measurement according to IFRS 9.[37]

Amortized cost refers to the acquisition costs minus any repayments and accumulated amortization of agios or disagios; the amortization of agios or disagios must be calculated using the effective interest method (IFRS 9.5.4).

Other comprehensive income (OCI) is an equity category that is used for changes in the value of assets or liabilities that should not affect the income statement.

3.1.5 Current assets

Any asset that is not non-current is current (§ 247 sect. 2).

The current assets consist of inventories, accounts receivable and securities, as well as cash and cash equivalents. Whereas inventories are often tangible assets, all the others are financial assets of different kinds.

This chapter explains the general approach for subsequent measurement as there are no specific rules for recognition and initial measurement. Specifics on

---

36 IFRS 9.4.4.

Coenenberg et al., 2021 (1), p. 296.

37 Coenenberg et al., 2021 (1), p. 301.

financial instruments and hedge accounting are highlighted in Chapter 3.1.5.3 or in Chapter 3.1.10.3.

Subsequent measurement

Because current assets do not continuously serve the business, i.e. they are used only once for operations, they are not depreciated or amortized. However, they must be impaired, if necessary.

For all current assets, the **strict lower-of-cost-or-market principle** must be applied (§ 253 sect. 4): The initial value (acquisition or production cost) must be compared with a market price at the closing date; if a market price is not available, a fair value is used. The lower value of the two must be recognized (based on the principle of prudence).[38]

In contrast to non-current assets, this must also be applied for only temporary decreases in value (that is why it is called **strict** lower-of-cost-or-market principle).

If the reason for an impairment is no longer valid, the impairment must be reversed (§ 253 sect. 5).

The value from which fair value is derived depends on the kind of current asset:[39]

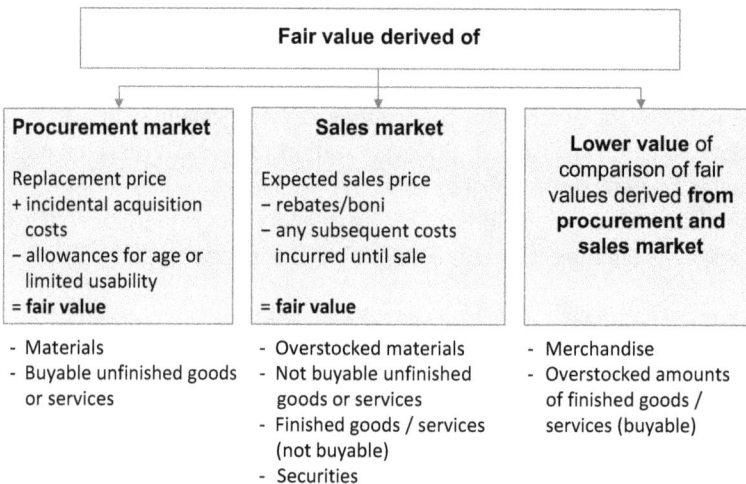

Fair value derived of		
Procurement market	**Sales market**	**Lower value** of comparison of fair values derived **from procurement and sales market**
Replacement price + incidental acquisition costs − allowances for age or limited usability = **fair value**	Expected sales price − rebates/boni − any subsequent costs incurred until sale = **fair value**	
- Materials - Buyable unfinished goods or services	- Overstocked materials - Not buyable unfinished goods or services - Finished goods / services (not buyable) - Securities	- Merchandise - Overstocked amounts of finished goods / services (buyable)

Fig. 3.2: Fair values for measurement of current assets.

---

38 *Beck'scher Bilanzkommentar*, § 253, nos. 501–505.
39 *Beck'scher Bilanzkommentar*, § 253, nos. 510–520.

Important differences to German tax law

See the remarks on non-current assets. Under tax law, there is an impairment option only for permanent decreases in value. This will often result in differences between the commercial balance sheet and the tax balance sheet because the strict lower-of-cost-or-market principle requires impairment also for only temporary decreases in value.

Important differences to IFRS

The remarks on the impairment of assets according to IAS 36 apply as well to current assets (see above) if they are not inventories, financial assets or assets resulting from contracts with customers (IFRS 15).

3.1.5.1 Inventories

Recognition

For inventories the general principles of recognition of assets must be used (see Chapter 2.4.1).

Because inventories are often owned for only a short time and may be moved from one location to another, the question of economic ownership is very important. Typical issues that arise are the following:

- Transfer of risks: Depending on the terms of trade (e.g. as the international standard Incoterms), the reporting entity can be liable for goods that have not reached its premises. If for example goods are to be delivered under the condition "free on board" (fob), the purchaser is responsible for the goods and bears the risk of loss or destruction when the goods cross the railing of the ship on which they are loaded, even if the goods are far away.
- Economic ownership: Even if the goods are physically on the premises of the reporting entity, they may not be recognized in the balance sheet, for example if they are used on commission or a similar arrangement, i.e. the reporting entity does not own the inventories economically.

Initial measurement

As for all assets, the measurement basis is acquisition costs (if purchased) or production costs (if produced). Thus, for proprietary products the definition of production costs and the use of the available options is a central topic of accounting policy (see Chapter 2.4.2.2).

Because inventories are often purchased or produced frequently or in large quantities, the principle of individual measurement is applicable only after exerting considerable effort. Imagine a box containing 5,000 identical screws that were delivered at different times and prices – it would be very costly to keep track of the value of each specific screw. To keep the accounting cost effective, several simplifications are possible:

- Constant-value approach: For raw materials and similar supplies a constant-value approach can be used (§ 240 sect. 3); this is the same approach as for tangible non-current assets and requires the same conditions (see Chapter 3.1.3.5).
- Group measurement: This can be used for similar inventories; similar means similar in kind or similar in use or function (§ 240 sect. 4). If applicable, the inventories are measured using the periodic weighted average or with the moving average:[40]
  - Periodic average: One average value is calculated for the complete reporting period, that is

$$\text{Average price} = \frac{\text{Opening balance } + \text{ value of all additions}}{\text{Opening amount } + \text{ amounts of all additions}}.$$

    This average price is used to measure the inventories and the cost of goods sold.
  - Moving average: Basically, the same calculation is done, but after each addition a new average is calculated and used until the next addition.
- Cost formulas: For similar items of inventories, cost formulas can be used (§ 256); cost formulas assume a certain usage pattern, that is, the real usage pattern can be different or is not known (as long as the GAAP are respected):[41]
  - Last in, first out (LIFO): It is assumed that the goods acquired/produced last are used/sold first; this implies that the goods in stock at the closing date are assumed to be the oldest or the oldest prices are used to measure the closing amount. In times of inflation this typically results in hidden reserves because the newer and higher prices are used to measure the cost of goods sold, whereas the older and lower prices are used to measure the stock.
  - First in, first out (FIFO): It is assumed that the goods acquired/produced first are used/sold first; this implies that the goods in stock at closing date are assumed to be the newest or the newest prices are used to measure the closing amount.

Subsequent measurement

As for all current assets, the strict lower-of-cost-or-market principle must be applied at each closing date (see above).

---

40 *Beck'scher Bilanzkommentar*, § 240, nos. 130–139.
    This can be applied to other moveable assets or liabilities if they are similar in kind or value (§ 240 sect. 4); a rule of thumb for goods that are similar in value is a ±20% price difference.
41 *Beck'scher Bilanzkommentar*, § 256.

Presentation
If the previously described simplifications are used and market prices exist for these goods, corporations must report the total difference for each group of goods measured using these methods between the latest market price before closing date and the initial measurement in the notes, if this difference is material (§ 284 sect. 2 no. 3).

Important differences to German tax law
LIFO is applicable for tax purposes if the real sequence of consumption does not contradict LIFO. FIFO is applicable for tax purposes only if it is the actual sequence of consumption, meaning it cannot be used as a simplification (§ 6 sect. 1 no. 2a EStG).

Important differences to IFRS
The applicable standard is IAS 2 "Inventories". Important differences exist
- with regard to the initial measurement: LIFO is not applicable according to IAS 2.25;
- with regard to subsequent measurement: Inventories are measured with their net realizable value at the closing date if that is below the initial acquisition or production costs (IAS 2.34). The net realizable value is strictly sales market oriented (even for materials), i.e. price decreases on a procurement market are not directly relevant for an impairment but may be an indicator of decreasing sales prices; in consequence, materials are not impaired (even if the procurement prices have decreased) as long as the finished products can be sold above the production costs (IAS 2.28–33).

3.1.5.2 Accounts receivable

Recognition
Accounts receivable are recognized as any other asset if they fulfil the recognition criteria. For any receivable, but in particular for trade receivables, the revenue recognition criteria must be fulfilled (completed contract method; Chapter 2.3.3.3.1).

Initial measurement
Accounts receivable are measured at their nominal value (acquisition cost).

Subsequent measurement
The principle of individual measurement and the lower-of-cost-or-market principle must be applied here as well. There is no specific legally required approach. In combination with the requirements of German tax law, this leads to a three-step approach as common practice:

1. Specific valuation allowance
    (a) Complete loss of a receivable
    (b) Partial loss of a receivable
2. General valuation allowance

In detail:[42]

1. Specific valuation allowanceBased on the principle of individual measurement, any risks known for specific receivables are taken into account. Because market prices for receivables are usually not observable, the collectible amount must be estimated.
    (a) Complete loss of a receivableIf a receivable is completely lost, it is derecognized and the VAT can be corrected (§ 17 sect. 2 UStG).
    (b) Partial loss of a receivableIf a receivable is not lost completely, a correction of the VAT is not possible, i.e. only the net values may be corrected to the extent the receivable is expected to be uncollectible.
2. General valuation allowanceApart from specific risks, i.e. knowledge about risks for specific receivables, typically a general risk exists, i.e. a certain percentage of receivables will become uncollectible even if at the closing date no specific risks were known. This general risk is reflected by a general valuation allowance. As in case 1.b. the VAT may not be corrected. The net values of all receivables for which no specific valuation allowances were recognized serve as the basis for the general valuation allowance;[43] the formula is as follows:

    Net value of all receivables
    − Net value of receivables with specific valuation allowance
    = **Net value of receivables with no specific valuation allowance**
    × Percentage of general valuation allowance
    = **General valuation allowance**

The percentage is an estimate of the risks of these receivables; typically it is based on past experience.

---

42 *Beck'scher Bilanzkommentar*, § 253, nos. 560–596.

43 Otherwise, a receivable with a partial loss, for example a 30% specific valuation allowance, would be included, with the remaining value of 70% in the basis of the general valuation allowance; that would result in a double valuation allowance (specific and general). This is not acceptable: The risks are accounted for either specifically or in general, but not both together.

Presentation

If receivables have a remaining term of more than 1 year, corporations must report this per balance sheet item in the balance sheet or in the notes (§ 268 sect. 4).[44]

Further reading

IDW RS HFA 8 "Zweifelsfragen in der Bilanzierung von asset backed securities-Gestaltungen und ähnlichen Transaktionen" – Specific questions about the accounting for transactions with asset-backed securities and similar transactions.

IDW RS HFA 22 "Zur einheitlichen oder getrennten handelsrechtlichen Bilanzierung strukturierter Finanzinstrumente" – Aggregated or separated accounting for structured financial instruments according to the Commercial Code.

IDW RH HFA 1.1014 "Umwidmung und Bewertung von Forderungen und Wertpapieren nach HGB" – Reclassification and measurement of receivables and securities according to the Commercial Code.

Important differences to German tax law and IFRS

See earlier remarks on impairment and financial assets.

3.1.5.3 Securities and cash/cash equivalents

Securities are financial assets that are in a specific form that allows for trading on stock exchanges (independently of whether or not they are traded).

Cash is the legal currency of the corresponding country; most amounts will not be held in cash on hand but in positive bank accounts. Cash equivalents are financial assets that can be converted to cash in the short term and at very little risk.

Recognition

Securities and cash/cash equivalents are recognized when they fulfil the general criteria for recognition.

Initial and subsequent measurement

Securities are measured initially by their acquisition costs, cash by its nominal value. For subsequent measurement the general rules for impairments must be applied.

Presentation

There are no specific requirements.

---

44 *Beck'scher Bilanzkommentar*, § 268, nos. 25–28.

Important differences to German tax law and IFRS
See earlier remarks on impairment and financial assets.

3.1.6 Equity

From an accounting point of view, equity equals net assets, i.e. it is the residual of assets and liabilities. From a legal perspective, equity defines on the one hand the claims of shareholders on the company; on the other hand it defines what is liable to creditors in case of insolvency. A third perspective is the controlling view: How much of the equity was paid in from the outside (i.e. individual claims of shareholders on the company, in particular voting rights) and how much was earned and retained in the company (i.e. can be claimed by the shareholders)?

For **proprietorships and partnerships,** there are no specific requirements regarding how to report equity; the GAAP, in particular the principle of clarity and transparency, must be fulfilled. Because these legal forms have at least one natural person that is fully personally liable, further regulation is not considered necessary.

Corporations, on the other hand, have limited liability, and more detailed information is required: The reporting of equity is twofold: on the one hand, subscribed capital and capital reserves, which have been paid in from outside, and on the other hand, revenue reserves, retained earnings and net profit/loss which have been earned by the company.

3.1.6.1 Subscribed capital and capital reserves

Subscribed capital
Subscribed capital is capital that is liable to creditors. For corporations, it is registered in the company register. It is recognized at its nominal value (§ 268 sect. 1).

Under German company law, corporations can be founded with only partial payment of the subscribed capital:

Tab. 3.9: Minimum capital requirements.

	Minimum capital	Minimum payment
Stock company	€50,000	Min. 25%
(Aktiengesellschaft AG)	(§ 7 AktG)	(§ 36a sect. 1 AktG)
Limited liability company	€25,000	Min. 50%*
(Gesellschaft mit beschränkter Haftung GmbH)	(§ 5 GmbHG)	(§ 7 sect. 2 GmbHG)

* To be more precise: For each share at least 25% must be paid in (i.e. the ratio can be different for each share), but in total for all shares 50% of the minimum capital must be reached.

If this option for partial payment is used, shareholders are nevertheless personally liable for the money that has not been paid in so far. For a creditor on the other hand, it is important to know both: the total amount of subscribed capital and the amount that is at the moment available to the company because if it becomes necessary to obtain the portion that has not been paid in so far, the legal enforcement will take more time and usually increase expenses.

Thus, the Commercial Code prescribes reporting in the balance sheet both the subscribed capital and the amount that has not been paid in and was not called up (§ 272 sect. 1):[45]

Example

A stock company is founded with the minimum capital of €50,000; the shareholders agree to pay in only 50% of that, and they do so. The reporting is as follows (figures in Euros):

Tab. 3.10: Example of partial payment (1).

A.	Equity		
	1.	Subscribed capital	50,000
		– Not paid-in and not called-up capital	25,000
		Called-up capital	25,000

If additional capital is called up by the company, but not yet paid in, it is recognized as being receivable from shareholders (i.e. as an asset and increased equity; § 272 sect. 1).

Let us continue the **example**:

Assume the shareholders decide to call up additional capital of €10,000 but do not pay until the closing date. The reporting changes as follows:

Tab. 3.11: Example of partial payment (2).

A.	Equity		
	1.	Subscribed capital	50,000
		– Not paid-in and not called-up capital	15,000
		Called-up capital	35,000

---

45 *Beck'scher Bilanzkommentar*, § 272, nos. 30–41.

Capital reserves

Capital reserves are any additional payments by shareholders in equity that do not increase the subscribed capital.

The most common case is the issuance of new shares for a price that is higher than the nominal value; this excess price is called *agio*. The agio is completely recognized in the capital reserves.

An agio can be combined with partial payment of subscribed capital, but the agio must always be paid in fully (§ 36a sect. 1 AktG).[46] Capital reserves are measured at their nominal value.

Special topic: Acquisition and sale of own shares

A corporation can acquire and later resell its own shares. Legally, this is not restricted to listed shares, but this is the most common case. For stock companies, in most cases the acquisition is limited to 10% of total issued shares (§ 71 sect. 2 AktG).

For the acquisition and sale of its own shares, specific rules must be observed:
- When a company acquires its own shares, the nominal value of these shares must be deducted from the subscribed capital, and the difference between the nominal value and the acquisition cost must be deducted from the revenue reserves. Incidental acquisition costs are expenses from the period (§ 272 sect. 1a).[47]
- If the shares are resold, the deductions are reversed. If a gain is realized (i.e. sales price is higher than acquisition price), this gain is recognized in the capital reserves. A loss remains as a reduction in revenue reserves. Costs for the sale are expenses from the period (§ 272 sect. 1b).[48]

3.1.6.2 Revenue reserves and retained earnings

Revenue reserves are profits of a company that are formally transferred to revenue reserves to be retained within the company (§ 272 sect. 3). They are measured at their nominal value.[49]

Revenue reserves are affected by the point in time when the shareholders decide how to use the profit:
- No decision about use of profit
  Shareholders have not decided how to use the profit until the preparation of the financial statements. The categories of equity look as follows (this is the structure of § 266):

---

46 *Beck'scher Bilanzkommentar*, § 272, nos. 160–200.
47 *Beck'scher Bilanzkommentar*, § 272, nos. 130–139.
48 *Beck'scher Bilanzkommentar*, § 272, nos. 141–150.
49 *Beck'scher Bilanzkommentar*, § 272, nos. 230–279.

Tab. 3.12: Presentation of equity given no decision about the use of profit.

A. **Equity**
I.   **Subscribed capital**
II.   **Capital reserves**
III.   **Revenue reserves**
1.   Legal reserves
2.   Reserves for shares of a controlling entity
3.   Statutory reserves
4.   Other revenue reserves
IV.   **Profit/loss carry forward**
V.   **Net profit/loss of year**

–   Decision on total use of profit (§ 268, sect. 1)
    When financial statements are prepared, the shareholders may have already decided that the complete profit will either be paid out as a dividend or allocated to revenue reserves; no funds will remain. Then the categories of equity look as follows: There are no profit/loss carry forward and net profit/loss for the year because the money is completely allocated.[50]

Tab. 3.13: Presentation of equity given total use of profit.

A. **Equity**
I.   **Subscribed capital**
II.   **Capital reserves**
III.   **Revenue reserves**
1.   Legal reserves
2.   Reserves for shares of a controlling entity
3.   Statutory reserves
4.   Other revenue reserves

–   Decision on the partial use of profit (§ 268 sect. 1)
    When the financial statements are prepared, the shareholders may have decided already that a part of profit (and/or profit carried forward) is either paid out as dividend or allocated to the revenue reserves, but there is an amount left. This remaining amount is aggregated and recognized as "retained earnings".[51]

---

50 *Beck'scher Bilanzkommentar*, § 268, nos. 8 and 9.
    The dividend that has to be paid out is reported as liability.
51 *Beck'scher Bilanzkommentar*, § 268, nos. 4–7.

Tab. 3.14: Presentation of equity given partial use of profit.

A.	**Equity**	
	I.	**Subscribed capital**
	II.	**Capital reserves**
	III.	**Revenue reserves**
		1. Legal reserves
		2. Reserves for shares of a controlling entity
		3. Statutory reserves
		4. Other revenue reserves
	IV.	**Retained earnings**

Presentation

If the equity of a corporation is more than offset by losses, the excess losses (i.e. those losses not covered by the equity) must be reported on the asset side as "Losses not covered by equity" (§ 268 sect. 3).[52]

If equity is presented given a partial use of profit, the different components of retained earnings must be reported in the balance sheet or in the notes (§ 268 sect. 1).

Stock companies must extend the income statement by the following items to reconcile net profit/loss with retained earnings (if applicable; § 158 AktG); the reconciliation can be carried out in the notes as well:

   Net profit/loss of the period
± Profit/loss carry forward
+ Transfers from capital reserves
+ Transfers from revenue reserves
– Transfers to revenue reserves
– Profit distributions
= **Retained earnings**

Important differences to IFRS

An additional category of equity according to IFRS is other comprehensive income (OCI). Changes in the value of assets or liabilities that should not affect the income statement are directly recognized in OCI (IAS 1.82A). This is not possible according to the Commercial Code.

---

52 *Beck'scher Bilanzkommentar*, § 268, nos. 11–20.

   Of course, this item is not an asset (no economic benefit, no separate marketability), but an accounting is necessary; otherwise, negative equity would be needed to balance the balance sheet.

3.1.7 Provisions

In the first part of the next section, the general approach to accounting for provisions is explained. In the second part, the specific topics concerning provisions for pensions and similar obligations are explained.

3.1.7.1 Accounting for provisions

Recognition

Provisions are uncertain liabilities. The uncertainty may relate to the reason or the amount of the obligation. Because of the principle of completeness, uncertain liabilities need to be included in financial statements if they are probable. Probable means, typically, that there are more arguments for their existence than against.[53]

The principle of individual measurement must be applied as much to provisions as to any other assets and liabilities. On the other hand, if there are many similar transactions that might result in future expenses, for example product warranties, the only way to measure them reasonably and effectively is to group them together; this is acceptable because the group measurement (§ 240 sect 4.) can be applied to provisions as well.[54]

The recognition of a provision (or its increase) results in an expense in the current period, but not in an expenditure or cash outflow because payment will be made in the future (similar to depreciation or amortization).

§ 249 defines all reasons for the recognition of a provision; for any other reason, a provision may not be recognized (§ 249 sect. 2; see Fig. 3.3).

Provisions for uncertain liabilities (§ 249 sect. 1 sent. 1)

Any liability that is uncertain, but probable in reason or amount, must be recognized. There is no legal recognition option, but a factual one: If the probability is estimated too low, a recognition is not possible.[55]

Uncertain liabilities include not only legal but also constructive obligations, which are obligations that arise from past behavior that cannot be avoided by a company.[56] Uncertain liability implies, nevertheless, that a liability already exists, meaning a past event results in an obligation in the future. Due to the matching principle (as part of the realization principle), expenses need to be recognized

---

53 In more detail, a distinction can be made between the probability that the obligation exists and the probability that the obligation must be fulfilled; for a recognition both must be probable. *Beck'-scher Bilanzkommentar*, § 249, nos. 42–44.

54 *Beck'scher Bilanzkommentar*, § 253, no. 162.

55 *Beck'scher Bilanzkommentar*, § 249, nos. 24–45.

56 *Beck'scher Bilanzkommentar*, § 249, no. 31.

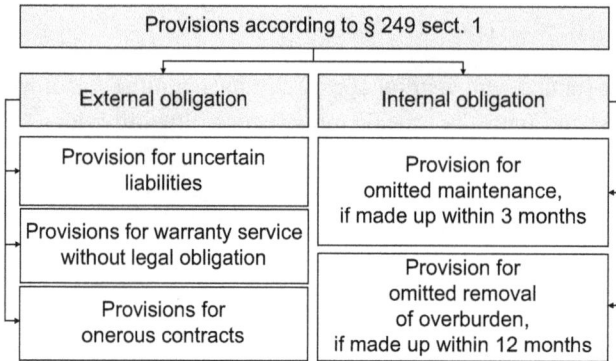

Fig. 3.3: Provisions.

corresponding to the income, meaning if a past event (e.g. sale of a product) re-sulted in income and will probably result in future expenses (e.g. warranty serv-ices), these expenses should be recognized in the same period as the income or in the earliest period when they become probable.[57]

Typical examples for provisions for uncertain liabilities are

- provisions for litigation,
- provisions for (legal) warranty services,
- provisions for taxes,
- provisions for pensions (see below).

Provisions for warranty service without legal obligation (§ 249 sect. 1 no. 2)

These obligations are partially included in the provisions for uncertain liabilities as long as a constructive obligation exists. With this specific regulation, warranty serv-ices without legal obligation and without constructive obligation must also be rec-ognized as provisions. The legislator wanted to make sure that any provision for warranty services will be tax deductible (because of the principle of congruence).[58]

Provisions for onerous contracts (§ 249 sect. 1 sent. 1)

Whereas a provision for uncertain liabilities is recognized for the uncertain effects of a past event, a provision for an onerous contract is recognized for an expected future loss of a pending transaction. A pending transaction is one in which none of the parties has fulfilled its obligations (e.g. under a sales contract, the seller has not delivered the products and the buyer has not paid). Usually, pending transactions are not accounted for because it is assumed that the assets or services exchanged

---

57 *Beck'scher Bilanzkommentar* § 249, no. 34.
58 *Beck'scher Bilanzkommentar*, § 249, nos. 112–115.

are at least of equal value, i.e. no loss will be incurred. Sometimes, even if the transaction is still pending, a loss may be expected when the contract is fulfilled; this situation is called an *onerous contract*. Because of the imparity principle, a loss must be recognized when it becomes probable; thus, a provision for onerous contracts must be recognized in such a case.[59]

Pending transactions and, in consequence, onerous contracts can occur in all areas of business:[60]

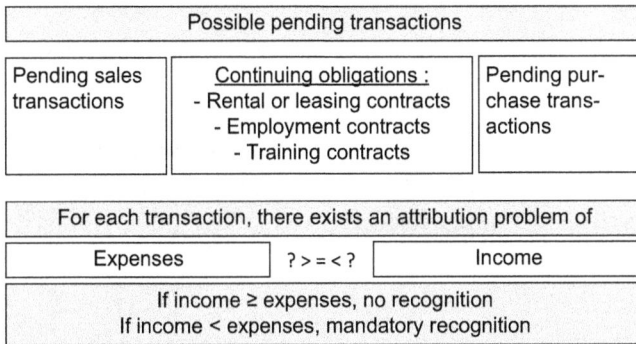

Possible pending transactions		
Pending sales transactions	Continuing obligations : - Rental or leasing contracts - Employment contracts - Training contracts	Pending purchase transactions

For each transaction, there exists an attribution problem of		
Expenses	? > = < ?	Income

If income ≥ expenses, no recognition   If income < expenses, mandatory recognition

Fig. 3.4: Provision for onerous contracts.

Provisions for omitted maintenance or removal of overburden (§ 249 sect. 1 no. 1)

So far, all provisions have been external obligations, i.e. obligations to a third party. In two specific cases, only internal obligations must be recognized as well: If maintenance was omitted, meaning it would have been necessary but was not carried out, and if it is made up within 3 months after the closing date, the upcoming maintenance expense must be recognized as provision.[61]

Because of the explicit time limit, a factual recognition option exists here: If the omitted maintenance is scheduled within 3 months, it must be recognized. If it is scheduled later, it is not allowed to be recognized.

The same logic applies to omitted removal of overburden that is made up within 12 months.[62]

---

59 *Beck'scher Bilanzkommentar*, § 249, no. 51.
60 *Beck'scher Bilanzkommentar*, § 249, nos. 52–80.
61 *Beck'scher Bilanzkommentar*, § 249, nos. 101–111.
62 *Beck'scher Bilanzkommentar*, § 249, no. 111.

Initial measurement

According to § 253 sect. 1, provisions are measured with the settlement amount necessary to fulfil the obligation based on reasonable commercial assessment. This implies[63]

- a necessity to estimate; the estimation of a range is possible; nevertheless, deliberate over- or undervaluations are not allowed;
- an estimation of the complete settlement amount. One's own potential claims or receivables may not be deducted, but must be recognized as assets if they fulfil the recognition criteria;
- the estimation of future price and cost developments, i.e. the settlement amount must be estimated for the time of settlement.

In addition, long-term provisions must be discounted to the present value using a 7-year-average market rate congruent with the term of the provision. This rate is published monthly by the German central bank (§ 253 sect. 2).[64]

Subsequent measurement

If the estimate for the settlement amount changes, the measurement of the provision must be adjusted (increase and decrease).[65]

Changes in the term of the provision or in the interest rates will lead to changes in the present value. The corresponding changes must be reported as interest income or expense in the income statement (§ 277 sect. 5).

If the reasons for a provision no longer exist, it must be reversed (§ 249 sect. 2).

Presentation

Corporations must present a split of "other provisions" in the notes if they are material (§ 285 no. 12).[66]

Further reading

IDW RS HFA 4 "Zweifelsfragen zum Ansatz und zur Bewertung von Drohverlustrückstellungen" – Specific questions about the recognition and measurement of provisions for onerous contracts.

IDW RS HFA 34 "Einzelfragen zur handelsrechtlichen Bilanzierung von Verbindlichkeitsrückstellungen" – Specific questions about the accounting for provisions for uncertain liabilities according to the Commercial Code.

---

63 *Beck'scher Bilanzkommentar*, § 253, nos. 151–163.
64 *Beck'scher Bilanzkommentar*, § 253, nos. 180–195.
65 *Beck'scher Bilanzkommentar*, § 253, no. 151.
66 *Beck'scher Bilanzkommentar*, § 285, nos. 430 and 431.

IDW RH HFA 1.009 "Rückstellungen für die Aufbewahrung von Geschäftsunterlagen sowie für die Aufstellung, Prüfung und Offenlegung von Abschlüssen und Lageberichten nach § 249 Abs. 1" – Provisions for storage of documents and for preparation, auditing and publication of financial statements and management reports according to § 249 sect. 1.

Important differences to German tax law
The recognition of provisions for onerous contracts is prohibited under tax law (§ 5 sect. 4a EStG).

Long-term provisions must be discounted at a discount rate of 5.5% – independent of any market situations (§ 6 sect. 1 no. 3a EStG).

Expected future price or cost increases may not be included in the settlement amount; the calculation of the settlement amount must be based on current conditions (§ 6 sect. 1 no. 3a EStG).

Important differences to IFRS
IAS 37 defines the general accounting for provisions, but there are specific rules in other standards, for example IAS 19 for employee benefits. Provisions for internal obligations (omitted maintenance or waste disposal, warranty services without obligation) cannot be recognized (IAS 37.14). For provisions in connection with restructuring, specific criteria for recognition exist (IAS 37.72).

Some transactions that are typically classified as provisions according to the Commercial Code are classified as accruals (and, in consequence, debt), according to IAS 37.11, for example non-invoiced audit fees for current financial statements or vacation leave not taken are reported as provision according to the Commercial Code, but as accrual according to IFRS. Long-term provisions must be discounted at a market-oriented pre-tax rate that reflects the risks of the provision (IAS 37.45 and 47) if the effect of discounting is material.

3.1.7.2 Specifics for pension provisions

Recognition
A company can use different ways to grant its employees retirement benefits in the future:[67]
- Defined contribution plans, where the employer must pay certain contributions but does not guarantee a specific retirement benefit. This is the case if, for example, the employer pays insurance premiums on behalf of its employees.

---

[67] Coenenberg et al., 2021, p. 464.

These contributions paid are expenses from the given period; no provision is recognized.

– Pension trusts: An independent organization guarantees a certain retirement benefit. The employer pays defined contributions. If the employer is not liable for retirement benefits (in case the pension trust cannot fulfil its obligations), this is treated as an expense from the given period. If the employer is liable for a defined level of retirement benefits, this is called an indirect pension agreement.

– Direct pension agreements: The employer promises to pay its employees defined retirement benefits directly; this is an uncertain liability and must be recognized as provision.

The accounting for pension provisions has changed over time; due to the long term of the provisions, the transitional rules remain relevant in some cases:[68]

– Direct pension agreements granted before 1 January 1987: recognition option according to Art. 28 sect. 1 EGHGB.

– Direct pension agreements granted on or after 1 January 1987: recognition requirement (§ 249 sect. 1).

– Indirect pension agreements: These are contingent liabilities and need not be recognized (see subsequent discussion in Chapter 3.1.9). In addition, there exists a recognition option whereby, even if such liabilities change from contingent to effective, they do not have to be recognized (Art. 28 sect. 1 EGHGB).

§ 246 sect. 2 requires that assets be deducted from the pension provision (plan assets) if

– these assets are not accessible to creditors and

– these assets serve only the purpose of fulfilling liabilities of pensions or similar obligations.

If the value of the assets is higher than the provision, a specific balance sheet item "asset surplus from netting" must be used (§ 266 sect. 2).[69]

Initial and subsequent measurement

A provision must be recognized at its settlement amount based on reasonable commercial assessment (as any other provision). The Commercial Code does not prescribe a specific measurement method. This implies that

– trends in salary and pension development,

– employee fluctuation and

– probabilities of employee mortality or invalidity

---

68 *Beck'scher Bilanzkommentar,* § 249, nos. 164–168.
69 *Beck'scher Bilanzkommentar,* § 246, nos. 120–122.

must be taken into account and that the value must be discounted. If an employee has already retired, the present value of future payments is recognized.[70] If the employee is working for the company and will retire sometime in the future, the provision is accumulated because it is assumed that the employee will earn the retirement benefits over time. This means that the present value of the future retirement benefits is distributed over the working time of the employee. The methods differ in how this distribution is done in detail:[71]

- Partial-value method: The present value is distributed over the employee's entire working life (even if the retirement benefits were granted later). Typically, this results in a higher one-time expense at the beginning if the start of work for the company differs from the date of granting of retirement benefits.
- Current-value method: The present value is distributed over the time period from the granting of retirement benefits until retirement.
- Projected unit credit method (IAS 19): Only that part of the present value that corresponds to the work history (i.e. has already been earned) is discounted to the closing date.

Any change in the value of the provision must be recognized as an expense (or, in the rare circumstances of a decrease, as an income).

The discount rate is a 10-year average corresponding to the remaining term of the provision; for simplification purposes a remaining term of 15 years can be assumed (§ 253 sect. 2). The discount rate is published by the German central bank.[72]

If plan assets are used, they must be measured at their fair value, even if the value increases above the acquisition costs (§ 253 sect. 1). This is an explicit contradiction of the realization principle; to make sure, these gains above the acquisition costs cannot be paid out as dividend; for corporations, a profit distribution restriction exists for them (§ 268 sect. 8).[73]

Presentation

Corporations must report in the notes the measurement method used and the actuarial assumptions applied, for example discount rate, salary trends and mortality probabilities (§ 285 no. 24).[74]

---

70 *Beck'scher Bilanzkommentar*, § 249, no. 197.
71 Coenenberg et al., 2021 (1), p. 467.
   Beck'scher Bilanzkommentar, § 249, nos. 195–199.
72 *Beck'scher Bilanzkommentar*, § 253, nos. 184 and 185.
73 *Beck'scher Bilanzkommentar*, § 253, no. 178 and § 268, no. 69.
74 *Beck'scher Bilanzkommentar*, § 285, nos. 740–748.

Further reading

IDW RS HFA 3 "Handelsrechtliche Bilanzierung von Verpflichtungen aus Altersteil-zeitregelungen" – Accounting for partial retirement obligations according to the Commercial Code.

IDW RS HFA 30 neue Fassung (new version)"Handelsrechtliche Bilanzierung von Altersversorgungsverpflichtungen" – Accounting for retirement obligations according to the Commercial Code.

Important differences to German tax law

§ 6a EStG defines the recognition and measurement for pension provisions:

- A pension provision may be recognized only for employees who are at least 27 years old.
- The partial value method must be applied.
- A discount rate of 6% must be used.

Important differences to IFRS

IAS 19 defines recognition and measurement for pension provisions:

- If an obligation is a defined benefit plan, it must be recognized (no option for indirect obligations).
- The projected unit credit method must be applied.
- The discount rate must reflect the interest rate of high-quality corporate bonds (if those are not available, then of government bonds).
- Changes in actuarial assumptions (i.e. actuarial gains and losses) are recognized in other comprehensive income, that is, directly in equity, not in the income statement.

3.1.8 Debt/payables

Recognition

Debt and payables are certain liabilities (in contrast to provisions as uncertain liabilities). They are recognized if the general recognition criteria are fulfilled. If debt is taken on with a disagio, meaning the outpayment amount is lower than the repayment amount, then § 250 sect. 3 provides a recognition option: The disagio can be recognized in the first period completely as an interest expense or it is recognized as a deferred expense and distributed over the term of the debt.[75] If debt is

---

75 *Beck'scher Bilanzkommentar*, § 250, nos. 35–52.

taken on with an agio, the agio must always be recognized as deferred income and distributed over the term of the debt.[76]

Initial measurement

Debt is measured using the settlement amount (253 sect. 1). Debt that is repaid in annuities is measured at the present value of the future payments. The discount rate applicable is a 7-year average corresponding to the term of the obligation; as a simplification a term of 15 years can be assumed (§ 253 sect. 2). Other long-term debt (except with repayment in annuities) is not discounted.[77]

Subsequent measurement

The higher-of-cost-or-market principle must be applied, i.e. if the value of a debt or payable increases, this increase must be recognized as an expense, whereas a decrease in value is only recognized when it is realized (§ 252 sect. 1 no. 4).[78]

Presentation

Corporations may deduct openly the received advance payments on orders (§ 266 sect. 3 C.3) from inventories[79] if the advance payment is for inventories; this results in a reduction of total assets and (all else being equal) an improved equity ratio.

In addition, corporations must report:[80]

–   All debt with a term of less than 1 year for each balance sheet item (in the balance sheet or in the notes; § 268 sect. 5);
–   All debt with a term of more than 1 year for each balance sheet item (in the balance sheet or in the notes; § 268 sect. 5);
–   All debt with a term of more than 5 years for each balance sheet item (in the notes; § 285 no. 1.a);
–   All debt that is collateralized by mortgages, pledged assets or similar rights for each balance sheet item with a description of the collateral used (in notes; § 285 no. 1.b);
–   All debt that comes into existence legally after the closing date if the amount is material (in the balance sheet or in the notes; § 268 sect. 5).

Typically, all these details are aggregated in one table reported in the notes.

---

76 *Beck'scher Bilanzkommentar*, § 250, nos. 53–56.
77 *Beck'scher Bilanzkommentar*, § 253, nos. 501–100 and nos. 188–191.
78 *Beck'scher Bilanzkommentar*, § 252, nos. 29–50.
79 *Beck'scher Bilanzkommentar*, § 268, no. 40.
80 *Beck'scher Bilanzkommentar*, § 268, nos. 35–39 and § 285, nos. 10–25.

If a disagio is recognized as a deferred expense, a corporation must report the corresponding amount separately in the balance sheet or in the notes (§ 268 sect. 6).[81]

Further reading
IDW RS HFA 22 "Zur einheitlichen oder getrennten handelsrechtlichen Bilanzierung strukturierter Finanzinstrumente" – Aggregated or separated accounting for structured financial instruments according to the Commercial Code.

Important differences to German tax law
The principle for measuring debt under tax law is different: All debt must be discounted at 5.5% (like long-term provisions) except if (§ 6 sect. 1 no. 3 EStG)
- it is short term (i.e. less than 1 year),
- it carries interest itself or
- it is an advance payment.

A disagio may not be recognized as interest in the first period but must always be recognized as deferred expenses and then distributed over the term of the debt.

Important differences to IFRS
See remarks on financial instruments in Chapter 3.1.4.

3.1.9 Contingent liabilities

Contingent liabilities are obligations that are currently not an economic burden (i.e. their fulfillment is not probable at the moment), but they may become a liability depending on future events. Typical examples are as follows:
- Collateral for third-party liabilities: As long as the third party fulfils its obligations, the collateral is not used and therefore there is no liability; but if the third party fails to fulfil its obligations, the provider of the collateral must fulfil the obligation on its own; under this condition, the collateral becomes a liability;
- Guarantees for a third party;
- Guarantees for a bill of exchange or a check.

Recognition
Contingent liabilities are not recognized in the balance sheet (§ 251).

---

81 *Beck'scher Bilanzkommentar*, § 268, nos. 45–48.

Presentation

All companies must report the total of contingent liabilities "below" the balance sheet (because they need not prepare notes). Contingent assets or receivables may not be offset from contingent liabilities (§ 251).[82]

Corporations must report the contingent liabilities in the notes (§ 268 sect. 7):[83]

– Split up into the different categories of contingent liabilities,
– Contingent liabilities related to pension provisions or affiliated or associated companies must be reported separately.

Further reading

IDW RH HFA 1.013 "Handelsrechtliche Vermerk- und Berichterstattungspflichten bei Patronatserklärungen" – Necessary reporting about letters of comfort according to the Commercial Code.

3.1.10 Specific topics

3.1.10.1 Deferrals and accruals

Recognition

Deferrals and accruals must be recognized if the recognition of an expense or income and the corresponding payment or remuneration differ. This follows the principle of completeness and the accrual basis.

Deferrals

Expenditures before the closing date must be recognized as deferred expenses if they correspond to expenses for a certain time after the closing date (§ 250 sect. 1). This is necessary in order to report the expenses in the period in which they occur.

It is important that the time, typically a time period, of the expenses is known and reliably fixed, for example based on a contract; a fixed minimum period is considered sufficient, but a simple estimate is not. Otherwise, a recognition as a deferred expense is not possible and the expenditure is recognized as an expense of the current period (based on the imparity principle).[84]

Typical examples are
– prepaid rent,

---

82 *Beck'scher Bilanzkommentar*, § 251, nos. 1–50.
83 *Beck'scher Bilanzkommentar*, § 268, nos. 50–59.
84 *Beck'scher Bilanzkommentar*, § 250, nos. 1–23.

- prepaid interest,
- prepaid insurance premiums or taxes if the tax is paid for a period of time, such as a vehicle tax.

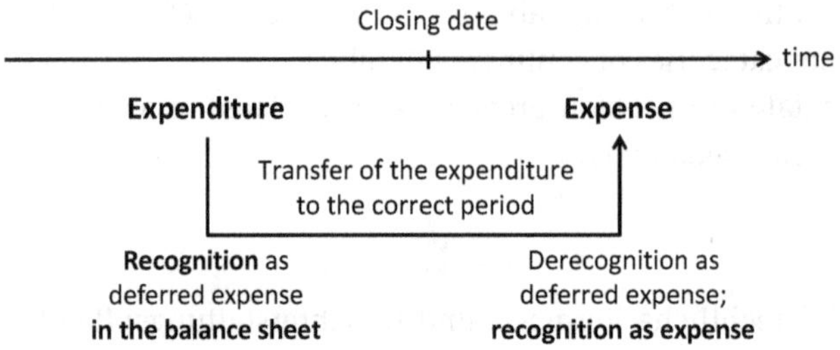

Fig. 3.5: Deferred expense.

For deferred income, basically the same deliberations apply. Proceeds before the closing date must be recognized as deferred income if they correspond to income for a certain time after the closing date (§ 250 sect. 2). Based on the realization principle, deferred income is recognized more easily even if the time period is not defined but could be defined, meaning deferred income must be recognized if it is obvious that a part of the proceeds is not income from the current period.[85]

Accruals

Accrued receivables or liabilities must be recognized if income or an expense was incurred in the current period but the corresponding proceeds or expenditures will occur in the future (see Fig. 3.6).

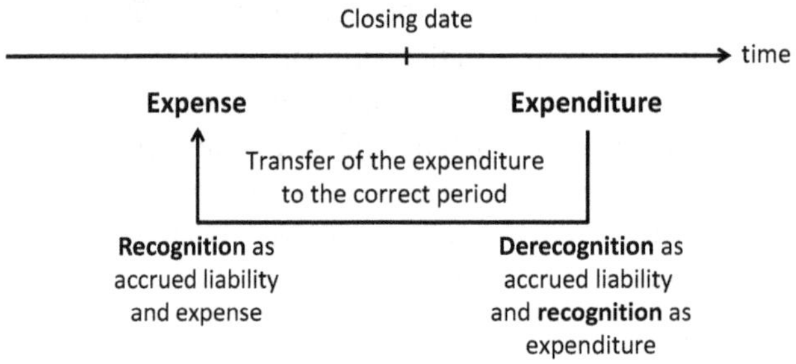

Fig. 3.6: Accrued liability.

---

85 *Beck'scher Bilanzkommentar*, § 250, nos. 24–26.

Typical examples are
- rent that is paid at the end of the rental period,
- interest that is paid at the end of the borrowing period.

Initial measurement
There are no specific measurement rules.

Subsequent measurement
The deferred items must be reversed to the extent that the expense or income is realized.

Presentation
No specific requirements.

3.1.10.2 Deferred taxes

Recognition
Deferred taxes arise if the value of a balance sheet item in the commercial balance sheet differs from the value in the tax balance sheet. The consequence is that the tax that must be paid (called a current tax) will not match the pre-tax profit in the commercial income statement, i.e. depending on the kind of difference, the current tax is relatively too high or too low. Corporations must recognize deferred tax liabilities and have an option to recognize deferred tax assets (§ 274).

Example

Recall the accounting option for internally generated, non-current, intangible assets: Assume a company recognizes an internally generated software that will be used for its own internal organization (value 100 T€, useful life of 4 years); in the tax balance sheet such an asset may not be recognized. Therefore, we have a difference, more precisely a temporary difference, because the difference will even out as the software is amortized. Let us assume there are no other differences between the commercial and tax balance sheet; the applicable tax rate is 30% and the pre-tax profit before recognition is in both cases 200 T€. For simplicity, it is assumed there is no amortization in the first year.

Situation without deferred taxes, year 1:[86]

The additional income of 100 in the commercial income statement may not be recognized in the taxable profit. On the other hand, the current tax is based on the taxable profit of 200 T€: that results in a tax rate of 30% in a current tax expense of 60 T€. This is recognized in the commercial

---

[86] For an easier understanding, the effects are demonstrated on the income statement; theoretically, the differences are calculated based on temporary differences between commercial and tax balance sheet and merely the consequences are reflected in the income statement.

Tab. 3.15: Example of deferred taxes (1).

In T€	Commercial income statement	Tax income statement	
Profit before taxes and recognition of software	200	200	
+ Income from recognition of software	100	–	
= Pre-tax profit	300	200	
– Current tax	–60	–60	30% of 200
Net result	240	140	

income statement. Thus, the effective tax rate shown in the commercial income statement is 60/300 = 20%, which is too low.

In the following years, the situation changes as follows (all else remains equal; only the amortization of the software must be recognized):

Tab. 3.16: Example of deferred taxes (2).

In T€	Commercial income statement	Tax income statement	
Profit before taxes and recognition of software	200	200	
– Amortization of software	–25	–	
= Pre-tax profit	175	200	
– Current tax	–60	–60	30% of 200
Net result	115	140	

Because the software could not be recognized in the tax balance sheet, the amortization is not allowed to reduce the taxable profit. Thus, the current tax does not change. In the commercial balance sheet, the effective tax rate is now too high: 60/175 = 34.3%.

Comparing the two years we see that in year 1 the company underreported their taxes (compared to the commercial pre-tax profit) and in the subsequent years the company overreported their taxes. This can be offset by a deferred tax liability that is recognized when recognizing the software and reversed corresponding to its amortization. This deferred tax liability is calculated by applying the tax rate to the difference between the commercial and tax balance sheet.

Situation with deferred tax, year 1

Tab. 3.17: Example of deferred taxes (3).

In T€	Commercial income statement	Tax income statement	
Profit before taxes and recognition of software	200	200	
+ Recognition of software	100	–	
= Pre-tax profit	300	200	
– Current tax	–60	–60	30% of 200

Tab. 3.17 (continued)

In T€	Commercial income statement	Tax income statement
– Deferred tax expense	–30	30% of 100 Temporary difference
Net result	210	140

In consequence, the effective tax rate shown is 90/300 = 30%, as expected.
In the subsequent years, the effect reverses because the deferred tax liability is reversed:

Tab. 3.18: Example of deferred taxes (4).

In T€	Commercial income statement	Tax income statement	
Profit before taxes and recognition of software	200	200	
– Amortization of software	– 25	–	
= Pre-tax profit	175	200	
– Current tax	– 60	– 60	30% of 200
+ Deferred tax income	+ 7.5		30% of 25
Net result	122.5	140	

In consequence, the effective tax rate shown is again 52.5/175 = 30%, as expected.

As in the example, a **deferred tax liability** reflects a **future tax burden**, i.e. in the future the current tax is too high compared to the commercial values.

On the other hand, a **deferred tax asset** reflects a **future tax relief**, i.e. in the future the current tax is too low compared to the commercial values.

As in the example, the deferred tax is calculated by multiplying the applicable tax rate by the difference between the commercial and tax balance sheet, but only temporary differences are used. Temporary differences are differences that will reverse over time (not necessarily on a scheduled basis like a difference in depreciation, but at a certain point in time, such as by a sale). Permanent differences cannot be basis for a deferred tax calculation. The Commercial Code applies the temporary concept like IFRS.[87]

---

[87] Coenenberg et al., 2021 (1), p. 518.

A future tax relief exists
- if assets in the commercial balance sheet are valued lower than in the tax balance sheet or
- if liabilities in the commercial balance sheet are valued higher than in the tax balance sheet.
 This results in a deferred tax asset.

A future tax burden exists (conversely)
- if assets in the commercial balance sheet are valued higher than in the tax balance sheet or
- if liabilities in the commercial balance sheet are valued lower than in the tax balance sheet.
 This results in a deferred tax liability.

In overview:

	Assets	Liabilities
CBS > TBS	Deferred tax liability	Deferred tax asset
CBS < TBS	Deferred tax asset	Deferred tax liability

CBS – commercial balance sheet
TBS – tax balance sheet

Fig. 3.7: Deferred tax assets and liabilities.

Tax loss carry forwards that also represent a future tax relief can serve as the basis for deferred tax assets if they can be recovered within 5 years, i.e. if in the next 5 years sufficient taxable profit will be generated (§ 274 sect. 1 sent. 4).

For deferred tax assets there exists a recognition option; for deferred tax liabilities recognition is mandatory.[88]

Typical examples of transactions that result in deferred taxes according to German GAAP and German tax laws are given in the Tab. 3.19:[89]

---

88 *Beck'scher Bilanzkommentar*, § 274, nos. 1–17.
89 Coenenberg et al., 2021 (1), p. 520.

Tab. 3.19: Examples of deferred tax assets and liabilities.

Commercial balance sheet	Tax balance sheet
Resulting in an optional deferred tax asset	
Recognition of a provision for onerous contracts	Recognition prohibited
Discounting of provisions with a discount rate of lower than 5.5% (6% for pension provisions)	Discounting with 5.5% (6% for pension provisions) mandatory
Recognition of a disagio as direct expense	Recognition of a disagio as deferred expense mandatory
Amortization of goodwill with a useful life of less than 15 years	Amortization of 15 years mandatory
Impairment of an asset for only temporary decreases in value (financial assets or current assets)	Impairment prohibited
Tax loss carry forward	Not applicable
Resulting in a deferred tax liability	
Recognition of internally generated, non-current, intangible assets	Recognition prohibited
Discounting of provisions with a discount rate of higher than 5.5% (6% for pension provisions)	Discounting with 5.5% (6% for pension provisions) mandatory

Initial measurement and subsequent measurement

As mentioned earlier, a deferred tax asset or liability is calculated by multiplying the temporary differences between commercial and tax balance sheet by the applicable tax rate (on an item-by-item basis). The applicable tax rate is the one that will probably be valid when the difference reverses, i.e. enacted but not yet applicable changes in the tax law must be taken into account. Deferred tax assets or liabilities are not discounted. If a future tax relief or burden can no longer be expected, the corresponding deferred tax must be reversed.[90]

Presentation

For one legal entity, usually either a deferred tax asset or a deferred tax liability is reported. In § 274 sect. 1 a presentation option is included, i.e. it is possible to report deferred tax assets and liabilities separately.[91]

---

90 *Beck'scher Bilanzkommentar*, § 274, nos. 55–68.
91 *Beck'scher Bilanzkommentar*, § 274, no. 14.

Important differences to IFRS

IAS 13 follows the same concept. Material differences will result primarily from differences in balance sheet items.

3.1.10.3 Hedge accounting

Hedge accounting is a fairly new topic in the Commercial Code; it was first implemented in 2009. Before that it was accepted practice under restrictive conditions, but a legal regulation was lacking.[92]

The principle of prudence and the realization and the imparity principle derived from it necessitate a regulation for hedge accounting: If, for example, a company plans to offset changes in value in a specific asset with a financial instrument, without hedge accounting any gains (e.g. of the financial instrument) may not be recognized until realized (realization principle), whereas the corresponding losses (e.g. of the asset) must be recognized (imparity principle). This would lead to an inappropriate and misleading reporting.

§ 254 states that companies can aggregate underlying transactions with financial instruments to a valuation unit for the purpose of offsetting opposite changes in value or cash flow due to similar risks. For the valuation unit certain measurement rules do not apply to the extent and for the time that the changes in value or in the cash flows offset each other.

This should be interpreted as an option, i.e. hedge accounting can be used, but does not have to be used; other opinions (i.e. a requirement of hedge accounting) exist.[93]

Underlying transactions[94]

§ 254 states that the following underlying transactions can be part of a valuation unit:
- assets; this excludes goodwill or contingent assets;
- liabilities; this excludes equity or contingent liabilities;
- pending transactions;
- expected transactions that have a high probability, i.e. anticipating hedges are explicitly included.

Financial instruments

Underlying transactions can be aggregated with financial instruments to a valuation unit (if all conditions are met). The term *financial instruments* is not defined in the Commercial Code. A financial instrument can be viewed as any contractual

---

92 *Beck'scher Bilanzkommentar*, § 254, nos. 1–3.
93 *Beck'scher Bilanzkommentar*, § 254, no. 3 with further references to deviating opinions.
94 *Beck'scher Bilanzkommentar*, § 254, nos. 10–14

arrangement that gives one party a claim to cash or cash equivalents and the other party an obligation to pay cash or cash equivalents or that leads to an equity instrument of the latter party. This includes, typically, for example, receivables of any kind, debt and payables of any kind, securities, money market instruments and financial derivatives. Commodity derivatives are explicitly included (§ 254 sent. 2).[95]

Hedge relationship

A valuation unit may be created only if the purpose of the financial instruments is to offset similar risks of the underlying transaction. This implies[96]

- a dedicated hedge intention of the company, which should be documented;
- similar risks of the underlying and the financial instrument, for example interest, currency, default or other risks are relevant for both;
- micro and macro/portfolio hedges are acceptable;
- the development of the financial instrument will probably offset changes in value or changes in cash flows of the underlying transaction (prospective effectivity);
- partial hedging of amounts or times seems acceptable;
- the hedge relationship is (retrospectively) effective; but the Commercial Code does not prescribe specific methods or thresholds to measure effectivity.

Documentation

§ 254 does not require a specific document for the closing date, nor is the documentation necessary to create the valuation unit. Nevertheless, based on general documentation principles and to give the necessary information for the notes (see below), it is necessary to prepare solid documentation of

- the underlying transactions and the financial instruments of a valuation unit,
- the hedge intention for creating the valuation unit,
- the prospective effectivity of the hedge and
- the retrospective effectivity of the hedge.[97]

Accounting for hedges

For the valuation unit the following measurement rules are applied differently:

- principle of individual measurement (§ 252 sect. 1 no. 3);
- principle of prudence, realization and imparity principle (§ 252 sect. 1 no. 4);
- acquisition or production cost as ceiling for assets (§ 253 sect. 1);
- impairment of assets (§ 253 sects. 3 and 4);
- recognition of provision for onerous contracts (§ 249 sect. 1).

---

95 *Beck'scher Bilanzkommentar*, § 254, nos. 20–24.
96 *Beck'scher Bilanzkommentar*, § 254, nos. 25–29, 42 and 43.
97 *Beck'scher Bilanzkommentar*, § 254, nos. 40 and 41.

Theses rules are not applied to each part of the valuation unit (underlying transactions and financial instruments) individually but to the combination of the parts to the extent that a hedge relationship exists and is effective.

The Commercial Code does not prescribe a specific accounting method. For the effective part of a hedge, the recommended method is the net hedge presentation method: Unrealized gains and losses are not recognized because they offset each other ("freezing method"). Other methods are possible under certain conditions. The ineffective part of a hedge must be treated according to the usual rules.[98]

Notes

Corporations must furnish additional information if they use hedge accounting (§ 285 no. 23):

a) Description of valuation units:
   - At what values are assets, liabilities, pending transactions or high-probability transactions included;
   - in what kinds of valuation units; possible categories are micro hedge, macro hedge and portfolio hedge;
   - to hedge against what risks;
   - as well as the amount of risks hedged with the valuation units; this is the amount of impairment of an asset or the higher valuation of a liability that has not been recognized because of the hedge accounting.[99]

b) Explanation of hedged risks
   Why, to what extent and for what risks do changes in value or changes in cash flows offset each other, including the methods of measuring? Possible methods for a micro hedge are the critical term match method or, for complex hedges, statistical correlations or sensitivity analysis, as well as the dollar offset method or the hypothetical derivative method.[100]

c) Explanation of transactions expected to occur with a high probability that are included in valuation units.

This information can be given in the notes or in the management report.

Further reading

IDW RS HFA 35 "Handelsrechtliche Bilanzierung von Bewertungseinheiten" – Accounting for valuation units according to the Commercial Code.

---

98 *Beck'scher Bilanzkommentar*, § 254, nos. 50–59.
99 *Beck'scher Bilanzkommentar*, § 285, nos. 705–708.
100 *Beck'scher Bilanzkommentar*, § 285, nos. 710–715.

Important differences to German tax law

Whereas the accounting in the commercial balance sheet is in general the basis for the tax balance sheet, different views exist about specific topics of hedge accounting because of the rather new rules and so far lacking court decisions.[101]

Important differences to IFRS

IFRS 9 defines the possibilities and necessities for hedge accounting.

Underlying transactions for hedge accounting can be (IFRS 9.6.3.1)[102]

– firm commitments,
– forecast transactions or
– a net investment in a foreign operation.

As hedging instruments, most financial instruments classified as "at fair value through profit or loss" can be used (IFRS 9.6.2.1–9.6.2.3).[103]

To aggregate several underlying transactions and to hedge the risk for this portfolio is possible only under restrictive conditions (IFRS 9.6.6. –9.6.6.6).

The intention of a hedge can be to hedge the fair value of the underlying transaction (i.e. the values recognized in the balance sheet),or to hedge future cash flows, or to hedge a net investment in a foreign entity (IFRS 9.6.5.2).

Formal requirements for a hedge accounting are:

– All hedged items and hedging instruments are eligible to hedge accounting.
– At inception the hedging instrument is formally designated to the hedge and the hedge relationship is documented.
– The hedge relationship fulfils all of the following criteria of hedge effectivity:[104]
    – There is an economic relationship between the hedged item and the hedging instrument that results systematically in an opposing development of values (IFRS 9.B6.4.4–9.B6.4.6),
    – Credit risk does not dominate the total changes in value within the economic relationship,
    – "the hedge ratio of the hedging relationship is the same as that resulting from the quantity of the hedged item that the entity actually hedges and the quantity of the hedging instrument that the entity actually uses to hedge that quantity of hedged item" (IFRS 9.6.4.1).

---

101 *Beck'scher Bilanzkommentar*, § 254, no. 4.
102 Coenenberg et al., 2021 (1), p. 341
103 Coenenberg et al, 2021 (1), p. 341
104 Coenenberg et al., 2021 (1), p. 342

Measurement of a fair-value hedge (IFRS 9.6.5)[105]

The hedging instrument is measured at fair value through profit or loss. The hedged item is measured at fair value through profit or loss as well – independent of the measurement without hedge accounting. Only in the case of equity instruments that are designated as "at fair value through other comprehensive income" are the changes in value of the hedged item and hedging instrument recognized in other comprehensive income.

Measurement of a cash flow hedge (IFRS 9.6.5.11)[106]

With a cash flow hedge, future cash flows are hedged, i.e. there is no corresponding item in the balance sheet that should be offset. Therefore, the effective part of a cash flow hedge is recognized directly in equity (other comprehensive income); only the ineffective part is recognized in the income statement.

3.1.10.4 Accounting for leases

To give an overview, this chapter presents mainly the perspective of the lessee.

The Commercial Code contains no specific rules for accounting for leases. Based on the principle of completeness (§ 246 sect. 1), i.e. that all assets and liabilities that belong economically to a company must be included in financial statements, any lease contract must be analyzed from the point of view of who owns the leased assets economically.

In practice, the classification rules developed for tax purposes (so-called leasing orders) are used for the commercial balance sheet as well.

Explanation of different terms:

For **full amortization contracts**, the economic ownership of the leased assets can be derived from the following figure:[107]

Useful life refers to the useful life used in the depreciation tables for tax purposes.

The decrease in the value of moveable assets is calculated using the remaining book value and the remaining useful life, i.e. the depreciation for the remaining period. For buildings, 75% of the regular market lease is used.

For **partial amortization contracts of moveable assets**, it is assumed that the term of the lease contracts is also between 40 and 90% of the useful life of the

---

105 Coenenberg et al., 2021 (1), p 344
106 Coenenberg et al, 2021 (1), p. 346
107 BMF-Schreiben as of 19 April 1971.

Tab. 3.20: Relevant terms in accounting for leases.[108]

Special leasing	Leasing of assets that are customized to the needs of the lessee to an extent that their use by somebody else is not possible in an economically sensible way.
Minimum lease term	Time period in which the leasing contract is not cancellable.
Full amortization contracts	The lessor recovers all costs, i.e. acquisition costs, financing costs and any incidental costs, over the minimum lease term.
Partial amortization contracts	The lessor recovers only a part of his costs over the minimum lease term.
Purchase option	At the end of the minimum lease term the lessee has the option to buy the asset; typically the purchase price is predefined in the lease contract.
Lease extension option	At the end of the minimum lease term the lessee has the option to extend the lease term; typically the leasing fee applicable for the extended term is predefined in the lease contract.

leased asset. For partial amortization contracts, additional clauses may be agreed to reach a full amortization.[109]

1. Put option of lessor

   The lessor has a put option at the end of the minimum lease term. If the lessee does not want to extend the contract after the minimum lease term, the lessor can execute the put option and the lessee must purchase the asset for a predefined price.

   Whereas the lessee has the risk of a decrease in value at the end of lease term, the lessor has the chance of an increase in value at his discretion. For that reason economic ownership is always assumed to be with the lessor.

2. Distribution of sales proceeds

   In this kind of contract, the leased asset is sold at the end of the minimum lease term by the lessor to a third party. If the sales proceeds do not cover the outstanding amortization of the contract, i.e. total costs of the lessor minus all payments of the lessee, the lessee must cover this outstanding amortization. If the sales proceeds are higher than the outstanding amortization, the excess amount is distributed between lessor and lessee.

   If the lessor receives at least 25%, i.e. the lessee receives at most 75%, economic ownership is with the lessor because he still participates substantially in the increase in value. If the lessor receives less than 25%, economic ownership is with the lessee.

---

108 Coenenberg et al., 2021 (1), p. 204.
109 BMF-Schreiben as of 22 December 1975.
   Coenenberg et al., 2021 (1), p. 205.

Economic ownership of leased assets with lessor or lessee				
		Kind of leased assets		
		Movable assets & buildings		
Kind of leasing contract		Minimum lease term 40 – 90 % of useful life	Minimum lease term <40% or >90% of useful life	Land
Without lease extension or purchase option	Special leasing	**Lessee**	**Lessee**	Lessor
	No special leasing	Lessor		
With purchase option	Special leasing		**Lessee**	As building
	No special leasing	Purchase price < book value at sale	**Lessee**	
		Purchase price > book value at sale	Lessor	
With lease extension option	Special leasing		**Lessee**	Lessor
	No special leasing	Extended lease < decrease in value	**Lessee**	
		Extended lease > decrease in value	Lessor	

Fig. 3.8: Economic ownership of leased assets (full amortization contracts).[110]

3. Cancellation right of lessee and partial netting of sales proceeds
   In this kind of contract, the lessee has the right to cancel the contract after a minimum lease term. The lessee must cover the outstanding amortization, but 90% of the sales proceeds of the leased assets are deducted. If the sales proceeds are higher than the outstanding amortization, the lessor receives the complete proceeds.

   The lessor is the economic owner in this case because he participates completely in any increases in value.

If the minimum lease term is above 90%, economic ownership is with the lessee; otherwise it is with the lessor.[111]

   The categorization of **partial amortization contracts for land and buildings** is similar:[112]

---

110 Coenenberg et al., 2021 (1), p. 204.
   Mujkanovic, 2014, p. 8.
   Beck'scher Bilanzkommentar, § 246, nos. 41–46.
111 Mujkanovic, 2014, p. 13.
112 BMF-Schreiben as of 23 December 1991.
   Mujkanovic, 2014, p. 18.

1. If the minimum lease term is above 90% of the useful life or, in the case of a lease extension option, the lease rate of the extension is less than 75% of the market lease rate, then the building is under the economic ownership of the lessee (otherwise it is under the economic ownership of the lessor).
2. If the minimum lease term is above 90% of the useful life or, in the case of a purchase option, the option price is below the remaining book value, then the building is under the economic ownership of the lessee (otherwise it is under the economic ownership of the lessor).
3. If there are additional obligations for the lessee in favor of the lessor in combination with a lease extension or purchase option, then the building is under the economic ownership of the lessee.[113]

Land is in the aforementioned cases always classified according to the building.

This is a rather casuistic approach. If a contract cannot be classified in these categories, the general criteria of economic ownership must be applied.

Accounting for leases[114]

If the economic ownership of a leased asset is with the lessor, the lessee recognizes the lease payments as an expense of the period.

If the economic ownership of a leased asset is with the lessee, the lessee must recognize the asset in his balance sheet. The asset is recognized with its acquisition costs, which are usually calculated as the present value of the lease payments of the minimum lease term. The present value of the lease contract is recognized as a liability as well; typically it is reported as "trade payables". The asset is depreciated over its useful life. The regular lease payments are split into interest and repayment. The interest portion is recognized as an interest expense, whereas the repayment is deducted from the lease liability.[115]

Important differences to IFRS

IFRS 16 must be applied to all lease agreements, with certain exceptions, in particular licenses of intellectual property and similar rights (IFRS 15 and IAS 38), leases in exploration industries and leases of biological assets (IAS 41).

From the lessee perspective, a uniform approach is used: all leases must be accounted for according to the use-of-rights approach unless
– the lease is short term (a minimum lease term of less than 12 months; IFRS 16.5) or

---

113 For more details: Mujkanovic, 2014, p. 19.
114 Mujkanovic, 2014, p. 23
115 *Beck'scher Bilanzkommentar*, § 246, no. 48.

- the leased goods are of low value (IFRS 16.5). A precise definition of low-value goods is missing, but some indicators are given:[116]
    - The value must be determined on an absolute basis, not based on materiality for the company (IFRS 16.B4).
    - The value must be assessed as if the asset were new (even if it is not), i.e. an asset that is currently of low value but was not when it was new does not qualify as a low-value asset (IFRS 16.B3 and B6).
- If the intention is to sublet the asset, it does not qualify as being of low value (IFRS 16.B7).
- Examples may be tablet or personal computers, small items of office furniture or telephones (IFRS 16.B8).

If a lease is included in a contract, this lease needs to be accounted for separately; several leases in one lease agreement must be separated as well (IFRS 16.9–16). The lessee must recognize a rights-of-use asset and a lease liability at the beginning of the lease agreement. The lease liability is the present value of the minimum lease payments; the rights-of-use asset corresponds to the lease liability plus incidental costs of the lease agreement minus any incentives at the beginning (IFRS 16.22–28). The rights-of-use asset is then measured at cost (IAS 16) unless the revaluation approach is used or the fair-value approach is used for investment property (IFRS 16. 29–35, IAS 40.33). The lease liability is increased according to the interest effect and decreased by the lease payments (IFRS 16.36).

3.2 Income statement

For all companies, the Commercial Code does not prescribe any rules for the income statement except that it must include all income and expenses from the period (§ 242 sect. 2 and § 246 sect. 1). In particular, no minimum structure is required, but the GAAP must be applied.

For corporations there are more detailed rules:
- The income statement must be prepared in vertical format, i.e. all items are in lines: income is added, expenses are deducted; an account format is unacceptable (§ 275 sect. 1).[117]
- The income statement can be prepared according to either a total-cost format or cost-of-sales format (see below); the formats may not be mixed.

---

116 IFRS 16.BC100 refers to an initial value of up to US$5,000 as an indication of a low-value lease.
117 The vertical format is more useful because meaningful subtotals can be calculated (e.g. earnings before interest and taxes, or EBIT); thus, the account format, even if allowed for partnerships, is hardly used.

The two formats look as follows:[118]

Tab. 3.21: Formats for income statement.

Total-cost format (§ 275 sect. 2)	Cost-of-sales format (§ 275 sect. 3)
1. Sales revenue	1. Sales revenue
2. Increase or decrease in finished and unfinished products	2. Production costs[a] of services rendered to generate the sales revenue
3. Other own work capitalized	3. Gross margin of sales revenue
4. Other operating income	4. Distribution costs
5. Material expenses	5. General administrative costs
a) Expenses for raw materials and merchandise	6. Other operating income
b) Expenses for acquired services	7. Other operating expenses
6. Personnel expenses	
a) Wages and salaries	
b) Expenses for social security and retirement and other benefitsthereof for retirement benefits	
7. Depreciation, amortization and impairment	
a) of intangible and tangible non-current assets	
b) of current assets if they exceed the usual impairments	
8. Other operating expenses	
9. Income from participationsthereof from affiliated companies	8. Income from participationsthereof from affiliated companies
10. Income from non-current securities and borrowingsthereof from affiliated companies	9. Income from non-current securities and borrowingsthereof from affiliated companies
11. Other interest income and similar incomethereof from affiliated companies	10. Other interest income and similar incomethereof from affiliated companies
12. Amortization and impairment of financial assets	11. Amortization and impairment of financial assets
13. Interest expenses and similar expensesthereof for affiliated companies	12. Interest expenses and similar expensesthereof for affiliated companies
14. Income taxes	13. Income taxes
15. Profit/loss after income tax	14. Profit/loss after income tax

---

118 *Beck'scher Bilanzkommentar*, § 275.

Tab. 3.21 (continued)

Total-cost format (§ 275 sect. 2)	Cost-of-sales format (§ 275 sect. 3)
16. Other taxes[b]	15. Other taxes[b]
17. Net profit/loss	16. Net profit/loss

[a]This is the literal translation; even if the Commercial Code uses the term *costs* here, expenses are meant (in general, the use of the terms expenses and costs is not completely consistent in the legal text).

[b]The legal structure requires a separate reporting of taxes, which do not depend on profit; a widespread practice is reporting them as other operating expenses (apart from taxes that relate directly to sales revenue and must be deducted from sales revenue (§ 277 sect. 1)); see *Beck'scher Bilanzkommentar*, § 275, no. 167.

The formats have the following features:[119]
- Change in inventory
  A change in inventory is reported as a separate line item in the total-cost format (no. 2), whereas it is netted with production costs in the cost-of-sales format (no. 2).This adjustment is necessary if produced amounts do not match the sold amounts. In this situation two possible solutions exist:
  - adjustment of income: total-cost format
  - adjustment of expense: cost-of-sales format.
  Depending on how the inventory changed, this can be an income or an expense:
  - inventory increased → income,
  - inventory decreased → expense.
- The total-cost format is structured according to the kind of expense (e.g. material expenses, personnel expenses, depreciation), whereas the cost-of-sales format is structured according to the functional areas in which the costs occur (production costs, distribution costs, administrative costs).
- After the operating income and expenses, the two formats are identical; net profit/loss is identical, i.e. the formats are only a different form of presenting the information but do not lead to a different result.
- Extraordinary items are not reported in the income statement but must be reported in the notes (§ 285 no. 31).
- For any line item, the previous year's figure must be reported. Blank lines may be neglected.

Important differences to IFRS
IAS 1 does not require a specific format or structure of the income statement but requires certain minimum information (IAS 1.81–82A).

---

119 Coenenberg et al., 2021 (1), p. 547.

In addition, the income statement must be enlarged to a statement of comprehensive income including any changes in OCI that reflect changes in the value of assets or liabilities that are not classified as income or expenses and directly posted to equity (IAS 1.82A).[120]

3.3 Notes

3.3.1 Overview

Notes must be prepared only by corporations (§ 264 sect. 1).

The central content of the notes is defined in §§ 284 and 285, but many other regulations of the Commercial Code require information in the notes, if applicable. In addition, laws for specific legal forms (e.g. Aktiengesetz for stock companies) require additional information; the explanations here are focused on the Commercial Code.

The notes serve several purposes:[121]

– **Interpretation**
  The notes need to give information that allows the user to interpret the financial statements, i.e. to understand how the information in the financial statements was prepared and what conclusions can be drawn from it.

Example

§ 284 sect. 2 no. 1 requires a description of the recognition and measurement methods applied to the balance sheet and income statement.

– **Correction**
  If the financial statements do not provide a true and fair view, even if the legal rules and GAAP were applied, additional information must be given to enable a true and fair view. This may occur only in very rare circumstances.[122]
– **Relief**
  Some information that is required in the balance sheet or in the income statement can be given in the notes, i.e. the balance sheet and income statement are relieved from that information (§ 284 sect. 1); that may improve clarity and transparency.

---

120 Coenenberg et al., 2021 (1), p. 541.
121 Coenenberg et al., 2021 (1), p. 888.
122 Coenenberg et al. give the example of a small company with very high hidden reserves (land that was acquired in the distant past and with a very high increase in its market value). No information about these hidden reserves must be given according to the legal rules; nevertheless, this may be misleading (Coenenberg et al., 2021 (1), p. 895).

Example

Receivables reported as "other assets" that come into legal existence after the closing date must be reported separately if material (§ 268 sect. 4). This can be done in the balance sheet, for example "trade receivables €X million, which came into legal existence after the closing date, €Y million", or the information "which came . . . " is transposed to the notes.

– **Addition**

   In the notes, additional information must be given.

   (a) Details on balance sheet or income statement

      This can be more detailed information about the balance sheet or income statement.

Example

§ 285 no. 4 requires splitting up the sales revenue by business unit and by geographical markets served.

   (b) Additional information not related to balance sheet or income statement Additional information that itself is not part of the financial statements is included to give users of the financial statements a wider picture of the company.

Example

§ 285 no. 7 requires reporting the average number of employees split into relevant groups.

Requirements that are only relevant to specific industries are neglected here.

3.3.2 General information (§ 284)

Tab. 3.22: General information in notes.

§ 264 sect. 1a	Name and location of company, company register in which company is registered and registration number.
§ 264 sect. 2	Additional information for financial statements that are compliant with the legal rules and GAAP if they do not provide a true and fair view to provide a true and fair view.
§ 265 sect. 1	Description of any changes in naming or structure of financial statements and reasons for changes.
§ 265 sect. 4	If the company is active in different industries and must apply different structures in the financial statements:Description of necessary additions to structure to comply with requirements for all industries.

Tab. 3.22 (continued)

§ 284 sect. 2 no. 1	Description of recognition and measurement methods for all items of balance sheet and income statement.
§ 284 sect. 2 no. 2	Description of any changes in recognition and measurement methods and reasons for changes; effects on financial or performance situation must be reported separately.
§ 284 sect. 2 no. 4	Information about whether borrowing costs are included in the definition of production costs.

3.3.3 Additional information about balance sheet and income statement[123]

Tab. 3.23: Additional information about balance sheet and income statement.

General	
§ 265 sect. 3	If a transaction should be reported in several balance sheet items: The balance sheet item in which it is reported as well as the balance sheet items in which it should be reported
§ 265 sect. 7 no. 2	Splitting up of items in balance sheet or income statement that were reported only aggregated for clarity
§ 265 sect. 2	Description and explanation of previous year's figures that are not comparable with the current year or of adjusted previous year's figures
§ 285 no. 33	Description of material subsequent events that were not included in the balance sheet or the income statement and their financial consequences

Tab. 3.24: Additional information on balance sheet.

Balance sheet	
§ 284 sect. 3	Development of non-current assets from opening balance to closing balance for all items (for details see Chapter 3.1.3.3).
§ 285 no. 13	Explanation of useful lives used to amortize goodwill.
§ 285 no. 22	If internally generated, non-current, intangible assets are recognized: Total amount of research and development costs and the portion that is recognized as asset.

---

[123] Under specific circumstances, information can be omitted to avoid adverse effects (§ 286); for details see *Beck'scher Bilanzkommentar*, § 286

Tab. 3.24 (continued)

Balance sheet	
§ 285 no. 18	For non-current financial instruments that were not impaired because of only a temporary decrease in value: – book value and fair value of assets, – reasons to classify decrease in value as temporary.
§ 285 no. 19	For each category of financial instruments not measured at fair value: – category and amount, – fair value, if it can be derived reliably, including the method used, –book value and balance sheet item in which it is recognized, –reasons why a fair value cannot be derived.[a]
§ 285 no. 25	If plan assets are deducted from pension provisions:
§ 285 no. 20a	– Acquisition costs and fair values of the assets, settlement amount of provision and any netted income and expenses, – methods and assumptions for measurement of fair value.
§ 268 sect. 4	The amount, if a material portion of "other assets" comes into legal existence after the closing date.
§ 284 sect. 2 no. 3	If group measurement or cost formulas are used: The difference between the applied measurement and a measurement based on the last market value, if the difference is substantial.
§ 268 sect. 6	The amount of a disagio recognized as deferred expense.
§ 285 no. 23	If hedge accounting is used: – description of valuation units, – description of hedged risks, – description of transactions expected with high probability. For details see Chapter 3.1.10.3.
§ 285 no. 29	If deferred taxes are recognized: The differences causing the deferred taxes and the applicable tax rates.[b]
§ 268 sect. 1	If equity is reported with partial use of profits: The different components of "retained earnings".
§ 285 no. 28	If a profit distribution restriction exists: – the total amount of restricted profit, – the split based on various reasons.
§ 285 no. 34	Proposal as to how the profit should be used or the decision about how the profit is used.
§ 268 sect. 5	For each category of debt and payables and the total:[c]
§ 285 nos. 1 and 2	– portion with remaining term of less than 1 year, – portion with remaining term between 1 and less than 5 years, – portion with remaining term of 5 years or more, – portion collateralized and description of collateral. For details see Chapter 3.1.8.

Tab. 3.24 (continued)

Balance sheet	
§ 285 no. 12	Splitting up and description of "other provisions", if material.
§ 285 no. 24	If pension provisions exist: –actuarial calculation methods, – assumptions for calculation, such as interest rate, salary trends, mortality probabilities.
§ 285 no. 15a	If any profit participation certificates, convertible bonds, option bonds, options or similar securities or rights exist: – volume of these financial instruments and – claims on company they involve.

[a]Further reading: IDW RH HFA 1.005 "Anhangangaben nach § 285 Nr. 18 und 19 zu bestimmten Finanzinstrumenten" – Disclosures according to § 285 nos. 18 and 19 on specific financial instruments.
[b]In § 285 no. 30 a deferred tax liability and changes to the previous year need to be reported. Due to changes in the structure of the balance, this is obsolete; *Beck'scher Bilanzkommentar*, § 285, nos. 845–847.
[c]Concerning the aggregation of these requirements, see *Beck'scher Bilanzkommentar*, § 268, nos. 35–39.

Tab. 3.25: Additional information about income statement.

Income statement	
§ 285 no. 4	Splitting up of sales revenue according to – different industries/business units, – geographical markets, if material differences exist.
§ 285 no. 8	If cost-of-sales method is used: – splitting up of material expenses according to total-cost format, – splitting up of personnel expenses according to total-cost format.
§ 285 no. 31	Amount and kind of extraordinary income or expenses, if material.
§ 285 no. 32	Amount and kind of income or expenses related to prior periods, if material.
§ 277 sect. 3	Impairment of non-current assets.
§ 285 no. 17	Remuneration of auditors: – total amount, – portion for auditing of financial statements, – portion for tax consulting, – portion for other services, if not included in consolidated notes.[a]

[a]Further reading: IDW RS HFA 36 neue Fassung (new version) and "Anhangangaben nach §§ 285 Nr. 17, 314 Abs. 1 Nr. 9 über das Abschlussprüferhonorar" – Disclosures according to §§ 285 no. 17, 314 sect. 1 no. 9 on the remuneration of auditors.

3.3.4 Additional information not related to balance sheet or income statement

Tab. 3.26: Additional information not included in balance sheet or income statement.

Transactions not included in financial statements	
§ 285 no. 3	For transactions not included in financial statements: – kind and purpose of transactions, – risks and chances of transactions, if the risks and rewards are material and their disclosure is necessary to provide a true and fair view.[a]
§ 285 no. 3a	Total amount of other financial obligations[b] not included in balance sheet and not contingent liabilities, if material. Obligations for retirement benefits and to affiliated or associated companies must be reported separately.
§ 268 sect. 7	Description and amounts of contingent liabilities: – total amount, – for each category and in relation to retirement benefits separately.
§ 285 no. 27	For contingent liabilities: Reasons why a claim of contingent liability is not probable.

Additional information	
§ 285 no. 7	Number of employees: – total average in reporting period, – split up into relevant groups.

[a]Further reading: IDW RS HFA 32 "Anhangangaben nach §§ 285 Nr. 3, 314 Abs. 1 Nr. 2 HGB zu nicht in der Bilanz enthaltenen Geschäften" – Disclosure according to §§ 285 no. 2, 314 sect. 1 no. 2 on transactions not included in balance sheet.
[b]These are typically pending transactions, e.g. orders of assets (that are not fulfilled by both parties and for which no future loss is expected).

Tab. 3.27: Additional information about affiliated companies and participations.

Affiliated companies and participations	
§ 285 no. 11	For participations: – name and location of company, – equity and net profit as of last available financial statements, – share of equity reflected by participation.
§ 285 no. 11a	Name and location of companies whose general partner is the reporting entity.
§ 285 no. 11b	For capital-market-oriented companies: Any share in a large corporation that exceeds 5% of voting rights.

Tab. 3.27 (continued)

Affiliated companies and participations	
§ 285 no. 14	Name and location of parent company of reporting entity that prepares the consolidated financial statements with the **largest** consolidation scope and the place where these consolidated financial statements can be accessed.
§ 285 no. 14a	Name and location of parent company of reporting entity that prepares the consolidated financial statements with the **smallest** consolidation scope and the place where these consolidated financial statements can be accessed.
§ 285 no. 15	If the company is a partnership whose general partners are only corporations with limited liability: Name, location and equity of corporations that are general partners.

Tab. 3.28: Additional information on corporate governance.

Governance	
§ 285 no. 9	For members of executive board, supervisory board or similar bodies of governance:[a] – total salary split up into its different components, – the total salary split up into its different components for former members, – advance payments or loans granted.
§ 285 no. 10	For members of executive board and supervisory board: – first name and last name, – profession, – in case of a listed company: membership on boards of other companies, – chairman and deputies of supervisory board and chairman of executive board, if they exist.
§ 285 no. 16	For stock companies: That the declaration of conformity with the German Corporate Governance Code was given and where it is available for the public.
§ 285 no. 21	Any transactions with related parties (persons or companies) that are not agreed on or performed by the parties of the transaction under market conditions, if material; 100% subsidiaries that are included in a consolidated financial statement may be excluded. The transactions may be aggregated if separate reporting is not necessary to assess the consequences for the financial position.[b]

[a]This is a fairly complex and detailed requirement; for an overview it is simplified here. For full details, see *Beck'scher Bilanzkommentar*, § 285, nos. 245–341.
[b]Further reading: IDW RS HFA 33 "Anhangsangaben nach §§ 285 Nr. 21, 314 Abs. 1 Nr. 13 zu Geschäften mit nahe stehenden Unternehmen und Personen" – Disclosures according to §§ 285 no. 21, 314 sect. 1 no. 13 about transactions with related parties.

3.4 Cash flow statement

3.4.1 Purpose and methods

The Commercial Code requires a cash flow statement for **consolidated** financial statements (§ 297 sect. 1).

If a company is capital-market oriented (§ 264d and § 2 sect. 6 WpHG) and does not prepare consolidated financial statements, it must supplement its financial statements with a cash flow statement (§ 264 sect. 1).

The purpose of the cash flow statement is to present and explain the changes in cash and cash equivalents by cash inflows and cash outflows; it is intended to furnish information about how the cash flows were generated and the extent to which the company will be able to generate future cash flows to cover its financial needs. In contrast to the other financial statements, the cash flow statement focuses on cash movements, not on income and expenses.

What follows is an overview of the interdependencies of the cash flow statement, balance sheet and income statement:[124]

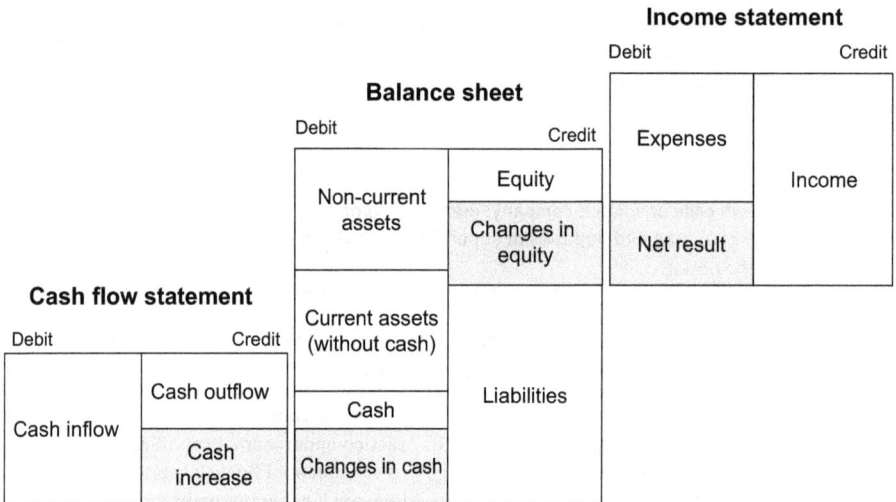

Fig. 3.9: Cash flow statement and financial statements.

124 Coenenberg et al., 2021 (1), p. 817.
Coenenberg et al., 2021 (2), p. 21

The income statement is a subledger of equity and the net result (here a profit, i.e. income is larger than expense) changes equity (in this example there are no external changes in equity, i.e. capital is not increased or decreased by shareholders).[125]

The cash flow statement explains the changes in cash and cash equivalents (in the figure just cash for short). If the cash flow statement is prepared according to the direct method (see below), it is a subledger to cash and cash equivalents because the detailed accounting information is used. If the indirect method is used (which is much more common), it is derived from the income statement and balance sheet.

The Commercial Code does not prescribe a specific method or structure of the cash flow statement. The German accounting standard 21 (DRS 21) details the legal requirement and is best practice in preparing a cash flow statement.[126]

Two methods are possible:
–   Direct method
    Each recorded transaction, i.e. each accounting entry, is analyzed for its cash effects, and the cash flows are categorized.
–   Indirect method
    Cash flows are calculated by eliminating non-cash transactions from the income statement and by comparing balance sheet items. That means (in a simplified version):

Net result
+ Expenses that are not a cash outflow
   eg depreciation amortization or impairment increase in provisions
– Income that is not a cash inflow
   eg reversal of impairment reversal of unused provisions
– Increases in assets or decreases in liabilities assumption of cash outflow
+ Decreases in assets or increases in liabilities assumption of cash inflow

According to DRS 21.25, the indirect method can be used to determine cash flow from operating activities; the direct method must be used for cash flows from investing and financing activities.

---

125 According to German GAAP, all changes in value of assets or liabilities are reflected as income or expense in the income statement; there is no recognition as "other comprehensive income" directly in equity as in IFRS.

126 With its application it is assumed that all GAAP are retained (§ 342 sect. 2); nevertheless, it is not directly applicable law, and financial statements (or here, a cash flow statement) can be prepared with deviations from a DRS.

3.4.2 Structure of cash flow statement

The basic structure of a cash flow statement is as follows:[127]

    Cash flow from operating activities

+ Cash flow from investing activities

+ Cash flow from financing activities

= **Cash–flow–based changes in cash and cash equivalents**

± Changes in cash and cash equivalents due to exchange rate measurement or consolidation scope changes

+ Cash and cash equivalents at beginning of period

= **Cash and cash equivalents at end of period**

Cash inflows are reported with a plus sign (+), cash outflows with a minus sign (-). The detailed structure using the indirect method is as follows:[128]

Tab. 3.29: Detailed structure of cash flow statement using indirect method (DRS 21).

1.	+/–	Net profit/loss
2.	+/–	Depreciation/amortization/impairment of non-current assets and reversal of impairment
3.	+/–	Increase/decrease in provisions
4.	+/–	Other non-cash-relevant expenses/income
5.	–/+	Increase/decrease in inventories, trade receivables and other assets not related to investment or financing activities
6.	+/–	Increase/decrease in trade payables and other liabilities not related to investment or financing activities
7.	–/+	Profit/loss from sale of non-current assets
8.	+/–	Interest expenses/income
9.	–	Other income from participations
10.	+/–	Extraordinary expenses/income
11.	+/–	Income tax expense/income
12.	+	Cash inflows related to extraordinary income
13.	–	Cash outflows related to extraordinary expenses
14.	–/+	Income tax payments/refunds
15.	**=**	**Cash flow from operating activities (sum of items 1 to 14)**
16.	+	Cash inflows from disposal of intangible non-current assets
17.	–	Cash outflows for investment in intangible non-current assets
18.	+	Cash inflows from disposal of tangible non-current assets
19.	–	Cash outflows for investment in tangible non-current assets
20.	+	Cash inflows from disposal of financial non-current assets
21.	–	Cash outflows for investment in financial non-current assets

---

127 DRS 21 annex 1; DRS 21 focuses on cash flow statements for consolidated financial statements; with slight changes this structure can be used for individual financial statements as well, i.e. by neglecting those items that are only relevant for consolidation.

128 DRS 21 annex 1.

Tab. 3.29 (continued)

22.	+	Cash inflows from disposals out of consolidation scope
23.	–	Cash outflows for additions to consolidation scope
24.	+	Cash inflows from short-term financial investments
25.	–	Cash outflows for short-term financial investments
26.	+	Cash inflows related to extraordinary income
27.	–	Cash outflows related to extraordinary expenses
28.	+	Received interest
29.	+	Received dividends
30.	**=**	**Cash flow from investment activities (sum of items 16 to 29)**
31.	+	Cash inflows from capital increases by shareholders of parent company
32.	+	Cash inflows from capital increases by other shareholders
33.	–	Cash outflows for capital decreases to shareholders of parent company
34.	–	Cash outflows for capital decreases to other shareholders
35.	+	Cash inflows from issuance of bonds or taking out of loans
36.	–	Cash outflows for repayment of bonds or loans
37.	+	Cash inflows from received grants or subsidies
38.	+	Cash inflows related to extraordinary income
39.	–	Cash outflows related to extraordinary expenses
40.	–	Paid interest
41.	–	Dividends paid to shareholders of parent company
42.	–	Dividends paid to other shareholders
43.	**=**	**Cash flow from financing activities (sum of items 31 to 42)**
44.	**=**	**Cash-flow-based changes of cash and cash equivalents (sum of items 15, 30, 43)**
45.	+/–	Changes in cash and cash equivalents due to exchange rate or measurement differences
46.	+/–	Changes in cash can cash equivalents due to changes in consolidation scope
47.	+	Cash and cash equivalents at beginning of period
48.	**=**	**Cash and cash equivalents at end of period (sum of items 44 to 47)**

If the direct method is used, the items of the operating cash flow change; all others are identical; therefore, only items of operating cash flow are listed:[129]

Tab. 3.30: Structure of cash flow from operating activities using direct method (DRS 21).

1.	+	Cash inflows from customers from sale of products and services
2.	–	Cash outflows to suppliers and employees
3.	+	Other cash inflows not related to investment or financing activities
4.	–	Other cash outflows not related to investment or financing activities
5.	+	Cash inflows related to extraordinary income
6.	–	Cash outflows related to extraordinary expenses
7.	–/+	Income tax payments/refunds
8.	**=**	**Cash flow from operating activities (sum of items 1 to 7)**

---

129 DRS 21 annex 1.

Important differences to IFRS and German tax law

German tax law does not require a cash flow statement.

DRS 21 requires that received interest and dividends be presented within the cash flow from investment activities and that paid interest and dividends be presented within the cash flow from financing activities (DRS 21.44 and 21.48). IAS 7 requires a classification of received and paid interest and dividends as being from operating, investment or financing activities; this may result in differences.

3.5 Management report

3.5.1 Purpose and principles

Corporations are required to prepare a management report (§ 264 sect. 1) in addition to the financial statements, meaning the management report is not part of the financial statements.

The general rule is that the management report should give a true and fair view of the state of the company; this true and fair view is not limited by the GAAP, in contrast to the financial statements; therefore, prospective information may be included. Primarily the management report should give an overall assessment of the company, including three perspectives:
- history (reporting period),
- current situation (closing date),
- future.[130]

The management report should give a balanced and comprehensive analysis of the course of business and the current situation of the company; depending on the complexity of the business, financial indicators should be included and linked to the financial statements (§ 289 sect. 1).

Large corporations must give, in addition to the financial indicators, non-financial indicators, e.g. about environmental or social topics, if this is relevant for an understanding of the course of business or the current situation (§ 289 sect. 3).[131]

DRS 20 defines the following principles for a consolidated management report, which nevertheless can be applied to an individual management report as well (on the proposed structure, see below):[132]

---

130 Coenenberg et al., 2021 (1), p. 958.
131 This requirement is not specified in detail; examples on what could be reported are found in *Beck'scher Bilanzkommentar*, § 315, nos. 205–213; DRS 20.117.
132 *Beck'scher Bilanzkommentar*, § 289, no. 30.

Tab. 3.31: Principles of management reports according to DRS 20.

Completeness	DRS 20.12–16	The management report must include all information relevant for a true and fair view. It must be self-contained, i.e. require no additional or supplementary information. Positive and negative aspects must be reported separately.
Reliability and balance	DRS 20.17–19	Any information must be correct and verifiable; facts and opinions must be distinguished clearly. Positive and negative aspects must be reported in a balanced manner, i.e. no particular emphasis on one side. Information must be plausible, consistent and without contradiction of the financial statements.
Clarity and transparency	DRS 20.20–30	The management report must be clearly separated from the financial statements and be titled "management report". It must have a clear structure with headings identifying the following content. Content and structure should be kept uniform over time; differences must be explained.
Presentation of view of management	DRS 20.31	The management report should present the view of management on the business and the company.
Materiality	DRS 20.32 and 33	The management report should focus on material information.
Gradation of information	DRS 20.34 and 35	Length and amount of details depend on the specific conditions, in particular the kind and size of the business and the use of capital markets.

3.5.2 Structure and content

DRS 20 provides a structure that includes all requirements of § 289. In an overview:[133]

---

133 *Beck'scher Bilanzkommentar*, § 289, nos. 40–206.
   Beck'scher Bilanzkommentar, § 289a, nos. 1–63.

Tab. 3.32: Recommended structure of management report according to DRS 20.

Fundamentals of the company/the group	DRS 20. 36–52	This is the basis for the following information; typical sub-items are descriptions of – the business model, – subsidiaries, – goals and strategies, – management system, – research and development activities.
Business report	DRS 20. 53–113	This is the core of the management report; typical sub-items are descriptions of – economic and industrial conditions and developments; – the course of business within the reporting period, – situation of company/group at closing date split into asset situation, financial situation and performance situation; – financial and non-financial key performance indicators.
Subsequent events	DRS 20.114	Material events that happened after the closing date but are relevant for a presentation of a true and fair view need to be reported.
Forecast and report about chances and risks	DRS 20. 116–167	The foreseeable development of the company/group must be reported along with its likelihood and risks. The risk management system of the company/group must be explained (only relevant for capital-market-oriented companies).
Internal control system and risk management system of accounting process	DRS 20. K168–K178	The internal control system and the risk management system specifically for the (group) accounting process must be described.Relevant only for capital-market-oriented companies.
Risk report about the use of financial instruments	DRS 20. 179–187	The risks of the use of financial instruments must be reported separately with the sub-items: – kind of risks (price, default, liquidity risks), – risk management goals and methods and use of hedge accounting.

Tab. 3.32 (continued)

Share capital and control	DRS 20. K188–K223	Capital-market-oriented companies must give additional information, e.g. about share capital, any additional rights or limitations on rights of shareholders, prospects that the executive board will issue new shares or acquire the company's own shares, material contracts with change-of-control clauses.
Declaration about corporate governance	DRS 20. K224–K231c § 289a	Capital-market-oriented stock companies must prepare a declaration about corporate governance, which must include – compliance with German Corporate Governance Code, – relevant information about management practices exceeding legal requirements, – description of working procedures of executive and supervisory board and their committees, – required goals to increase quota of women on executive and supervisory boards, if goals were met and, if not, the reasons why.
Assurance of legal representatives	DRS 20. K232–K235	For capital-market-oriented companies, legal representatives must provide assurance that the management report is prepared with the best of their knowledge to provide a true and fair view.

3.5.3 Non-financial statement/CSR reporting

Directive 2014/95/EU of the EU[134] was transferred into national law beginning of 2017; the extended CSR reporting needs to be prepared for business years beginning after December 31, 2016.[135]

The changes require a so-called non-financial statement by certain companies.[136] Companies that

---

134 Directive 2014/95/EU of the European parliament and of the council of 22 October 2014.
135 Gesetz zur Stärkung der nichtfinanziellen Berichterstattung der Unternehmen in ihren Lage- und Konzernlageberichten (CSR-Richtlinie-Umsetzungsgesetz) as of 11 April 2017.
136 For more details see Beisheim, CSR-Compliance: Neue Herausforderungen im Reporting, in: Schulz et al., *Compliance Management*, pp. 363–392.

- are large corporations according to § 267,
- are capital-market oriented according to § 264d and
- employ more than 500 people on average,

must provide a non-financial statement together with its individual financial statements; it may be included in the management report as a separate section or integrated into it. Alternatively, a separate non-financial report can be prepared (§ 289b).[137]

If consolidated financial statements need to be prepared, a non-financial group statement must be included in the group management report; alternatively, a separate non-financial group report must be prepared and published (§§ 315b and c).

The non-financial statement needs to include the following aspects (§289c):[138]

- environmental aspects,e.g. emission of greenhouse gases, use of water, air pollution, use of renewable and non-renewable energy, protection of biological diversity;
- employee interests,e.g. measures to ensure gender equality, to execute agreements of International Labor Organization, respect rights of employees;
- social interests,e.g. information about dialogue on local or regional level to protect and develop communities;
- respect for human rights,e.g. how violations of human rights can be avoided;
- avoidance of corruption and bribery,e.g. information about measures to avoid corruption and bribery.

The company must provide information on the aforementioned aspects to the extent that it is relevant to understanding the course of the business, the current situation and the effects of the business on these aspects, i.e. the reporting includes two perspectives (§ 289c sect. 3):[139]

- aspects relevant to understanding the business **and**
- effects of business on these aspects.

The latter represents a substantial increase in reporting requirements.

The information must include for each aspect (§289c sect. 3)

- the concepts and control processes used,
- the results of these concepts and control processes,
- material risks for the company itself that will very likely have a severe negative impact on the aforementioned aspects,
- material risks of the company's own business relations, products or services that will very likely have a severe negative impact on these aspects,

---

137 Beck'scher Bilanzkommentar, § 289b.
138 Beck'scher Bilanzkommentar, § 289c, nos. 20–26.
139 Beck'scher Bilanzkommenter, § 289c, nos. 55–72.

- the most important non-financial indicators relevant for the business,
- as much as necessary for understanding, references to values in the financial statements and further explanations.

No specific methodology is required, but accepted frameworks, e.g. Global Compact, OECD guidelines, German Sustainability Codex, may be used (§ 289d).[140]
Required information may be neglected (§ 289e)[141]
- if it might harm the company based on reasonable commercial judgment and
- if its omission does not inhibit a true and fair view of the course of business, the current situation and effects on the business.

Important differences to German tax law and IFRS
German tax law and IFRS do not require a management report.

---

140 Beck'scher Bilanzkommenter, § 289d.
141 Beck'scher Bilanzkommenter, § 289e.

4 Consolidated financial statements

4.1 Purpose

In many cases, larger businesses do not consist of one legal company only but of many companies, i.e. business is conducted by a group of companies. Each of these companies may have (depending on the rules explained earlier) to prepare financial statements; these individual financial statements cover only the specific part of the group's business.

To furnish information about the business of the entire group, groups are obliged (under certain conditions – see below) to prepare consolidated financial statements.

§ 297 sect. 3 requires that consolidated financial statements present the financial and performance situation of all group companies as if they were only one company (the so-called one-entity theory). Therefore, the consolidated financial statements follow the economic entity, not the legal entity.[1]

The purpose of consolidated financial statements is to provide information about the group; additional purposes of individual financial statements, such as serving as a basis for payments (profit distribution to shareholders or taxes), do not exist.[2]

4.2 Legal requirements

4.2.1 Mandatory preparation

A legal obligation to prepare consolidated financial statements exists only for
– corporations (and limited liability partnerships, see earlier in Chapter 2.1.4)
– sole proprietorships and partnerships if the Disclosure Act must be applied (see earlier in Chapter 2.1.2.2).

If such a company is a parent company of a group, it must prepare consolidated financial statements. A parent company is any company that can exercise, directly or indirectly, a controlling influence over another company (a so-called subsidiary; § 290 sect. 1).

A controlling influence of the parent company is always assumed (the so-called control concept) if[3]

---

1 Coenenberg et al., 2021 (1), p. 6644.
2 Coenenberg et al. 2021 (1), p. 644.
3 *Beck'scher Bilanzkommentar*, § 290, nos. 30–76.

https://doi.org/10.1515/9783110744170-004

- the parent company has the majority of voting rights of the subsidiary (§ 290 sect. 2 no. 1),
- it is a shareholder and has the right to appoint or dismiss the majority of persons that constitute the governing body (e.g. executive board) that determines the business and financial policy of the subsidiary (§ 290 sect. 2 no. 2),
- it has the right to control the business and financial policy of the subsidiary because of an existing controlling agreement with the subsidiary or a specific clause in the articles of association of the subsidiary (§ 290 sect. 2 no. 3) or
- it bears, from an economic perspective, the majority of risks and rewards of a company, which facilitates the realization of a limited and precisely defined goal of the parent company (special-purpose entity; § 290 sect. 2 no. 4).

This is applied to direct interests in subsidiaries as well as to indirect interests, i.e. the rights a parent company has are added directly to the rights other subsidiaries may have; thus, group structures with several levels of subsidiaries are recognized as one group if the ultimate parent company has a controlling influence in them.

A company can therefore be both subsidiary and parent company of a subgroup. Whether this subgroup must prepare consolidated financial statements depends on whether the parent company of the subsidiary prepares so-called exempting consolidated financial statements, i.e. consolidated financial statements that exempt the company from its own obligations.

Exempting consolidated financial statements for a company exist if[4]

- the parent company of the subsidiary is located within the European Economic Area and prepares and publishes itself consolidated financial statements and a consolidated management report in German (§ 291)[5]
  - that include the company and its subsidiaries,
  - that are compliant with the corresponding EU directives or the applicable IFRS and that are audited according to the corresponding EU Directives,
  - whose notes include the following information:
    - name and location of the parent company that prepares the exempting consolidated financial statements,
    - information about the exemption from the requirement to prepare consolidated financial statements for the company,
    - explanation of applied recognition, measurement or consolidation rules that deviate from German GAAP.

---

4 Coenenberg et al., 2021 (1), p. 656.
5 *Beck'scher Bilanzkommentar*, § 291.

–   the parent company of the subsidiary is not located within the European Economic Area and prepares and publishes itself consolidated financial statements and a consolidated management report in German (§ 292)[6]
  –   that fulfils the criteria from above or
  –   that is prepared and audited in an equivalent manner.[7]

For small groups, this may be quite a burden, so size-dependent simplifications exist here as well. The logic of the criteria is the same as for individual financial statements (two criteria fulfilled in two consecutive years). A specialty is that consolidated figures or non-consolidated figures can be used. The difference in the values is assumed to cover the consolidation effects.

Larger **groups controlled by a proprietorship or a partnership** must prepare consolidated financial statements as well according to the Disclosure Act; the limits are identical to those of the individual financial statements. Such groups need not prepare a consolidated cash flow statement and a consolidated changes-in-equity statement unless they are capital-market oriented (§ 13 sect. 3 PublG).[8]

Tab. 4.1: Size classes for consolidated financial statements.

Consolidation mandatory	Total assets (€)	Sales revenue (€)	Average number of employees
Corporations			
Unconsolidated values of group (sum; § 293 sect. 1 no. 1)	> 24,000,000	> 48,000,000	> 250
Consolidated values of group (§ 293 sect. 1 no. 2)	> 20,000,000	> 40,000,000	> 250
Proprietorships and partnerships			
Consolidated values of group (§ 11 PublG)	> 65,000,000	> 130,000,000	> 5,000

Important differences to IFRS
The general approach of IFRS 10 is also control based, but control is defined differently. It requires (IFRS 10.6 and 7):
–   "power over the investee;

---

6 *Beck'scher Bilanzkommentar*, § 292.
7 This is the legal intention, but the legal description is a bit more complex to cover all possibilities; for simplicity, this is neglected here.
8 *Beck'scher Bilanzkommentar*, § 293.

–   exposure, or rights, to variable returns from its involvement with the investee
    (. . .); and
–   the ability to use its power over the investee to affect the amount of the invest-
    or's returns (. . .)."

This can result in a different classification depending on whether control is given
over a specific subsidiary.

Special-purpose entities are defined as "structured entities" (IFRS 12.A) in a
way that may lead to different conclusions about whether or not control is given.

IFRS 3 or 10 do not provide any size-dependent exemptions.

4.2.2 Applicable rules

Consolidated financial statements can be prepared either
–   according to the Commercial Code (§§ 290–315):
    This is what the following explanations will focus on;
or
–   according to IFRS (§ 315a):[9]
    Capital-market-oriented parent companies must prepare their consolidated fi-
    nancial statements **according to those IFRS** that have been adopted by the EU.
    Other parent companies can choose to apply IFRS.

4.3 Elements and content

Consolidated financial statements consist of (§ 297 sect. 1)[10]
–   a consolidated balance sheet,
–   a consolidated income statement,
–   consolidated notes (see Chapter 4.7),
–   a consolidated cash flow statement (see Chapter 3.4) and
–   a changes-in-equity statement.

The consolidated financial statement may be extended by a segment reporting.

In addition to the consolidated financial statements, a consolidated management report must be prepared (see Chapter 3.5).

---

9 *Beck'scher Bilanzkommentar*, § 315a.
10 *Beck'scher Bilanzkommentar*, § 297, nos. 10–16.

Apart from the changes-in-equity statement and a possible segment reporting, all other elements have the same content as individual financial statements.

According to § 297 sect. 1a the name, location, commercial register and number of registration of the parent company must be reported. If the parent company is in a liquidation process, this must be reported as well.

Changes-in-equity statement

The Commercial Code provides no specific details about the changes-in-equity statement. DRS 22 recommends that corporations present the changes-in-equity statement in the following way.[11]

Columns:
   Subscribed capital
− Own shares (treasury shares)
− Non – called – up capital
= (Corrected) subscribed capital
+ Capital reserves
+ Revenue reserves
± Equity difference due to currency conversion
± Consolidated net profit/loss attributable to parent company
= Consolidated equity of parent company
+ Minority interests
= Consolidated equity

Lines:
   Opening balance
± Capital increases/decreases
+ Call for/payment of non-called contributions
± Allocation to/withdrawal from reserves
− Dividends/profit distribution
± Currency conversion
± Other changes
± Changes in consolidation scope
± Consolidated net profit/loss
= Closing balance

---

11 DRS 22, annex 1.
   DRS 22 must be applied to all business years starting January 1st, 2017 or later (before that: DRS 7).

The bases for the changes-in-equity statement are the consolidated balance sheet and the consolidated income statement. The balance sheet provides the structure of the columns and the first and last lines, i.e. the opening and closing balances of the individual items. All changes are reported in the lines in between; the consolidated net profit/loss must match the figure in the consolidated income statement.[12]

Segment reporting

Segment reporting is an optional element and – like the management report – an addition to the consolidated financial statements. Its purpose is to give more details about the segments in which a group operates in order to supplement the consolidated financial statements.[13]

The Commercial Code does not specify any details about segment reporting. DRS 3 defines segments as follows:[14]

- The definition of segments follows the management approach, i.e. the organizational structure that is used to manage the company (DRS 3.9).
- The typical structures to report are product-oriented segments and geographical segments (DRS 3.8).
- Segments must be reported if they fulfil one of the following criteria (DRS 3.15):
  - External sales are at least 10% of total external and intersegmental sales,
  - The segment result is at least 10% of all positive or negative segment results,
  - The segment assets (not netted with liabilities) are at least 10% of all segment assets.

For each segment that must be reported, the following information needs to be given:
- sales revenues (divided into third parties and intersegmental revenues);
- segment results (typically earnings before interest and taxes (EBIT) or earnings before interest, taxes, depreciation and amortization (EBITDA) are used); depending on results figures, additional information must be given;
- cash flows per segment (recommended);
- segment assets and investments in non-current assets (without netting with liabilities);
- segment liabilities.

---

12 *Beck'scher Bilanzkommentar*, § 297, nos. 100–146.
13 *Beck'scher Bilanzkommentar*, § 297, nos. 10 and 11. Coenenberg et al., 2021 (1), p. 933.
14 *Beck'scher Bilanzkommentar*, § 297, nos. 151–176.

A reconciliation from the segment data with the data in the consolidated financial statements must be given; typically, there will be consolidation effects between the segments that need to be reported.

Important differences to IFRS
Segment reporting is mandatory according to IFRS (IFRS 8).

4.4 General principles[15]

Tab. 4.2: Principles of consolidated financial statements.

Principle	Content	Codification
Completeness	The parent company and all subsidiaries must be included to give a true and fair view of the financial and performance situation of the group.	§ 294 sect. 1
	This implies that for all companies included all assets and liabilities are recognized and included in the consolidated financial statements.	§ 300
Clarity and transparency	The consolidated financial statements should be clear and transparent (like the individual financial statements). This applies to all elements, in particular to those not relevant to individual financial statements (cash flow statements, changes-in-equity statement and eventually segment reporting). If the corresponding DRS are applied, this is assumed to be clear and transparent.	§ 297 sect. 2
One-entity theory	The consolidated financial statements present the information of the consolidated companies as if they were one entity, i.e. all transactions within the consolidation scope must be eliminated by consolidation procedures.	§ 297 sect. 3 sent. 1
Uniform closing date	Resulting from the one-entity theory, all companies within the consolidation scope should prepare the consolidated data at the same closing date as the parent company (simplifications see below).	§ 299 sect. 1

---

15 *Beck'scher Bilanzkommentar,* § 297, nos. 180–203
   Coenenberg et al., 2021 (1), p. 647

Tab. 4.2 (continued)

Principle	Content	Codification
Uniform recognition and measurement	Resulting from the one-entity theory, all consolidated companies should apply the same recognition and measurement methods; otherwise the consolidated data will (at least partially) not be comparable. The consequence is that recognition and measurement options can be applied differently in individual and consolidated financial statements (i.e. the individual financial statements may have to be restated for consolidation based on the group accounting policy).	§ 300 sect. 2 § 308
Comparability of consolidation procedures	The applied consolidation procedures must be applied in the same way as in the earlier consolidated financial statements. If a deviation is necessary, this must be described and explained in the notes.	§ 297 sect. 3 sent. 2
Materiality	Because the consolidated financial statements are used for information purposes only, materiality is more important than for individual financial statements. This principle is codified in many specific rules that are intended to keep the effort for preparation in line with the additional information gained.	Codified in many specific rules[a]

[a]*Beck'scher Bilanzkommentar*, § 297, no. 195.

4.5 Consolidation scope

The consolidation scope comprises all subsidiaries that need to be included and the parent company. § 294 sect. 1 requires that the parent company and all subsidiaries, i.e. all companies that can be controlled by the parent company according to § 290, must be included.

A subsidiary need not be included (§ 296 sect. 1 and 2)[16] if
- there exist substantial and continuing restrictions in exercising the rights of the parent company with regard to the management or transfer of assets,
- information necessary for the preparation of the consolidated financial statements can be provided only with disproportionately high costs or delays in time,
- shares of the subsidiary are held for the sole purpose of reselling them or
- the subsidiary is not material for the consolidated financial statements.

---

16 *Beck'scher Bilanzkommentar*, § 296.

If a subsidiary is not included in the consolidated financial statement, this must be justified in the consolidated notes.

Further reading

DRS 19 "Pflicht zur Konzernrechnungslegung und Abgrenzung des Konsolidierungskreises" – Mandatory consolidated financial statements and definition of consolidation scope

4.6 Consolidation procedures

The Commercial Code provides several methods of consolidation: Full consolidation, proportional consolidation and at-equity consolidation. The regular case, if an entity is controlled, is full consolidation.

4.6.1 Full consolidation

If an entity is controlled, it is included completely in the consolidated financial statements. That is done by the method of full consolidation (§§ 300–309).

4.6.1.1 Comparability of data

A consequence of the one-entity theory is that the financial statements that are consolidated must be prepared applying identical methods, i.e. the data need to be comparable. Typically, this leads to adjustments in the financial statements of the subsidiaries (so-called adjusted financial statements; the only purpose of these financial statements is integration with the consolidated financial statements[17]). This means:

Identical closing date[18]

The consolidated financial statements must be prepared for the closing date of the parent company (§ 299 sect. 1).

---

17 This is the so-called HB2 (Handelsbilanz 2); HB1 refers to the individual financial statements according to German GAAP, whereas the HB2 are the adjusted financial statements for consolidation purposes.
18 Coenenberg et al., 2021 (1), p. 669
   Beck'scher Bilanzkommentar, § 299

The financial statements included in the consolidated financial statements should be prepared for the closing date of the parent company. A consolidation is acceptable if the closing date of the subsidiary is not more than 3 months earlier than the closing date of the parent company. Otherwise, interim financial statements must be prepared for consolidation purposes. Because this is an extra burden for the subsidiary, the closing dates are usually changed to the closing date of the parent company (if possible according to local GAAP).

If financial statements with a different closing date are included in the consolidated financial statements and incidents of particular importance for the financial or performance situation of the subsidiary occur between its own closing date and the closing date of the parent company, these effects must be reported in the consolidated balance sheet and income statement (i.e. must be included additionally) or in the consolidated notes.[19]

Uniform recognition

Assets and liabilities in the financial statements that will be consolidated by the parent company must be recognized in a uniform way (§ 300 sect. 2).[20] This means:
-   Application of the Commercial Code
    Foreign subsidiaries applying their national GAAP for accounting must restate the adjusted financial statements according to German GAAP. All assets and liabilities that must be recognized according to the Commercial Code must be included (independently of local GAAP).
-   Uniform use of recognition options
    Any recognition options in the Commercial Code must be applied according to the accounting policy of the parent company.

    This implies that recognition options can be used differently in the individual financial statements and in the consolidated financial statements.

Example

A subsidiary recognizes internally generated software in its individual financial statements according to § 248 sect. 2. The parent company follows a different accounting policy and does not recognize such assets. For the consolidated financial statements, the subsidiary must restate its individual financial statements to adjusted financial statements that comply with the group accounting policy: The asset is derecognized; the expenses recognized in the balance sheet in the first year remain expenses, any amortization in subsequent years must be reversed.

---

19 Note that these incidents must be important for the individual subsidiary, not only for the group, i.e. even if an incident is not material for the group but material for the subsidiary, it must be reported additionally; *Beck'scher Bilanzkommentar*, § 299, no. 33; Coenenberg et al., 2021 (1), p. 670.
20 *Beck'scher Bilanzkommentar*, § 300, nos. 11–51.
    Coenenberg et al., 2021 (1), p. 670.

Uniform measurement

Assets and liabilities in the financial statements that will be consolidated by the parent company must be measured in a uniform way (§ 308).[21] This means:
- Application of the Commercial Code

  Foreign subsidiaries applying their national GAAP for accounting must restate the adjusted financial statements according to German GAAP. All assets and liabilities that must be measured according to the Commercial Code (independently of local GAAP).
- Uniform use of measurement options

  Any measurement options in the Commercial Code must be applied according to the accounting policy of the parent company.

  This implies that measurement options can be used differently in the individual financial statements and in the consolidated financial statements.

  No adjustment is necessary if there is no material effect on the true and fair view or if there are specific reasons for not adjusting. The latter case must be reported and explained in the consolidated notes.

Example[22]

A subsidiary measures its inventories using the FIFO method. The parent company applies the periodic average. If there are no specific reasons that would justify a deviation (e.g. the subsidiary handles perishable goods for which FIFO is more adequate than an average), the subsidiary must restate its inventories using the periodic average method.

Group accounting manual

To fulfil these requirements, parent companies typically furnish their subsidiaries with a group accounting manual (or guideline) that explains the accounting procedures to be used by subsidiaries. On the one hand, it defines how any recognition or measurement options are to be used for the adjusted financial statements. On the other hand, it defines the consolidation procedures and any preparatory steps (e.g. a reconciliation of intercompany transactions; see below).

Further reading

IDW RS HFA 44 "Vorjahreszahlen im handelsrechtlichen Konzernabschluss und Konzernrechnungslegung bei Änderung des Konsolidierungskreises" – Prior year

---

21 *Beck'scher Bilanzkommentar*, § 308.

Coenenberg et al., 2021 (1), p. 672.

22 Coenenberg et al., 2021 (1), p. 673.

figures in consolidated financial statements according to Commercial Code and changes in consolidation scope

IDW RH HFA 1.018 "Einheitliche Bilanzierung und Bewertung im handelsrecht-lichen Konzernabschluss" – Uniform recognition and measurement in consolidated financial statements according to the Commercial Code.

IDW RH HFA 1.019 "Handelsrechtliche Konzernrechnungslegung bei unter-schiedlichen Abschlussstichtagen" – Consolidated financial statements according to the Commercial Code with differing closing dates.

DRS 13 "Grundsatz der Stetigkeit und Berichtigung von Fehlern" – Principle of comparability and correction of errors

4.6.1.2 Currency conversion

Subsidiaries prepare their financial statements typically in their local currency, whereas the consolidated financial statements must be prepared in Euros according to the Commercial Code (§ 298 sect. 1 in combination with § 244).

Therefore, the adjusted financial statements of the subsidiaries that are pre-pared in another currency must be converted to Euros. § 308a defines the method of currency conversion:[23]

- Assets and liabilities are converted with the average spot rate on the closing date (i.e. the average between bid and ask rates).
- Equity is converted with historic rates, i.e. the rate that was relevant when the specific equity item was recognized. The net result of the reporting period is converted using the average rate of the reporting period.
- Income and expenses of the reporting period are converted using the average rate of the reporting period; typically, a weighted monthly average rate is used.[24]

Because different rates are used to convert the different parts of the financial state-ments, typically a difference arises in equity (the converted net result of the income statement does not match the equity difference in the balance sheet). This difference is reported as a separate item, "Equity difference from currency conversion", in equity.

If a subsidiary leaves the consolidation scope partially or completely, the corre-sponding part of the equity difference must be posted to the income statement (i.e. is transferred backed to equity via income or expense).

---

23 *Beck'scher Bilanzkommentar*, § 308a.
    Coenenberg et al., 2021 (1), p. 675.
24 *Beck'scher Bilanzkommentar*, 308a, nos. 35 and 36.

Important differences to IFRS

IAS 21 defines a functional currency for the financial statements. For simplicity, it is assumed that any subsidiary will prepare its financial statements in its functional currency. The conversion to a different presentation currency is then done in the following way (IAS 21.39):

– Assets and liabilities are converted using the spot rate at closing date.
– Income and expense are converted using an average rate for the reporting period.
– Any differences are recognized in OCI.

4.6.1.3 Capital consolidation

The first step of the consolidation procedure is the so-called capital consolidation: The shares of a subsidiary recognized by the parent company (typically as shares in affiliated companies) are offset with the corresponding portion of equity acquired. This must be done a first time when control is gained (a so-called initial consolidation); the results of the initial consolidation must then be updated for subsequent periods.

Initial consolidation[25]

Whereas the acquisition costs of the shares are known because they are recognized at that value in the financial statement of the parent company, the corresponding equity must be calculated.

The Commercial Code prescribes in § 301 the so-called acquisition (or purchase) method, i.e. it is assumed that by gaining control over a subsidiary all assets and liabilities of this subsidiary are acquired and therefore consolidated in the consolidated financial statements. The acquired equity is therefore calculated in the following way:

Assets at time value (including any deferrals, accruals and deferred taxes)
– Liabilities at time value (including any deferrals, accruals and deferred taxes)
= Acquired equity.

The measurement at time value implies that any hidden reserves or burdens are disclosed and included in the measurement.

A positive difference between the acquisition costs of the shares and the corresponding proportion of the acquired equity is goodwill (i.e. if 100% of the share capital of the subsidiary is acquired, the complete acquired equity is used; if the

---

25 *Beck'scher Bilanzkommentar,* § 301, nos. 10–176
   Coenenberg et al., 2021 (1), p. 705

percentage is less, only the corresponding fraction of the acquired equity is used). A negative difference (a "lucky buy" or "badwill") must be reported on the credit side of the balance sheet below equity as "Difference from capital consolidation".

The date of initial consolidation is the date when the parent company gains control over the subsidiary. This implies that the subsidiary must prepare financial statements at the date of initial consolidation. If consolidated financial statements are prepared the first time, the values at the point in time when the subsidiary is included must be used. The same applies if a subsidiary was excluded from the consolidation scope and is then included again (§ 301 sect. 2).

Subsequent consolidation

The initial consolidation must be repeated at the initial values, i.e. the acquired equity does not change, because it reflects the acquisition costs from a group perspective.

In a second step, any uncovered hidden reserves or burdens must be transferred to income and expense depending on the development of the underlying items, e.g. if at the date of initial consolidation there existed a hidden reserve in a machine, this hidden reserve is depreciated corresponding to the machine.

In a third step, goodwill must be amortized according to § 309 over its useful life.[26] If the useful life cannot be estimated (in rare cases), it must be amortized over 10 years. A "difference from capital consolidation" may be reversed to income if that corresponds to a true and fair view (basically, depending on whether it is judged as a lucky buy or as badwill).

Shares of a consolidated company that are not owned by the parent company must be reported as "non-controlling interests" in the equity (separately from the equity of the parent company). The share of the net result corresponding to the "non-controlling interests" must be reported separately in the income statement below the net result (§ 307).[27]

Further reading

DRS 4 "Unternehmenserwerbe im Konzernabschluss" – Business combinations in consolidated financial statements

DRS 23 "Kapitalkonsolidierung" – Capital consolidation

DRS 24 "Immaterielle Vermögensgegenstände im Konzernabschluss" – Intangible assets in the consolidated financial statements

---

26 *Beck'scher Bilanzkommentar*, § 309.
27 *Beck'scher Bilanzkommentar*, § 307.

Important differences to IFRS

The general logic of IFRS 3 is identical to that of the Commercial Code, but there are differences in the details (which are out of scope of the discussion here).

According to IFRS 3.19, there exists an option to account for goodwill either by including the fair value of non-controlling interests (i.e. a so-called full goodwill) or by including non-controlling interests as a proportionate share of identifiable net assets (i.e. as proportionate goodwill). The resulting goodwill is not amortized but tested only for impairment according to IAS 36.

For the following topics (see Chapters 4.6.1.4, 4.6.1.6 and 4.6.1.7) there are no material differences to IFRS.

4.6.1.4 Liability consolidation

§ 303 states that any borrowings and receivables, provisions and liabilities as well as corresponding deferred items (so-called intercompany transactions) that exist between companies within the consolidation scope must be eliminated.[28] An elimination can be neglected if the effect is not material for a true and fair view.

Basically, any intercompany receivable of one group company should have a corresponding intercompany liability of another group company. Thus, an exact elimination should be possible. The basis for that is a detailed and precise reconciliation of all intercompany transactions.

In real life, differences often exist:[29]

– Formal or temporary differences
  Usually, these differences result from different dates of delivery and reception (before and after closing date).
– Substantial differences
  A typical example are intercompany provisions: One company recognizes a provision (due to the principle of prudence), whereas the other cannot recognize a receivable yet (because there is no asset).
– Currency differences
  Using different exchange rates, intercompany differences can result.[30]

Based on the one-entity theory, a judgment must be made as to how these differences can be resolved and which way the consolidated financial statements need to be adjusted.

---

28 *Beck'scher Bilanzkommentar*, § 303.
29 Coenenberg et al., 2021 (1), p. 763.
30 The best way to avoid this problem is to reconcile the intercompany transactions not only in the functional currency of each company but also in the underlying transaction currency. If the figures in the transaction currency match, the differences are purely due to exchange rate differences and can be neglected.

4.6.1.5 Consolidation of intercompany profits

Assets that have been acquired from a group company must be measured as if the group were one legal entity, i.e. intercompany profits must be eliminated; put differently: assets must be measured using the group acquisition or production costs (§ 304). Elimination of intercompany profits may be neglected if it is not material for a true and fair view.[31]

Important differences to IFRS

Because the group production costs for the assets must be determined, there may be differences to the extent that IFRS and Commercial Code define production costs differently (see Chapter 2.4.2.2).

4.6.1.6 Income consolidation

The income statement needs to be consolidated in two ways (§ 305):[32]
1. Sales revenue resulting from deliveries or services to group companies must be consolidated with the corresponding expenses (in the financial statements of the receiving company) unless they are recognized as inventories or non-current assets.
2. Any other income resulting from deliveries or services to group companies must be consolidated with the corresponding expenses (in the financial statements of the receiving company) unless they are recognized as inventories or non-current assets.

Any intercompany income that is recognized as inventory or non-current assets must be reclassified as a change in inventory or own work capitalized; in addition, any intercompany profits must be eliminated (see above).

The elimination of intercompany income and expenses may be neglected if it is not material for a true and fair view.

4.6.1.7 Deferred taxes on consolidation procedures

§ 306 extends the concept of deferred taxes from § 274 to the consolidation procedures; the basic logic is the same as for individual financial statements (see Chapter 3.1.10.2).[33]

---

31 *Beck'scher Bilanzkommentar*, § 304.
   Coenenberg et al., 2021 (1), p. 766.
32 *Beck'scher Bilanzkommentar*, § 305.
   Coenenberg et al., 2021 (1), p. 788.
33 *Beck'scher Bilanzkommentar*, § 306.
   Coenenberg et al., 2021 (1), p. 799.

Because the consolidation procedures may change the value of balance sheet items, these changes can result in a temporary difference in the tax base. If that happens, deferred taxes must be recognized. The following differences exist compared to the individual financial statements:

- The rules of § 306 apply only to temporary differences resulting from consolidating procedures.
- There is no accounting option for deferred tax assets, i.e. any deferred tax must be recognized.
- There is no recognition of a deferred tax for goodwill.

Further reading
DRS 18 "Latente Steuern" – Deferred taxes

4.6.2 Proportional consolidation

For joint ventures, a consolidation option exists. According to § 310, they can be included by

- proportional consolidation or
- at-equity consolidation (see below).

A joint venture is defined as a company[34]

- that is managed by at least two so-called parent companies.
  Joint ownership is not sufficient, but current management must be done jointly. Typically, joint management implies that each of the parent companies owns the same share of the joint venture; unequal shares are possible if management is based on mutual understanding and if this is contractually agreed; and
- that is owned by at least one shareholder not included in the consolidated financial statements.

If proportional consolidation is chosen for a joint venture, the financial statements of the joint venture are included only according to the relative share the parent company owns, i.e. if a parent company owns 50% of a joint venture, 50% of the financial statements of the joint venture are included in the consolidated financial statements.[35]

---

34 *Beck'scher Bilanzkommentar*, § 310, nos. 10–38.
35 *Beck'scher Bilanzkommentar*, § 310, nos. 50–74.
  Coenenberg et al., 2021 (1), p. 748.

This implies:
- Capital consolidation
  Hidden reserves and burdens are only recognized proportionally; resulting goodwill (or badwill) is recognized on this basis;
- Liability consolidation
  Receivables and liabilities are consolidated only proportionally, i.e. the portion of the other owners of the joint venture remains unconsolidated and must be reclassified to receivables/liabilities from/to third parties;
- Income consolidation/elimination of intercompany profits
  The same applies to the income consolidation and intercompany profits: only the proportional values are eliminated.

Further reading

DRS 9 "Bilanzierung von Anteilen an Gemeinschaftsunternehmen im Konzernabschluss" – Accounting for shares in joint ventures in consolidated financial statements

Important differences to IFRS

IFRS 11 describes joint arrangements: A joint arrangement is a contractual arrangement that gives two or more parties joint control over an arrangement (IFRS 11.5):
- Joint operations
  A joint operation is an arrangement in which the partners have not only joint control but rights to the assets or liabilities of the arrangement (IFRS 11.15);
- Joint venture
  In contrast to joint operations, in a joint venture, the partners have rights only to the **net** assets of the joint venture (IFRS 11.16).

For joint operations, proportional consolidation is required (IFRS 11.20), whereas for joint ventures at-equity consolidation is required (IFRS 11.24).

4.6.3 Associated companies/at-equity consolidation

An associated company is a company in which the parent company has a substantial share (typically assumed at more than 20%), has substantial influence on its conduct of business, but cannot control it (§ 311).[36]

An associated company must be included in the consolidated financial statements on an at-equity basis (§ 312). This means that the acquisition costs of the participation

---

36 *Beck'scher Bilanzkommentar*, § 311.

are replaced by the proportionate equity of the associated company (so-called one-line consolidation).

Based on the most recently available financial statements of the associated company, hidden reserves and burdens are identified in the corresponding balance sheet items. Based on that, goodwill (or badwill) is calculated. These values are amortized over time corresponding to the balance sheet items.

In addition, changes in the equity of an associated company are added or subtracted. This results in the following scheme:

For the initial consolidation:[37]

    Share of accounted equity

+   Share of hidden reserves/burdens

+   Goodwill

=   **Acquisition costs of participation**

The sole purpose of this calculation is to identify the hidden reserves/burdens and the goodwill. The initial measurement is nevertheless the acquisition costs of the participation.

For the subsequent consolidation, the different preceding components must be adjusted for any changes:[38]

    Acquisition costs of participation

−/+ Amortization of hidden reserves/hidden burdens

−   Amortization of goodwill

+/− Portion of net profit/loss of associated company

−   Received dividend payments of associated company

−   Impairment of participation

+   Reversal of impairment

=   **At−equity value of participation**

An adjustment of the financial statements of the associated company to the group accounting policy (uniform recognition and measurement) is not mandatory (§ 312 sect. 5).

---

36 *Beck'scher Bilanzkommentar*, § 311.

37 *Beck'scher Bilanzkommentar*, § 312, nos. 5–25.

    Coenenberg et al., 2021 (1), p. 751.

38 *Beck'scher Bilanzkommentar*, § 312, nos. 29–58.

    Coenenberg et al., 2021 (1), p. 752.

At-equity consolidation may be neglected if it is not material for a true and fair view (§ 311 sect. 2).

Further reading

DRS 8 "Bilanzierung von Anteilen an assoziierten Unternehmen im Konzernabschluss" – Accounting for shares in associated companies in the consolidated financial statements

Important differences to IFRS

IAS 28 requires a method that differs in its details and that might lead to different initial values. Because goodwill is not impaired according to IAS 36 (impairment only approach) and it is not reported separately in case of an associated company, the whole investment must be tested for impairment. IAS 28 requires uniform recognition and measurement, if possible; otherwise, this information must be disclosed in the notes.

4.7 Consolidated notes

Consolidated notes are a mandatory component of consolidated financial statements (§ 297 sect. 1). As a simplification, the notes of the individual financial statements of the parent company and the consolidated notes can be combined. If that is done, the individual financial statements of the parent company and the consolidated financial statements must be published together, and there must be clear indications about which information refers to the parent company and which to the whole group (§ 298 sect. 2).[39]

The function of the consolidated notes is comparable to the notes of the individual financial statements (see Chapter 3.3.1).

Information can be omitted if the information might lead to disadvantages for the group or the subsidiary; this is not possible for capital-market-oriented companies. Information may be omitted if it is not material for a true and fair view (§ 313 sect. 3).[40]

---

39 *Beck'scher Bilanzkommentar*, § 298, nos. 95–97.
40 *Beck'scher Bilanzkommentar*, § 313, nos. 290–300.

General information

Tab. 4.3: General information in consolidated notes.

§ 313 sect. 1 no. 1	Description of recognition and measurement methods applied to items in consolidated balance sheet and consolidated income statement.
§ 313 sect. 1 no. 2	Any changes in recognition, measurement and consolidation methods must be described and justified. The effects on the financial and performance situation of the group must be reported separately.

Information on consolidation scope

Tab. 4.4: General information in consolidated notes.

§ 297 sect. 1a	Name, location, commercial registry and registration number of parent company must be reported. If the parent company is in liquidation, this must be reported.
§ 313 sect. 2 no. 1	For all subsidiaries: – name and location, – share capital owned by parent company, – share capital owned by persons acting for these companies. If a subsidiary is not included in the consolidation scope, this must be reported.
§ 313 sect. 2 no. 2	For all associated companies: – name and location, – share capital owned by parent company and other subsidiaries, – share capital owned by persons acting for these companies.
§ 313 sect. 2 no. 3	For all proportionally consolidated companies: – name and location, – share capital owned by parent company and other subsidiaries, – share capital owned by persons acting for these companies.
§ 313 sect. 2 no. 4	For any other participation (according to § 271): – name and location, – share capital owned by parent company and other subsidiaries, – share capital owned by persons acting for these companies, – total share capital of participation.
§ 313 sect. 2 no. 6	For any company whose general partner is the parent company or another company that is included in the consolidated financial statements: – name and location, – legal form.

Tab. 4.4 (continued)

§ 313 sect. 2 no. 7	Name and location of company that prepared the consolidated financial statements with the **largest** consolidation scope in which the parent company is included and the place where these consolidated financial statements can be accessed.
§ 313 sect. 2 no. 8	Name and location of company that prepared the consolidated financial statements with the **smallest** consolidation scope in which the parent company is included and the place where these consolidated financial statements can be accessed.

Tab. 4.5: Additional information about consolidated balance sheet.

Balance sheet	
§ 313 sect. 4 in combination with § 284 sect. 3	Development of non-current assets from opening balance to closing balance for all items (for details see Chapter 3.1.3.3).
§ 313 sect. 4 in combination with § 284 sect. 2 no. 4	Description of whether borrowing costs are included in production costs.
§ 314 sect. 1 no. 20	Explanation of useful lives used to amortize goodwill.
§ 314 sect. 1 no. 14	If internally generated, non-current, intangible assets are recognized: The total amount of research and development costs and the portion that is recognized as asset.
§ 314 sect. 1 no. 10	For non-current financial instruments not impaired because of a temporary decrease in value: – book value and fair value of the assets, – reasons for classifying the decrease in value as temporary.
§ 314 sect. 1 no. 11	For each category of financial instruments not measured at fair value: – category and amount, – fair value, if it can be derived reliably, including the method used, – book value and balance sheet item in which it is recognized, – reasons why a fair value cannot be derived[a].
§ 314 sect. 1 no. 17	If plan assets are deducted from pension provisions: – Acquisition costs and fair value of assets, settlement amount of provision and any netted income and expenses, – methods and assumptions for measurement of fair value.
§ 314 sect. 1 no. 15	If hedge accounting is used: – description of valuation units, – description of hedged risks,

Tab. 4.5 (continued)

Balance sheet	
	– description of transactions expected with high probability. For details see Chapter 3.1.10.3.
§ 314 sect. 1 nos. 21 and 22	If deferred taxes are recognized: – differences from which deferred taxes result and applicable tax rates, – structure and development of deferred taxes in reporting period.
§ 314 sect. 1 no. 26	Proposal on how profit should be used or decision on how profit is used.
§ 314 sect. 1 no. 7	For the company's own shares acquired by the parent company or a subsidiary: – number and nominal capital of acquired shares, – portion of total capital.
§ 314 sect. 1 no. 7a	For issued shares of parent company based on authorized capital increase within reporting period: – number of shares, – category of shares.
§ 314 sect. 1 no. 1	For all debt and payables and each category: – portion with remaining term of less than 5 years, – portion with remaining term of 5 years or more, – portion collateralized and a description of collateral. Compare to Chapter 3.1.8.
§ 314 sect. 1 no. 16	If pension provisions exist: – actuarial calculation methods, – assumptions behind calculation, such as interest rate, salary trends, mortality probabilities.
§ 314 sect. 1 no. 7b	If any profit participation certificates, convertible bonds, option bonds, options or similar securities or rights exist: – volume of these financial instruments and – claims on company they involve.

[a] Further reading: IDW RH HFA 1.005 "Anhangangaben nach § 285 Nr. 18 und 19 zu bestimmten Finanzinstrumenten" – Disclosures according to § 285 nos. 18 and 19 about specific financial instruments.

Tab. 4.6: Additional information about consolidated income statement.

Income statement	
§ 314 sect. 1 no. 3	Splitting up of sales revenue according to – different industries/business units, – geographical markets, if material differences exist. This is not necessary if a segment reporting is prepared (§ 314 sect. 2).
§ 314 sect. 1 no. 23	Amount and kind of extraordinary income or expenses, if material.
§ 314 sect. 1 no. 24	Amount and kind of income or expenses related to prior periods, if material.
§ 314 sect. 1 no. 9	Remuneration of auditors: – total amount, – portion for auditing of financial statements, – portion for tax consulting, – portion for other services.[a]

[a] Further reading: IDW RS HFA 36 neue Fassung (new version) and "Anhangangaben nach §§ 285 Nr. 17, 314 Abs. 1 Nr. 9 über das Abschlussprüferhonorar" – Disclosures according to §§ 285 no. 17, 314 sect. 1 no. 9 on the remuneration of auditors.

Tab. 4.7: Additional information not included in balance sheet or income statement.

Transactions not included in consolidated financial statements	
§ 314 sect. 1 no. 2	For transactions by parent company or subsidiaries not included in consolidated financial statements: – kind and purpose of transactions, – risks and rewards of transactions, if the risks and chances are material and the disclosure is necessary to provide a true and fair view.[a]
§ 314 sect. 1 no. 2a	Total amount of other financial obligations[b] not included in consolidated balance sheet and not a contingent liability, if material. Obligations for retirement benefit and to affiliated or associated companies must be reported separately.
§ 298 sect. 1 § 314 sect. 1 no. 19	Description and amounts of contingent liabilities: – total amount, – for each category and in relation to retirement benefits separately, – reasons why a claim of contingent liability is not probable.
§ 314 sect. 1 no. 25	For subsequent events not included in the consolidated balance sheet or income statement, if material: – kind of subsequent event and – its financial effects.

Tab. 4.7 (continued)

Transactions not included in consolidated financial statements

Additional information

§ 314 sect 1. No. 4	Number of employees: – total average for reporting period, – split into relevant groups, – separately for proportionally consolidated companies. If not reported separately in the income statement: expenses for – salaries and wages, – social security and – retirement benefits.

[a] Further reading: IDW RS HFA 32 "Anhangangaben nach §§ 285 Nr. 3, 314 Abs. 1 Nr. 2 HGB zu nicht in der Bilanz enthaltenen Geschäften" – Disclosure according to §§ 285 no. 2, 314 sect. 1 no. 2 on transactions not included in balance sheet.
[b] These are typically pending transactions, e.g. orders of assets (not fulfilled by both parties and for which no future loss is expected).

Tab. 4.8: Additional information on corporate governance.

Governance

§ 314 sect. 1 no. 6	For members of executive board, supervisory board or similar bodies of governance:[a] – total salary breakdown into various components, – total salary breakdown into various components for former members, – advance payments or loans granted.
§ 314 sect. 1 no. 8	For any listed stock company included in consolidated financial statements: That the declaration of conformity with the German Corporate Governance Code was given and where it is available for the public.
§ 314 sect. 1 no. 13	Any transactions with related parties (persons or companies) that are not agreed to or performed under market conditions, if material; 100% wholly owned subsidiaries included in a consolidated financial statement may be excluded. The transactions may be aggregated if separate reporting is not necessary to assess the effects on the financial position.[b]

[a] This is a fairly complex and detailed requirement; for an overview it is simplified here. For the full details, see *Beck'scher Bilanzkommentar*, § 314, nos. 70–118.
[b] Further reading: IDW RS HFA 33 "Anhangsangaben nach §§ 285 Nr. 21, 314 Abs. 1 Nr. 13 zu Geschäften mit nahe stehenden Unternehmen und Personen" – Disclosures according to §§ 285 no. 21, 314 sect. 1 no. 13 about transactions with related parties.

Part II: **Exercises**

The following exercises are mainly from
Nothhelfer/Bacher/Rade/Scholz, *Klausurtraining für Bilanzierung und Finanzwirtschaft*,
1st edition, De Gruyter Oldenbourg, Berlin, 2015

5 Exercises on individual topics with solutions

5.1 Bookkeeping and basic terms

Exercise 1: Basic accounting terms

Category: Knowledge/Application
Time to solve: 10 minutes

a) *Exercise*

You are working in the accounting team of a company at the end of March 20X1. Classify the different transactions as cash in-/outflow, expenditures/proceeds, income/expenses or output/cost. Neglect VAT.

1. Delivery of 3,000 kg of raw material for €8/kg on credit.
2. Cash sale of goods that were produced in March for €12,000.
3. Payment of wages and salaries from bank account of €16,700 for March plus a payment of €3,300 for February.
4. Payment of receivables of €25,000.
5. Sale of a used machine for €26,800 on credit. The book value of the machine is €21,800.
6. Overdue notice from raw material supplier. The management decides to pay in April.
7. Purchase and storage of low-value goods in cash of €5,000.
8. Receipt of an invoice of around €700 from tax consultant. The consulting was conducted in early March.
9. Sale and invoicing of goods produced in March worth €48,000; the customer paid €40,000 in advance. The balance is paid in March.
10. Donation of €300 to church in cash.
11. For the company owner an imputed salary of €8,000/month is recognized.

b) *Solution*
See next page.

c) *Hints*
Hint for 1: Because the raw materials have not been used (so far), this is only an expenditure, not an expense.

Hint for 3: The late payment for February is just a cash outflow because it was an expenditure, expense and cost in February (even if not paid).

Hint for 5: Selling non-current assets will usually not be output because it is not the primary goal of the company; in rare cases selling of non-current assets could be

https://doi.org/10.1515/9783110744170-005

Tab. 5.1: Solution to exercise 1.

	Cash outflow	Expenditure	Expense	Cost	Cash inflow	Proceeds	Income	Output
1.		24,000						
2.					12,000	12,000	12,000	12,000
3.	20,000	16,700	16,700	16,700				
4.					25,000			
5.						26,800	5,000	(5,000)
6.	Not relevant							
7.	5,000	5,000	(5,000)	(5,000)				
8.		700	700	700				
9.					8,000	48,000	48,000	48,000
10.	300	300	300					
11.				8,000				

part of the business model, i.e. it is done on a regular, planned basis. Then this transaction could be included in output.

Hint for 7: For simplicity, low-value goods are often directly expensed (i.e. expense and cost in brackets); from a theoretical perspective this is just cash outflow and expenditure.

Hint for 9: Because €40,000 was paid in advance, the cash inflow is only €8,000; nevertheless, this advance payment was not proceeds because no change in net financial assets occurred (increase in cash and corresponding increase in liabilities, thus net effect 0).

d) *References*
Coenenberg et al., 2021 (2), p. 12
Jung, p. 1028
Wöhe/Döring, p. 631

Exercise 2: Basic accounting terms

Category: Knowledge/Application
Time to solve: 10 minutes

a) *Exercise*
The company you are working for buys a new company car. Explain all numbered transactions corresponding to Fig. 5.1 below and give an example (e.g. field 1 is a transaction that is a cash outflow but not an expenditure).

b) *Solution*
Cell 1: Cash outflow, but not an expenditure
The company bought the car in the previous reporting period on credit. This results in an expenditure in the previous period, but not in a cash outflow. In the current

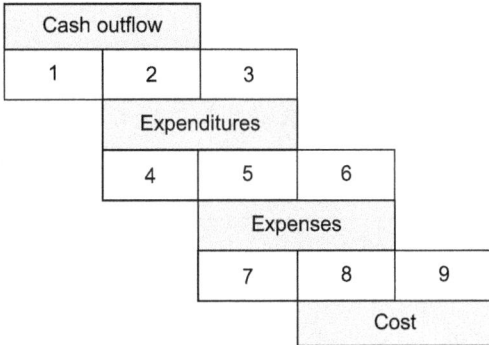

Fig. 5.1: Connection between basic terms.

period, the payment is made. This is a cash outflow, but not an expenditure: cash decreases, but debt decreases as well – in total, net financial assets do not change.

Another example is an advance payment that is paid to the car dealer. Cash is reduced, but a corresponding receivable is recognized (if the car dealer cannot deliver the car, the advance payment will be called back). Therefore, no change in financial assets occurred (i.e. no expenditure).

Cell 2: Cash outflow and expenditure
This is a purchase in cash, that is, the car is bought and paid for immediately. Cash is reduced, receivables and debt are unchanged, so net financial assets decrease as well.

Cell 3: No cash outflow, but expenditure
This is a purchase on credit in the current period. No changes in cash and receivables, but an increase in debt; therefore, this is an expenditure and will result in a cash flow (when paid; see Cell 1).

Cell 4: Expenditure, no expense
An expense is a decrease in net assets; in the context of the purchase of a car, it is the depreciation of the car. In the first year, only a part of the initial expenditure is expensed (assuming a useful life of more than one year). Therefore, the part of the expenditure that is not expensed in the first year is the remaining book value.

Cell 5: Expenditure and expense
This is the depreciation of the first year, which was also an expenditure.

Cell 6: No expenditure, but expense
This is the depreciation in all subsequent periods. The expenditure occurred in the first period, but the depreciation continues until the end of the useful life.

This part is particularly important to understand because it will be used for the preparation of a cash flow statement.

Cell 7: Expense, but no cost

This is a theoretical case, because under current laws it is (in this context) not possible. If there were a purely tax-induced higher depreciation that is included in the financial accounting (which is currently not the case), it might not be included in cost accounting because it might distort the figures.

Another theoretical example could be that the car is not used for operating purposes (it is owned by the company but used by a charity organization – similar to a donation).

Cell 8: Expense and cost

This is the depreciation when (which is the usual case) the car is used for company purposes.

Cell 9: Cost, but not expense

These are imputed costs not included in financial accounting. A typical example would be additional depreciation based on replacement costs: If the company expects the price on a car replacement after the car's useful life to be higher than the acquisition costs, it wants to include these expected additional expenditures in the current cost accounting (which is used, for example, to define minimum prices for price negotiations).

c) *References*

Coenenberg et al., 2021 (2), p. 12

Jung, p. 1028

Wöhe/Döring, p. 631

Exercise 3: Balance sheet

Category: Knowledge/Application

Time to solve: 5 minutes

a) *Exercise*

Calculate from the following inventory the net assets and prepare the balance sheet!

In T€, on 31 December X0	
Land	575
Bank loans	300
Machines	125
Inventories	400
Trade receivables	100
Bank/cash	50
Trade payables	350
Other payables	75

b) *Solution*

Calculation of net assets:

Assets		
	Land	575
	Machines	125
	Inventories	400
	Trade receivables	100
	Bank/cash	50
Total assets		**1,250**
Liabilities	Bank loans	300
	Trade payables	350
	Other payables	75
Total liabilities		**725**
Net assets (assets – liabilities)		**525**

Now the figures need to be rearranged to produce a balance sheet: All assets on the debit side, equity and all liabilities on the credit side:

Tab. 5.2: Solution to exercise 3 – balance sheet.

Debit (T€)		Balance sheet	Credit (T€)
Land	575	Equity (net assets)	525
Machines	125	Bank loans	300
Inventories	400	Trade payables	350
Trade receivables	100	Other payables	75
Bank/Cash	50		
Total assets	1,250	Total equity and liabilities	1,250

c) *References*

Coenenberg et al., 2021 (2), p. 61

Jung, p. 1032

Exercise 4: Asset accounts

Category: Knowledge/Application

Time to solve: 5 minutes

a) *Exercise*

Post the following transactions to the account "trade receivables" (in Euros):

Opening balance	7,500
Sale to customer on credit	15,500
Bank transfer by customer	12,000
Cash payment by customer	1,000

What is the closing balance? Close the account assuming no other transactions occurred.

b) *Solution*
The opening balance of an asset account is on the debit side. The sale increases the receivables and must be posted on the debit side, whereas the bank transfer and the cash payment reduce the receivables (because they are settled) and are thus posted on the credit side.

Tab. 5.3: Solution to exercise 4 – trade receivables.

Debit (€)		Trade receivables	Credit (€)
Opening balance	7,500	Bank	12,000
Sales revenue	15,500	Cash	1,000
Total debits	23,000	Total credits	13,000

After posting the transactions the account is not balanced: the sum of all debit entries is larger than the sum of all credit entries, i.e. the account has a debit balance. At year end this is called the closing balance. To close the account, this balance must be transferred to the closing balance sheet with the following journal entry:

Debit balance sheet 10,000
    Credit trade receivables 10,000

This results in the following balanced account:

Tab. 5.4: Solution to exercise 4 – closed account.

Debit (€)		Trade receivables	Credit (€)
Opening balance	7,500	Bank	12,000
Sales revenue	15,500	Cash	1,000
		Closing balance	10,000
Total debits	23,000	Total credits	23,000

Note:
For an asset account, the opening balance is typically on the debit side and the closing balance is typically on the credit side.

c) *References*
Coenenberg et al., 2021 (2), p. 95
Weygandt et al., 2015, p. 54

Exercise 5: Liability accounts

Category: Knowledge/Application
Time to solve: 5 minutes

a) *Exercise*
Post the following transactions to the account "trade payables" (in Euros):

Opening balance	9,000
Purchase from supplier on credit	13,000
Bank transfer to supplier	7,000
Cash payment to supplier	800

What is the closing balance? Close the account assuming no other transactions occurred.

b) *Solution*
The opening balance of a liability account is on the credit side. The purchase increases the payables and must be posted on the credit side, whereas the bank transfer and the cash payment reduce the payables (because they are settled) and are
thus posted on the debit side.

Tab. 5.5: Solution to exercise 5 – liability account.

Debit (€)		Trade payables	Credit (€)
Bank	7,000	Opening balance	9,000
Cash	800	Purchase	13,000
Total debits	7,800	Total credits	22,000

After posting the transactions the account is not balanced: the sum of debit entries
is smaller than the sum of all credit entries, i.e. the account has a credit balance.
At year end this is called the closing balance. To close the account, this balance
must be transferred to the closing balance sheet with the following journal entry:

Debit trade payables	1 4,200	
Credit balance sheet		1 4,200

This results in the following balanced account:

Tab. 5.6: Solution to exercise 5 – closed account.

Debit (€)		Trade payables	Credit (€)
Bank	7,000	Opening balance	9,000
Cash	800	Purchase	13,000
Closing balance	14,200		
Total debits	22,000	Total credits	22,000

Note:
For a liability account, the opening balance is typically on the credit side and the closing balance is typically on the debit side.

c) *References*
Coenenberg et al., 2021 (2), p. 95
Weygandt et al., 2015, p. 54

Exercise 6: Accounting procedures

Category: Knowledge/Application
Time to solve: 15 minutes

a) *Exercise*
Split the following balance sheet into asset and liability accounts (i.e. open the accounts), journalize and post the transactions. Finally, close the accounts and prepare the closing balance sheet (ignore VAT).

Tab. 5.7: Solution to exercise 6 – opening balance.

Debit (T€)		Balance sheet	Credit (T€)
Tangible assets	125	Equity	100
Inventory	50	Loans	80
Bank	100	Trade payables	120
Cash	25		
Total assets	300	Total equity and liabilities	300

Transactions to be posted:
1. Purchase of a machine on credit for €15,000.
2. Transfer of trade payables in a medium-term loan; volume €8,000.
3. Purchase of inventories with cash for €1,000.
4. Payment of a supplier invoice by bank transfer: €9,000.

b) *Solution*

Step 1: Opening of accounts

Opening an account means transferring the opening balance from the opening balance sheet to the individual account:[1]

Tab. 5.8: Solution to exercise 6 – opening of accounts (1).

Debit (T€)	Tangible assets		Credit (T€)
Opening balance	125		

Tab. 5.9: Solution to exercise 6 – opening of accounts (2).

Debit (T€)	Inventory		Credit (T€)
Opening balance	50		

Tab. 5.10: Solution to exercise 6 – opening of accounts (3).

Debit (T€)	Bank		Credit (T€)
Opening balance	100		

Tab. 5.11: Solution to exercise 6 – opening of accounts (4).

Debit (T€)	Cash		Credit (T€)
Opening balance	25		

Tab. 5.12: Solution to exercise 6 – opening of accounts (5).

Debit (T€)	Equity		Credit (T€)
		Opening balance	100

---

1 This could be done with journal entries as well, for example for tangible assets

       Debit tangible assets   125

           Credit opening balance sheet   125

For simplicity, this is omitted here.

Tab. 5.13: Solution to exercise 6 – opening of accounts (6).

Debit (T€)	Loans	Credit (T€)
	Opening balance	80

Tab. 5.14: Solution to exercise 6 – opening of accounts (7).

Debit (T€)	Trade payables	Credit (T€)
	Opening balance	120

Step 2: Journalizing and posting
The journal entries for the transactions are as follows:

1. Debit tangible assets	15 T€	
Credit trade payables		15 T€
2. Debit trade payables	8 T€	
Credit loans		8 T€
3. Debit inventory	1 T€	
Credit cash		1 T€
4. Debit trade payables	9 T€	
Credit bank		9 T€

Posting these entries to the accounts leads to:

Tab. 5.15: Solution to exercise 6 – posting to accounts (1).

Debit (T€)	Tangible assets	Credit (T€)
Opening balance	125	
Transaction 1	15	

Tab. 5.16: Solution to exercise 6 – posting to accounts (2).

Debit (T€)	Inventory	Credit (T€)
Opening balance	50	
Transaction 3	1	

Tab. 5.17: Solution to exercise 6 – posting to accounts (3).

Debit (T€)		Bank	Credit (T€)
Opening balance	100	Transaction 4	9

Tab. 5.18: Solution to exercise 6 – posting to accounts (4).

Debit (T€)		Cash	Credit (T€)
Opening balance	25	Transaction 3	1

Tab. 5.19: Solution to exercise 6 – posting to accounts (5).

Debit (T€)	Loans		Credit (T€)
	Opening balance		80
	Transaction 2		8

Tab. 5.20: Solution to exercise 6 – posting to accounts (6).

Debit (T€)		Trade payables	Credit (T€)
Transaction 2	8	Opening balance	120
Transaction 4	9	Transaction 1	15

This leads to the following balances:

Tangible assets:	Debit balance	140 T€	
Inventory:	Debit balance	51 T€	
Bank:	Debit balance	91 T€	
Cash:	Debit balance	24 T€	
Equity:	Credit balance	100 T€	(unchanged)
Loans:	Credit balance	88 T€	
Trade payables:	Credit balance	118 T€	

Step 3: Closing the accounts and preparing the closing balance sheet

At year end, the closing balances are transferred back to the closing balance sheet by the following closing journal entries:

1. Debit closing balance	140 T€		
Credit tangible assets		140 T€	
2. Debit closing balance	51 T€		
Credit inventory		51 T€	
3. Debit closing balance	91 T€		
Credit bank		91 T€	
4. Debit closing balance	24 T€		
Credit cash		24 T€	
5. Debit equity	100 T€		
Credit closing balance			100 T€
6. Debit loans	88 T€		
Credit closing balance			88 T€
7. Debit trade payables	118 T€		
Credit closing balance			118 T€

The closed accounts look as follows:

Tab. 5.21: Solution to exercise 6 – closing of accounts (1).

Debit (T€)		Tangible assets	Credit (T€)
Opening balance	125	**Closing balance**	**140**
Transaction 1	15		
Total debits	140	Total credits	140

Tab. 5.22: Solution to exercise 6 – closing of accounts (2).

Debit (T€)		Inventory	Credit (T€)
Opening balance	50	**Closing balance**	**51**
Transaction 2	1		
Total debits	51	Total credits	51

Tab. 5.23: Solution to exercise 6 – closing of accounts (3).

Debit (T€)		Bank	Credit (T€)
Opening balance	100	Transaction 4	9
		Closing balance	**91**
Total debits	100	Total credits	100

Tab. 5.24: Solution to exercise 6 – closing of accounts (4).

Debit (T€)		Cash	Credit (T€)
Opening balance	25	Transaction 3	1
		Closing balance	**24**
Total debits	25	Total credits	25

Tab. 5.25: Solution to exercise 6 – closing of accounts (5).

Debit (T€)		Equity	Credit (T€)
Closing balance	**100**	Opening balance	100
Total debits	100	Total credits	100

Note in this case that the opening balance equals the closing balance because there were no transactions.

Tab. 5.26: Solution to exercise 6 – closing of accounts (6).

Debit (T€)		Loans	Credit (T€)
Closing balance	**88**	Opening balance	80
		Transaction 2	8
Total debits	88	Total credits	88

Tab. 5.27: Solution to exercise 6 – closing of accounts (7).

Debit (T€)		Trade payables	Credit (T€)
Transaction 2	8	Opening balance	120
Transaction 4	9	Transaction 2	15
Closing balance	**118**		
Total debits	135	Total credits	135

This results in the following closing balance sheet:

Tab. 5.28: Solution to exercise 6 – closing balance.

Debit (T€)		Balance sheet	Credit (T€)
Tangible assets	140	Equity	100
Inventory	51	Loans	88
Bank	91	Trade payables	118
Cash	24		
Total assets	306	Total equity and liabilities	306

c) *References*
Coenenberg et al., 2021 (2), p. 95
Weygandt et al., 2015, p. 54

Exercise 7: Income and expense accounts

Category: Knowledge/Application
Time to solve: 5 minutes

a) *Exercise*
Journalize the following transactions (neglect VAT):

1. Rendering of services on credit: €200,000.
2. Bank transfer of wages and salaries: €135,000.
3. Bank transfer of insurance premiums: €4,500.
4. Incoming bank transfer for a sublet office: €800.
5. Transfer of monthly rent for a warehouse: €2,500.

b) *Solution*
This results in the following journal entries (values in €:)

1.	Debit trade receivables	200,000	
	Credit sales revenue		200,000
2.	Debit wages and salaries	135,000	
	(or: Personnel expenses)		
	Credit bank		135,000
3.	Debit insurance expenses	4,500	
	Credit bank		4,500
4.	Debit bank	800	
	Credit rental income		800
5.	Debit rental expenses	2,500	
	Credit bank		2,500

c) *Hints*

Recall that income is defined as an increase in net assets, i.e. of equity. Equity increases require a credit entry, so income is recorded on the credit side. Conversely, expenses are defined as a decrease in equity, which is recorded on the debit side. Thus, expenses are entered on the debit side.

d) *References*

Coenenberg et al., 2021 (2), p. 106
Weygandt et al., 2015, p. 54

Exercise 8: Income and expense accounts (2)

Category: Knowledge/Application
Time to solve: 10 minutes

a) *Exercise*

Journalize the following transactions of an automotive supplier that produces steel springs (neglect VAT).
1. Purchase of steel bars for €25,000 and other materials for €800; both purchases are on credit.
2. Requisition of these materials from storage for production of steel springs.
3. Bank transfer of wages and salaries of €15,000.
4. Sale of finished products for €75,000 on credit.

Close the income and expense accounts and post the change in equity. Does the company make a profit or a loss?

b) *Solution*

The journal entries are as follows (values in €):

1.	Debit raw materials	25,800	
	Credit trade payables		25,800
2.	Debit material expenses	25,800	
	Credit raw materials		25,800
3.	Debit salaries and wages	15,000	
	Credit bank		15,000
4.	Debit trade receivables	75,000	
	Credit sales revenue		75,000

Assuming no other transactions occurred, the closing balances are debit balances for material expenses (€25,800) and salaries and wages (€15,000) and a credit balance for sales revenue (€75,000). This results in the following closing entries:

1.	Debit income statement	25,800	
	Credit material expenses		25,800
2.	Debit income statement	15,000	
	Credit salaries and wages		15,000
3.	Debit sales revenue	75,000	
	Credit income statement		75,000

The income statement shows as a consequence a credit balance:

Sales revenue	75,000	(credit)
– Material expenses	– 25,800	(debit)
– Salaries and wages	– 15,000	(debit)
= profit	**34,200**	**(credit)**

The income statement shows a credit balance because the sum of the credit entries is larger than the sum of the debit entries, i.e. all income entries are larger than all expense entries; thus, the company makes a profit of 34,200 €. This profit increases equity (recall that equity is reported on the credit side and therefore credit entries increase equity); the entry is as follows:

| Debit income statement | 34,200 | |
| Credit equity | | 34,200 |

c) *References*
Coenenberg et al., 2021 (2), p. 106
Weygandt et al., 2015, p. 54

Exercise 9: Selling and purchasing with VAT

Category: Knowledge/Application
Time to solve: 5 minutes

a) *Exercise*
Journalize the following transactions.
1. Purchase of raw materials on credit for €25,000 in total.
2. Sale of products for €35,000 net against direct bank transfer.
3. Reception of an invoice from the tax consultant of €1,500 net.
4. Invoicing of service fees of a total of €4,500.
5. Received advance payment of a customer of €11,900.
6. Made advance payment of €15,000 to a supplier.

b) *Solution*

This results in the following journal entries (values in €):

1.	Debit raw materials	21,008.40	
	IT	3,991.60	
	Credit trade payables		25,000.00

Hint

If the total amount is €25,000, it includes the VAT (assuming the regular rate of 19%). To calculate the net amount, the total must be divided by 1.19 (119%). The corresponding input tax is calculated by multiplying the net amount by 0.19 (19%).

2.	Debit bank	41,650.00	
	Credit sales revenue		35,000.00
	VAT		6,650.00
3.	Debit administration expenses	1,500.00	
	IT	285.00	
	Credit trade payables		1,785.00
4.	Debit trade receivables	4,500.00	
	Credit Sales revenue		3,781.51
	VAT		718.49
5.	Debit bank	11,900.00	
	Credit received adv. payments		10,000.00
	VAT		1,900.00
6.	Debit paid adv. payments	12,605.04	
	IT	2,394.96	
	Credit bank		15,000.00

Hint

On the one hand, advance payments are subject to VAT (if the underlying transaction is subject to VAT); thus only the net value is recorded in the advance payment account. On the other hand, this is a pure balance sheet transaction, i.e. a received advance payment is a liability, because the customer could request the money back if the company does not fulfil the sales contract (consequently, a paid advance payment is a receivable because the company will request the money back if the supplier does not fulfil the purchase contract).

c) *References*

Coenenberg et al., 2021 (2), p. 138

Exercise 10: Discounts

Category: Knowledge/Application

Time to solve: 10 minutes

a) *Exercises*

Journalize the following transactions:

1. Purchase of merchandise for €18,000 net. The supplier grants a cash discount of 1% that is used.
2. Sale of products on credit for €7,500 net. The company grants a cash discount of 2% to the customer. The customer uses the discount.

b) *Solution*

Values in €

	1.a) Purchase		
	Debit merchandise	18,000.00	
	IT	3,420.00	
	Credit trade payables		21,420.00
	1.b) Payment		
	Debit trade payables	21,420.00	
	Credit bank		21,205.80 (less discount of 1%)
	Merchandise		180.00 (adjustment to acquisition costs: net value)
	IT		34.20 (adjustment of input tax because of adjustment to acquisition costs)
	2.a) Sale		
	Debit trade receivables	8,925.00	
	Credit sales revenue		7,500.00
	VAT		1,425.00
	2.b) Payment		
	Debit bank	8,746.50	(less discount of 2%)
	Sales revenue	150.00	(adjustment of sales, only net value)
	VAT	28.50	(adjustment of VAT because of adjustment of sales revenue)
	Credit trade receivables		8,925.00

c) *References*

Coenenberg et al., 2021 (2), pp. 152 and 156

Exercise 11: Comprehensive exercise on accounting procedures

Category: Knowledge/Application

Time to solve: 20 minutes

a) *Exercise*

A company submits the following balance sheet at the beginning of the business year:

Tab. 5.29: Solution to exercise 11 – opening balance.

Debit (€)		Balance sheet	Credit (€)
Tangible assets	375,000	Equity	300,000
Inventory	125,000	Loans	290,000
Trade receivables	175,000	Trade payables	210,000
Bank	125,000		
Total assets	800,000	Total equity and liabilities	800,000

The following transactions occur:
1. Purchase of a new machine on credit: €27,500 net.
2. Purchase of raw materials on credit: €15,000 net; a cash discount of 2% is offered and used. After a couple of days, all of the material is used for production.
3. Payment of interest for loans: €5,000.
4. Taking out a new loan: €30,000.
5. Sale of products for €45,000 net on credit; a cash discount of 2% is offered and used.

Questions
(a) Open the accounts.
(b) Journalize transactions.
(c) Post transactions to the accounts and close all accounts.

b) *Solution*
Values in €
(a) The opening balances are transferred to the accounts; see the detailed accounts in (c).
(b) Journal entries:

1. Debit tangible assets		27,500	
IT		5,225	
Credit trade payables			32,725
2.a) Purchase			
Debit raw materials		15,000	
IT		2,850	
Credit trade payables			17,850
b) Payment			
Debit trade payables		17,850	
Credit bank			17,493
Raw materials			300
IT			57
c) Use of material			
Debit material expenses		14,700	
Credit raw materials			14,700

Note that only the real acquisition costs (€15,000 initial purchase price minus the cash discount of €300) can be expensed.

3.	Debit interest expense	5,000	
	Credit bank		5,000
4.	Debit bank	30,000	
	Credit loans		30,000
5.a)	Sale		
	Debit trade receivables	53,550	
	Credit sales revenue		45,000
	VAT		8,550
b)	Payment		
	Debit bank	52,479	
	Sales revenue	900	
	VAT	171	
	Credit trade receivables		53,550

(c) Posting and closing of accounts

The accounts, including the posting of the transactions and the closing balances, look as follows:

Tab. 5.30: Solution to exercise 11 – posting and closing of accounts (1).

Debit (€)		Tangible assets	Credit (€)
Opening balance	375,000	**Closing balance**	**402,500**
Transaction 1	27,500		
Total debits	402,500	Total credits	402,500

Tab. 5.31: Solution to exercise 11 – posting and closing of accounts (2).

Debit (€)		Inventory	Credit (€)
Opening balance	125,000	Transaction 2b	300
Transaction 2a	15,000	Transaction 2c	14,700
		Closing balance	**125,000**
Total debits	140,000	Total credits	140,000

Tab. 5.32: Solution to exercise 11 – posting and closing of accounts (3).

Debit (€)		Trade receivables	Credit (€)
Opening balance	175,000	Transaction 5b	53,550
Transaction 5a	53,550	**Closing balance**	**175,000**
Total debits	228,550	Total credits	228,550

Tab. 5.33: Solution to exercise 11 – posting and closing of accounts (4).

Debit (€)		Bank	Credit (€)
Opening balance	125,000	Transaction 2b	17,493
Transaction 4	30,000	Transaction 3	5,000
Transaction 5b	52,479	**Closing balance**	**184,986**
Total debits	207,479	Total credits	207,479

Tab. 5.34: Solution to exercise 11 – posting and closing of accounts (5).

Debit (€)		Input tax	Credit (€)
(Opening balance	0)	Transaction 2b	57
Transaction 1	5,225	**Closing balance**	**8,018**
Transaction 2a	2,850		
Total debits	8,075	Total credits	8,075

Note that the account input tax is closed to the account VAT because the balance is lower than the balance on the VAT account (i.e. in total it is a liability).

Tab. 5.35: Solution to exercise 11 – posting and closing of accounts (6).

Debit (€)		Equity	Credit (€)
Closing balance	**324,400**	Opening balance	300,000
		Profit	24,400
Total debits	324,400	Total credits	324,400

For the profit, see the income statement below.

Tab. 5.36: Solution to exercise 11 – posting and closing of accounts (7).

Debit (€)		Loans	Credit (€)
Closing balance	320,000	Opening balance	290,000
		Transaction 4	30,000
Total debits	320,000	Total credits	320,000

Tab. 5.37: Solution to exercise 11 – posting and closing of accounts (8).

Debit (€)		Trade payables	Credit (€)
Transaction 2b	17,850	Opening balance	210,000
Closing balance	242,725	Transaction 1	32,725
		Transaction 2a	17,850
Total debits	260,575	Total credits	260,575

Tab. 5.38: Solution to exercise 11 – posting and closing of accounts (9).

Debit (€)		VAT	Credit (€)
Transaction 5b	171	(Opening balance	0)
Input tax	8,018	Transaction 5a	8,550
Closing balance	361		
Total debits	8,550	Total credits	8,550

Tab. 5.39: Solution to exercise 11 – posting and closing of accounts (10).

Debit (€)		Sales revenue	Credit (€)
Transaction 5b	900	Transaction 5a	45,000
Closing balance	44,100		
Total debits	45,000	Total credits	45,000

Tab. 5.40: Solution to exercise 11 – posting and closing of accounts (11).

Debit (€)		Material expenses	Credit (€)
Transaction 2c	14,700	Closing balance	14,700
Total debits	14,700	Total credits	14,700

Tab. 5.41: Solution to exercise 11 – posting and closing of accounts (12).

Debit (€)		Interest expenses	Credit (€)
Transaction 3	5,000	Closing balance	5,000
Total debits	5,000	Total credits	5,000

Note that all income and expense accounts are closed to the income statement:

Tab. 5.42: Solution to exercise 11 – posting and closing of accounts (13).

Debit (€)		Income statement	Credit (€)
Material expenses	14,700	Sales revenue	44,100
Interest expenses	5,000		
Closing balance	24,400		
Total debits	44,100	Total credits	44,100

Note that the income statement is closed to equity (see above). This results in the following closing balance sheet:

Tab. 5.43: Solution to exercise 11 – closing balance.

Debit (€)		Balance sheet	Credit (€)
Tangible assets	402,500	Equity	324,400
Inventory	125,000	Loans	320,000
Trade receivables	175,000	Trade payables	242,725
Bank	184,986	VAT	361
Total assets	887,486	Total equity and liabilities	887,486

c) *References*
Coenenberg et al., 2021 (2), p. 95

5.2 Exercises on fundamental concepts and GAAP

Exercise 1: Generally Accepted Accounting Principles

Category: Knowledge
Time to solve: 5 minutes

a) *Exercise*
The GAAP contain the principle of comparability. Explain this principle. What is its purpose?

b) *Solution*
§ 252 sect. 1 nos. 1 and 6,
additionally for corporations and partnerships according to § 264a:
§ 265 sect. 1, § 284 sect. 2 no. 3

The principle of comparability has as its purpose ensuring that the information in the financial statements is comparable to the information in the earlier financial statements.

The rules described in what follows for corporations apply also to partnerships that do not have at least one natural person as general partner (§ 264a).

Comparability can be distinguished further in:

Formal comparability
Comparability in presentation: The structure of the financial statements of a corporation must be retained unless there are good reasons for not doing so; good reasons are typically that the true and fair view is improved. For corporations the detailed structures of §§ 266, 275 must be applied; any changes in the structure must be explained in the notes.

Substantial comparability
Measurement methods must be retained, corporations must present deviations in the notes with additional explanations of how the changes affect the asset, financial, and income situation of the company.

c) *References*
Bacher, Chapter 3.2
Beck'scher Bilanzkommentar, §§ 252, 265 and 284
Coenenberg et al., 2021 (1), p. 43

Exercise 2: Generally Accepted Accounting Principles

Category: Knowledge
Time to solve: 5 minutes

a) *Exercise*
The following transactions violate the GAAP. Please name the relevant principles in detail!

Example: When measuring assets, one machine is measured by its liquidation (break-up) value.
Violation of the going concern principle!

Several provisions are grouped together and measured in sum:

Violation of . . . .!

The trade receivables are netted with the trade payables:

Violation of . . . .!

Expenses are always recognized when they are paid:

Violation of . . . .!

On the closing date, inventories are measured at their acquisition cost because lower market values are considered temporary:

Violation of . . . .!

b) *Solution*
Several provisions are grouped together and measured in sum:

Violation of the **principle of individual measurement!**
§ 252 sect. 1 no. 3
If not specifically allowed, any asset or liability must be measured separately from all others.

The trade receivables are netted with the trade payables:

Violation of the **principle of no offsetting**!
§ 246 sect. 2 sent. 1
Assets and liabilities must be reported separately; only under rare circumstances is netting acceptable.

Expenses are always recognized when they are paid:

Violation of the **principle of accrual basis!**
§ 252 sect. 1 no. 5

Income and expenses are reported on an accrual basis, not a cash basis, i.e. income or expenses are recognized if and when they occur, not when paid.

On the closing date, inventories are measured at their acquisition cost because lower market values are considered temporary:

Violation of the **principle of prudence/imparity principle (strict lower-of-cost-or-market principle)**!
§ 252 sect. 1 no. 4
Losses must be recognized if they are probable. For current assets this is applied as the strict lower-of-cost-or-market principle, which means that any decrease in value must be recognized. This is true even if the decrease in value is only temporary.

c) *References*
Bacher, Chapter 3.2
Beck'scher Bilanzkommentar, see the named §§ in the solution
Coenenberg et al., 2021 (1), p. 40

Exercise 3: Size classes

Category: Knowledge/Application
Time to solve: 5 minutes

a) *Exercise*
Singleholiday.com GmbH has the following data:

Tab. 5.44: Exercise 3.

	20X1	20X2
Balance Sheet Total (in million €)	4,100	6,500
Sales Revenue (in million €)	8,100	12,750
Average number of employees	50	50

1. Can the company use size-dependent simplifications for the 20X2 financial statements?
2. What would happen if the company showed the same data in 20X3 as in 20X2?
3. What would happen if the company had placed a listed bond?

b) *Solution*
§ 267
1. Singleholiday.com GmbH is a corporation, i.e. if applicable it could use size-dependent simplifications. The criteria for a medium-sized company according to

§ 267 are fulfilled in 20X2 (total assets > €6,000 million and sales revenue > €12,000 million), but only for 1 year. Therefore, the company is still classified as small and can use the corresponding simplifications.

2. Now the company fulfils the criteria for a medium-sized company in two consecutive years and is therefore classified as medium-sized.
3. A capital-market-oriented company is treated as a large company, independently of any size criteria. A company is capital-market oriented if it has shares, bonds or other securities that are listed on a stock exchange.

c) *References*
Bacher, Chapter 2.1
Beck'scher Bilanzkommentar, § 267
Coenenberg et al., 2021 (1), p. 29

Exercise 4: Acquisition and production costs

Category: Knowledge
Time to solve: 10 minutes

a) *Exercise*
Describe similarities and important differences between acquisition costs and production costs. Name the different components that must, may or need not be included.

b) *Solution*
§ 255 sect. 1, 2, 2a and 3
Acquisition costs and production costs are both measures of the initial valuation of assets. Whereas acquisition costs are used for acquired assets, production costs are used for assets produced by the company itself.

Acquisition costs include any costs that are directly attributable to the acquisition of the asset until the acquired asset is ready for use. Production costs include also the direct costs of production, but also indirect costs.

Detailed definition of acquisition costs:
Purchase price
− Discounts and rebates
+ Incidental acquisition costs
+ Subsequent acquisition costs
= Acquisition costs of asset

Only values net of VAT are included in the acquisition costs.

Detailed definition of production costs:

Direct material costs
+ A fair part of indirect material costs
+ Direct manufacturing costs
+ A fair part of indirect manufacturing costs
+ Special direct costs of manufacturing
+ A fair part of depreciation of non-current assets used in production
= Minimum value of production costs
+ A fair part of general administrative costs (optional)
+ A fair part of voluntary social security and employee benefits (optional)
+ Borrowing costs for the production process (optional only if a direct link to the specific production process exists)
= Maximum value of production costs

Not to be included are research costs and sales and distribution costs.

c) *References*
Bacher, Chapter 3.2.2.4
Beck'scher Bilanzkommentar, § 255
Coenenberg et al., 2021 (1), p. 99

Exercise 5: Acquisition costs

Category: Knowledge/Application
Time to solve: 10 minutes

a) *Exercise*
Import AG purchases a stable, stationary crane for the unloading of containers. The crane costs €595,000 including VAT. Included in this amount are service costs for the first year after installation of €7,140, costs for test runs including the used materials of €4,640. For transport, Drive Inn GmbH charged €5,950 including VAT. The transportation risk was borne by Import AG itself. The controlling department posted imputed costs of €8,120 for this. For the evaluation of several technical facilities, an expert, Dr. Weiß, charged €3,940 including VAT. For a security check and acceptance of the crane, TÜV charged €9,520 including VAT. For installation and electrical connection, Import AG received invoices from other service companies totaling €10,000 net. The invoiced purchasing price was paid by Import AG in accordance with the sales contract after deducting a 10% discount.

What acquisition costs of the crane must be recognized?

b) *Solution*
§ 255 sect. 1

Tab. 5.45: Solution to exercise 5.

Value in €	Description/explanation
+500,000	Purchase price, net of VAT
−6,000	Service costs for first year (net) included in purchase price. The service costs included are for services after the crane is installed, so they may not be included in the acquisition costs. On the other hand, the costs for test runs are necessary to attain operations readiness and, thus, remain included.
+5,000	Transport of crane to premises (net), necessary for operations readiness, and so included. Transportation risk is not insured, so no insurance premium is paid. Purely imputed costs are not allowed to be included in the financial accounting. Dr. Weiß inspected several facilities; therefore, the costs related to his services are not directly attributable to this purchase and are not included.
+8,000	A security check by TÜV (Technischer Überwachungsverein – Technical survey organization) is necessary for operations readiness and therefore included.
+10,000	Installation – see above.
−49,400	Discounts must be deducted from the acquisition costs (if directly attributable, which is the case here). Because the purchase price was reduced by the service costs, the discount rate can be applied to the reduced value only, i.e. 10 % of 494,000.
= 467,600	**Acquisition costs of crane**

c) *Hints*

The precise calculation of acquisition costs can be a quite difficult and time-consuming task in real life – particularly when large and complex assets, such as ships, (large) buildings and power plants, are acquired.

d) *References*
Bacher, Chapter 3.2.2.4
Beck'scher Bilanzkommentar, § 255
Coenenberg et al., 2021 (1), p. 99

Exercise 6: Revenue recognition

Category: Knowledge
Time to solve: 5 minutes

a) *Exercise*
On the basis of what criteria can it be judged whether or not a revenue or gain has been realized or whether or not a receivable already exists?

b) *Solution*

Based on the realization principle, income or revenue can be recognized only when realized. To put that in concrete terms, four criteria must be fulfilled:

1. **A contract exists:** There exists a legally binding agreement. In legal terms, there are no specific requirements concerning the form of the agreement for most cases, a purely oral or an implicit agreement is sufficient; because of the lack of evidence, this is usually not best practice.

2. **Goods delivered/services rendered:** The seller or service provider fulfilled all his obligations completely, so that the buyer now owes payment.

3. **Risks have been transferred:** In case of moveable goods, the goods must be at the disposal of the buyer or a transfer of risk must have occurred, i.e. the risk of accidental loss or destruction must have been transferred to the buyer.

4. **The contract can be billed:** If the contract defines additional conditions about the delivery of a good or the rendering of services (e.g. successful test run of a machine), they must be fulfilled before payment is due, and all the additional conditions must be met before revenue is realized.

c) *Hints*

German accounting follows the "completed-contract method": As the name implies, a contract must be completed before revenue can be recognized. In international accounting other recognition principles, e.g. percentage of completion, are acceptable and used.

The exact definition of transfer of risk is particularly important for exporting or importing transactions over long distances because of the transportation risk. Therefore, the International Chamber of Commerce in Paris edited the so-called Incoterms that clearly define the conditions of delivery for a contract. Within the conditions of delivery, the definition of the transfer of risk is an essential element.

d) *References*
Bacher, Chapter 3.2.1
Beck'scher Bilanzkommentar, § 252 no. 44

5.3 Exercises on non-current assets

Exercise 7: Definition of non-current assets

Category: Knowledge
Time to solve: 5 minutes

a) *Exercise*
Define the term non-current assets. In which way, or to what extent, can a company influence the classification of assets as non-current?

b) *Solution*
§ 247 sect. 2
All assets that are intended to serve a business continuously must be classified as non-current. Thus, classification depends on the business purpose of each asset. To the extent the company can and wants to influence this purpose (subjectively, depending on its individual intentions), the classification can be influenced. For example, an acquired piece of land can be split into two parts, where one part is used continuously for the business and is therefore reported as a non-current asset, whereas the other part can be sold on short notice and so is classified as a current asset. Whether the piece of land is split up and one part is sold depends on the wishes and decision of the company.

c) *References*
Bacher, Chapter 3.2.1.1
Beck'scher Bilanzkommentar, § 247 nos. 350–361
Coenenberg et al., 2021 (1), p. 143

Exercise 8: Structure of non-current assets

Category: Knowledge
Time to solve: 5 minutes

a) *Exercise*
What is the structure of non-current assets? Give two practical examples of each category.

b) *Solution*
§ 266 sect. 2 A
  The typical structure according to § 266 is as follows:
–   Intangible assets, such as patents, software, licenses or goodwill.
–   Tangible assets, such as land and buildings, machines, vehicles or office equipment.
–   Financial assets, such as shares in or loans to affiliated companies, participations and loans to them, other long-term loans.
The legal structure requires further details for each category.

c) *Hints*
This structure is mandatory for corporations. Sole proprietorships and partnerships do not have a specific legal requirement to detail non-current assets (§ 247 sect. 1); nevertheless this structure is commonly used by them as well.

Advance payments are reported corresponding to the asset that has been paid for in advance, i.e. if the company pays in advance for a software that will be classified as non-current, and the advance payment is reported as an intangible asset (in a separate line item of the intangible assets).

d) *References*
Bacher, Chapter 3.3.1.1
Beck'scher Bilanzkommentar, § 266, nos. 59–82
Coenenberg et al., 2021 (1), p. 143

Exercise 9: Goodwill

Category: Knowledge
Time to solve: 10 minutes

a) *Exercise*
Is goodwill an asset? Explain your judgment briefly and explain the rules for measuring goodwill in the commercial balance sheet and in the tax balance sheet.

b) *Solution*
Recognition in commercial balance sheet § 246 sect. 1 sent. 4
Measurement in commercial balance sheet § 253 sect. 1 sent. 1 and 2
Recognition in tax balance sheet § 5 sect. 2 EStG
Measurement in tax balance sheet § 6 sect. 1 no. 1 EStG, § 7 sect. 1 sent. 3 EStG

There is a distinction between acquired goodwill and internally generated goodwill.

For internally generated goodwill, a recognition is prohibited by both the Commercial Code and German tax law. Internally generated goodwill comes into existence during the usual course of business by creating an organization for the business, a customer base or the quality or experience of employees. It does not fulfil the recognition criteria for an asset (see below).

Acquired goodwill is the difference between the consideration for a purchased business and the identifiable net assets acquired; a bit informal: if you pay more for a business than you can identify as assets and liabilities, this premium is goodwill.

Acquired goodwill does not fulfil the general recognition criteria as an asset but is treated like an asset with a definite useful life. The general recognition criteria are as follows:

Economic benefit: This is fulfilled usually because goodwill represents the future profit potential of the acquired business that cannot be attributed to individual assets or liabilities.

Separate measurability: This is fulfilled, and the value can be measured as the difference between the value of the acquired business (purchase price/consideration) and the acquired net assets.

Independent marketability: This cannot be fulfilled because goodwill cannot be sold independently of its business.

Commercial Code: According to § 246 sect. 1 sent. 4, acquired goodwill is treated as an asset with a definite useful life and must be measured according to the general rules of § 253 sect. 3, i.e. it must be amortized over its useful life. If a presumably permanent decrease in value occurs, an additional impairment to the lower fair value is mandatory. If the reasons for an earlier impairment no longer exist, the lower value must be kept, i.e. there is no reversal of impairment for acquired goodwill. The latter is a difference from all other assets.

German tax law: Acquired goodwill must be recognized according to § 5 sect. 2 EStG and must be amortized over 15 years according to § 7 sect. 1 sent. 3 EStG. As for all assets, an impairment option exists if a permanent decrease in value occurs.

c) *Hints*

The estimated useful life of goodwill must be explained in notes (§ 285 no. 13).

If – applicable only in rare cases – the useful life of goodwill cannot be estimated, 10 years must be used (§ 253 sect 3 sent. 3 and 4).

If the useful life applied according to the Commercial Code differs from the 15 years that must be used under German tax law (which will usually be the case), this will result in temporary differences, which may result in deferred taxes. If the useful life according to the Commercial Code is shorter, this results in a deferred tax asset; if the useful life according to the Commercial Code is longer (which can hardly be the case), it would result in a deferred tax liability.

If goodwill appears in consolidated financial statements, i.e. due to a share deal, no deferred taxes are recognized (§ 306 sent. 3).

d) *References*

Bacher, Chapter 3.1.1 and Chapter 3.3.1.1

Beck'scher Bilanzkommentar, § 246, nos. 82 and 83 as well as § 253, nos. 212–279 and 676

Coenenberg et al., 2021 (1), p. 190

Exercise 10: Goodwill

Category: Knowledge/Application
Time to solve: 10 minutes

a) *Exercise*
Akquise AG acquires the business of Target GmbH with all assets and liabilities for
a purchase price of €500,000 (asset deal). Target GmbH reports assets with a book
value of €800,000 and equity of €100,000. The following information is additionally available:
– land: hidden reserves of €120,000,
– internally generated brand with a fair value of €250,000.
– After acquisition the legal department of Target GmbH will no longer be needed.
  The expected severance payments amount to €200,000.

Prepare the balance sheet of Target GmbH before acquisition.
    How is the asset deal to be recognized in the books of Akquise AG? Show the
journal entry for the integration of the transaction (one debit or credit item per
line).

b) *Solution*
§ 246 sect. 1 sent. 4
Balance sheet of Target GmbH before acquisition:

Tab. 5.46: Solution to exercise 10.

Debit (T€)		Balance sheet	Credit (T€)
Assets	800	Equity (net assets)	100
		Liabilities	700
Total assets	800	Total equity and liabilities	800

Calculation of goodwill:

Purchase price		500 T€
Minus net assets at time value, i.e.		
Assets	800 T€	
+ Hidden reserve in land	120 T€	
+ Internally generated brand	250 T€	
– Liabilities	700 T€	
– Provision for severance payments	200 T€	
= Net assets at time value		+270 T€
= Goodwill (purchase price – net assets)		+230 T€

Journal entry:

Debit assets	800 T€		
Debit hidden reserves	120 T€		
Debit internally generated brand	250 T€		
Debit goodwill	230 T€		
		Credit liabilities	700 T€
		Credit severance provision	200 T€
		Credit purchase price payable	500 T€
Total debits	1,400 T€	Total credits	1,400 T€

c) *References*
Bacher, Chapters 3.1.1 and 3.3.1.1
Coenenberg et al., 2021 (1), p. 190

Exercise 11: Presentation of non-current financial assets

Category: Knowledge
Time to solve: 5 minutes

a) *Exercise*
Describe briefly in key words the differences between the following balance sheet items:
- Shares in affiliated companies
- Participations
- Non-current securities

b) *Solution*
§ 271

Shares in affiliated companies
Affiliated companies are companies that are consolidated within the same consolidated financial statements. They are controlled by the parent company that owns the shares or one controls the other (§ 290). An investment must be reported here if a controlling interest exists in another company depending on the specific legal form, e.g. common stock for a stock company.

Shares in affiliated companies typically represent a majority of voting rights.

Participations
Participations are shares of companies (s.a.), in which the reporting company has a substantial interest, but no control, e.g. because it does not hold the majority of voting rights. Nevertheless the shares are intended to serve as a permanent connection among the businesses.

Participations typically represent voting rights of 20 % up to 49.9% – so substantial influence is given, but no control.

Non-current securities

Securities that are intended to continuously serve the business, i.e. are held long term, are reported in this item. It is essential that the claims be securitized and, therefore, tradable. Equity instruments, such as shares, and debt instruments, such as bonds, are reported in this item. But an instrument is reported here only if it is tradable and cannot be classified as being related to affiliated companies (shares in affiliated companies or borrowings to affiliated companies) or to participations (participations or borrowings to participations), i.e. if the voting rights usually do not exceed 20%.

c) Reference
Beck'scher Bilanzkommentar, § 266, nos. 69–82 and § 271
Coenenberg et al., 2021 (1), p. 276

Exercise 12: Deferred tax assets

Category: Knowledge/Application
Time to solve: 5 minutes

a) Exercise
Name at least three transactions that result in deferred tax assets.

b) Solution
1. Recognition of a provision for onerous contracts. Under the Commercial Code, recognition is mandatory; under German tax law, it is forbidden.
2. Higher measurement of (pension) provisions under the Commercial Code than under German tax law, e.g. because of discounting of provisions according to the Commercial Code with an interest rate that is lower than the 5.5% (6%) applicable under tax law.
3. Use of the option to expense a disagio fully in the first period according to the Commercial Code, whereas a recognition as deferred expenses according to the matching principle is mandatory under German tax law.
4. Use of higher depreciation under the Commercial Code, e.g. declining balance method, which is currently not allowed under German tax law.
5. Tax losses carried forward if they are expected to be used in the next 5 years.

c) Hints
To the extent that the recognition and measurement criteria in the Commercial Code and German tax law are not identical, deferred taxes are used to correct the

measurement of taxes under the Commercial Code. Theoretically, the result before taxes under the Commercial Code multiplied by the tax rate should be identical to the tax expense or income (both current and deferred) presented in the income statement.

Deferred tax assets are expected future tax relief, i.e. the result under the Commercial Code is reduced today by expenses that will be tax deductible in the future. In consequence, today's result under German tax law is higher than under the Commercial Code, and therefore current taxes are higher than would be expected when looking at the result according to the Commercial Code. This situation can be corrected for corporations if the recognition option (§ 274) is used. Recognition of deferred tax liabilities is mandatory.

A good way to remember what kind of difference will turn into what kind of deferred tax is the following matrix. If you remember one square, all the other possibilities can be derived because the adjacent squares lead to the opposite result.

The rules for deferred taxes are specified in § 274 and are therefore applicable only for corporations.

	Assets	Liabilities
CBS > TBS	Deferred tax liability	Deferred tax asset
CBS < TBS	Deferred tax asset	Deferred tax liability

CBS – commercial balance sheet
TBS – tax balance sheet

Fig. 5.2: Deferred tax assets and liabilities.

d) *References*
Bacher, Chapter 3.3.5
Beck'scher Bilanzkommentar, § 274
Coenenberg et al., 2021 (1), p. 508

Exercise 13: Internally generated intangible assets

Category: Knowledge/Application
Time to solve: 5 minutes

a) *Exercise*

A company has developed a new production technique. The development costs are €160,000 and are included as expenses in the income statement. This production technique was patented and approved. The company likes to use the production technique in its own production department (beginning in January of the next year).

How could this transaction be accounted for? How will the profit at the closing date be influenced by recognition (and amortization) in the next 4 years (neglect deferred taxes)? Assume a useful life of 4 years and linear/straight-line amortization.

b) *Solution*

§ 248 sect. 2

§ 255 sect. 2a

The Commercial Code offers a recognition option for self-produced intangible assets that are non-current: These assets can be recognized as assets but do not have to be (§ 248 sect. 2).

In the current case:

patent	intangible asset
developed by company	internally generated
used in production	non-current (no intention to sell patent)

A recognition is possible only if the development costs can be clearly distinguished from research costs (§ 255 sect. 2a); this is the case here, so a recognition as a non-current intangible asset would be possible.

The effects of a recognition look as follows:

Tab. 5.47: Solution to exercise 13.

	Effect on net result	Comment
Year 0	+ 160, 000	Recognition of asset
Year 1 of use	− 40, 000	Amortization in year 1
Year 2 of use	− 40, 000	Amortization in year 2
Year 3 of use	− 40, 000	Amortization in year 3
Year 4 of use	− 40, 000	Amortization in year 4
Sum	0	

For simplicity a partial amortization of year 0 is neglected.

c) *Hints*

Note that the sum of the annual effects is 0. Using the accounting option affects the results of individual periods, but for the total period it is always neutral, i.e. if you increase your profit today, you will reduce your profit in upcoming periods (and vice versa).

d) *References*

Bacher, Chapter 3.3.1.1

Beck'scher Bilanzkommentar, § 248, nos. 10–46

Coenenberg et al., 2021 (1), p. 186

Exercise 14: Depreciation methods

Category: Knowledge

Time to solve: 5 minutes

a) *Exercise*

Name briefly and precisely the most important advantages of both the linear depreciation method and the declining balance method.

b) *Solution*

Advantages of linear depreciation:
- It satisfies current tax requirements if the useful life is identical for commercial and tax balance sheet. In that case, no additional tax calculations are necessary and no deferred taxes exist.
- It is easy to calculate and to understand.
- It assumes a continuous use of the asset, which is often the most plausible assumption if better information is not available.

Advantages of declining balance depreciation:
- It represents better a disproportionate decrease in value at the beginning of the useful life (e.g. after purchase of a company car).
- It is better suited to keep the total expenses of an investment constant; over time maintenance expenses, for example, typically increase and can be compensated by the decreasing depreciation.
- It transfers tax payments to the future if tax deductible (currently, for new investment not the case in Germany).

c) *References*

Jung, p. 1043

Exercise 15: Depreciation methods

Category: Knowledge/Application
Time to solve: 10 minutes

a) *Exercise*
A car is bought on 15 January 20X1 and will probably be used for 5 years or 200,000 km. The acquisition costs amount to €40,000. The mileage is distributed as follows:

Year 1	35,000 km
Year 2	25,000 km
Year 3	30,000 km
Year 4	65,000 km
Year 5	45,000 km

Compare the development of the depreciation for linear, declining balance (30%) and performance-oriented depreciation.

b) *Solution*
The depreciation schedules look as follows (all values in €):

Tab. 5.48: Solution to exercise 15 – linear depreciation.

Linear depreciation			
Year	Remaining book value at beginning	Depreciation	Remaining book value at end
1	40,000	8,000	32,000
2	32,000	8,000	24,000
3	24,000	8,000	16,000
4	16,000	8,000	8,000
5	8,000	8,000	0
Total		40,000	

Tab. 5.49: Solution to exercise 15 – declining balance depreciation.

Declining balance depreciation (30%)				
Year	Remaining book value at beginning	Depreciation	Remaining book value at end	Corresponding linear depreciation
1	40,000	12,000	28,000	8,000
2	28,000	8,400	19,600	7,000
3	19,600	(Declining: 5,880) **Linear: 6,533**	13,067	6,533
4	13,067	6,533	6,534	
5	6,534	6,534	0	
Total		40,000		

The corresponding linear depreciation is calculated as the remaining book value at the beginning divided by the remaining useful life (i.e. for year 2: 28,000/ 4 = 7,000). When this corresponding linear depreciation is larger than the declining balance depreciation, you must switch to linear (in this example in period 3: 6,533 > 5,880).

Tab. 5.50: Solution to exercise 15 – performance-oriented depreciation.

Performance-oriented depreciation					
Year	Performance	Performance (%)	Remaining book value at beginning (€)	Depreciation (€)	Remaining book value at end (€)
1	35,000	17.5	40,000	7,000	33,000
2	25,000	12.5	33,000	5,000	28,000
3	30,000	15.0	28,000	6,000	22,000
4	65,000	32.5	22,000	13,000	9,000
5	45,000	22.5	9,000	9,000	0
Total	200,000			40,000	

The annual depreciation is calculated by multiplying the initial acquisition costs (€40,000) with the performance as a percentage (i.e. percentage of annual performance (for year 1: 35,000 km) and total performance (200,000 km)).

The total amount depreciated is always the same: 40,000. But the distribution over the reporting periods varies substantially.

c) *References*
Bacher, Chapter 3.3.1.1
Coenenberg et al., 2021 (1), p. 164

5.4 Exercises on current assets

Exercise 16: Inventories

Category:　　Knowledge/Application
Time to solve:　10 minutes

a) *Exercise*
Gert Glitz is a jeweler in Pforzheim and at a summer auction purchases gold for €100,000 and diamonds for €50,000. In spring of the following year he prepares his balance sheet. The price for gold increased, so that he could have sold his gold for €120,000 on 31 December. Unfortunately, the diamonds are of minor quality. Their market value decreases continuously: on 31 December they are valued at

€40,000, and in February of the following year they are worth only €30,000. How will the gold and diamonds be valued on 31 December in the commercial and the tax balance sheets? Give reasons for your answer.

b) *Solution*
§ 252 sect. 1 no. 4
§ 253 sect. 4

Because Gert Glitz is a jeweler, it can be assumed that gold and diamonds are current assets for him, i.e. he plans to use them for his own production and wants to sell the related products to customers.

Measurement of the gold:
The value remains at the acquisition costs of €100,000 on the closing date. This corresponds to the realization principle as one part of the principle of prudence: Gains may be recognized only if they are realized. Due to the principle of congruence, this applies to the tax balance sheet as well.

Measurement of the diamonds:
The diamonds must be recognized at the lower market value; this corresponds to the imparity principle as the other part of the principle of prudence. For current assets any decrease in value at the closing date must be recognized as an expense (strict lower-of-cost-or-market principle). In addition, we must apply the closing date principle, i.e. the market conditions on the closing date are relevant. According to this principle, the diamonds must be recognized at €40,000. The even lower value in February can only be used in the following financial statements (if still relevant). If this decrease in value is considered permanent, it can be recognized for tax purposes as well. Only temporary decreases in value must not be recognized for tax purposes.

c) *References*
Bacher, Chapter 3.3.1.2
Coenenberg et al., 2021 (1), p. 239

Exercise 17: Inventories (2)

Category: Knowledge
Time to solve: 5 minutes

a) *Exercise*
What methods can be used for the initial measurement of acquired inventories according to the Commercial Code? Explain the methods briefly.

b) *Solution*
§ 240 sect. 3 and 4
§ 256

Acquired inventories must be measured by their acquisition costs. The basic principle to be applied is individual measurement (each part separately). Because this is
not practical for large quantities, the following simplifications are possible if they
are in line with GAAP:
1.   Group measurement of similar inventories:
  –   **Periodic average**
      The periodic average is calculated using only one average per reporting period:
      The total value of all additions and the opening balance is divided by the total
      amount of all additions and the opening balance. This average is applied to all
      withdrawals/consumptions and the closing balance.
  –   **Moving average**
      After each new addition a new average is calculated: The total value of the ad-
      dition and assets in stock divided by the total amount of addition and assets in
      stock. This average is used for all withdrawals/consumptions until the next ad-
      dition. To do this properly, you need precise information about the timing of
      additions and withdrawals.
  –   **Last in, first out**
      (LIFO) Under LIFO, it is assumed that the inventories acquired last are used
      first. Thus, to measure the closing balance, you need to take the oldest addi-
      tions (including the opening balance).
  –   **First in, first out**
      (FIFO) Under FIFO, it is assumed that the inventories acquired first (or the
      opening balance) are used first. Thus, to measure the closing balance you need
      to use the newest/latest additions.

2. Constant-value approach for raw materials and similar items:
Raw materials and other materials (i.e. not finished or unfinished products) may be
recognized at a constant value under strict conditions. Then you can retain the
value of the prior year and show all acquisitions directly as expenses.

c) *Hints*
Conditions for group measurement:
The inventories must be similar. Similarity means similar in kind (e.g. screwdrivers of
different sizes) or function (e.g. screws and nails can both be used to fix two things
together).

This approach can also be used for moveable non-current assets or moveable current assets other than inventories if they are similar in kind (see above) or similar in

value. Similar in value is interpreted as belonging to the same category of asset with a price difference of less than 20%.

Conditions for the constant-value approach:
Raw materials and tangible non-current assets can be measured at a constant value if
–   their value is of minor importance,
–   their structure fluctuates only slightly and
–   they are continuously being used and replaced.

An example could be nails and screws for a roofer (if business does not grow and working processes do not change). Another example (for non-current assets) are cutlery, table linen or bed sets for a hotel.

d) *References*
Bacher, Chapter 3.3.1.2
Coenenberg et al., 2021 (1), p. 239

Exercise 18: Inventories (3)

Category: Knowledge/Application
Time to solve: 10 minutes

a) *Exercise*
Ride-a-Bike GmbH produces bicycles for children. At the balance sheet date the company has 1,800 identical steering bars in stock, which are from different purchases in the business year. It is not possible to allocate the individual parts to the different purchases. Records show the following information:

Opening balance	1 January 20X1:	1,400 pcs to €48 per piece
Increase	10 April 20X1	2,000 pcs to €45 per piece
Increase	15 September 20X1	3,500 pcs to €43 per piece
Increase	10 December 20X1	2,800 pcs to €46 per piece
Total decrease:		7,900 pcs

1. What is the balance sheet amount if the weighted periodic average is used?
2. What other calculation methods are allowed under the Commercial Code? Calculate the book values according to those. What calculation method would you choose if you wanted to show as high a profit as possible?
3. What measurement methods are allowed under German tax law?

b) *Solution*
§ 240 sect. 4
§ 256

Tab. 5.51: Solution to exercise 18.

	Amount (pc.)	Price (€/pc.)	Value (€)	LIFO	FIFO
Opening balance	1,400	48	67,200	67,200	
Increase 1	2,000	45	90,000	18,000	
Increase 2	3,500	43	150,500		
Increase 3	2,800	46	128,800		82,800
Total	9,700	**45**	436,500		
Consumption	7,900	45	355,500	351,300	353,700
Closing Balance	1,800	45	81,000	85,200	82,800

1. If the periodic average is used, one average is calculated for the whole year: All increases and the opening balance are summed up and the total value is divided by the total amount. This results in an average of €45/pc. This average is applied to the consumption and the closing balance. Thus, the value of the consumption is €355,500 and the value of the closing balance is €81,000.
2. According to Commercial Code, LIFO and FIFO can also be applied (if in line with the GAAP). When applying LIFO, it is assumed that the latest increases are used first, i.e. the oldest items are still in stock. This results in a value of 85,200: the total amount of the closing balance is 1,800 pc., of which 1,400 pc. are from the opening balance with a value of €67,200, and the remaining 400 pc. are from increase 1 with a value of €18,000. Thus, the total value is €85,200. When applying FIFO, it is exactly the converse, i.e. it is assumed that the newest items are still on hand: Thus, the closing balance is measured using the price of increase 3, i.e. 1,800 pc. at €46/pc., that is €82,800. To show as high a profit as possible, the assets should be measured as high as possible, i.e. LIFO should be used.
3. According to tax law, periodic average and LIFO are possible (LIFO only if the real sequence of consumption does not contradict LIFO).

c) *Hints*

The moving average could be used from a legal perspective, but it cannot be used in practice here because the exact timing of the consumption/usage of the parts is not known.

For accounting policy, you must keep in mind that these simplifications apply only to the initial measurement. If the market value at year end is lower, the lower value must be recognized (independently of the method chosen for the initial measurement – strict lower-of-cost-or-market principle).

d) *References*
Bacher, Chapter 3.3.1.2
Coenenberg et al., 2021 (1), p. 239

Exercise 19: Inventories (4)

Category: Knowledge
Time to solve: 5 minutes

a) *Exercise*
A carpenter has a steady business. His total assets amount to €100,000, of which €3,000 is for glues and colors.

At the closing date of 31 December 20X1 he wants to simplify the preparation of his financial statements, and he wants to use the constant-value approach for the glues and colors.

Is that possible? What is the consequence?

b) *Solution*
§ 240 sect 3.

– it is applied to (raw) materials:	that is the case here
– the materials are of minor importance:	3% of total assets are in general considered minor
– the materials are continuously replaced:	unknown
– the materials fluctuate in value and composition only slightly:	unknown

The constant-value approach can be used if
The first two criteria are fulfilled. The two additional criteria need to be fulfilled as well; only if all criteria are fulfilled can the constant-value approach be used.

If the constant-value approach is used, the consequence is that for these assets a constant value is used, i.e. the book value no longer changes and acquisitions of new material are directly shown as expenses.

c) *Hints*
The constant-value approach is also a simplification for stock taking because a physical stock taking must be done only after 3 years, not every year.

d) *References*
Beck'scher Bilanzkommentar, § 240, nos. 71–126
Coenenberg et al., 2021 (1), p. 246

Exercise 20: Measurement of receivables

Category: Knowledge/Application
Time to solve: 10 minutes

a) *Exercise*
Maria Hilig owns a wholesaling business for statues of saints and other devotional items. On 31 December 20X1, her trade receivables amount to €520,625. The following specific information is available:

- An "Italian" shop for "original relics" in Hamburg owes her €11,900 (gross). The invoices have been returned to sender "address unknown". Who the owner of the shop has been cannot be clarified. Her lawyer recommends that Maria not attempt any additional legal enforcement because it will very probably not be successful and generate additional costs.
- The customer, Hillbilly GmbH, filed for insolvency. At the moment it is unclear what the insolvency rate will be. Her lawyer estimates that she will receive 40% of the original receivable of €7,140.
- Customer Meier lost all his private belongings in gambling and is currently in a closed section of a psychiatric hospital. It is very improbable that he will pay his invoice total of €2,380.
- In recent years, the tax authorities have accepted a general valuation allowance of 2%.

In March 20X2, Maria prepares her financial statements. What will be the value of the receivables in the balance sheet? What will be the amount of valuation allowance in the income statement?

b) *Solution*
§ 253 sect. 4

Tab. 5.52: Solution to exercise 20.

	Receivables (gross) (€)	Receivables (net) (€)	Valuation allowance as expense (€)
Before Valuation	520,625	437,500	
"Italian" shop	−11,900	− 10,000	10,000
Hillbilly GmbH	− 3,600	− 3,600	3,600
Mr. Meier	− 2,380	− 2,000	2,000
General valuation allowance	− 8,390	− 8,390	8,390
After valuation	494,355	413,510	23,990

The measurement of receivables according to German laws follows a three-step approach:
1. Specific valuation allowances take into account individual risks of receivables:
    (a) A complete loss is expected and very probable: The corresponding VAT may be corrected, i.e. valuation allowance based on the gross value.
    (b) Only a partial loss is expected: Valuation is based on the net receivable; no correction of the VAT is allowed.
2. A general valuation allowance takes into account the general risk of receivables and is based on past experience. It may be based only on the net receivables for which no specific valuation allowance has been recognized (otherwise the valuation allowances would double).

For the "Italian" shop and Mr. Meier, a complete loss of the receivable is very probable; therefore 100% of the receivable (including the VAT) is deducted.

For Hillbilly GmbH, only a partial loss is probable: Maria will receive 40%, i.e. she will lose 60%; therefore 60% of the net receivable is deducted.

A general valuation of 2% of all receivables for which no specific valuation allowance has been recognized:

Net value of receivables	437,500
– Receivable "Italian" shop	– 10,000
– Receivable Hillbilly GmbH	– 6,000
– Receivable Meier	– 2,000
Net value of receivables without specific valuation allowance	419,500, of which 2%: 8,390.

Therefore, the receivables shown in the balance sheet on 31 December 20X1 amount to €494,355. The valuation allowances recognized in the income statement amount to €23,990.

c) *References*
Bacher, Chapter 3.3.1.2
Beck'scher Bilanzkommentar, § 253, nos. 560–608
Coenenberg et al., 2021 (1), p. 286

5.5 Exercises on equity

Exercise 21: Accounting for equity

Category: Knowledge
Time to solve: 5 minutes

a) *Exercise*

Explain how capital increases of a corporation are accounted for. What do partial payment and agio mean in this context?

b) *Solution*

§ 272 sect. 1 and 2

The equity of a corporation is split into shares that have a nominal value (for a stock company the nominal value of all shares must be identical). The subscribed capital is the sum of the nominal value of all shares.

If the equity of a company is increased, this is often done by issuing new shares. The nominal value of these new shares is added to the subscribed capital. If the investors who buy the new shares pay in more than the nominal value, i.e. they pay an agio or a premium, this agio is recognized as capital reserve.

Under German company law, it is possible to found a corporation with only partial payment of subscribed capital.

The minimum equity of a limited liability company (GmbH) is €25,000. Of this €25,000, 50% must be paid in upon founding of the company. The rest can be called up later by the company.

The minimum equity of a stock company (AG) is €50,000, of which 25% must paid in when founding the company.

Nevertheless, the shareholders of the company are required to pay in the complete subscribed capital in the case of insolvency. Thus, in the financial statements the subscribed capital is reported with the complete amount, and the part that has not been paid in and is not called up is deducted, i.e. the effectively paid-in or called-up capital is calculated openly in the balance sheet and called "Paid-in/called-up capital".

For an agio, partial payment is not possible. If the company is founded with partial payment of the nominal capital, a possible agio must always be paid in full.

c) *References*

Bacher, Chapter 3.3.2

Beck'scher Bilanzkommentar, § 272

Coenenberg et al., 2021 (1), p. 355

Exercise 22: Accounting for equity (2)

Category: Knowledge

Time to solve: 5 minutes

a) *Exercise*

What is the difference between capital reserves and revenue reserves in accounting and in financing?

b) *Solution*

§ 272 sect. 2 and 3

A capital reserve is an additional capital contribution of shareholders that does not increase the nominal capital (and therefore typically does not increase voting rights). It often occurs together with a capital increase if an agio is paid. The nominal value of the capital increase increases the subscribed capital, while the agio, i.e. the additionally paid-in capital, increases the capital reserves.

Revenue reserves are profits of either the current period or former periods that are kept in the company and formally transferred to the revenue reserves, i.e. they are not paid out as dividends or other form of profit distribution.

From a financing perspective, a change of capital reserves is external financing because there is cash flow from the outside to the company. On the other hand, revenue reserves are internal financing because the additional capital is generated by the business process of the company.

c) *References*

Bacher, Chapter 3.3.2

Beck'scher Bilanzkommentar, § 272

Coenenberg et al., 2021 (1), p. 355

Exercise 23: Accounting for a company's own shares

Category: Knowledge/Application

Time to solve: 10 minutes

a) *Exercise*

The price for shares of High Tech AG decreased in recent months. Therefore, the executive board decided to purchase company shares to stabilize the price. On 31 December 20X1 the equity was shown as follows:

Subscribed capital	€100 million
Capital reserves	€800 million
Revenue reserves	€600 million

On 30 November 20X2, the company buys one million shares with a nominal value of €1/share for a total price of €12 million. How does this transaction have to be shown in the balance sheet as of 31 December 20X2?

On 15 January 20X3 the company is able to sell the shares again for a price of €15 million. How should this be accounted for in the upcoming balance sheet?

b) *Solution*

§ 272 sect. 1a and 1b

Tab. 5.53: Solution to exercise 23.

In million €	31 Dec. 20X1	Acquisition	31 Dec. 20X2	Resale	31 Dec. 20X3
Subscribed capital	100	− 1	99	+ 1	100
Capital reserve	800		800	+ 3	803
Revenue reserve	600	− 11	589	+ 11	600
Total	**1,500**	**− 12**	**1,488**	**+15**	**1,503**

If a corporation acquires its own shares (typically it is a listed stock company that purchases its own shares on a stock exchange, but the logic applies to any acquisition of its own shares by a company), the value of these shares must be deducted openly from equity.

More precisely: The acquired nominal amounts must be deducted from subscribed capital, and any agio that has been paid must be deducted from revenue reserves (see column "acquisition").

If the shares are sold again, the original deduction must be reversed. If an additional gain is made, this gain is shown as capital reserve (because it has been paid in additionally by third parties; see column "resale").

c) *Hints*

The presentation of a company's own shares as financial assets would be misleading: On the one hand, there is an asset because the shares could be sold again and – usually – were acquired against cash. On the other hand, equity would be overstated in doing this: To the extent that the company acquired its own shares, the company belongs to itself; in the case of insolvency, not all equity would be available for creditors because the shares would be worthless. Therefore, to present the value of equity that is available to third parties, the company's own shares are netted with equity.

Any expenses incurred during the acquisition are not treated as an incidental acquisition cost but as expenses from the period.

d) *References*

Beck'scher Bilanzkommentar, § 272, nos. 130–150

Coenenberg et al., 2021 (1), p. 383

5.6 Exercises on provisions

Exercise 24: Important differences between provisions and debt

Category: Knowledge
Time to solve: 5 minutes

a) *Exercise*
What is the difference between a provision and a debt in accounting? Give one example for each case.

b) *Solution*
§ 249

Provisions are liabilities, i.e. they are based on an obligation to a third party (e.g. customers, suppliers, employees). Unlike debt, they are uncertain to some extent: The reason or the settlement amount can be uncertain (or both). Nevertheless, the obligation and its fulfillment must be probable.

Examples for provisions
Pension provision: A company promises employees (all or only some) to pay additional retirement benefits. There is a lot of uncertainty in this promise: Which employees will reach retirement within the company? What is their salary at that time? What will the retirement benefit be in the future (based on, for example, price changes or salary increases)? Nevertheless, it is probable that there will be future payments, and therefore a provision must be recognized.

Warranty provision: Some products of a company may be faulty or damaged. In that case, customers will make use of warranty services. Insofar as the expenses incurred by the warranty services are probable and predictable, a provision for warranties must be recognized.

Examples for debt
Bank loan: The loan agreement with the bank states clearly what the obligation is and how and when it must be fulfilled. There is very little uncertainty – thus, it is a debt, not a provision.

Trade payables: When a company receives an invoice from a supplier and it has received the goods or services, there is very little uncertainty regarding what amount must be paid and when.

c) *Hints*
The obligation to recognize provisions results from the realization principle and the imparity principle: Probable and predictable losses must be recognized when known, not when realized (i.e. as early as possible). If there is a concrete connection from future expenses to a past event, the realization principle (matching principle)

requires the recognition of a provision for uncertain liabilities. If future expenses are not covered by future income, but cannot be avoided because of an existing contract, a provision for onerous contracts must be recognized; it is based on the imparity principle.

Apart from provisions for uncertain liabilities and onerous contracts, § 249 requires the recognition of another category of provisions: In two specific circumstances, expense provisions must be recognized:

– If necessary maintenance was omitted and is brought up to date within 3 months or
– if necessary waste disposal was omitted and is brought up to date within 12 months, a provision must be recognized. In contrast to the provisions for uncertain liabilities or for onerous contracts, there exists no outside obligation in these cases; whether or not the maintenance or the waste disposal is brought up to date is a decision of company management.

d) *References*
Bacher, Chapter 3.3.3.2
Beck'scher Bilanzkommentar, § 249
Coenenberg et al., 2021 (1), p. 455

Exercise 25: Recognition of provisions

Category: Knowledge/Application
Time to solve: 10 minutes

a) *Exercise*
Please determine in which of the following cases the recognition of a provision is required by the Commercial Code, and classify the type of provision.

1. Due to the strong increase in demand for ITL Care i5 computers, in October a dealer orders 10,000 units at €1,000 per unit; delivery will occur in January. In December the next-generation model ITL Care i6 surprisingly appears on the market, so the sales prices for the acquired units decrease to €500 per unit. How does the dealer account for that at the balance sheet date? What happens if the computers were delivered in November, but not sold?
2. A car producer sold 10,000 cars in the last business year. The revenue from the sales was €500 million. Based on past experience, the company must calculate on the basis of 2% usage of guarantee services. How does the company account for this at the balance sheet date?
3. A production machine of producer X needs urgent maintenance, but the maintenance was neglected due to the currently high order volume. Producer X came to an agreement with craftsman Y that Y will maintain the machine for a fixed price of €800. Y can do the maintenance after the balance sheet date. How should X account for that?

b) *Solution*

§ 249

1. A purchase contract exists, but neither the buyer nor the seller has fulfilled his obligations, so the transaction is pending. Usually, pending transactions are not accounted for, with one exception: If a loss is expected to be realized on this transaction, then the loss must be recognized already now as a provision for onerous contracts. In the current case, the dealer expects a loss of €500 per unit because of the decreased sales price. Therefore, he must recognize a provision for onerous contracts in the amount of €5 million. If the computers were already delivered and in stock, the transaction is no longer pending. The computers are recognized as assets (merchandise) with their acquisition costs and must be revalued to the lower market price at year end (strict lower-of-cost-or-market principle). In this case, the value of the computers must be reduced to €5 million by an impairment. The effect on the income statement is identical, but the balance sheet position is different (reduction of an asset instead of increase in a provision). An additional provision could be recognized only if the expected loss is greater than the value of the corresponding assets (which is not the case here).

2. Expected warranty services are a typical case for a provision for an uncertain liability. A car producer expects, based on experience, that in the future 2% of current sales will be used for warranty services. Therefore, he must recognize a provision for uncertain liabilities (more specifically, for warranty services) of 2% of the current sales, or €10 million.

3. The maintenance of the machine should have been done earlier but was neglected. If the maintenance is done by the craftsman within the first quarter after the closing date, it must be recognized as a provision. If it is done later, a recognition is prohibited.

c) *Hints*

In the last case, a factual accounting option exists: Depending on the timing (within the first quarter, after the first quarter) it is a recognition requirement or prohibition. If the timing is flexible, it can be used for accounting policy. But keep in mind that the correctness can be checked easily afterwards – thus, if this is to be used for the accounting policy, the timing must be precise and kept constant.

d) *References*

Bacher, Chapter 3.3.3.2
Beck'scher Bilanzkommentar, § 249
Coenenberg/Haller/Schultze, p. 455

Exercise 26: Discounting of provisions

Category: Knowledge/Application
Time to solve: 5 minutes

a) *Exercise*
Customers of a production company were not satisfied with the quality of the products and claimed damages. The company does not accept the claims and seeks a legal decision in court; nevertheless, the company expects that it will probably have to pay €12 million in damages in about 3 years after closing date (the decision of the court in all instances will take that amount of time).

The German central bank published the following rates according to § 253 sect. 2:

Tab. 5.54: Exercise 26.

	Maturity in years								
	1	**2**	**3**	**4**	**5**	**6**	**7**	**8**	**9**
Dec. X1	1.2%	1.5%	1.8%	2.0%	2.2%	2.3%	2.4%	2.5%	2.6%

What is the value of the provision at the closing date? What is the value 1 year later assuming that nothing has changed (same settlement amount and same interest rates)?

b) *Solution*
§ 253 sect. 2

At closing date
The expected settlement amount must be discounted for 3 years by the corresponding interest rate:

$$\text{Present value of provision} = \frac{\text{Expected settlement amount}}{(1 + \text{interest rate})^{\text{maturity}}} = \frac{\text{€12 million}}{1,018^3}$$

$$= \text{€11, 374, 647}$$

The value to be recognized is €11,374,647, i.e. the effect of discounting is €625,353.

One year later

$$\text{Present value of provision} = \frac{\text{Expected settlement amount}}{(1 + \text{interest rate})^{\text{maturity}}} = \frac{€12 \text{ million}}{1,015^3}$$

$$= €11,647,940$$

The maturity is reduced by 1 year because settlement is now expected in 2 years, and the interest rate must be adjusted according to the changed maturity.

The increase must be shown as interest expense because it stems from the changes in maturity and interest rate (if there were any changes in the settlement amount, these would be recognized as operating expenses or income); the corresponding journal entry is as follows:

```
Debit interest expense    273,293
       Credit provision                273,293
```

c) *References*
Beck'scher Bilanzkommentar, § 253, nos. 180–191
Coenenberg et al., 2021 (1), p. 462

5.7 Exercises on debt

Exercise 27: Presentation of tax liabilities

Category: Knowledge/Application
Time to solve: 5 minutes

a) *Exercise*
A company must recognize a tax liability of €100,000 at the closing date. How is this transaction presented in the three cases? What is the exact balance sheet item in each case and the recognized amount?

1. The company has paid €80,000 in advance and has filed its tax return, but the final tax assessment by the tax authorities remains open.
2. The company has paid €80,000 in advance and the tax assessment was received (100 T€); the amount is due in the middle of January.
3. The company has paid €140,000 in advance and has filed its tax return.

b) *Solution*
§ 266
1. This results in a tax provision of €20,000 because the final assessment of the tax authorities is open; there is some uncertainty that the assessed amount could be lower or higher than the tax return.

2. This results in a tax payable of €20,000, shown as "other payables, to tax authorities", because the exact amount and timing are known.
3. This results in a tax receivable of €40,000, shown as "other receivables" because a refund is expected from the tax authorities.

c) *References*
Beck'scher Bilanzkommentar, § 247 and § 266

Exercise 28: Accounting for a disagio

Category: Knowledge/Application
Time to solve: 10 minutes

a) *Exercise*
Your company needs a loan of €100,000 for an investment. Your bank offers a loan at a 7% annual interest rate. As an alternative, it offers a low-rate variant (5% interest) with a discount of 6%, i.e. outpayment is 94%. The term of the loan is 3 years and is to be repaid in full at the end of the term. You choose the discount alternative; the outpayment is in early January.

How can this loan be accounted for (under the Commercial Code and German tax law)? What is the interest expense in each year and in total?

b) *Solution*
§ 250 sect. 3

Commercial Code
§ 250 sect. 3 provides an accounting option for a disagio: It can be recognized as an expense in the first period or be recognized as a deferred expense and be distributed over the term of the loan.

Expense in first period
Values in €

Outpayment: Debit bank	94,000	
Interest expense	6,000	
Credit bank loan		100,000
End of year 1: Debit interest expense	5,000	
Credit bank		5,000
End of year 2: Debit interest expense	5,000	
Credit bank		5,000
End of year 3: Debit interest expense	5,000	
Bank loan	100,000	
Credit bank		105,000

Thus, in the first year €11,000 in interest expense are recognized, and in the two following years only €5,000, in total €21,000.

Recognition of deferred expense

Outpayment: Debit bank	94,000	
Deferred expense	6,000	
Credit bank loan		100,000
End of year 1: Debit interest expense	5,000	
Credit bank		5,000
Debit interest expense	2,000	
Credit deferred expense		2,000
End of year 2: Debit interest expense	5,000	
Credit bank		5,000
Debit interest expense	2,000	
Credit deferred expense		2,000
End of year 3: Debit interest expense	5,000	
Bank loan	100,000	
Credit bank		105,000
Debit interest expense	2,000	
Credit deferred expense		2,000

Thus, using the deferred expenses, the interest expenses are spread equally over all periods (€7,000 each), again in total €21,000.

Tax law:
Only the second alternative is acceptable.

c) *Hints*
The effects of any accounting options are neutral when you look at the total period: In total €21,000 of interest were paid over 3 years; just the distribution between the years varies. The use of accounting options does not produce additional profits or gains; it can only influence the accounting for these profits and gains and in particular when they must be shown.

Only if an accounting option is tax deductible and results in lower tax payments today and higher tax payments in the future can there be a positive interest effect (more liquidity today, i.e. more interest income or less interest expense) that is not neutral, but an additional profit.

d) *References*
Bacher, Chapter 3.3.3
Beck'scher Bilanzkommentar § 250
Coenenberg et al., 2021 (1), p. 505

5.8 Exercises on deferred items and deferred taxes

Exercise 29: Accounting for deferrals and accruals

Category: Knowledge
Time to solve: 5 minutes

a) *Exercise*
When is the recognition of a deferral or an accrual necessary? Give an example for each possible case.

b) *Solution*
§ 250 and § 252 sect. 1 no. 5

Deferrals and accruals must be recognized when payment (cash in-/outflow or proceeds/expenditure) and received or rendered service occur in different reporting periods; the services received or rendered must refer to a specific time period. This is a consequence of accrual accounting (in contrast to cash accounting), which requires income and expenses to be recognized when they occur (and not when they are paid).

Four cases can be distinguished:
Cash outflow/expenditure now, expense in next period: In this case, a deferred expense must be recognized (if an asset is acquired, the asset is recognized; here we are discussing services we will receive and that cannot be recognized as an asset). Typical examples are prepaid rent or prepaid insurance premiums.
Cash inflow/proceeds now, income the next period: In this case a deferred income must be recognized. A typical example is prepaid rent when the landlord receives payment in advance.

> Deferrals are also called *transitory items* because they are recognized in the balance sheet, even if they are not an asset or a liability, just to shift the expense and income to the correct period in the future.

Expense now, cash outflow/expenditure in next period: In this case, the expense must be recognized now (must be accrued now) and a corresponding other liability is recognized. A typical example is when rent is paid at the end of the rental period or when interest is paid at the end of the borrowing period.
Income now, cash inflow/proceeds in next period: In this case, the income must be recognized now (must be accrued now) and a corresponding other receivable is recognized. A typical example is when rent is received at the end of the rental period.

> Accruals are also called anticipative items because the income or expenses are recognized before payments are due (i.e. shifted to the current period).

c) *References*
Bacher, Chapter 3.3.4
Beck'scher Bilanzkommentar, § 250 and § 252, nos. 51–54
Coenenberg et al., 2021 (1), p. 505

Exercise 30: Accounting for deferrals and accruals

Category: Knowledge/Application
Time to solve: 10 minutes

a) *Exercise*
Identify the balance sheet positions, on 31 December 20X1, of the following transactions and journalize them:
1.   Advanced payments (paid) for rental expenses of the year 20X2 of €12,000.
2.   Received advance payment of €34,000 for delivery in 20X2.
3.   An amount of €25,000 must be paid for delivered raw material supplies.
4.   Taking out a loan from a bank at a nominal amount of €100,000, 90% of which is paid out.
5.   Received lease payments of €300 for the first quarter of 20X2.
6.   The rent for a storage building used last year was not paid until now (€15,000). On 30 November 20X1 the company no longer used this storage building.
7.   A bond was issued with a volume of €1 million. The interest of 4% must paid at the end of each quarter. The payment for the last quarter of 20X1 was made on 3 January 20X2.

b) *Solution*
§ 250 and § 252 sect. 1 no. 5
1.   Deferred expenses of €12,000

> Debit deferred expenses   12,000
>   Credit rental expenses or bank   12,000

Whether rental expenses or the bank is used as the credit entry depends on the status of the accounting: If the payment was already journalized as rental expenses, then the rental expenses must be corrected. If this is the first entry of the transaction, then the payment must be recognized, i.e. bank is the credit entry.
2.   Received advance payments of €34,000

> Debit bank   34,000
>   Credit received advance payments   34,000

An advance payment for a delivery does not refer to a specific time period, so it must be recognized as regular liability, because the customer will probably claim it back if the company is not able to deliver the products (§ 266).

3. Payable of €25,000 for delivered materials

Debit raw materials	25,000	
Credit trade payables		25,000

See answer 2. As these advance payments relate to inventories, they will be shown as a subitem of inventories (§ 266).

4. According to § 250 sect. 3, there exist options for a disagio.

Alternative 1: full recognition of the disagio as interest expense

Debit bank	90,000	
Interest expense	10,000	
Credit bank loan		100,000

Alternative 2: Recognition as deferred expense

Debit bank	90,000	
Deferred expense	10,000	
Credit bank loan		100,000

5 Deferred income of €300

Debit rental income/bank	300	
Credit deferred income		300

See answer 1.

6 Trade payable of €15,000

Debit rental expense	15,000	
Credit trade payable		15,000

This is not a deferral or accrual because everything has already happened. The building was used and the rent should have been paid. Because that did not happen, a liability must be recognized.

7 Other liability of €10,000

Debit interest expense	10,000	
Credit other liability		10,000

This is a typical accrual: The money borrowed through the bond is available and used by the company, so the benefits of the money are recognized in the reporting period. The matching principle requires recognizing expenses corresponding to the income, i.e. the interest of the money used must be recognized, even if payment occurs in the next period.

c) *References*
Bacher, Chapter 3.3.4
Beck'scher Bilanzkommentar, § 250 and § 252, nos. 51–54
Coenenberg et al., 2021 (1), p. 505

Exercise 31: Deferred taxes

Category: Knowledge/Application
Time to solve: 10 minutes

a) *Exercise*
In the balance sheet of Karlsruhe Beteiligungs GmbH, a provision for onerous contracts in the amount of €100,000 is recognized. The income tax rate at the time the difference will even out (trade tax, corporation tax, solidarity surcharge) is 30%.
1.   Is there a temporary difference?
2.   Does this result in deferred tax assets or liabilities?
3.   What is the amount of the deferred taxes?
4.   Do any options exist regarding the accounting for deferred assets in this case?
5.   How is the use or reversal of the provision accounted for if a deferred tax asset has been recognized?

b) *Solution*
1.   Yes. A provision for onerous contracts must be recognized according to the Commercial Code and is forbidden under German tax law. Thus, there is a difference. The difference will even out: Either the loss is realized, in which case it will be taxed as well, or the provision needs to be reversed because it is no longer necessary. Therefore, it is a temporary difference.
2.   Deferred tax assets. The loss was already recognized as an expense in the commercial balance sheet but will be tax deductible only when it occurs in the future. Therefore, the future tax payments will be too low compared to the result in the commercial income statement. A deferred tax asset can correct this future tax relief (lower future tax payments).
3.   A deferred tax asset or liability is calculated by multiplying the temporary difference by the applicable tax rate: €100,000 temporary difference × 30% tax rate = €30,000 deferred tax asset.
4.   For deferred tax assets there exists an accounting option, i.e. the asset can be recognized or not; a partial recognition is not possible.
5.   When the provision is used or reversed, there is no longer any temporary difference: In the case of use, the loss was realized and is tax deductible. In the case of reversal, there was no loss, but because of the reversal there is no longer any provision.
       Because the temporary difference no longer exists, the resulting deferred tax asset must be reversed as well.

c) *References*
Bacher, Chapter 3.3.5
Beck'scher Bilanzkommentar, § 274
Coenenberg et al., 2021 (1), p. 508

5.9 Exercises on income statement and cash flow statement

Exercise 32: Income statement

Category: Knowledge
Time to solve: 5 minutes

a) *Exercise*
Explain the differences between the total-cost format and cost-of-sales format.

b) *Solution*
§ 275

According to § 275, two alternative formats for the preparation of the income statement are possible for corporations. Partnerships and sole proprietorships have no
specific formats but can use any structure that satisfies GAAP (the concepts of § 275
can be viewed as best practices, which are often used by partnerships or sole proprietorships as well, but often with less detail).

Total-cost format
In the total-cost format, the change in inventory, i.e. the increase or decrease in finished and unfinished products, is reported as a separate income item. The expenses
are structured according to the type of expense, e.g. material expenses, personnel
expenses, depreciation and amortization.

Cost-of-sales format
In the cost-of-sales format, the change in inventory is netted with the cost of goods
sold, i.e. this income or expense is not shown separately. In addition, the expenses
are structured according to the functional area in which they occur, e.g. cost of goods
sold, distribution costs, research and development costs, administrative costs.

c) *Hints*
The net result is necessarily the same in both formats. The differences concern only
the way the information is presented, not the substance of the transactions.
    For example, personnel expenses in the total-cost format include all personnel
expenses of the company: e.g. for production, for distribution, for administration,
whereas, for example, the distribution costs according to the cost-of-sales format

include all material and personnel expenses as well as depreciation that were incurred for the distribution department (marketing, sales and sales logistics).

d) *References*
Bacher, Chapter 3.4
Beck'scher Bilanzkommentar, § 275
Coenenberg et al., 2021 (1), p. 547

Exercise 33: Income statement

Category: Knowledge/Application
Time to solve: 10 minutes

a) *Exercise*
For a company the following information is available:

Tab. 5.55: Exercise 33.

Business year 20X1, T€			
Sales revenue	+20,000		
	Production	**Sales**	**Administration**
Material expenses	− 2,000		
Salaries and wages	− 4,000	− 2,000	− 1,000
Depreciation	− 3,000	− 1,000	− 1,000
Increase in inventory	+500		

What does the income statement look like according to the total-cost format and
according to the cost-of-sales format?

b) *Solution*
§ 275

Total-cost format (values in T€):
–   The change in inventory is shown as a separate income item.
–   The structure of expenses accords with the kind of expense (i.e. in lines).

Sales revenue	20,000
Change of inventory	500
Material expenses	− 2,000
Salaries and wages	− 7,000
Depreciation	− 5,000
Operating profit	**6,500**

Cost-of-sales format (values in T€):

- The change in inventory is netted with cost of good sold.
- The structure of expenses accords with the functional area (i.e. in columns).

Sales revenue	20,000
Costs of goods sold	− 8,500
Gross profit	11,500
Distribution costs	− 3,000
Administration costs	− 2,000
Operating Profit	**6,500**

c) *References*

Bacher, Chapter 3.4

Beck'scher Bilanzkommentar, § 275

Coenenberg et al., 2021 (1), p. 547

Exercise 34: Cash flow statement

Category: Knowledge/Application

Time to solve: 10 minutes

a) *Exercise*

1. What is an expense? Give an example of an expense that is also a cash outflow and an example of an expense that is not a cash outflow.

2. How is the operating cash flow calculated (using the indirect method)? Explain the basic logic, not the full detail schedule.

3. What is the cash flow from financing if
   - cash at the beginning of the period is 2,500
   - operating cash flow is 3,300
   - investment cash flow is − 1.250 and
   - cash at the end of the period is 3.075?

b) *Solution*

DRS 21

1. An expense is a decrease in net assets, i.e. a decrease in equity caused by the operations of the company and not an external cash outflow. An expense is not necessarily at the same time a cash outflow.

   Expense and cash outflow are identical, for example, for received services that are paid for in cash or for wages or salaries paid for in the same reporting period.

   Expense and cash outflow are not identical, for example, for depreciation (cash outflow occurred when the asset was acquired or produced) or when a service is purchased on credit.

2. The indirect method means that the cash flow statement is calculated from the balance sheet and income statement and not directly from the cash flows of the company.

   The indirect method calculates the operating cash flow as follows (general method):

   Net profit
   + Depreciation, amortization, impairment (minus any reversals)
   + Increase in provisions (minus any decreases)
   − Increase in net working capital (plus any decreases)
   = Cash flow from operating activities

3. The general formula for the cash flow statement is as follows:

   Cash at beginning of period
   + Cash flow from operating activities
   + Cash flow from investing activities
   + Cash flow from financing activities
   = Cash at end of period

   Rearranging we get

Cash at end of period	+3,075
− Cash at beginning	−2,500
− Cash flow from operating activities	−3,300
− Cash flow from investing activities	+1,250
= Cash flow from financing activities	= −1,475

c) *References*
DRS 21
Coenenberg et al., 2021 (1), p. 832

Exercise 35: Cash flow statement

Category: Knowledge/Application
Time to solve: 15 minutes

a) *Exercise*
Example AG shows the following balance sheet and income statement for the business year 20X1 (values in €):

Tab. 5.56: Exercise 35 balance sheet.

Debit	31 Dec. 20X1	31 Dec. 20X0	Credit	31 Dec.20X1	31 Dec. 20X0
Non-current assets	400,000	320,000	Equity	260,000	200,000
Inventories	80,000	70,000	Provisions	70,000	50,000
Trade receivables	100,000	120,000	Bank loans	250,000	200,000
Cash	90,000	80,000	Trade payables	90,000	140,000
Total Assets	**670,000**	**590,000**	**Total equity + Liabilities**	**670,000**	**590,000**

In the change in non-current assets are included – apart from the depreciation – expenditures for investments of €130,000 and proceeds from the disposal of assets of €40,000.

The change in bank loans results from proceeds of €70,000 due to new loans and repayments of €20,000. In addition, a dividend of €70,000 was paid for the previous year.

The balance sheet items "inventories", "trade receivables", "bank loans" and "trade payables" do not include any changes that are non-cash oriented.

Tab. 5.57: Exercise 35 income statement.

Values in €	1 Jan. 20X1–31 Dec. 20X1
Sales revenue	940,000
Material expenses	– 300,000
Personnel expenses	– 340,000
Depreciation/amortization	– 50,000
Net result of other expenses/income	– 50,000
Financial result	– 70,000
Tax expenses	– 40,000
Net result	90,000

In the income statement all income and expenses apart from depreciation and changes in provisions are cash oriented.

Prepare the cash flow statement for year X1.

b) *Solution*

Using the indirect method for the calculation of the cash flow from operating activities, in a first step the net result must be adjusted for any non-cash items in the income statement. In a second step, additional cash flows must be calculated by comparing balance sheet items.

Tab. 5.58: Exercise 35 solution.

Item	Value in €	Explanation
Net result	90,000	
+ Depreciation	50,000	
+ Increase in provisions	20,000	Calculate increase from current and prior balance sheet
− Increase in inventories	− 10,000	Calculate increase from current and prior balance sheet
+ Decrease in trade receivables	+ 20,000	Calculate decrease from current and prior balance sheet
− Decrease in trade payables	− 50,000	Calculate decrease from current and prior balance sheet
= Cash flow from operating activities	**120,000**	
− Expenditures for non-current assets	−130,000	See text; basis: cash flows
+ Proceeds from disposal of non-current assets	+ 40,000	See text; basis: cash flows
= Cash flow from investing activities	**−90,000**	
+ Proceeds from new loans	70,000	See text; basis: cash flows
− Repayment of loans	− 20,000	See text; basis: cash flows
− Payment of dividend	− 70,000	See text; basis: cash flows
= Cash flow from financing activities	**−20,000**	
Total change of cash	**+10,000**	**Sum of partial cash**
Cash at beginning	80,000	See balance sheet, prior year
Cash at end	90,000	**See balance sheet, current year**

c) *References*

DRS 21

Coenenberg et al., 2021 (1), p. 832

6 Case studies

Case 1: Depreciation and advance payments

Carpenter Karl Dach needs a new van. The van will be delivered on 18 January 20X1, payable within 1 week at a 1% discount or within 4 weeks net. Karl Dach does not use the discount; the van costs €28,800 net. For transfer and registration, the dealer charges €400 net. The useful life is estimated at 5 years. The reselling value after 5 years for the used vehicle is estimated roughly at €3,000.

1. Calculate the depreciation and prepare the depreciation schedule according to the straight-line (linear) method. Assume that Karl uses all usual options!
2. At the beginning of 20X2, Karl Dach upgrades the car with a navigation system for €2,000. What effect does this have on the depreciation schedule?
3. Continuation of 2: Assume that, due to new emission regulations, the market value of a comparable (used) vehicle decreases to €6,000 on 31 December 20X2. Which value must be recognized in the balance sheet on 31 December 20X2 and what are the values on the following closing dates? Why?
4. Continuation of 3: At the beginning of December 20X3, Karl Dach receives an offer from a car dealer from Eastern Europe to buy the car for €16,000. To reinforce his offer, the dealer pays €8,000 in advance in mid-December. Karl agrees and the deal is finalized in January. How is the advance payment recognized in the balance sheet? At what value is the car recognized in the balance sheet on 31 December 20X3?

Case 2: Accounting policy of Victoria AG

Victoria AG is a mid-sized company that is specialized in the production of industrial components. The company faced high revenue decreases in 20X1 but does not want to report a loss because of an upcoming rating. Therefore, any accounting options or margins of estimation/judgment should be used in the form of a **progressive/aggressive accounting policy** to report **the highest net result possible**. Explain your accounting of the following transactions of Victoria AG, and name the relevant legal regulations according to the Commercial Code and if necessary the balance sheet item.

1. Based on the bad revenue situation, the finished products in stock increased significantly compared to the previous year. The following data for the products in stock are known:
   - Material for production: €20,000.
   - Storage costs for material: €2,000.
   - Hourly wages of production workers: €40,000.

https://doi.org/10.1515/9783110744170-006

- Overtime premiums of production workers: €5,000.
- Depreciation on production machines: €8,000.
- Proportionate share of voluntary pension benefits for administration employees: €14,000.
- Storage costs of finished products: €6,000.
- Proportionate share of costs of company day care center: €10,000.
- Costs of research department: €12,000.
- Idle time costs due to continuous low orders: €16,000.

2. Victoria AG has acquired the operating business of Bastian GmbH for €250,000; legal and economic integration are completed. The book value of net assets at acquisition time was €100,000. The inventories are recognized at €20,000, which is €10,000 below market value. The warehouse is fully depreciated, whereas the market value amounts to €80,000. Does this result in goodwill?

3. Victoria AG has owned a 30% share of Jonas AG for 3 years. The shares are recognized at their acquisition costs of €200,000. The net profit of Jonas AG was constant at €30,000 during that time, so an increase in the near future cannot be expected. The relevant discount rate is 6%.

4. In 20X1 a new patent for an innovative production process is developed and registered. The direct costs attributable to the patent are €40,000, and the proportionate indirect costs of the research and development department amount to €60,000.

5. The crude oil stock developed as follows in 20X1:

Tab. 6.1: Case 2 5. Development of crude oil stock.

	Crude oil in barrels	€/barrel
Opening balance	100,000	48
Purchase 5 May 20X1	100,000	56
Purchase 7 July 20X1	300,000	68
Purchase 9 Sept. 20X1	200,000	62
Total use	400,000	

Calculate the value of the use of oil and of the closing balance according to LIFO and periodic average. Which method should be used based on the intention behind the accounting policy?

What values are acceptable in the balance sheet if the replacement costs on the closing date are

(a) €66.30/barrel or

(b) €60/barrel.

6. Victoria AG has machinery that was not maintained properly because of a bad liquidity situation. On the closing date, it is not foreseeable when the maintenance will be done. Cost estimates range from €60,000 to €100,000.
7. On 1 January 20X1, a long-term loan with a volume of €500,000 was taken out. Outpayment 95%, term 10 years, nominal interest 5%, full repayment at the end.

Case 3: Accounting policy of bits and pieces GmbH

Bits and Pieces GmbH is a company that produces and sells gift items. The head of accounting, Mr. C. Orrect, is preparing the financial statements as of 31 December 20X1 in March 20X2.

Explain the recognition and measurement under the Commercial Code for the following transactions of Bits and Pieces GmbH. Name the relevant legal regulations and whether there are any options or margins of estimation/judgment. Options and margins of estimation should be used in such a way that the **net profit is the lowest possible**.

1. Mr. C. Orrect discovered in December 20X1 that the roof of the production building was leaking; he reported the leak immediately to the executive board. The cheaper estimate of repair costs was €11,900 (including VAT), the more expensive €23,800 (including VAT). The executive board decides that maintenance will be done the following year; the exact schedule is open.
2. Based on the good financial and profitability situation, C. Orrect acquired during 20X1 500 shares of a listed blue chip company for a total of €20,000; this is considered a long-term investment. On the closing date the quoted share price is €30, but financial analysts are very positive about the future development of the company and its share price.
3. The procurement department received merchandise valued at US$10,000 from an American supplier on 1 December 20X1. C. Orrect recognizes the goods on the same day at an exchange rate of US$1 = €0.6. The executive board wants to use the supplier's entire credit of 6 weeks. On the closing date the exchange rate is US$1 = €0.8.
4. At the beginning of 20X1, a new production machine was acquired for €48,000 and recognized in the balance sheet item "machines". So far it has not been depreciated because there are no experience values for this kind of machine. The head of production estimates a useful life of 10 to 15 years, assuming constant and continuous usage.
5. According to the information of the machine's manufacturer, a general overhaul will be necessary in 4 years. The costs for this measure in year 20X4 will probably be €20,000.
6. Bits and Pieces GmbH signed a sales contract with Light and Sound GmbH on 12 October 20X1 to produce and deliver a light organ (delivery date 30 March 20X2,

price €60,000). The start of production is scheduled for January 20X2. The head of accounting, C. Orrect, was on vacation when the offer was calculated and signed, and he realizes now that his apprentice forgot to include the wages for the production workers in the calculation. The direct costs for material and production already amount to €70,000; in addition, indirect costs can be attributed to the light organ: €3,000 for material and €2,000 for production.

7. For a new warehouse, a monthly rent of €5,000 is charged from 1 December 20X1 onwards. So far, no rent has been paid because of minor defects that the landlord must fix. Nevertheless, the building is used. The rental contract states that the rent must be paid 3 months in advance.

Case 4: Accounting for inventories

Charlene Coal is managing director of Drilling Equipment Trading GmbH and supplies production companies with twist drills and diamond abrasive blocks. In autumn, she buys from an insolvent company first-class twist drills for €100,000 and diamond abrasive blocks for €200,000.

1. In March of the following year she prepares his financial statements.
    – The price on the twist drills has increased, so she has good arguments that the acquired drills could have been sold by 31 December for at least €120,000.
    – Crises in Russia and Africa have led to huge price pressures for diamond abrasive blocks. The value of the blocks drops to €98,000 on 31 December, in February of the following year their market value is only €88,000. Charlene Coal keeps the blocks because she thinks the prices will recover sometime in the future.

At which values must the products be recognized under the Commercial Code on 31 December? Why? Would it be different under German tax law? Is there any effect on the income statement?

2. Continuation of question 1: In the following summer, the price for the diamond abrasive blocks rises again to €150,000 and stays there until the end of the year. Nevertheless, Charlene Coal does not want to sell below her acquisition costs. How are the abrasive blocks recognized in the following financial statements and why? Is there an effect in the income statement (only Commercial Code)?

Case 5: Accounting for intangible assets

The champagne winery Wochenheim AG has developed a new technology for producing champagne that is free of alcohol; the new technology should be used from the beginning of 20X1 until the end of 20X5. The technology was registered as a patent at the end of 20X0. In the context of the innovation, the following costs (in Euros) were incurred:

- Personnel expenses, research part of project: 500,000
- Operating expenses, research part of project (e.g. material): 200,000
- Personnel expenses, development part of project: 750,000
- Operating expenses, development part of project (e.g. material): 300,000

The R&D department worked only on this technology.

The company is a large corporation; its effective tax rate is 30%.

(a) What accounting options exist for this new technology in the **commercial balance sheet** as of 31 December 20X0? Explain the different options briefly and journalize possible entries.

(b) What accounting options exist for this new technology in the **tax balance sheet** as of 31 December 20X0? Explain the different options briefly and journalize possible entries.

(c) What must be considered in this context for the commercial balance sheet as of 31 December 20X0 in addition? Explain briefly possible consequences and journalize possible entries.

Case 6: Accounting policy

Explain and argue for the following topics if there exist any legal or factual accounting options or margins of judgment. Show as well how the use of any options or margins of judgment can influence the net result or the equity ratio:

(a) Acquisition costs
(b) Provisions
(c) Impairment of non-current financial assets
(d) Measurement simplifications for current assets

Case 7: Accounting for inventories (2)

The Electronic Parts GmbH is a midsized corporation and is currently preparing its balance sheet. One standard product of the company is the electric engine Pro-2; it is continuously in large but changing amounts in stock and stored in an open-shelf system. Additions to stock and the purchase price development are shown in the table later in the chapter. Withdrawals from stock occur when needed and cannot be allocated to specific additions.

Tab. 6.2: Case 7 – Development of product amounts and purchase prices.

Date	Movement	Amount in pieces	Purchase price € per piece
01.01.	Opening balance	38	271.00
12.02.	Addition	40	269.00
13.06.	Addition	120	317.00
27.09.	Addition	20	324.00
29.11.	Addition	40	319.00
31.12.	Closing balance	66	

(a) Calculate the value of the closing balance for the electric engine! List the possible variants according to the German Commercial Code. The market price on December 31 is 325 €.
(b) Which measurement approach would you choose, if the company wants to report a profit that is as high as possible?
(c) Is the statement correct that FIFO creates hidden reserves when you assume continuously increasing prices?

Case 8: Consolidated financial statements (1)

The Wine & Champagne Group consists of a parent company, Riesling AG, located in Deidesheim in Rhineland-Palatinate, and Distribution GmbH located in Pforzheim.

The parent company (PC) recognized, apart from the shares in affiliated companies of €300,000, other assets of €700,000. The PC has a capital structure of 50% equity and 50% liabilities.

The subsidiary (SUB) recognizes equity of €80,000 and liabilities of €320,000. Its assets include a piece of land with a book value of €100,000 (fair value at acquisition by the PC of €200,000).

(a) What consolidation methods do you know?
(b) Prepare the balance sheets of the PC and the SUB.
(c) Prepare the consolidated balance sheet and journalize the necessary entries.

Case 9: Consolidated financial statements (2)

Snow AG has acquired the shares of Ski GmbH on 31 December 20X1 for €2 million, which will enable the company not only to offer ski clothing but also ski equipment. The purchase price was paid on 31 December 20X1.

Preliminary balance sheet of Snow AG of 31 December 20X1 **prior** to acquisition of Ski GmbH:

Tab. 6.3: Case 9 – balance sheet of Snow AG prior to acquisition.

Debit (€)		Balance sheet Snow AG	Credit (€)
Non-current assets	950,000	Equity	1,520,000
Current assets	5,100,000	Liabilities	4,530,000
Total assets	6,050,000	Total equity and liabilities	6,050,000

Balance sheet of Ski GmbH from 31 December 20X1:

Tab. 6.4: Case 9 – balance sheet Ski GmbH.

Debit (€)		Balance sheet Ski GmbH	Credit (€)
Non-current assets	250,000	Equity	400,000
Current assets	2,100,000	Liabilities	1,950,000
Total assets	2,350,000	Total equity and liabilities	2,350,000

Additional information about the financial statements of Ski GmbH:
- The non-current assets include a fully depreciated machine that the company will continue to use; its reproduction value amounts to €200,000 on the acquisition date.
- Equity includes the full net profit of €80,000 for the business year 20X1.
- Provisions: pension provisions of €100,000 have not been recognized yet.
- Ski GmbH sells its products largely under the brand name "Solo", which the company had created itself. Industry experts estimate the brand's value at €500,000.

Questions

(a) Prepare consolidated financial statements and carry out the capital consolidation (equity) consolidation. What are the corresponding journal entries?

(b) In which case is a purchase price allocation in the individual financial statements necessary?

7 Solutions for case studies

Solution to case 1: Depreciation and advance payments

Category: Knowledge/Application/Analysis
Time to solve: 15 minutes

Keywords: Acquisition costs, depreciation and impairment, reversal of impairment, advance payments

The carpenter Karl Dach needs a new van. The van will be delivered on 18 January 20X1, payable within 1 week with a 1% discount or within 4 weeks net. Karl does not use the discount, so the van costs €28,800 net. For transfer and registration, the dealer charges €400 net. The useful life is estimated to be 5 years. The resale value after 5 years for the used vehicle is estimated at roughly €3,000.

1. Calculate the depreciation and prepare the depreciation schedule according to the straight line (linear) method. Assume that Karl uses all usual options!
Acquisition costs (€):

Purchase price	28,800
+ Transfer and registration	400
= Acquisition costs	29,200

The residual value cannot be used for the financial accounting because it can be estimated only roughly (due to the principle of prudence, a reliable and precise estimation is necessary). Thus, the basis for the depreciation is the acquisition costs. With a useful life of 5 years the linear depreciation amounts to €5,840/year. Because the acquisition takes place in January it is common practice to start with the depreciation at the beginning of January, i.e. include January completely.

Tab. 7.1: Solution to case 1 1.

Year	Remaining book value at beginning (€)	Depreciation (€)	Remaining book value at end (€)
20X1	29,200	5,840	23,360
20X2	23,360	5,840	17,520
20X3	17,520	5,840	11,680
20X4	11,680	5,840	5,840
20X5	5,840	5,840	0

https://doi.org/10.1515/9783110744170-007

2. At the beginning of 20X2, Karl Dach upgrades the car with a navigation system for €2,000. What effect does this have on the depreciation schedule?

The navigation system improves the usability of the car, so the costs are subsequent acquisition costs that increase the remaining book value in January 20X2 and afterwards the annual depreciation.

Tab. 7.2: Solution to case 1 2.

Year	Remaining book value at beginning (€)	Depreciation (€)	Remaining book value at end (€)
20X1	29,200	5,840	23,360
20X2	**25,360**	**6,340**	19,020
20X3	19,020	6,340	12,680
20X4	12,680	6,340	6,340
20X5	6,340	6,340	0

3. Continuation of 2: Assume that, due to new emission regulations, the market value of a comparable (used) vehicle decreases to €6,000 on 31 December 20X2. What value must be recognized in the balance sheet on 31 December 20X2 and what are the values on the following closing dates? Why?

Because the value of the van decreases due to a new legal regulation, a permanent decrease in value is probable. Therefore, the car must be impaired to the lower market value (§ 253 sect. 3): the moderate lower-of-cost-or-market principle.

The new regulation or case gives no indication that the useful life is or should be reduced. Therefore, the depreciation continues for the remaining useful life based on the new remaining book value after impairment.

Tab. 7.3: Solution to case 1 3.

Year	Remaining book value at beginning (€)	Depreciation (€)	Remaining book value at end (€)
20X1	29,200	5,840	23,360
20X2	25,360	Depreciation 6,340	6,000
		Impairment 13,020	
20X3	6,000	2,000	4,000
20X4	4,000	2,000	2,000
20X5	2,000	2,000	0

4. Continuation of 3: At the beginning of December 20X3, Karl Dach receives an offer from a car dealer in Eastern Europe to buy the car for €16,000. To reinforce his offer, the dealer pays €8,000 in advance in mid-December. Karl agrees and the deal is finalized in January.

How is the advance payment recognized in the balance sheet? At what value is the car recognized in the balance sheet on 31 December 20X3?

The advance payment is recognized separately from the non-current assets: If Karl is unable to deliver the van according to the contract, the car dealer will request that the advance payment be returned (and is entitled to do so):

Debit bank	8,000	
Credit received advance payments		8,000

Because of the explicit and then binding offer the reason for the impairment no longer exists. Thus, the impairment must be reversed (§ 253 sect. 5). The ceiling for the reversal stems from the historic costs, i.e. the acquisition costs reduced by the original depreciation (as if no impairment had occurred).

The historic costs at the end of 20X3 are 12.680 € (see 2). This results in a reversal of impairment of €8,680 at the end of 20X3.

Tab. 7.4: Solution to case 1 4.

Year	Remaining book value at beginning (€)	Depreciation (€)		Remaining book value at end (€)
20X1	29,200		5,840	23,360
20X2	25,360	Depreciation	6,340	6,000
		Impairment	13,020	
20X3	6,000	Depreciation	2,000	12,680
		Reversal of impairment	−8,680	

The planned sale has no further effect on the accounting (apart from the reversal of impairment). The realization principle must be applied (§ 252 sect. 1 no. 4), i.e. any proceeds and gain from the sale are to be recognized if and when they are realized (if and when the sales price becomes a receivable; in the actual situation, this is typically the case after handing over the car and car documents).

Solution to case 2: Accounting policy of Victoria AG

Category: Knowledge/Application/Analysis
Time to solve: 30 minutes

Keywords: production costs, goodwill, measurement of participations/financial assets, self-generated intangible non-current assets, measurement of inventories, disagio, provisions.

Victoria AG is a mid-sized company that is specialized in production of industrial components. The company had to face high revenue decreases in 20X1 but does not want to report a loss because of an upcoming rating. Therefore, any accounting options or margins of estimation/judgment should be used in the way of a **progressive/aggressive accounting policy** *to report* **the highest net result possible.** *Explain your accounting of the following transactions of Victoria AG, and name the relevant legal regulations according to the Commercial Code and, if necessary, the balance sheet item.*

1. Based on the bad revenue situation, the finished products in stock increased significantly compared to the previous year. The following data for the products in stock are known:
- *Material for production €20,000 €*
- *Storage costs for material €2,000*
- *Hourly wages of production workers €40,000*
- *Overtime premiums production workers €5,000*
- *Depreciation on production machines €8,000*
- *Proportionate share of voluntary pension benefits for administration employees €14,000*
- *Storage costs of finished products €6,000*
- *Proportionate share of costs of company day care center €10,000*
- *Costs of research department €12,000*
- *Idle time costs because of continuous low orders €16,000*

Production costs as basis for measurement of the company's own products are defined in § 255 sect. 2 and 3:
- The minimum values are the direct and indirect costs for materials and for production as well as the proportionate depreciation of the production machines.
- For the maximum values, voluntary social benefits and proportionate administrative costs are added.
- Costs of distribution and sales or research are not allowed to be included.
- Idle time costs may not be included because the usual production conditions, in particular a standard use of the production capacity, must be assumed.

	Material of production	€20,000
	Storage costs of material	€2,000
	Hourly wages of production workers	€40,000
	Their overtime premiums	€5,000
	Depreciation of production machines	€8,000
=	**Minimum production costs**	**€75,000**

	Voluntary pension benefits	€14,000
	Costs for day care center	€6,000
=	**Maximum production costs**	**€95,000**

To report as high a profit as possible, the finished products should be measured using the maximum value of production costs.

2. Victoria AG has acquired the operating business of Bastian GmbH for €250,000; legal and economic integration is complete. The book value of the net assets at acquisition time was €100,000. The inventories are recognized at €20,000, which is €10,000 below market value. The warehouse is fully depreciated, whereas the market value amounts to €80,000. Does this result in goodwill?

If a business is acquired, goodwill results from a purchase price that is higher than the acquired net assets. Relevant for the calculation are the net assets at time value, not at book value:

	Purchase price	250,000
–	Book value of net assets	– 100,000
–	Hidden reserves inventory	– 10,000
–	Hidden reserves warehouse	– 80,000
=	**Goodwill**	**60,000**

Goodwill must be recognized (§ 246 sect. 1) and amortized over its useful life. To report as high a net profit as possible, the useful life should be estimated to be as long as possible.

3. Victoria AG has owned a 30% share of Jonas AG for 3 years. The shares are recognized at their acquisition costs of €200,000. The net profit of Jonas AG was a constant €30,000 during that time, an increase in the near future cannot be expected. The relevant discount rate is 6%.

This is a question of subsequent measurement of shares. If a permanent decrease in value exists, an impairment to the lower value must be recognized (§ 253 sect. 3).

The imputed value of the shares can be calculated by the present value of a perpetual annuity because the expected profits remain constant at €30,000.

$$PV = \frac{A}{i} = \frac{€\,30,000}{6\%} = €\,500,000$$

where

PV = present value of perpetual annuity

A = annuity

i = discount rate

The value of the complete business of Jonas AG is €500,000, the proportionate value of 30% of the shares is therefore €150,000. An impairment of €50,000 must be recognized because the decrease in value is probably permanent (otherwise it must be explained why this decrease is assumed to be only temporary).)

4. In 20X1 a new patent for an innovative production process was developed and registered. The direct costs attributable to the patent are €40,000, the proportionate indirect costs of the research and development department amount to €60,000.

An accounting option exists for non-current intangible assets that are internally generated (§ 248 sect. 2); to use this option, a clear distinction between research and development costs is necessary because only the development costs can be recognized (§ 255 sect 2), whereas research costs are prohibited from being recognized. This can be assumed here, because the direct costs of the patent and corresponding indirect costs are given.

On that basis, an option exists to recognize the patent at €100,000. To report as high a profit as possible, that option should be used.

In the tax balance sheet, a recognition is prohibited for this kind of asset. Therefore, a recognition in the commercial balance sheet results in a deferred tax liability that partially offsets the increase in the profit and a profit distribution restriction (§268 sect. 8).

5. The crude oil in stock developed as follows in 20X1:

Tab. 7.5: Solution to case 2 5. Development of crude oil stock.

	Crude oil in barrels	€/barrel
Opening balance	100,000	48
Purchase 5 May 20X1	100,000	56
Purchase 7 July 20X1	300,000	68
Purchase 9 Sept. 20X1	200,000	62
Total use	400,000	

Calculate the value of the use of oil and of the closing balance according to LIFO and periodic average. Which method should be used based on the intention of the accounting policy?

First, the total value of the opening balance and purchases must be calculated:

Tab. 7.6: Solution to case 2 5. Development of crude oil stock – total values.

	Crude oil in barrels	€/barrel	Value in €
Opening balance	100,000	48	4,800,000
Purchase 5 May 20X1	100,000	56	5,600,000
Purchase 7 July 20X1	300,000	68	20,400,000
Purchase 9 Sept. 20X1	200,000	62	12,400,000
Total use	400,000		

The closing balance is calculated as follows:

$$\text{Closing balance} = \text{Opening balance} + \text{Purchases} - \text{Use}$$
$$= 100,000 \text{ barrels} + 600,000 \text{ barrels} - 400,000 \text{ barrels}$$
$$= 300,000 \text{ barrels}$$

LIFO = Last in, first out

LIFO is a measurement method that assumes a specific sequence of use: LIFO assumes that the amounts purchased last are used first; that means the unused amounts (in stock) are the oldest ones:

A total of 400,000 barrels were used, according to LIFO:

from the last purchase:	200,000 barrels ×€62/barrel = €12,400,000
from the second last purchase:	200,000 barrels ×€68/barrel = €13,600,000
Total value of use:	€26,000,000
Average price per barrel:	€65/barrel

Measurement of closing balance of 300,000 according to LIFO:

from opening balance:	100,000 barrels ×€48/barrel = €4,800,000
from the first purchase:	100,000 barrels ×€56/barrel = €5,600,000
from the second purchase:	100,000 barrels ×€68/barrel = €6,800,000
Total value of closing balance	€17,200,000
Average price per barrel	€57.33/barrel

Periodic average: In this method, an average of the opening balance and all purchases is calculated. This average is used to measure all uses and the closing balance:

$$\text{Periodic average} = \frac{\text{Value opening balance} + \text{Purchases}}{\text{Amount opening balance} + \text{Purchases}}$$
$$= \frac{€43,200,000}{700,000 \text{ barrels}} = €61.71/\text{barrel}$$

This results in a value of the closing balance of 300,000 barrels × €61.71/barrel = €18,513,000.

This results in a use value of 400,000 barrels × €61,71/barrel ≈ €24,687,000.[1]

With regard to the intention to report as high a profit as possible, the closing balance should be measured using the periodic average.

What values are acceptable in the balance sheet if the replacement costs on the closing date are

(a) *€66.30/barrel or*
(b) *€60/barrel?*

For current assets, the strict lower-of-cost-or-market principle must be applied, i.e. even only temporary decreases in value must be impaired (§ 255 sect. 4). In case (a), the market price is €66.30/barrel, so no changes need to be made because both valuations are below market price. In case (b), with a market value of €60/barrel, the closing balance must be impaired to €60/barrel if the periodic average is used; this results in an impairment of €513,000 (= €1.71/barrel ×300,000 barrels) to a market value of €18,000,000.

6. *Victoria AG has machinery that was not maintained properly because of a bad liquidity situation. As of the closing date, it is not foreseeable when the maintenance will be done. The cost estimates range from €60,000 to €100,000.*

Provisions for omitted maintenance must be recognized if the maintenance is executed within 3 months (§ 249 sect. 1 sent. 2).

The maintenance could be scheduled in such a way that no provision needs to be recognized because so far there are no detailed ideas when to do it, e.g. by scheduling it in May 20X2 (this is not a formal but a factual accounting option).

7. *On 1 January 20X1, a long-term loan with a volume of €500,000 was taken out, with the following details: outpayment 95%, term 10 years, nominal interest 5%, full repayment at end.*

The amount paid out is 95% below the amount that must be repaid, i.e. this is a disagio.

For a disagio there exists an accounting option (§ 250 sect. 3):

– recognition as interest expense in first period or
– recognition as deferred expense and distribution over loan term.

---

1 The result was rounded because the total amounts acquired are allocated completely to either closing balance or use; any differences due to rounding of the average price must be added; common practice is to use the precise value for the balance sheet and to adjust the use.

With regard to the intention to report as high a profit as possible, the disagio should be recognized as a deferred expense and distributed over time.

Solution case 3: Accounting policy of bits and pieces GmbH

Category: Knowledge/Application/Analysis
Time to solve: 20 minutes

Keywords: provisions, measurement of financial assets, acquisition costs and exchange rate losses, depreciation, deferred items

Bits and Pieces GmbH is a company that produces and sells gift items. The head of accounting, Mr. C. Orrect, is preparing the financial statements as of 31 December 20X1 in March 20X2.

*Explain the recognition and measurement under the Commercial Code for the following transactions of Bits and Pieces GmbH. Name the relevant legal regulations and whether there are any options or margins for estimation/judgment. Options and margins of estimation should be used in such a way that **net profit is minimized**.*

1. Mr. C. Orrect discovered in December 20X1 that the roof of the production building is leaking; he reported the leak immediately to the executive board. The cheaper estimate of costs is €11,900 (including VAT), the more expensive €23,800 (including VAT). The executive board decides that the maintenance will be done in the following year; the exact schedule is open.

A provision for omitted maintenance must be recognized if it is done within 3 months (§ 249 sect. 1). Nevertheless, there exists a factual accounting option because the timing of the maintenance can be chosen according to the accounting effect.

With the intention of reporting a profit as low as possible, the provision should be recognized and the maintenance should be scheduled for the first quarter. Because there are two plausible estimates, the higher one should be chosen (this also depends on the decision of management), but note that only net values can be recognized as a provision, i.e. €20,000 provision for omitted maintenance.

2. Based on the good financial and profitability situation of the company, during 20X1 C. Orrect acquired 500 shares of a listed blue chip company for a total of €20,000; this is considered a long-term investment. On the closing date the quoted share price is €30, but financial analysts are very optimistic about the future development of the company and its share price.

Based on the foregoing data, the acquisition costs per share are €40/share (€20,000/ 500 shares). The market price on the closing date is, at €30/share, significantly below that; but financial analysts remain optimistic about the future, so at that point in time this decrease in value is likely to be temporary.

For non-current financial assets there exists an accounting option: temporary decreases can be impaired but do not have to be (§ 253 sect. 3 sent. 4).

With regard to the intention to report as low a profit as possible, the shares should be impaired by €5,000 to the lower market value.

3. The procurement department received merchandise with a value of US$10,000 from an American supplier on 1 December 20X1. C. Orrect recognizes the goods on the same day at an exchange rate of US$1 = €0.6 €. The executive board wants to fully use the supplier credit of 6 weeks. On the closing date the exchange rate is US$1 = €0.8.

The measurement of the merchandise remains unchanged (acquisition costs = original value of payable, i.e. US$10,000 × €0.6/US$ = €6,000). Subsequent changes in the exchange rate are not part of the acquisition costs.

The trade payable must be increased to the higher market value based on the imparity principle (here: higher-of-cost-or-market principle): Recognition of an exchange rate loss of €2,000 to increase the payable (value of payable at closing date: US$10,000 × €0.8/US$ = €8,000).

There are no options in this case.

4. At the beginning of 20X1, a new production machine was acquired for €48,000 and recognized in the balance sheet item "machines". So far it has not been depreciated because there are no historical values for this kind of machine. The head of production estimates a useful life between 10 and 15 years assuming constant and continuous usage.

Because a machine is an asset with a definite useful life, its acquisition costs must be depreciated over the useful life (§ 253 sect. 3).

However, the useful life must be estimated, in particular when the user has no experience with this kind of asset. With linear depreciation (based on constant usage) the annual amount is between €4,800 and €3,200.

With regard to the intention to report as low a profit as possible, the machine should be depreciated using the shorter useful life, i.e. it should be depreciated faster at an annual amount of €4,800.

5. According to the information of the producer of the machine, a general overhaul will be necessary after 4 years. The costs for this measure in year 20X4 will probably be €20,000.

It is not possible to recognize a provision. All reasons for provisions are named in § 249 as a definitive list. Therefore, the measurement of the machine remains unchanged (apart from the annual depreciation). Whether or not subsequent acquisition costs will be incurred after a successful general overhaul (because of a substantial improvement or increase in useful life) must be decided in 20X4 and will be relevant for accounting then.

6. Bits and Pieces GmbH signed a sales contract with Light and Sound GmbH on 12 October 20X1 to produce and deliver a light organ (delivery date 30 March 20X2, fixed price of €60,000). The start of production is scheduled for January 20X2. Head of accounting C. Orrect was on vacation when the offer was calculated and signed and realizes now that his apprentice forgot to include the wages for the production workers in the calculation. The direct costs for material and production already amount to €70,000; in addition, indirect costs can be attributed to the light organ: €3,000 for material and €2,000 for production.

This is a pending transaction: Bits and Pieces GmbH has not delivered the light organ, nor has Light and Sound GmbH paid for it. Nevertheless, a loss is expected from the future fulfillment of the contract:

	Sales price	€60,000
−	Direct costs	−€70,000
−	Indirect costs	−€5,000
=	**Expected loss**	**−€15,000**

For onerous contracts, a provision must be recognized (§ 249 sect. 1). Possibilities for estimation exist only in the attribution of relevant costs, but not in the specific case here: Direct and indirect costs of material and production must be included.

7. For a new warehouse, a monthly rent of €5,000 is charged from 1 December 20X1 onwards. So far, no rent has been paid because of minor defects, which the landlord must fix. Nevertheless, the building is used. The rental contract states that the rent must be paid 3 months in advance.

Defects of or in a rented asset justify only to a slight and specific extent the right to reduce rent payments, in particular when the rented asset can be used. Thus, the minor defects here do not justify reduced payments.

Based on the principle of completeness, the complete payable (3 months at €5,000 each, i.e. in total €15,000) must be recognized. Based on the matching principle, only 1 month is reported as expense and 2 months in the next reporting period as deferred expenses (§ 250 sect. 1): Rental expense in 20X1 amounts to €5,000, deferred expense to €10,000.

Solution to case 4: Accounting for inventories

Category: Knowledge/Application/Analysis
Time to solve: 15 minutes

Keywords: measurement of inventories, lower-of-cost-or-market principle, closing-date principle

Charlene Coal is managing director of Drilling Equipment Trading GmbH and supplies production companies with twist drills and diamond abrasive blocks. In autumn, she buys from an insolvent company first-class twist drills for €100,000 and diamond abrasive blocks for €200,000.

1. In March of the following year she prepares her financial statements:
- *The price for twist drills increased, so that she has good arguments that the acquired drills could have been sold by 31 December for at least €120,000.*
- *Crises in Russia and Africa have led to significant price pressure for diamond abrasive blocks. The value of her blocks drops to €98,000 on 31 December; in February of the following year the market value is only €88,000. Charlene Coal keeps the blocks because she thinks the prices will recover sometime in the future.*

At what values do the products have to be recognized under the Commercial Code? Why? Is there a difference to German tax law? Is there an effect on the income statement?

Twist drills:
In this case, the realization principle must be applied (§ 252 sect. 1 no. 4), i.e. the gain may be recognized only if and when it is realized. On 31 December, the twist drills are still measured at their acquisition costs of €100,000. In addition, the acquisition cost principle is valid here as well: The acquisition costs are the upper limit of measurement for any asset (§ 253 sect. 1).

There is no effect on the income statement and no difference to German tax law.

Diamond abrasive blocks:
In this case, the imparity principle must be applied (see above), i.e. losses must be recognized if and when they are probable, even if not realized. On that basis, the strict lower-of-cost-or-market principle is the more detailed rule for current assets (§ 253 sect. 4). Therefore, the blocks must be impaired to the lower market value of €98,000. The even lower value of February cannot be used due to the closing-date principle (§ 252 sect. 1 no. 3).

There is an additional expense (the impairment) of €102,000 in the income statement. Under German tax law only permanent decreases in value may be impaired. Therefore, the tax treatment depends on the judgment of whether or not the decrease is permanent and, if it is considered permanent, whether the impairment option is used.

2. Continuation of question 1: In the following summer the price for the diamond abrasive blocks rises again to €150,000 and stays there until the end of the year. Nevertheless Charlene Coal does not want to sell below her acquisition costs. How are the

abrasive blocks recognized in the following financial statements and why? Is there an effect in the income statement (only Commercial Code)?

If the reasons for an impairment no longer exist, the impairment must be reversed (§ 253 sect. 1). Because the market price increased again, the impairment must be reversed partially to €150,000. The reversal of an impairment is an income in the income statement, i.e. income of €52,000 due to reversal of impairment.

Hints

If there exist measurement differences between the commercial balance sheet and the tax balance sheet, this may result in deferred taxes. In the current case of the diamond abrasive blocks, an impairment is necessary in the commercial balance sheet. Because a permanent decrease in value is not probable (the market prices increased again in the following year but did not recover completely), the impairment is probably not tax deductible. This is a temporary difference because it will reverse over time – at the latest, when the blocks are sold. Because the assets are valued lower in the commercial balance sheet, this will result in a deferred tax asset; for deferred tax assets in individual financial statements, there exists an accounting option (§ 274 sect. 1), i.e. the deferred tax asset can be recognized, but it does not have to be recognized.

Solution Case 5: Accounting for intangible assets

Category: Knowledge/Application/Analysis
Time to solve: 10 minutes

Keywords: recognition of intangible assets, definition of production costs, deferred taxes

The champagne winery Wochenheim AG has developed a new technology for producing champagne that is free of alcohol; the new technology should be used from the beginning of 20X1 until the end of 20X5. The technology was patented at the end of 20X0. In the context of the innovation the following costs were incurred:

– *Personnel expenses, research part of project:*	*€500,000*
– *Operational expenses, research part of project (e.g. material):*	*€200,000*
– *Personnel expenses, development part of project:*	*€750,000*
– *Operational expenses, development part of project (e.g. material):*	*€300,000*

The R&D department worked only on this technology.
The company is a large corporation; its effective tax rate is 30%.
(a) *What accounting options exist for this new technology in the **commercial balance sheet** as of 31 December 20X0? Explain the different options briefly and journalize the possible entries.*

This is an internally generated, intangible, non-current asset. For assets of this kind there exists an accounting option for the commercial balance sheet, i.e. the expenses for development (not for research) can be recognized as an asset (§ 248 sect. 1 and § 255 sect. 2a) or they remain expenses in the income statement.

If the technology is recognized as an asset, it must be amortized over the useful life, i.e. here probably 5 years.

Journal entry for recognition:

Debit internally generated, intangible, non-current assets 1,050,000
        Credit own work capitalized   1,050,000

(b) *What accounting options exist for this new technology in the **tax balance sheet** as of 31 December 20X0? Explain the different options briefly and journalize possible entries.*

In the tax balance sheet, there is no recognition option, i.e. research and development expenses are always expenses in the income statement of the period.

(c) *What must be considered in this context for the commercial balance sheet as of 31 December 20X0 in addition? Explain briefly the possible consequences and journalize possible entries.*

If the recognition option is not used, there are no differences between commercial and tax balance sheet: Nothing to consider.

If the recognition option is used, there exists a temporary difference between commercial and tax balance sheet; the difference is temporary because it will even out either by amortization or sale – at any rate, after a certain period of time, the commercial balance sheet and tax balance sheet will be in line again; the result is a deferred tax liability:

$$\text{Tax rate} \times \text{Temporary difference} = \text{Deferred tax (here: liability)}$$
$$30\% \ \times \quad \text{€ } 1,050,000 \quad = \quad \text{€ } 315,000$$

Corresponding to the amortization of the patent over time, the deferred tax liability is reduced/reversed. In addition, there is a restriction for profit distribution: The amount recognized as an asset minus the deferred tax liability may not be paid out as dividends: €1,050,000 – €315,000 = €735,000. Only profits in excess of this level may be distributed to the shareholders (§ 268 sect. 8).

Case study 6: Accounting policy

Category: Knowledge/Application/Analysis
Time to solve: 15 minutes

Keywords: accounting policy, acquisition costs, provisions, measurement of non-current assets, measurement of current assets

Explain and argue for the following topics if there exist any legal or factual accounting options or margins of judgment. Show as well how the use of any options or margins of judgment can affect the net result or the equity ratio:

(a) *Acquisition costs*
According to § 255 sect. 1, acquisition costs are defined as:

+ Purchase price
- Purchase price reductions (trade or cash discounts, rebates)
+ Incidental acquisition costs
- Subsequent acquisition costs
= Acquisition costs

All costs must be directly attributable to the acquisition (direct costs) and must be incurred until the acquired asset is ready to use (except subsequent acquisition costs – as implied by the name). Subsequent acquisition costs are incurred later but increase the usage potential of the asset or improve the asset substantially – but they are not an asset themselves. There are no legal accounting options but factual options, e.g. whether or not a cash discount is used or how a certain service is invoiced so it can or cannot be attributed to a specific acquisition (e.g. a security check can be invoiced or reported for each checked facility separately or summed up).

In addition, an estimation is necessary in different areas, e.g.
- at what point in time an asset is ready for use and
- whether a transaction is subsequent acquisition costs or just maintenance.

The higher the acquisition costs are (i.e. if factual options are used to increase the acquisition costs), the higher the net result typically is in the period of acquisition. The later the asset is ready for use, the later the depreciation or amortization starts and thus the higher the net profit in the period of acquisition. There is no clear effect on the equity ratio because this depends on the financing of the acquisition.

(b) *Provisions*
All reasons for recognizing a provision are listed in § 249; there are no legal options. Factual options exist for the provisions for omitted maintenance and waste disposal: They must be recognized if they are done within 3 months (maintenance) or 12 months (waste disposal); otherwise, they are prohibited. Thus, the scheduling influences the recognition.

Because provisions are uncertain liabilities, there are significant margins of judgment: Reason, amount and timing are uncertain and the settlement amount must be estimated. These estimations can be used for accounting policy; the limits are the GAAP (in particular the principle of correctness), i.e. arbitrary values that cannot be verified and understood by a third party are not allowed.

Recognition of provisions creates an additional liability and additional expenses and thus reduces net profit. In consequence, the equity ratio is reduced (this is a transaction purely on the credit side of the balance sheet).

(c) *Impairment of non-current financial assets*

For non-current assets in general, the moderate lower-of-cost-or-market principle must be applied, i.e. impairment must be done only if a presumably permanent decrease in value occurs; for temporary decreases in value, an impairment is not allowed. But there exists an accounting option for non-current financial assets: According to § 253 sect. 3, a non-current financial asset may be impaired even if the decrease in value is only temporary.

Margins of judgment exist in particular if no market prices are available, i.e. the value of a financial asset cannot be derived from a market price, e.g. from a stock exchange, but must be calculated using valuation models. The basic data and methods used for the valuation models typically require a lot of estimation, and so the result can be affected; typical examples are the discount rates used or the amount and timing of future cash flows that must be estimated.

All else being equal, an additional impairment or a higher impairment leads to a lower net profit and to a lower equity ratio.

(d) *Measurement simplifications for current assets*

Several accounting options exist:

- The general principle is individual measurement (§ 252 sect. 1).
- A constant-value approach is possible for raw materials (§ 240 sect. 3).
- Group measurement for similar inventories or other moveable assets with similar value (§ 240 sect. 4): Apart from the option to group items, there exists the option to choose between a periodic average or a moving average as the basis for the initial measurement.
- Cost formulas (sequence of consumption) can be used for similar inventories (§ 256): Apart from the option to group items, there exists the option to choose between FIFO and LIFO.

All methods are equivalent, i.e. can be used alternatively, if the legal requirements are met.

Specific margins of judgment do not exist in this context.

The effect on the net results depends on the method chosen and on the development of the asset prices, i.e. there is no general rule on whether a method increases or decreases the net results. There is no clear effect on the equity ratio because this depends on the financing of the acquisition.

Hint

There exist substantial accounting options or margins of judgment in connection with other topics concerning the measurement of current assets, in particular:

- definition of production costs: whether or not optional elements are included;
- subsequent measurement (measurement simplifications are relevant for initial measurement), i.e. the strict lower-of-cost-or-market principle at the closing date. For inventories and receivables, substantial estimates are necessary. For inventories a net realizable value must be calculated, i.e. a possible sales price minus any costs incurred until sale. For receivables, any expected losses must be estimated to recognize a valuation allowance.

But these topics were not addressed in this exercise.

Solution to Case 7: Accounting for inventories (2)

Category: Knowledge/Application/Analysis
Time to solve: 15 minutes

Keywords: accounting for current assets, inventories, cost formulas, accounting policy

The Electronic Parts GmbH is a midsized corporation and is currently preparing its balance sheet. One standard product of the company is the electric engine Pro-2; it is continuously in large but changing amounts in stock and stored in an open-shelf system. Additions to stock and the purchase price development are shown in the table later in the chapter. Withdrawals from stock occur when needed and cannot be allocated to specific additions.

Tab. 7.7: Case 7 Development of product amounts and purchase prices.

Date	Movement	Amount in pieces	Purchase price € per piece
01.01.	Opening balance	38	271.00
12.02.	Addition	40	269.00
13.06.	Addition	120	317.00
27.09.	Addition	20	324.00
29.11.	Addition	40	319.00
31.12.	Closing balance	66	

(a) *Calculate the value of the closing balance for the electric engine. List the possible variants according to the German Commercial Code. The market price on 31 December is 325 €.*

According to German Commercial Code the following variants of group measurements are possible: periodic average, LIFO, FIFO. LIFO and FIFO are presumably acceptable because there is no specific real sequence of consumption and the price changes are not likely to distort the true and fair view of the financial statements. The calculations are done in Tab. 7.8.

Tab. 7.8: Solution to case 7 measurement variants.

Date	Movement	Amount in pieces	Price € per piece	Value	FIFO	LIFO
01.01.	Opening balance	38	271.00	10,298.00		10,298.00
12.02.	Addition	40	269.00	10,760.00		7,532.00
13.06.	Addition	120	317.00	38,040.00	1,902.00	
27.09.	Addition	20	324.00	6,480.00	6,480.00	
29.11.	Addition	40	319.00	12,760.00	12,760.00	
	Total	258	303.64	78,338.00		
31.12.	Closing balance	66	303.64	20,040.24	21,142.00	17,830.00

For the periodic average, total value is divided through total amount. Measuring the closing balance with FIFO means that the newest items are in stock; whereas applying LIFO means the opposite.

The current market value is not relevant for the measurement, because this value (66 pieces x 325 € per piece = 21,450.00) is higher than the initial measurement. Due to the realization principle this current value cannot be used.

(b) *Which measurement approach would you choose, if the company wants to report a profit that is as high as possible?*

For a profit that is as high as possible, the expenses need to be as low as possible. The higher the initial measurement of the products, the lower the corresponding expenses for withdrawal of sold products, i.e. the products should be measured with FIFO.

(c) *Is the statement correct that FIFO creates hidden reserves when you assume continuously increasing prices?*

Creating hidden reserves with assets means measuring the assets with a value lower than their current market value. Since FIFO uses the most up-to-date prices to measure the assets, no hidden reserves can be created by doing so.

Note: If there is an increasing price trend, using LIFO for the initial measurement will create hidden reserves.

Solution to case 8: Consolidated financial statements (1)

Category: Knowledge/Application
Time to solve: 15 minutes

Keywords: consolidation methods, consolidated financial statements

The Wine & Champagne Group consists of a parent company, Riesling AG, located in Deidesheim in Rhineland-Palatinate, and Distribution GmbH located in Pforzheim.

The parent company (PC) recognized, apart from the shares in affiliated companies of €300,000, other assets of €700,000. The PC has a capital structure of 50% equity and 50% liabilities.

The subsidiary (SUB) recognizes equity of €80,000 and liabilities of €320,000. Its assets include a piece of land with a book value of €100,000 (fair value at acquisition by the PC of €200,000).

(a) *Which consolidation methods do you know?*
Full consolidation (§§ 300)
Proportional consolidation (§ 310)
At-equity consolidation (recognition as associated company, § 312)
(b) *Prepare the balance sheets of the PC and the SUB.*

Tab. 7.9: Solution to case 8 – balance sheet parent company.

Debit (€)		Balance sheet PC	Credit (€)
Shares in affiliates	300,000	Equity	500,000
Other assets	700,000	Liabilities	500,000
Total assets	1,000,000	Total equity and liabilities	1,000,000

Tab. 7.10: Solution to case 8 – balance sheet subsidiary.

Debit (€)		Balance sheet SUB	Credit (€)
Land	100,000	Equity	80,000
Other assets	300,000	Liabilities	320,000
Total assets	400,000	Total equity and liabilities	400,000

(c) *Prepare the consolidated balance sheet and journalize the necessary entries.*
Step 1: Preparation of an aggregated balance sheet
Aggregated balance sheet of the Wine & Champagne Group (€), column form

Tab. 7.11: Solution to case 8 – aggregated balance sheet (column form).

Assets	PC	SUB	Sum
Land		100,000	100,000
Shares in affiliates	300,000		300,000
Other assets	700,000	300,000	1,000,000
Total assets	1,000,000	400,000	1,400,000
Equity and liabilities			
Equity	500,000	80,000	580,000
Liabilities	500,000	320,000	820,000
Total equity and liabilities	1,000,000	400,000	1,400,000

In addition, in account form:

Tab. 7.12: Solution to case 8 – aggregated balance sheet (account form).

Debit (€)		Aggregated balance sheet group	Credit (€)
Land	100,000	Equity	580,000
Share in affiliates	300,000	Liabilities	820,000
Other assets	1,000,000		
Total assets	1,400,000	Total equity and liabilities	1,400,000

Step 2: Capital (equity) consolidation
Offsetting shares in affiliates with equity of subsidiary (€):

Debit equity	80,000	
Debit asset difference	220,000	
Credit shares in affiliates		300,000

Step 3: Allocation of asset difference
Allocation of asset difference to revalued assets and liabilities as well as goodwill
(purchase price allocation):

Debit land	100,000	
Debit goodwill	120,000	
Credit asset difference		220,000

Step 4: Preparation of consolidated balance sheet (integration of steps 2 and 3 in step 1)

Tab. 7.13: Solution to case 8 – consolidated balance sheet.

Debit (€)		Consolidated balance sheet group	Credit (€)
Land	200,000	Equity	500,000
Goodwill	120,000	Liabilities	820,000
Other assets	1,000,000		
Total assets	1,320,000	Total equity & liabilities	1,320,000

Solution to case 9: Consolidated financial statements (2)

Category: Knowledge/Application
Time to solve: 15 minutes

Keywords: Consolidation methods, consolidated financial statements

Snow AG acquired the shares of Ski GmbH on 31 December 20X1 for €2 million to be able in the future to offer not only ski clothes but also ski equipment. The purchase price was paid on 31 December 20X1.

*Preliminary balance sheet of Snow AG of 31 December 20X1 **prior** to acquisition of Ski GmbH:*

Tab. 7.14: Solution to *case 9 – balance sheet of Snow AG prior to acquisition.*

Debit (€)		Balance sheet Snow AG	Credit (€)
Non-current assets	950,000	Equity	1,520,000
Current assets	5,100,000	Liabilities	4,530,000
Total assets	6,050,000	Total equity and liabilities	6,050,000

Balance sheet of Ski GmbH from 31 December 20X1:

Tab. 7.15: Solution to case 9 – balance sheet of Ski GmbH.

Debit (€)		Balance sheet Ski GmbH	Credit (€)
Non-current assets	250,000	Equity	400,000
Current assets	2,100,000	Liabilities	1,950,000
Total assets	2,350,000	Total equity and liabilities	2,350,000

Additional information about the financial statements of Ski GmbH:
- *The non-current assets include a fully depreciated machine that the company will continue to use; its reproduction value amounts to €200,000 at the acquisition date.*
- *The equity includes the full net profit of €80,000 for the business year 20X1.*
- *Provisions: pension provisions of €100,000 have not been recognized yet.*
- *Ski GmbH sells its products largely under the brand name "Solo", which was created by the company itself. Industry experts estimate the brand value at €500,000.*

Questions:

(a) *Prepare the consolidated financial statements and carry out the capital consolidation (equity). What are the corresponding journal entries?*
All values in T€.
Step 1: Recognition of acquired shares

Debit shares in affiliates	2,000	
Credit cash		2,000

This results in the following adjusted balance sheet of Snow AG:

Tab. 7.16: Solution to case 9 – balance sheet of Snow AG after acquisition.

Debit (T€)	Balance sheet Snow AG		Credit (T€)
Non-current assets	2,950	Equity	1,520
Current assets	3,100	Liabilities	4,530
Total assets	6,050	Total equity & liabilities	6,050

Step 2: Preparation of aggregated balance sheet for the group
Preparation of an aggregated balance sheet by adding up the corresponding items of the individual balance sheets.
In T€, PC = parent company, SUB = subsidiary

Tab. 7.17: Solution to case 9 – aggregated balance sheet (column form).

Assets	PC	SUB	Sum
Non-current assets	2,950	250	3,200
Current assets	3,100	2,100	5,200
Total assets	**6,050**	**2,350**	**8,400**
Equity and liabilities			
Equity	1,520	400	1,920
Liabilities	4,530	1,950	6,480
Total equity and liabilities	**6,050**	**2,350**	**8,400**

In addition, in account form:

Tab. 7.18: Solution to case 9 – aggregated balance sheet (account form).

Debit (T€)		Aggregated balance sheet group	Credit (T€)
Non-current assets	3,200	Equity	1,920
Current assets	5,200	Liabilities	6,480
Total assets	8,400	Total equity & liabilities	8,400

Step 3: Calculation of asset difference (capital/equity consolidation)
Calculation of asset difference between purchase price for shares and acquired equity:

Debit equity	400	
Debit asset difference	1,600	
Credit shares in affiliates		2,000

Step 4: Allocation of asset difference
Allocation of asset difference to revalued assets and liabilities as well as goodwill (as residual); this is called purchase price allocation:

Debit non-current assets (tangible assets)	200	
Debit non-current assets (brand)	500	
Debit goodwill	1,000	
Credit liabilities (pension provision)		100
Credit asset difference		1,600

Step 5: Integration of steps 3 and 4 in aggregated balance sheet

Tab. 7.19: Solution to case 9 – consolidated balance sheet.

Debit (T€)		Consolidated balance sheet group	Credit (T€)
Non-current assets	2,900	Equity	1,520
Current assets	5,200	Liabilities	6,580
Total assets	8,100	Total equity and liabilities	8,100

(b) *In what case is a purchase price allocation in the individual financial statements necessary?*

If a business is acquired through the acquisition of all assets and liabilities, but not a legal entity, i.e. if a so-called asset deal occurs, the goodwill must be recognized in the individual financial statements (including the purchase price allocation); see § 246 sect. 1 sent. 4.

Part III: **Additional information**

8 Translation of German legal accounting rules

Translation of the accounting part of the German Commercial Code (individual and consolidated financial statements) as enacted in June 2021.

For historic reasons a central term in the Commercial Code is "Kaufmann", literally translated as "merchant". "Kaufmann" is in the legal understanding a wide term that refers to any person operating a commercial business. "Merchant" in the English language is associated with trading or retailing business, thus a literal translation would give a misleading impression. For this reason "Kaufmann" is translated as "businessman" implying a wide range of commercial activities. The legal text is not gender neutral, so the translation is not either.

This translation covers the regulations directly relevant for accounting and that are used as references in the book chapters. Additional topics like auditing, disclosure procedures and penalties have been left out because they are not within the scope of this book.

This translation is not an authoritative or official translation. The authoritative text is available in German only. The author used his best knowledge to prepare a complete and correct translation of the legal text. Nevertheless, for any decision with legal or operational consequences the official text should be used.

Drittes Buch. Handelsbücher	Book Three. Commercial books
Erster Abschnitt. Vorschriften für alle Kaufleute	**First section. Regulations for all businessmen**
Erster Unterabschnitt. Buchführung; Inventar	**First subsection. Bookkeeping; inventory**
§ 238 Buchführungspflicht (1) Jeder Kaufmann ist verpflichtet, Bücher zu führen und in diesen seine Handelsgeschäfte und die Lage seines Vermögens nach den Grundsätzen ordnungsmäßiger Buchführung ersichtlich zu machen. Die Buchführung muß so beschaffen sein, daß sie einem sachverständigen Dritten innerhalb angemessener Zeit einen Überblick über die Geschäftsvorfälle und über die Lage des Unternehmens vermitteln kann. Die Geschäftsvorfälle müssen sich in ihrer Entstehung und Abwicklung verfolgen lassen.	**§ 238 Accounting obligation** (1) Every businessman is obliged to keep books and to make his commercial transactions and the situation of his assets apparent in these books in accordance with the generally accepted accounting principles. The bookkeeping must be such that it can provide an expert third party with an overview of the business transactions and the situation of the enterprise within a reasonable period of time. The business transactions must be traceable in their origin and processing.

https://doi.org/10.1515/9783110744170-008

(continued)

---

(2) Der Kaufmann ist verpflichtet, eine mit der Urschrift übereinstimmende Wiedergabe der abgesandten Handelsbriefe (Kopie, Abdruck, Abschrift oder sonstige Wiedergabe des Wortlauts auf einem Schrift-, Bild- oder anderen Datenträger) zurückzubehalten.

(2) The businessman is obliged to retain a reproduction of the dispatched commercial letters (copy, imprint, transcript or other reproduction of the wording on a written, visual or other data carrier) which corresponds to the original.

---

§ 239 Führung der Handelsbücher

(1) Bei der Führung der Handelsbücher und bei den sonst erforderlichen Aufzeichnungen hat sich der Kaufmann einer lebenden Sprache zu bedienen. Werden Abkürzungen, Ziffern, Buchstaben oder Symbole verwendet, muß im Einzelfall deren Bedeutung eindeutig festliegen.

(2) Die Eintragungen in Büchern und die sonst erforderlichen Aufzeichnungen müssen vollständig, richtig, zeitgerecht und geordnet vorgenommen werden.

(3) Eine Eintragung oder eine Aufzeichnung darf nicht in einer Weise verändert werden, daß der ursprüngliche Inhalt nicht mehr feststellbar ist. Auch solche Veränderungen dürfen nicht vorgenommen werden, deren Beschaffenheit es ungewiß läßt, ob sie ursprünglich oder erst später gemacht worden sind.

(4) Die Handelsbücher und die sonst erforderlichen Aufzeichnungen können auch in der geordneten Ablage von Belegen bestehen oder auf Datenträgern geführt werden, soweit diese Formen der Buchführung einschließlich des dabei angewandten Verfahrens den Grundsätzen ordnungsmäßiger Buchführung entsprechen. Bei der Führung der Handelsbücher und der sonst erforderlichen Aufzeichnungen auf Datenträgern muß insbesondere sichergestellt sein, daß die Daten während der Dauer der Aufbewahrungsfrist verfügbar sind und jederzeit innerhalb angemessener Frist lesbar gemacht werden können. Absätze 1 bis 3 gelten sinngemäß.

§ 239 Keeping of commercial books

(1) In keeping the commercial books and in the otherwise required records, the businessman has to use a living language. If abbreviations, numbers, letters or symbols are used, their meaning must be clearly established for the specific case.

(2) Entries in books and otherwise required records must be complete, correct, timely and orderly.

(3) An entry or record may not be altered in such a way that the original content can no longer be determined. Nor may such alterations be made whose nature makes it uncertain whether they were made originally or only later.

(4) The commercial books and the otherwise required records may also consist of the orderly filing of documents or be kept on data carriers, provided that these forms of bookkeeping, including the procedure used, comply with the generally accepted accounting principles. In keeping the commercial books and the otherwise required records on data carriers, it must be ensured in particular that the data are available for the duration of the retention period and can be made readable at any time within a reasonable period. Sections 1 to 3 shall apply mutatis mutandis.

(continued)

§ 240 Inventar	§ 240 Inventory

§ 240 Inventar

(1) Jeder Kaufmann hat zu Beginn seines Handelsgewerbes seine Grundstücke, seine Forderungen und Schulden, den Betrag seines baren Geldes sowie seine sonstigen Vermögensgegenstände genau zu verzeichnen und dabei den Wert der einzelnen Vermögensgegenstände und Schulden anzugeben.

(2) Er hat demnächst für den Schluß eines jeden Geschäftsjahrs ein solches Inventar aufzustellen. Die Dauer des Geschäftsjahrs darf zwölf Monate nicht überschreiten. Die Aufstellung des Inventars ist innerhalb der einem ordnungsmäßigen Geschäftsgang entsprechenden Zeit zu bewirken.

(3) Vermögensgegenstände des Sachanlagevermögens sowie Roh-, Hilfs- und Betriebsstoffe können, wenn sie regelmäßig ersetzt werden und ihr Gesamtwert für das Unternehmen von nachrangiger Bedeutung ist, mit einer gleichbleibenden Menge und einem gleichbleibenden Wert angesetzt werden, sofern ihr Bestand in seiner Größe, seinem Wert und seiner Zusammensetzung nur geringen Veränderungen unterliegt. Jedoch ist in der Regel alle drei Jahre eine körperliche Bestandsaufnahme durchzuführen.

(4) Gleichartige Vermögensgegenstände des Vorratsvermögens sowie andere gleichartige oder annähernd gleichwertige bewegliche Vermögensgegenstände und Schulden können jeweils zu einer Gruppe zusammengefaßt und mit dem gewogenen Durchschnittswert angesetzt werden.

§ 240 Inventory

(1) Every businessman has to, at the beginning of his commercial business, keep an accurate record of his real estate, his receivables and debts, the amount of his cash and his other assets, stating the value of each asset and debt.

(2) He has to prepare such an inventory for the end of each business year. The duration of the business year may not exceed twelve months. The inventory has to be prepared within a period corresponding to an orderly conduct of business.

(3) Tangible assets as well as raw materials and supplies may, if they are replaced regularly and their total value is of subordinate importance to the enterprise, be recognized at a constant quantity and a constant value, provided that their inventory is subject to only minor changes in quantity, value and composition. However, as a rule, a physical stock taking must be carried out every three years.

(4) Inventory assets that are similar in kind, and other movable assets and liabilities that are similar in kind or value, may be grouped together and recognized at the weighted average value.

(continued)

§ 241 Inventurvereinfachungsverfahren	§ 241 Simplification of stock taking procedures
(1) Bei der Aufstellung des Inventars darf der Bestand der Vermögensgegenstände nach Art, Menge und Wert auch mit Hilfe anerkannter mathematisch-statistischer Methoden auf Grund von Stichproben ermittelt werden. Das Verfahren muß den Grundsätzen ordnungsmäßiger Buchführung entsprechen. Der Aussagewert des auf diese Weise aufgestellten Inventars muß dem Aussagewert eines auf Grund einer körperlichen Bestandsaufnahme aufgestellten Inventars gleichkommen.	(1) When preparing the inventory, the stock of assets may also be determined in terms of type, quantity and value with the aid of recognized mathematical/statistical methods on the basis of samples. The method must comply with the generally accepted accounting principles. The informative value of the inventory prepared in this way must be equivalent to the informative value of an inventory prepared on the basis of a physical stock taking.
(2) Bei der Aufstellung des Inventars für den Schluß eines Geschäftsjahrs bedarf es einer körperlichen Bestandsaufnahme der Vermögensgegenstände für diesen Zeitpunkt nicht, soweit durch Anwendung eines den Grundsätzen ordnungsmäßiger Buchführung entsprechenden anderen Verfahrens gesichert ist, daß der Bestand der Vermögensgegenstände nach Art, Menge und Wert auch ohne die körperliche Bestandsaufnahme für diesen Zeitpunkt festgestellt werden kann.	(2) When preparing the inventory for the end of a business year, a physical stock taking of the assets for that date shall not be required if it is ensured by the application of another procedure in accordance with the generally accepted accounting principles that the inventory of the assets can be determined in terms of type, quantity and value even without the physical stock taking for that date.
(3) In dem Inventar für den Schluß eines Geschäftsjahrs brauchen Vermögensgegenstände nicht verzeichnet zu werden, wenn	(3) Assets need not be recorded in the inventory for the end of a business year if
1. der Kaufmann ihren Bestand auf Grund einer körperlichen Bestandsaufnahme oder auf Grund eines nach Absatz 2 zulässigen anderen Verfahrens nach Art, Menge und Wert in einem besonderen Inventar verzeichnet hat, das für einen Tag innerhalb der letzten drei Monate vor oder der ersten beiden Monate nach dem Schluß des Geschäftsjahrs aufgestellt ist, und	1. the businessman records their stock in a special inventory of their kind, quantity and value on the basis of a physical stock taking or on the basis of another procedure permissible under section 2 prepared for a day within the last three months before or the first two months after the end of the business year, and

(continued)

2. auf Grund des besonderen Inventars durch Anwendung eines den Grundsätzen ordnungsmäßiger Buchführung entsprechenden Fortschreibungs- oder Rückrechnungsverfahrens gesichert ist, daß der am Schluß des Geschäftsjahrs vorhandene Bestand der Vermögensgegenstände für diesen Zeitpunkt ordnungsgemäß bewertet werden kann.	2. it is ensured, on the basis of the special inventory, by the application of an updating or back-calculation procedure in accordance with the generally accepted accounting principles, that the stock of assets existing at the end of the business year can be properly measured for that date.

§ 241a Befreiung von der Pflicht zur Buchführung und Erstellung eines Inventars	**§ 241a Exemption from the obligation to keep books and to prepare an inventory**
Einzelkaufleute, die an den Abschlussstichtagen von zwei aufeinander folgenden Geschäftsjahren nicht mehr als jeweils 600 000 Euro Umsatzerlöse und jeweils 60 000 Euro Jahresüberschuss aufweisen, brauchen die §§ 238 bis 241 nicht anzuwenden. Im Fall der Neugründung treten die Rechtsfolgen schon ein, wenn die Werte des Satzes 1 am ersten Abschlussstichtag nach der Neugründung nicht überschritten werden.	Sole proprietorships which do not have more than €600,000 each in sales revenue and €60,000 each in net profit on the balance sheet dates of two consecutive business years do not need to apply §§ 238 to 241. In the case of a new foundation, the legal consequences shall already apply if the values in sentence 1 are not exceeded on the first reporting date after the new foundation.

Zweiter Unterabschnitt. Eröffnungsbilanz. Jahresabschluß	**Second subsection. Opening balance sheet. Financial statements**

Erster Titel. Allgemeine Vorschriften	**First title. General rules**

§ 242 Pflicht zur Aufstellung	**§ 242 Obligation of preparation**
(1) Der Kaufmann hat zu Beginn seines Handelsgewerbes und für den Schluß eines jeden Geschäftsjahrs einen das Verhältnis seines Vermögens und seiner Schulden darstellenden Abschluß (Eröffnungsbilanz, Bilanz) aufzustellen. Auf die Eröffnungsbilanz sind die für den Jahresabschluß geltenden Vorschriften entsprechend anzuwenden, soweit sie sich auf die Bilanz beziehen.	(1) At the beginning of his business and at the end of each business year, a businessman has to prepare financial statements showing the relationship between his assets and his liabilities (opening balance sheet, balance sheet). The rules applicable to the financial statements shall be applied mutatis mutandis to the opening balance sheet insofar as they relate to the balance sheet.
(2) Er hat für den Schluß eines jeden Geschäftsjahrs eine Gegenüberstellung der Aufwendungen und Erträge des Geschäftsjahrs (Gewinn- und Verlustrechnung) aufzustellen.	(2) At the end of each business year, he has to prepare a comparison of the expenses and income of the business year (income statement).
(3) Die Bilanz und die Gewinn- und Verlustrechnung bilden den Jahresabschluß.	(3) The balance sheet and the income statement form the financial statements.

(continued)

(4) Die Absätze 1 bis 3 sind auf Einzelkaufleute im Sinn des § 241a nicht anzuwenden. Im Fall der Neugründung treten die Rechtsfolgen nach Satz 1 schon ein, wenn die Werte des § 241a Satz 1 am ersten Abschlussstichtag nach der Neugründung nicht überschritten werden.	(4) Sections 1 to 3 shall not apply to sole proprietorships according to § 241a. In the case of a new foundation, the legal consequences according to sentence 1 shall already apply if the values of § 241a sentence 1 are not exceeded on the first balance sheet date after the new foundation.

§ 243 Aufstellungsgrundsatz (1) Der Jahresabschluß ist nach den Grundsätzen ordnungsmäßiger Buchführung aufzustellen. (2) Er muß klar und übersichtlich sein. (3) Der Jahresabschluß ist innerhalb der einem ordnungsmäßigen Geschäftsgang entsprechenden Zeit aufzustellen.	**§ 243 Principle of preparation** (1) The financial statements have to be prepared in accordance with the generally accepted accounting principles. (2) They must be clear and well structured. (3) The financial statements shall be prepared within the time necessary in the orderly course of business.

§ 244 Sprache. Währungseinheit Der Jahresabschluß ist in deutscher Sprache und in Euro aufzustellen.	**§ 244 Language. Currency unit** The financial statements have to be prepared in German and in Euros.

§ 245 Unterzeichnung Der Jahresabschluß ist vom Kaufmann unter Angabe des Datums zu unterzeichnen. Sind mehrere persönlich haftende Gesellschafter vorhanden, so haben sie alle zu unterzeichnen.	**§ 245 Signature** The financial statements shall be signed by the businessman, stating the date of signature. If there are several personally liable partners, they must all sign.

(continued)

Zweiter Titel Ansatzvorschriften	Title Two Recognition rules
§ 246 Vollständigkeit. Verrechnungsverbot	**§ 246 Completeness. Prohibition of offsetting**

Zweiter Titel Ansatzvorschriften
§ 246 Vollständigkeit. Verrechnungsverbot
(1) Der Jahresabschluss hat sämtliche Vermögensgegenstände, Schulden, Rechnungsabgrenzungsposten sowie Aufwendungen und Erträge zu enthalten, soweit gesetzlich nichts anderes bestimmt ist. Vermögensgegenstände sind in der Bilanz des Eigentümers aufzunehmen; ist ein Vermögensgegenstand nicht dem Eigentümer, sondern einem anderen wirtschaftlich zuzurechnen, hat dieser ihn in seiner Bilanz auszuweisen. Schulden sind in die Bilanz des Schuldners aufzunehmen. Der Unterschiedsbetrag, um den die für die Übernahme eines Unternehmens bewirkte Gegenleistung den Wert der einzelnen Vermögensgegenstände des Unternehmens abzüglich der Schulden im Zeitpunkt der Übernahme übersteigt (entgeltlich erworbener Geschäfts- oder Firmenwert), gilt als zeitlich begrenzt nutzbarer Vermögensgegenstand.
(2) Posten der Aktivseite dürfen nicht mit Posten der Passivseite, Aufwendungen nicht mit Erträgen, Grundstücksrechte nicht mit Grundstückslasten verrechnet werden. Vermögensgegenstände, die dem Zugriff aller übrigen Gläubiger entzogen sind und ausschließlich der Erfüllung von Schulden aus Altersversorgungsverpflichtungen oder vergleichbaren langfristig fälligen Verpflichtungen dienen, sind mit diesen Schulden zu verrechnen; entsprechend ist mit den zugehörigen Aufwendungen und Erträgen aus der Abzinsung und aus dem zu verrechnenden Vermögen zu verfahren. Übersteigt der beizulegende Zeitwert der Vermögensgegenstände den Betrag der Schulden, ist der übersteigende Betrag unter einem gesonderten Posten zu aktivieren.
(3) Die auf den vorhergehenden Jahresabschluss angewandten Ansatzmethoden sind beizubehalten. § 252 Abs. 2 ist entsprechend anzuwenden.

Title Two Recognition rules
§ 246 Completeness. Prohibition of offsetting
(1) The financial statements have to include all assets, liabilities, accruals and deferrals as well as expenses and income, unless otherwise provided by law. Assets shall be included in the owner's balance sheet; if an asset is not attributable to the owner, but is economically attributable to another party, the latter has to recognize it in its balance sheet. Liabilities shall be included in the balance sheet of the debtor. The difference by which the consideration transferred for the acquisition of an enterprise exceeds the value of the individual assets of the enterprise less the liabilities at the time of the acquisition (goodwill acquired for consideration) is considered to be an asset with a limited useful life.
(2) Items on the assets side may not be offset against items on the liabilities side, expenses may not be offset against income, and land rights may not be offset against land encumbrances. Assets that are not accessible to all other creditors and are used exclusively for the fulfillment of liabilities arising from pension obligations or comparable long-term obligations are to be offset against these liabilities; the associated expenses and income from discounting and from the assets to be offset are to be treated accordingly. If the fair value of the assets exceeds the amount of the liabilities, the excess amount shall be recognized in a separate item.
(3) The recognition methods applied to the previous financial statements have to be retained. § 252 sect. 2 shall be applied accordingly.

(continued)

§ 247 Inhalt der Bilanz	**§ 247 Contents of the balance sheet**

§ 247 Inhalt der Bilanz

(1) In der Bilanz sind das Anlage- und das Umlaufvermögen, das Eigenkapital, die Schulden sowie die Rechnungsabgrenzungsposten gesondert auszuweisen und hinreichend aufzugliedern.

(2) Beim Anlagevermögen sind nur die Gegenstände auszuweisen, die bestimmt sind, dauernd dem Geschäftsbetrieb zu dienen.

§ 247 Contents of the balance sheet

(1) In the balance sheet, the non-current and current assets, the equity, the liabilities and the accruals and deferrals must be shown separately and broken down sufficiently.

(2) In the case of non-current assets, only those items are to be reported which are intended to serve the business operations continuously.

§ 248 Bilanzierungsverbote und -wahlrechte

(1) In die Bilanz dürfen nicht als Aktivposten aufgenommen werden:

1. Aufwendungen für die Gründung eines Unternehmens,
2. Aufwendungen für die Beschaffung des Eigenkapitals und
3. Aufwendungen für den Abschluss von Versicherungsverträgen.

(2) Selbst geschaffene immaterielle Vermögensgegenstände des Anlagevermögens können als Aktivposten in die Bilanz aufgenommen werden. Nicht aufgenommen werden dürfen selbst geschaffene Marken, Drucktitel, Verlagsrechte, Kundenlisten oder vergleichbare immaterielle Vermögensgegenstände des Anlagevermögens.

§ 248 Recognition prohibitions and options

(1) The following may not be included in the balance sheet as assets:

1. Expenses for the establishment of a company,
2. Expenses for the procurement of equity and
3. Expenses for the conclusion of insurance contracts.

(2) Internally generated intangible non-current assets may be included as an asset item in the balance sheet. Internally generated trademarks, print titles, publishing rights, customer lists or comparable intangible non-current assets may not be included.

§ 249 Rückstellungen

(1) Rückstellungen sind für ungewisse Verbindlichkeiten und für drohende Verluste aus schwebenden Geschäften zu bilden. Ferner sind Rückstellungen zu bilden für

1. im Geschäftsjahr unterlassene Aufwendungen für Instandhaltung, die im folgenden Geschäftsjahr innerhalb von drei Monaten, oder für Abraumbeseitigung, die im folgenden Geschäftsjahr nachgeholt werden,
2. Gewährleistungen, die ohne rechtliche Verpflichtung erbracht werden.

(2) Für andere als die in Absatz 1 bezeichneten Zwecke dürfen Rückstellungen nicht gebildet werden. Rückstellungen dürfen nur aufgelöst werden, soweit der Grund hierfür entfallen ist.

§ 249 Provisions

(1) Provisions must be recognized for uncertain liabilities and for onerous contracts. Furthermore, provisions have to be recognized for

1. expenses for maintenance omitted in the business year, which are made up for in the following business year within three months, or for removal of overburden, which are made up for in the following business year,
2. warranties provided without legal obligation.

(2) Provisions may not be recognized for purposes other than those specified in section 1. Provisions may only be reversed to the extent that the reason for them no longer exists.

(continued)

§ 250 Rechnungsabgrenzungsposten

(1) Als Rechnungsabgrenzungsposten sind auf der Aktivseite Ausgaben vor dem Abschlußstichtag auszuweisen, soweit sie Aufwand für eine bestimmte Zeit nach diesem Tag darstellen.

(2) Auf der Passivseite sind als Rechnungsabgrenzungsposten Einnahmen vor dem Abschlußstichtag auszuweisen, soweit sie Ertrag für eine bestimmte Zeit nach diesem Tag darstellen.

(3) Ist der Erfüllungsbetrag einer Verbindlichkeit höher als der Ausgabebetrag, so darf der Unterschiedsbetrag in den Rechnungsabgrenzungs-posten auf der Aktivseite aufgenommen werden. Der Unterschiedsbetrag ist durch planmäßige jährliche Abschreibungen zu tilgen, die auf die gesamte Laufzeit der Verbindlichkeit verteilt werden können.

§ 250 Deferrals

(1) Expenditures prior to the balance sheet date are to be shown as deferred expenses on the assets side insofar as they represent expenses for a certain time after this date.

(2) On the liabilities side, proceeds before the balance sheet date must be shown as deferred income if they represent income for a certain period after that date.

(3) If the settlement amount of a debt is higher than the issue amount, the difference may be included in the deferred expenses on the assets side. The difference shall be amortized through scheduled annual depreciation, which may be spread over the entire term of the debt.

§ 251 Haftungsverhältnisse

Unter der Bilanz sind, sofern sie nicht auf der Passivseite auszuweisen sind, Verbindlichkeiten aus der Begebung und Übertragung von Wechseln, aus Bürgschaften, Wechsel- und Scheckbürgschaften und aus Gewährleistungsverträgen sowie Haftungsverhältnisse aus der Bestellung von Sicherheiten für fremde Verbindlichkeiten zu vermerken; sie dürfen in einem Betrag angegeben werden. Haftungsverhältnisse sind auch anzugeben, wenn ihnen gleichwertige Rückgriffsforderungen gegenüberstehen.

§ 251 Contingent liabilities

Liabilities arising from the issue and transfer of bills of exchange, from guarantees, bill and check guarantees and from warranty agreements as well as contingent liabilities arising from the provision of collateral for third-party debt shall be stated under the balance sheet, unless they are to be shown on the liabilities side; they may be stated in one amount. Contingent liabilities must also be stated if they are compensated by equivalent claims under a right of recourse.

Dritter Titel Bewertungsvorschriften

Title Three Measurement rules

§ 252 Allgemeine Bewertungsgrundsätze

(1) Bei der Bewertung der im Jahresabschluß ausgewiesenen Vermögensgegenstände und Schulden gilt insbesondere folgendes:

1. Die Wertansätze in der Eröffnungsbilanz des Geschäftsjahrs müssen mit denen der Schlußbilanz des vorhergehenden Geschäftsjahrs übereinstimmen.

§ 252 General measurement principles

(1) The following applies in particular to the measurement of the assets and liabilities shown in the financial statements:

1. The values in the opening balance sheet of the business year must be identical to those in the closing balance sheet of the previous business year.

(continued)

2. Bei der Bewertung ist von der Fortführung der Unternehmenstätigkeit auszugehen, sofern dem nicht tatsächliche oder rechtliche Gegebenheiten entgegenstehen.

2. The measurement shall be based on the assumption of a going concern, provided that there are no factual or legal circumstances to the contrary.

3. Die Vermögensgegenstände und Schulden sind zum Abschlußstichtag einzeln zu bewerten.

3. The assets and liabilities are to be measured individually on the balance sheet date.

4. Es ist vorsichtig zu bewerten, namentlich sind alle vorhersehbaren Risiken und Verluste, die bis zum Abschlußstichtag entstanden sind, zu berücksichtigen, selbst wenn diese erst zwischen dem Abschlußstichtag und dem Tag der Aufstellung des Jahresabschlusses bekanntgeworden sind; Gewinne sind nur zu berücksichtigen, wenn sie am Abschlußstichtag realisiert sind.

4. The measurement must be prudently, namely all foreseeable risks and losses which have arisen up to the balance sheet date must be taken into account, even if they become known only between the balance sheet date and the date of preparation of the financial statements; profits shall only be taken into account if they have been realized on the balance sheet date.

5. Aufwendungen und Erträge des Geschäftsjahrs sind unabhängig von den Zeitpunkten der entsprechenden Zahlungen im Jahresabschluß zu berücksichtigen.

5. Expenses and income for the business year shall be taken into account in the financial statements irrespective of the dates of the corresponding payments.

6. Die auf den vorhergehenden Jahresabschluss angewandten Bewertungsmethoden sind beizubehalten.

6. The measurement methods applied to the previous financial statements shall be retained.

(2) Von den Grundsätzen des Absatzes 1 darf nur in begründeten Ausnahmefällen abgewichen werden.

(2) The principles of paragraph 1 may only be deviated from in justified exceptional cases.

(continued)

§ 253 Zugangs- und Folgebewertung

(1) Vermögensgegenstände sind höchstens mit den Anschaffungs- oder Herstellungskosten, vermindert um die Abschreibungen nach den Absätzen 3 bis 5, anzusetzen. Verbindlichkeiten sind zu ihrem Erfüllungsbetrag und Rückstellungen in Höhe des nach vernünftiger kaufmännischer Beurteilung notwendigen Erfüllungsbetrages anzusetzen. Soweit sich die Höhe von Altersversorgungsverpflichtungen ausschließlich nach dem beizulegenden Zeitwert von Wertpapieren im Sinn des § 266 Abs. 2 A. III. 5 bestimmt, sind Rückstellungen hierfür zum beizulegenden Zeitwert dieser Wertpapiere anzusetzen, soweit er einen garantierten Mindestbetrag übersteigt. Nach § 246 Abs. 2 Satz 2 zu verrechnende Vermögensgegenstände sind mit ihrem beizulegenden Zeitwert zu bewerten. Kleinstkapitalgesellschaften (§ 267a) dürfen eine Bewertung zum beizulegenden Zeitwert nur vornehmen, wenn sie von keiner der in § 264 Absatz 1 Satz 5, § 266 Absatz 1 Satz 4, § 275 Absatz 5 und § 326 Absatz 2 vorgesehenen Erleichterungen Gebrauch machen. Macht eine Kleinstkapitalgesellschaft von mindestens einer der in Satz 5 genannten Erleichterungen Gebrauch, erfolgt die Bewertung der Vermögensgegenstände nach Satz 1, auch soweit eine Verrechnung nach § 246 Absatz 2 Satz 2 vorgesehen ist.

§ 253 Initial and subsequent measurement

(1) Assets have to be measured at no more than acquisition or production cost, minus depreciation in accordance with sections 3 to 5. Liabilities have to be recognized at their settlement amount and provisions shall be recognized at the settlement amount required by reasonable commercial judgment. Insofar as the amount of retirement benefit obligations is determined exclusively by the fair value of securities within the meaning of § 266 sect. 2 A. III. 5, provisions for this are to be recognized at the fair value of these securities to the extent that it exceeds a guaranteed minimum amount. Assets to be offset according to § 246 sect. 2 sent. 2 shall be measured at their fair value. Very small corporations (§ 267a) may only carry out a measurement at fair value if they do not make use of any of the simplifications provided for in § 264 sect. 1 sent. 5, § 266 sect. 1 sent. 4, § 275 sect. 5 and § 326 sect. 2. If a very small corporation makes use of at least one of the reliefs provided for in sentence 5, the assets shall be measured in accordance with sentence 1, even if offsetting is provided for in accordance with § 246 sect. 2 sent. 2.

(continued)

(2) Rückstellungen mit einer Restlaufzeit von mehr als einem Jahr sind abzuzinsen mit dem ihrer Restlaufzeit entsprechenden durchschnittlichen Marktzinssatz, der sich im Falle von Rückstellungen für Altersversorgungsverpflichtungen aus den vergangenen zehn Geschäftsjahren und im Falle sonstiger Rückstellungen aus den vergangenen sieben Geschäftsjahren ergibt. Abweichend von Satz 1 dürfen Rückstellungen für Altersversorgungsverpflichtungen oder vergleichbare langfristig fällige Verpflichtungen pauschal mit dem durchschnittlichen Marktzinssatz abgezinst werden, der sich bei einer angenommenen Restlaufzeit von 15 Jahren ergibt. Die Sätze 1 und 2 gelten entsprechend für auf Rentenverpflichtungen beruhende Verbindlichkeiten, für die eine Gegenleistung nicht mehr zu erwarten ist. Der nach den Sätzen 1 und 2 anzuwendende Abzinsungszinssatz wird von der Deutschen Bundesbank nach Maßgabe einer Rechtsverordnung ermittelt und monatlich bekannt gegeben. In der Rechtsverordnung nach Satz 4, die nicht der Zustimmung des Bundesrates bedarf, bestimmt das Bundesministerium der Justiz und für Verbraucherschutz im Benehmen mit der Deutschen Bundesbank das Nähere zur Ermittlung der Abzinsungszinssätze, insbesondere die Ermittlungsmethodik und deren Grundlagen, sowie die Form der Bekanntgabe.	(2) Provisions with a remaining term of more than one year shall be discounted at the average market interest rate corresponding to their remaining term, which in the case of provisions for retirement benefit obligations is derived from the past ten business years and in the case of other provisions from the past seven business years. In deviation from sentence 1, provisions for retirement benefit obligations or comparable long-term obligations may be discounted in less detail using the average market interest rate resulting from an assumed remaining term of 15 years. Sentences 1 and 2 shall apply accordingly to liabilities based on retirement obligations for which consideration is no longer expected. The discount rate to be applied in accordance with sentences 1 and 2 shall be determined by the Deutsche Bundesbank in accordance with a statutory ordinance and shall be published on a monthly basis. In the statutory ordinance pursuant to sentence 4, which shall not require the consent of the Bundesrat (Federal Council), the Federal Ministry of Justice and Consumer Protection shall, in consultation with the Deutsche Bundesbank, determine the details of the calculation of the discount rates, in particular the calculation method and its basis, as well as the form of publication.

(continued)

(3) Bei Vermögensgegenständen des Anlagevermögens, deren Nutzung zeitlich begrenzt ist, sind die Anschaffungs- oder die Herstellungskosten um planmäßige Abschreibungen zu vermindern. Der Plan muss die Anschaffungs- oder Herstellungskosten auf die Geschäftsjahre verteilen, in denen der Vermögensgegenstand voraussichtlich genutzt werden kann. Kann in Ausnahmefällen die voraussichtliche Nutzungsdauer eines selbst geschaffenen immateriellen Vermögensgegenstands des Anlagevermögens nicht verlässlich geschätzt werden, sind planmäßige Abschreibungen auf die Herstellungskosten über einen Zeitraum von zehn Jahren vorzunehmen. Satz 3 findet auf einen entgeltlich erworbenen Geschäfts- oder Firmenwert entsprechende Anwendung. Ohne Rücksicht darauf, ob ihre Nutzung zeitlich begrenzt ist, sind bei Vermögensgegenständen des Anlagevermögens bei voraussichtlich dauernder Wertminderung außerplanmäßige Abschreibungen vorzunehmen, um diese mit dem niedrigeren Wert anzusetzen, der ihnen am Abschlussstichtag beizulegen ist. Bei Finanzanlagen können außerplanmäßige Abschreibungen auch bei voraussichtlich nicht dauernder Wertminderung vorgenommen werden.	(3) In the case of non-current assets whose use is limited in time, the acquisition or production costs must be reduced by scheduled depreciation. The schedule must distribute the acquisition or production costs over the business years in which the asset is expected to be used. If, in exceptional cases, the expected useful life of an internally generated intangible non-current asset cannot be reliably estimated, scheduled amortization of the cost of production shall be carried out over a period of ten years. Sentence 3 shall apply mutatis mutandis to goodwill acquired for consideration. Irrespective of whether their use is limited in time, in the case of non-current assets, impairments are to be carried out in the event of an expected permanent reduction in value so that they are reported at the lower fair value on the balance sheet date. In the case of non-current financial assets, impairments may also be made in the event of a reduction of value that is not expected to be permanent.
(4) Bei Vermögensgegenständen des Umlaufvermögens sind Abschreibungen vorzunehmen, um diese mit einem niedrigeren Wert anzusetzen, der sich aus einem Börsen- oder Marktpreis am Abschlussstichtag ergibt. Ist ein Börsen- oder Marktpreis nicht festzustellen und übersteigen die Anschaffungs- oder Herstellungskosten den Wert, der den Vermögensgegenständen am Abschlussstichtag beizulegen ist, so ist auf diesen Wert abzuschreiben.	(4) In the case of current assets, impairments are to be carried out in order to report them at a lower value resulting from a stock exchange or market price on the balance sheet date. If a stock exchange or market price cannot be determined and the acquisition or production costs exceed the fair value on the balance sheet date, the assets must be impaired to this value.

(continued)

(5) Ein niedrigerer Wertansatz nach Absatz 3 Satz 5 oder 6 und Absatz 4 darf nicht beibehalten werden, wenn die Gründe dafür nicht mehr bestehen. Ein niedrigerer Wertansatz eines entgeltlich erworbenen Geschäfts- oder Firmenwertes ist beizubehalten.

(6) Im Falle von Rückstellungen für Altersversorgungsverpflichtungen ist der Unterschiedsbetrag zwischen dem Ansatz der Rückstellungen nach Maßgabe des entsprechenden durchschnittlichen Marktzinssatzes aus den vergangenen zehn Geschäftsjahren und dem Ansatz der Rückstellungen nach Maßgabe des entsprechenden durchschnittlichen Marktzinssatzes aus den vergangenen sieben Geschäftsjahren in jedem Geschäftsjahr zu ermitteln. Gewinne dürfen nur ausgeschüttet werden, wenn die nach der Ausschüttung verbleibenden frei verfügbaren Rücklagen zuzüglich eines Gewinnvortrags und abzüglich eines Verlustvortrags mindestens dem Unterschiedsbetrag nach Satz 1 entsprechen. Der Unterschiedsbetrag nach Satz 1 ist in jedem Geschäftsjahr im Anhang oder unter der Bilanz darzustellen.

(5) A lower value in accordance with section 3 sent. 5 or 6 and section 4 may not be retained if the reasons for it no longer exist. A lower value of goodwill acquired for consideration shall be retained.

(6) In the case of provisions for retirement benefit obligations, the difference between the measurement of the provisions according to the corresponding average market interest rate from the past ten business years and the measurement of the provisions according to the corresponding average market interest rate from the past seven business years shall be determined in each business year. Profits may only be distributed if the freely available reserves remaining after the distribution plus any profit carried forward and minus any loss carried forward at least correspond to the difference according to sentence 1. The difference according to sentence 1 shall be presented in the notes or under the balance sheet in each business year.

§ 254 Bildung von Bewertungseinheiten

Werden Vermögensgegenstände, Schulden, schwebende Geschäfte oder mit hoher Wahrscheinlichkeit erwartete Transaktionen zum Ausgleich gegenläufiger Wertänderungen oder Zahlungsströme aus dem Eintritt vergleichbarer Risiken mit Finanzinstrumenten zusammengefasst (Bewertungseinheit), sind § 249 Abs. 1, § 252 Abs. 1 Nr. 3 und 4, § 253 Abs. 1 Satz 1 und § 256a in dem Umfang und für den Zeitraum nicht anzuwenden, in dem die gegenläufigen Wertänderungen oder Zahlungsströme sich ausgleichen. Als Finanzinstrumente im Sinn des Satzes 1 gelten auch Termingeschäfte über den Erwerb oder die Veräußerung von Waren.

§ 254 Creation of measurement units

If assets, liabilities, pending transactions or transactions expected with a high degree of probability are combined with financial instruments to offset opposing changes in value or cash flows from the occurrence of comparable risks (measurement unit), § 249 sect. 1, § 252 sect. 1 nos. 3 and 4, § 253 sect. 1 sent. 1 and § 256a shall not apply to the extent and for the period in which the opposing changes in value or cash flows offset each other. Forward transactions on the purchase or sale of goods shall also be deemed to be financial instruments within the meaning of sentence 1.

(continued)

§ 255 Bewertungsmaßstäbe	§ 255 Measurement standards
(1) Anschaffungskosten sind die Aufwendungen, die geleistet werden, um einen Vermögensgegenstand zu erwerben und ihn in einen betriebsbereiten Zustand zu versetzen, soweit sie dem Vermögensgegenstand einzeln zugeordnet werden können. Zu den Anschaffungskosten gehören auch die Nebenkosten sowie die nachträglichen Anschaffungskosten. Anschaffungspreisminderungen, die dem Vermögensgegenstand einzeln zugeordnet werden können, sind abzusetzen.	(1) Acquisition costs are the expenses incurred to acquire an asset and to bring it to a condition ready for operation, insofar as they can be allocated individually to the asset. Acquisition costs also include incidental costs and subsequent acquisition costs. Reductions in the acquisition price that can be individually allocated to the asset are to be deducted.
(2) Herstellungskosten sind die Aufwendungen, die durch den Verbrauch von Gütern und die Inanspruchnahme von Diensten für die Herstellung eines Vermögensgegenstands, seine Erweiterung oder für eine über seinen ursprünglichen Zustand hinausgehende wesentliche Verbesserung entstehen. Dazu gehören die Materialkosten, die Fertigungskosten und die Sonderkosten der Fertigung sowie angemessene Teile der Materialgemeinkosten, der Fertigungsgemeinkosten und des Werteverzehrs des Anlagevermögens, soweit dieser durch die Fertigung veranlasst ist. Bei der Berechnung der Herstellungskosten dürfen angemessene Teile der Kosten der allgemeinen Verwaltung sowie angemessene Aufwendungen für soziale Einrichtungen des Betriebs, für freiwillige soziale Leistungen und für die betriebliche Altersversorgung einbezogen werden, soweit diese auf den Zeitraum der Herstellung entfallen. Forschungs- und Vertriebskosten dürfen nicht einbezogen werden.	(2) Production costs are the expenses incurred through the consumption of goods and the use of services for the production of an asset, its expansion or for a significant improvement beyond its original condition. This includes the material costs, the production costs and the special costs of production as well as appropriate parts of the material overheads, the production overheads and the consumption of non-current assets, insofar as this is caused by production. When calculating the production costs, reasonable parts of the costs of general administration as well as reasonable expenses for social facilities of the enterprise, for voluntary social benefits and for the company pension scheme may be included, insofar as these are attributable to the period of production. Research and distribution costs may not be included.

(continued)

(2a) Herstellungskosten eines selbst geschaffenen immateriellen Vermögensgegenstands des Anlagevermögens sind die bei dessen Entwicklung anfallenden Aufwendungen nach Absatz 2. Entwicklung ist die Anwendung von Forschungsergebnissen oder von anderem Wissen für die Neuentwicklung von Gütern oder Verfahren oder die Weiterentwicklung von Gütern oder Verfahren mittels wesentlicher Änderungen. Forschung ist die eigenständige und planmäßige Suche nach neuen wissenschaftlichen oder technischen Erkenntnissen oder Erfahrungen allgemeiner Art, über deren technische Verwertbarkeit und wirtschaftliche Erfolgsaussichten grundsätzlich keine Aussagen gemacht werden können. Können Forschung und Entwicklung nicht verlässlich voneinander unterschieden werden, ist eine Aktivierung ausgeschlossen.	(2a) Production costs of an internally generated intangible non-current asset are the expenses incurred in its development in accordance with section 2. Development is the application of research results or other knowledge for the new development of goods or processes or the further development of goods or processes by means of substantial modifications. Research is the independent and planned search for new scientific or technical knowledge or experience of a general nature, about whose technical usability and economic prospects generally no statements can be made. If research and development cannot be reliably distinguished from each other, recognition is prohibited.
(3) Zinsen für Fremdkapital gehören nicht zu den Herstellungskosten. Zinsen für Fremdkapital, das zur Finanzierung der Herstellung eines Vermögensgegenstands verwendet wird, dürfen angesetzt werden, soweit sie auf den Zeitraum der Herstellung entfallen; in diesem Falle gelten sie als Herstellungskosten des Vermögensgegenstands.	(3) Interest on borrowed capital is not included in production costs. Interest on borrowed capital used to finance the production of an asset may be recognized to the extent that it relates to the period of production; in this case, it is deemed to be the production cost of the asset.
(4) Der beizulegende Zeitwert entspricht dem Marktpreis. Soweit kein aktiver Markt besteht, anhand dessen sich der Marktpreis ermitteln lässt, ist der beizulegende Zeitwert mit Hilfe allgemein anerkannter Bewertungsmethoden zu bestimmen. Lässt sich der beizulegende Zeitwert weder nach Satz 1 noch nach Satz 2 ermitteln, sind die Anschaffungs- oder Herstellungskosten gemäß § 253 Abs. 4 fortzuführen. Der zuletzt nach Satz 1 oder 2 ermittelte beizulegende Zeitwert gilt als Anschaffungs- oder Herstellungskosten im Sinn des Satzes 3.	(4) The fair value corresponds to the market price. If there is no active market from which the market price can be determined, the fair value is determined using generally accepted valuation methods. If the fair value cannot be determined either in accordance with sentence 1 or sentence 2, the acquisition or production costs shall be carried forward in accordance with § 253 sect. 4. The most recently determined fair value according to sentence 1 or 2 shall be deemed to be acquisition or production costs within the meaning of sentence 3.

(continued)

§ 256 Bewertungsvereinfachungsverfahren Soweit es den Grundsätzen ordnungsmäßiger Buchführung entspricht, kann für den Wertansatz gleichartiger Vermögensgegenstände des Vorratsvermögens unterstellt werden, daß die zuerst oder daß die zuletzt angeschafften oder hergestellten Vermögensgegenstände zuerst verbraucht oder veräußert worden sind. § 240 Abs. 3 und 4 ist auch auf den Jahresabschluß anwendbar.	**§ 256 Measurement simplification procedures** Insofar as it is in accordance with the generally accepted accounting principles, it may be assumed for the measurement of similar assets of the inventory that the assets acquired or produced first or last were consumed or sold first. § 240 sect. 3 and 4 shall also apply to the financial statements.
§ 256a Währungsumrechnung Auf fremde Währung lautende Vermögensgegenstände und Verbindlichkeiten sind zum Devisenkassamittelkurs am Abschlussstichtag umzurechnen. Bei einer Restlaufzeit von einem Jahr oder weniger sind § 253 Abs. 1 Satz 1 und § 252 Abs. 1 Nr. 4 Halbsatz 2 nicht anzuwenden.	**§ 256a Currency conversion** Assets and liabilities denominated in foreign currencies shall be translated at the average spot exchange rate on the balance sheet date. In the case of a remaining term of one year or less, § 253 sect. 1 sent. 1 and § 252 sect. 1 no. 4 half-sent. 2 are not applicable.
Dritter Unterabschnitt Aufbewahrung und Vorlage	**Third subsection Retention and presentation**
§ 257 Aufbewahrung von Unterlagen; Aufbewahrungsfristen (1) Jeder Kaufmann ist verpflichtet, die folgenden Unterlagen geordnet aufzubewahren: 1. Handelsbücher, Inventare, Eröffnungsbilanzen, Jahresabschlüsse, Einzelabschlüsse nach § 325 Abs. 2a, Lageberichte, Konzernabschlüsse, Konzernlageberichte sowie die zu ihrem Verständnis erforderlichen Arbeitsanweisungen und sonstigen Organisationsunterlagen, 2. die empfangenen Handelsbriefe, 3. Wiedergaben der abgesandten Handelsbriefe, 4. Belege für Buchungen in den von ihm nach § 238 Abs. 1 zu führenden Büchern (Buchungsbelege). (2) Handelsbriefe sind nur Schriftstücke, die ein Handelsgeschäft betreffen.	**§ 257 Retention of documents; retention periods** (1) Every businessman is obliged to keep the following documents in an orderly manner: 1. Commercial books, inventories, opening balance sheets, financial statements, individual financial statements pursuant to § 325 sect. 2a, management reports, consolidated financial statements, group management reports as well as the work instructions and other organizational documents required for their understanding, 2. The commercial letters received, 3. Reproductions of the commercial letters sent, 4. Receipts for entries in the books to be kept by him in accordance with § 238 sect. 1 (vouchers). (2) Commercial letters are only documents that concern a commercial transaction.

(continued)

(3) Mit Ausnahme der Eröffnungsbilanzen und Abschlüsse können die in Absatz 1 aufgeführten Unterlagen auch als Wiedergabe auf einem Bildträger oder auf anderen Datenträgern aufbewahrt werden, wenn dies den Grundsätzen ordnungsmäßiger Buchführung entspricht und sichergestellt ist, daß die Wiedergabe oder die Daten

1. mit den empfangenen Handelsbriefen und den Buchungsbelegen bildlich und mit den anderen Unterlagen inhaltlich übereinstimmen, wenn sie lesbar gemacht werden,

2. während der Dauer der Aufbewahrungsfrist verfügbar sind und jederzeit innerhalb angemessener Frist lesbar gemacht werden können.

Sind Unterlagen auf Grund des § 239 Abs. 4 Satz 1 auf Datenträgern hergestellt worden, können statt des Datenträgers die Daten auch ausgedruckt aufbewahrt werden; die ausgedruckten Unterlagen können auch nach Satz 1 aufbewahrt werden.

(4) Die in Absatz 1 Nr. 1 und 4 aufgeführten Unterlagen sind zehn Jahre, die sonstigen in Absatz 1 aufgeführten Unterlagen sechs Jahre aufzubewahren.

(5) Die Aufbewahrungsfrist beginnt mit dem Schluß des Kalenderjahrs, in dem die letzte Eintragung in das Handelsbuch gemacht, das Inventar aufgestellt, die Eröffnungsbilanz oder der Jahresabschluß festgestellt, der Einzelabschluss nach § 325 Abs. 2a oder der Konzernabschluß aufgestellt, der Handelsbrief empfangen oder abgesandt worden oder der Buchungsbeleg entstanden ist.

(3) With the exception of the opening balance sheets and financial statements, the documents listed in section 1 may also be kept as a reproduction on an image carrier or on other data carriers if this complies with generally accepted accounting principles and it is ensured that the reproduction or the data

1. correspond visually with the commercial letters received and the vouchers and with the other documents in terms of content if they are made readable,

2. are available for the duration of the retention period and can be made readable at any time within a reasonable period of time.

If documents have been produced on data carriers on the basis of § 239 sect. 4 sent. 1, the data may also be kept in printed form instead of the data carrier; the printed documents may also be kept in accordance with sentence 1.

(4) The documents listed in section 1 nos. 1 and 4 shall be kept for ten years, the other documents listed in section 1 for six years.

(5) The retention period shall begin at the end of the calendar year in which the last entry was made in the commercial book, the inventory was prepared, the opening balance sheet or the financial statements were adopted, the individual financial statements in accordance with § 325 sect. 2a or the consolidated financial statements were prepared, the commercial letter was received or sent or the accounting voucher was created.

(continued)

§ 258 Vorlegung im Rechtsstreit

(1) Im Laufe eines Rechtsstreits kann das Gericht auf Antrag oder von Amts wegen die Vorlegung der Handelsbücher einer Partei anordnen.

(2) Die Vorschriften der Zivilprozeßordnung über die Verpflichtung des Prozeßgegners zur Vorlegung von Urkunden bleiben unberührt.

§ 258 Presentation in legal proceedings

(1) In the course of legal proceedings, the court may, on application or of its own motion, order the presentation of a party's commercial books.

(2) The provisions of the Code of Civil Procedure (Zivilprozeßordnung) on the obligation of the opposing party to produce documents shall remain unaffected.

§ 259 Auszug bei Vorlegung im Rechtsstreit

Werden in einem Rechtsstreit Handelsbücher vorgelegt, so ist von ihrem Inhalt, soweit er den Streitpunkt betrifft, unter Zuziehung der Parteien Einsicht zu nehmen und geeignetenfalls ein Auszug zu fertigen. Der übrige Inhalt der Bücher ist dem Gericht insoweit offenzulegen, als es zur Prüfung ihrer ordnungsmäßigen Führung notwendig ist.

§ 259 Extract on presentation in legal proceedings

If commercial books are presented in the course of legal proceedings, their contents shall be inspected in consultation with the parties insofar as they relate to the matter in dispute and, if appropriate, an extract shall be prepared. The remaining contents of the books shall be disclosed to the court to the extent necessary to examine their proper keeping.

§ 260 Vorlegung bei Auseinandersetzungen

Bei Vermögensauseinandersetzungen, insbesondere in Erbschafts-, Gütergemeinschafts- und Gesellschaftsteilungssachen, kann das Gericht die Vorlegung der Handelsbücher zur Kenntnisnahme von ihrem ganzen Inhalt anordnen.

§ 260 Presentation in case of distributions

In the case of asset distributions, in particular in cases of inheritance, joint property and division of partnerships, the court may order the presentation of the commercial books for the purpose of information about their entire contents.

§ 261 Vorlegung von Unterlagen auf Bild- oder Datenträgern

Wer aufzubewahrende Unterlagen nur in der Form einer Wiedergabe auf einem Bildträger oder auf anderen Datenträgern vorlegen kann, ist verpflichtet, auf seine Kosten diejenigen Hilfsmittel zur Verfügung zu stellen, die erforderlich sind, um die Unterlagen lesbar zu machen; soweit erforderlich, hat er die Unterlagen auf seine Kosten auszudrucken oder ohne Hilfsmittel lesbare Reproduktionen beizubringen.

§ 261 Presentation of documents on image or data carriers

Any person who can present documents to be kept only in the form of a reproduction on an image carrier or on other data carriers shall be obliged to provide at his own expense such aids as are necessary to make the documents readable; to the extent necessary, he shall print out the documents at his own expense or provide readable reproductions without aids.

(continued)

Vierter Unterabschnitt Landesrecht	Fourth subsection State law
§ 262 (weggefallen)	§ 262 (omitted)
§ 263 Vorbehalt landesrechtlicher Vorschriften Unberührt bleiben bei Unternehmen ohne eigene Rechtspersönlichkeit einer Gemeinde, eines Gemeindeverbands oder eines Zweckverbands landesrechtliche Vorschriften, die von den Vorschriften dieses Abschnitts abweichen.	§ 263 Reservation of state law regulations State law regulations that deviate from the regulations of this section shall remain unaffected in the case of enterprises without legal personality of a municipality, a municipality association or a special-purpose association.
Zweiter Abschnitt Ergänzende Vorschriften für Kapitalgesellschaften (Aktiengesellschaften, Kommanditgesellschaften auf Aktien und Gesellschaften mit beschränkter Haftung) sowie bestimmte Personenhandelsgesellschaften	Section Two Supplementary regulations for corporations (stock companies, partnerships limited by shares and limited liability companies) and certain commercial partnerships
Erster Unterabschnitt Jahresabschluß der Kapitalgesellschaft und Lagebericht	First subsection Financial statements of the corporation and management report
Erster Titel Allgemeine Vorschriften	First title General regulations
§ 264 Pflicht zur Aufstellung; Befreiung (1) Die gesetzlichen Vertreter einer Kapitalgesellschaft haben den Jahresabschluß (§ 242) um einen Anhang zu erweitern, der mit der Bilanz und der Gewinn- und Verlustrechnung eine Einheit bildet, sowie einen Lagebericht aufzustellen. Die gesetzlichen Vertreter einer kapitalmarktorientierten Kapitalgesellschaft, die nicht zur Aufstellung eines Konzernabschlusses verpflichtet ist, haben den Jahresabschluss um eine Kapitalflussrechnung und einen Eigenkapitalspiegel zu erweitern, die mit der Bilanz, Gewinn- und Verlustrechnung und dem Anhang eine Einheit bilden; sie können den Jahresabschluss um eine Segmentberichterstattung erweitern. Der Jahresabschluß und der Lagebericht sind von den gesetzlichen Vertretern in den ersten drei Monaten des Geschäftsjahrs für das vergangene Geschäftsjahr aufzustellen. Kleine	Section 264 Duty of preparation; exemption (1) The legal representatives of a corporation shall supplement the financial statements (§ 242) with notes, which form a unit with the balance sheet and the income statement, and shall prepare a management report. The legal representatives of a capital-market-oriented corporation that is not required to prepare consolidated financial statements shall supplement the financial statements with a cash flow statement and a statement of changes in equity, which form a unit with the balance sheet, income statement and the notes; they can supplement the financial statement with a segment reporting. The financial statements and the management report shall be prepared by the legal representatives in the first three months of the business year for the previous business year. Small corporations (§ 267 sect. 1) do not need to prepare the management report; they

(continued)

Kapitalgesellschaften (§ 267 Abs. 1) brauchen den Lagebericht nicht aufzustellen; sie dürfen den Jahresabschluß auch später aufstellen, wenn dies einem ordnungsgemäßen Geschäftsgang entspricht, jedoch innerhalb der ersten sechs Monate des Geschäftsjahres. Kleinstkapitalgesellschaften (§ 267a) brauchen den Jahresabschluss nicht um einen Anhang zu erweitern, wenn sie
1. die in § 268 Absatz 7 genannten Angaben,
2. die in § 285 Nummer 9 Buchstabe c genannten Angaben und
3. im Falle einer Aktiengesellschaft die in § 160 Absatz 3 Satz 2 des Aktiengesetzes genannten Angaben unter der Bilanz angeben.

(1a) In dem Jahresabschluss sind die Firma, der Sitz, das Registergericht und die Nummer, unter der die Gesellschaft in das Handelsregister eingetragen ist, anzugeben. Befindet sich die Gesellschaft in Liquidation oder Abwicklung, ist auch diese Tatsache anzugeben.

(2) Der Jahresabschluß der Kapitalgesellschaft hat unter Beachtung der Grundsätze ordnungsmäßiger Buchführung ein den tatsächlichen Verhältnissen entsprechendes Bild der Vermögens-, Finanz- und Ertragslage der Kapitalgesellschaft zu vermitteln. Führen besondere Umstände dazu, daß der Jahresabschluß ein den tatsächlichen Verhältnissen entsprechendes Bild im Sinne des Satzes 1 nicht vermittelt, so sind im Anhang zusätzliche Angaben zu machen. Die Mitglieder

may also prepare the financial statements later if this is in the proper course of business, but within the first six months of the business year. Very small corporations (§ 267a) do not need to supplement the financial statements with notes, if they report

1. the information referred to in § 268 sect. 7),
2. the information referred to in § 285 no. 9 lit. c and
3. in the case of a stock company the information specified in § 160 sect. 3 sent. 2 of the Stock Company Act (Aktiengesetz) under the balance sheet.

(1a) The financial statements shall state the company name, the registered office, the commercial register and the number under which the company is entered in the commercial register. If the company is in liquidation or being wound up, this fact shall also be stated.

(2) The financial statements of the corporation shall give a true and fair view of the asset, finance and income position of the corporation in accordance with generally accepted accounting principles. If special circumstances result in the financial statements not giving a true and fair view within the meaning of sentence 1, additional information shall be given in the notes. The members of the body authorized to represent a corporation which issues securities (§ 2 sect. 1 of the Securities

(continued)

des vertretungsberechtigten Organs einer Kapitalgesellschaft, die als Inlandsemittent (§ 2 Absatz 14 des Wertpapierhandelsgesetzes) Wertpapiere (§ 2 Absatz 1 des Wertpapierhandelsgesetzes) begibt und keine Kapitalgesellschaft im Sinne des § 327a ist, haben in einer dem Jahresabschluss beizufügenden schriftlichen Erklärung zu versichern, dass der Jahresabschluss nach bestem Wissen ein den tatsächlichen Verhältnissen entsprechendes Bild im Sinne des Satzes 1 vermittelt oder der Anhang Angaben nach Satz 2 enthält. Macht eine Kleinstkapitalgesellschaft von der Erleichterung nach Absatz 1 Satz 5 Gebrauch, sind nach Satz 2 erforderliche zusätzliche Angaben unter der Bilanz zu machen. Es wird vermutet, dass ein unter Berücksichtigung der Erleichterungen für Kleinstkapitalgesellschaften aufgestellter Jahresabschluss den Erfordernissen des Satzes 1 entspricht.

(3) Eine Kapitalgesellschaft, die nicht im Sinne des § 264d kapitalmarktorientiert ist und als Tochterunternehmen in den Konzernabschluss eines Mutterunternehmens mit Sitz in einem Mitgliedstaat der Europäischen Union oder einem anderen Vertragsstaat des Abkommens über den Europäischen Wirtschaftsraum einbezogen ist, braucht die Vorschriften dieses Unterabschnitts und des Dritten und Vierten Unterabschnitts dieses Abschnitts nicht anzuwenden, wenn alle folgenden Voraussetzungen erfüllt sind:

1. alle Gesellschafter des Tochterunternehmens haben der Befreiung für das jeweilige Geschäftsjahr zugestimmt;

2. das Mutterunternehmen hat sich bereit erklärt, für die von dem Tochterunternehmen bis zum Abschlussstichtag eingegangenen Verpflichtungen im folgenden Geschäftsjahr einzustehen;

Trading Act (Wertpapierhandelsgesetz)) as a domestic issuer (§ 2 sect. 14 of the Securities Trading Act) and which is not a corporation within the meaning of § 327a shall certify in a written statement to be attached to the financial statements that, to the best of their knowledge, the financial statements give a true and fair view within the meaning of sentence 1 or that the notes contain information in accordance with sentence 2. If a very small corporation makes use of the simplification pursuant to section 1 sentence 5, additional disclosures required pursuant to sentence 2 shall be made under the balance sheet. It shall be presumed that financial statements prepared taking into account the simplifications for very small corporations comply with the requirements of sentence 1.

(3) A corporation that is not capital-market oriented within the meaning of § 264d and is included as a subsidiary in the consolidated financial statements of a parent company with its registered office in a member state of the European Union or another contracting state to the Agreement on the European Economic Area need not apply the regulations of this subsection and the third and fourth subsections of this section if all of the following conditions are met:

1. all shareholders of the subsidiary have agreed to the exemption for the respective business year;

2. the parent company has agreed to guarantee the obligations entered into by the subsidiary up to the balance sheet date in the following business year;

(continued)

3. der Konzernabschluss und der Konzernlagebericht des Mutterunternehmens sind nach den Rechtsvorschriften des Staates, in dem das Mutterunternehmen seinen Sitz hat, und im Einklang mit folgenden Richtlinien aufgestellt und geprüft worden:
   a) Richtlinie 2013/34/EU des Europäischen Parlaments und des Rates vom 26. Juni 2013 über den Jahresabschluss, den konsolidierten Abschluss und damit verbundene Berichte von Unternehmen bestimmter Rechtsformen und zur Änderung der Richtlinie 2006/43/EG des Europäischen Parlaments und des Rates und zur Aufhebung der Richtlinien 78/660/EWG und 83/349/EWG des Rates (ABl. L 182 vom 29.6.2013, S. 19), die zuletzt durch die Richtlinie 2014/102/EU (ABl. L 334 vom 21.11.2014, S. 86) geändert worden ist,
   b) Richtlinie 2006/43/EG des Europäischen Parlaments und des Rates vom 17. Mai 2006 über Abschlussprüfungen von Jahresabschlüssen und konsolidierten Abschlüssen, zur Änderung der Richtlinien 78/660/EWG und 83/349/EWG des Rates und zur Aufhebung der Richtlinie 84/253/EWG des Rates (ABl. L 157 vom 9.6.2006, S. 87), die durch die Richtlinie 2013/34/EU (ABl. L 182 vom 29.6.2013, S. 19) geändert worden ist;
4. die Befreiung des Tochterunternehmens ist im Anhang des Konzernabschlusses des Mutterunternehmens angegeben und
5. für das Tochterunternehmen sind nach § 325 Absatz 1 bis 1b offengelegt worden:
   a) der Beschluss nach Nummer 1,
   b) die Erklärung nach Nummer 2,
   c) der Konzernabschluss,
   d) der Konzernlagebericht und
   e) der Bestätigungsvermerk zum Konzernabschluss und Konzernlagebericht des Mutterunternehmens nach Nummer 3.

3. the consolidated financial statements and the group management report of the parent company have been prepared and audited in accordance with the legal requirements of the country in which the parent company has its registered office and in compliance with the following guidelines:
   a) Directive 2013/34/EU of the European Parliament and of the Council of 26 June 2013 on the financial statements, consolidated financial statements and related reports of certain types of companies, amending Directive 2006/43/EC of the European Parliament and of the Council and repealing Council Directives 78/660/EEC and 83/349/EEC (OJ L 182, 29.6.2013, p. 19), as last amended by Directive 2014/102/EU (OJ L 334, 21.11.2014, p. 86),
   b) Directive 2006/43/EC of the European Parliament and of the Council of 17 May 2006 on statutory audits of financial statements and consolidated financial statements, amending Council Directives 78/660/EEC and 83/349/EEC and repealing Council Directive 84/253/EEC (OJ L 157, 9.6.2006, p. 87), as amended by Directive 2013/34/EU (OJ L 182, 29.6.2013, p. 19);
4. the exemption of the subsidiary is disclosed in the notes to the consolidated financial statements of the parent and
5. for the subsidiary have been disclosed in accordance with § 325 sect. 1 to 1b:
   a) the decision referred to in number 1,
   b) the declaration referred to in number 2,
   c) the consolidated financial statements,
   d) the group management report and
   e) the auditor's report on the consolidated financial statements and the group management report of the parent company in accordance with number 3.

(continued)

Hat bereits das Mutterunternehmen einzelne oder alle der in Satz 1 Nummer 5 bezeichneten Unterlagen offengelegt, braucht das Tochterunternehmen die betreffenden Unterlagen nicht erneut offenzulegen, wenn sie im Bundesanzeiger unter dem Tochterunternehmen auffindbar sind; § 326 Absatz 2 ist auf diese Offenlegung nicht anzuwenden. Satz 2 gilt nur dann, wenn das Mutterunternehmen die betreffende Unterlage in deutscher oder in englischer Sprache offengelegt hat oder das Tochterunternehmen zusätzlich eine beglaubigte Übersetzung dieser Unterlage in deutscher Sprache nach § 325 Absatz 1 bis 1b offenlegt.	If the parent company has already disclosed some or all of the documents referred to in sentence 1 number 5, the subsidiary shall not be required to disclose the relevant documents again if they can be found in the Federal Gazette (Bundesanzeiger) under the subsidiary; § 326 sect. 2 shall apply to this disclosure. Sentence 2 shall only apply if the parent company has disclosed the relevant document in German or in English or the subsidiary additionally discloses a certified translation of this document in German pursuant to § 325 sect. 1 to 1b.
(4) Absatz 3 ist nicht anzuwenden, wenn eine Kapitalgesellschaft das Tochterunternehmen eines Mutterunternehmens ist, das einen Konzernabschluss nach den Vorschriften des Publizitätsgesetzes aufgestellt hat, und wenn in diesem Konzernabschluss von dem Wahlrecht des § 13 Absatz 3 Satz 1 des Publizitätsgesetzes Gebrauch gemacht worden ist; § 314 Absatz 3 bleibt unberührt.	(4) Section 3 shall not apply if a corporation is the subsidiary of a parent company that has prepared consolidated financial statements in accordance with the regulations of the Disclosure Act (Publizitätsgesetz) and if the option under § 13 sect. 3 sent. 1 of the Disclosure Act has been exercised in those consolidated financial statements; § 314 sect. 3 shall remain unaffected.

§ 264a Anwendung auf bestimmte offene Handelsgesellschaften und Kommanditgesellschaften	**§ 264a Application to certain general partnerships and limited partnerships**
(1) Die Vorschriften des Ersten bis Fünften Unterabschnitts des Zweiten Abschnitts sind auch anzuwenden auf offene Handelsgesellschaften und Kommanditgesellschaften, bei denen nicht wenigstens ein persönlich haftender Gesellschafter	(1) The regulations of the first to fifth subsections of the second section shall also apply to general partnerships and limited partnerships in which there is not at least one general partner
1. eine natürliche Person oder	1. a natural person or
2. eine offene Handelsgesellschaft, Kommanditgesellschaft oder andere Personengesellschaft mit einer natürlichen Person als persönlich haftendem Gesellschafter	2. a general partnership, limited partnership or other partnership with a natural person as general partner
ist oder sich die Verbindung von Gesellschaften in dieser Art fortsetzt.	or the combination of companies continues in this way.

(continued)

(2) In den Vorschriften dieses Abschnitts gelten als gesetzliche Vertreter einer offenen Handelsgesellschaft und Kommanditgesellschaft nach Absatz 1 die Mitglieder des vertretungsberechtigten Organs der vertretungsberechtigten Gesellschaften.	(2) For the purposes of this section, the legal representatives of a general partnership and limited partnership under section 1 shall be the members of the representative body of the companies entitled to represent them.

§ 264b Befreiung der offenen Handelsgesellschaften und Kommanditgesellschaften im Sinne des § 264a von der Anwendung der Vorschriften dieses Abschnitts

§ 264b Exemption of general partnerships and limited partnerships within the meaning of § 264a from the application of the regulations of this section

Eine Personenhandelsgesellschaft im Sinne des § 264a Absatz 1, die nicht im Sinne des § 264d kapitalmarktorientiert ist, ist von der Verpflichtung befreit, einen Jahresabschluss und einen Lagebericht nach den Vorschriften dieses Abschnitts aufzustellen, prüfen zu lassen und offenzulegen, wenn alle folgenden Voraussetzungen erfüllt sind:	A commercial partnership within the meaning of § 264a sect. 1 that is not capital-market oriented within the meaning of § 264d is exempt from the obligation to prepare, have audited and disclose financial statements and a management report in accordance with the provisions of this section if all of the following requirements are met:

1. die betreffende Gesellschaft ist einbezogen in den Konzernabschluss und in den Konzernlagebericht
   a) eines persönlich haftenden Gesellschafters der betreffenden Gesellschaft oder
   b) eines Mutterunternehmens mit Sitz in einem Mitgliedstaat der Europäischen Union oder einem anderen Vertragsstaat des Abkommens über den Europäischen Wirtschaftsraum, wenn in diesen Konzernabschluss eine größere Gesamtheit von Unternehmen einbezogen ist;
2. die in § 264 Absatz 3 Satz 1 Nummer 3 genannte Voraussetzung ist erfüllt;
3. die Befreiung der Personenhandelsgesellschaft ist im Anhang des Konzernabschlusses angegeben und

1. the company concerned is included in the consolidated financial statements and in the group management report
   a) of a general partner of the company concerned, or
   b) of a parent company with its registered office in a member state of the European Union or another contracting state to the Agreement on the European Economic Area, if a larger group of companies is included in these consolidated financial statements;
2. the requirement specified in § 264 sect. 1 no. 3 is met;
3. the exemption of the commercial partnership is stated in the notes to the consolidated financial statements and

(continued)

4. für die Personenhandelsgesellschaft sind der Konzernabschluss, der Konzernlagebericht und der Bestätigungsvermerk nach § 325 Absatz 1 bis 1b offengelegt worden; § 264 Absatz 3 Satz 2 und 3 ist entsprechend anzuwenden.	4. for the commercial partnership, the consolidated financial statements, the group management report and the auditor's report have been disclosed in accordance with § 325 sect. 1 to 1b; § 264 sect. 3 sent. 2 and 3 shall apply accordingly.

§ 264c Besondere Bestimmungen für offene Handelsgesellschaften und Kommanditgesellschaften im Sinne des § 264a	**§ 264c Special regulations for general partnerships and limited partnerships within the meaning of § 264a**
(1) Ausleihungen, Forderungen und Verbindlichkeiten gegenüber Gesellschaftern sind in der Regel als solche jeweils gesondert auszuweisen oder im Anhang anzugeben. Werden sie unter anderen Posten ausgewiesen, so muss diese Eigenschaft vermerkt werden.	(1) As a rule, loans, receivables from and liabilities to shareholders must be shown separately as such or disclosed in the notes. If they are shown under other items, this characteristic must be noted.
(2) § 266 Abs. 3 Buchstabe A ist mit der Maßgabe anzuwenden, dass als Eigenkapital die folgenden Posten gesondert auszuweisen sind:	(2) § 266 sect. 3 lit. A shall apply provided that the following items shall be shown separately as equity:
I. Kapitalanteile	I. Capital shares
II. Rücklagen	II. Reserves
III. Gewinnvortrag/Verlustvortrag	III. Profit/loss carried forward
IV. Jahresüberschuss/Jahresfehlbetrag.	IV. Net profit/loss for the year.
Anstelle des Postens "Gezeichnetes Kapital" sind die Kapitalanteile der persönlich haftenden Gesellschafter auszuweisen; sie dürfen auch zusammengefasst ausgewiesen werden. Der auf den Kapitalanteil eines persönlich haftenden Gesellschafters für das Geschäftsjahr entfallende Verlust ist von dem Kapitalanteil abzuschreiben. Soweit der Verlust den Kapitalanteil übersteigt, ist er auf der Aktivseite unter der Bezeichnung "Einzahlungsverpflichtungen persönlich haftender Gesellschafter" unter den	Instead of the item "subscribed capital", the capital shares of the personally liable partners are to be reported; they may also be reported together. The loss for the business year attributable to the capital share of a personally liable shareholder shall be written off from the capital share. Insofar as the loss exceeds the capital share, it shall be reported separately on the assets side under the designation "payment obligations of personally liable partners" within the receivables, insofar as a payment obligation exists. If there is no payment obligation, the

(continued)

Forderungen gesondert auszuweisen, soweit eine Zahlungsverpflichtung besteht. Besteht keine Zahlungsverpflichtung, so ist der Betrag als "Nicht durch Vermögenseinlagen gedeckter Verlustanteil persönlich haftender Gesellschafter" zu bezeichnen und gemäß § 268 Abs. 3 auszuweisen. Die Sätze 2 bis 5 sind auf die Einlagen von Kommanditisten entsprechend anzuwenden, wobei diese insgesamt gesondert gegenüber den Kapitalanteilen der persönlich haftenden Gesellschafter auszuweisen sind. Eine Forderung darf jedoch nur ausgewiesen werden, soweit eine Einzahlungsverpflichtung besteht; dasselbe gilt, wenn ein Kommanditist Gewinnanteile entnimmt, während sein Kapitalanteil durch Verlust unter den Betrag der geleisteten Einlage herabgemindert ist, oder soweit durch die Entnahme der Kapitalanteil unter den bezeichneten Betrag herabgemindert wird. Als Rücklagen sind nur solche Beträge auszuweisen, die auf Grund einer gesellschaftsrechtlichen Vereinbarung gebildet worden sind. Im Anhang ist der Betrag der im Handelsregister gemäß § 172 Abs. 1 eingetragenen Einlagen anzugeben, soweit diese nicht geleistet sind.

(3) Das sonstige Vermögen der Gesellschafter (Privatvermögen) darf nicht in die Bilanz und die auf das Privatvermögen entfallenden Aufwendungen und Erträge dürfen nicht in die Gewinn- und Verlustrechnung aufgenommen werden. In der Gewinn- und Verlustrechnung darf jedoch nach dem Posten "Jahresüberschuss/Jahresfehlbetrag" ein dem Steuersatz der Komplementärgesellschaft entsprechender Steueraufwand der Gesellschafter offen abgesetzt oder hinzugerechnet werden.

amount shall be designated as "share of losses of personally liable partners not covered by capital contributions" and reported in accordance with § 268 sect. 3. Sentences 2 to 5 shall be applied mutatis mutandis to the contributions of limited partners, whereby these shall be reported separately in total from the capital shares of the personally liable partners. A receivable may, however, only be reported insofar as there exists a payment obligation; the same shall apply if a limited partner withdraws shares in profits while his capital share is reduced by loss below the amount of the contribution made, or insofar as the withdrawal reduces the capital share below the amount specified. Only such amounts are to be reported as reserves which have been formed on the basis of an agreement under company law. In the notes, the amount of the contributions registered in the commercial register pursuant to § 172 sect. 1 shall be stated to the extent that they have not been paid in.

(3) The other assets of the partners (private assets) may not be included in the balance sheet and the expenses and income attributable to the private assets may not be included in the income statement. However, in the income statement after the item "net profit/loss for the year", a tax expense of the partners corresponding to the tax rate of the general partner company may be openly deducted or added.

(continued)

(4) Anteile an Komplementärgesellschaften sind in der Bilanz auf der Aktivseite unter den Posten A.III.1 oder A.III.3 auszuweisen. § 272 Abs. 4 ist mit der Maßgabe anzuwenden, dass für diese Anteile in Höhe des aktivierten Betrags nach dem Posten "Eigenkapital" ein Sonderposten unter der Bezeichnung "Ausgleichsposten für aktivierte eigene Anteile" zu bilden ist.	(4) Shares in general partner companies are reported in the balance sheet on the assets side within the items A.III.1 or A.III.3. § 272 sect. 4 is to be applied with the regulation that a special item is to be reported for these shares in the amount of the recognized amount after the item "equity" under the designation "adjustment item for recognized own shares".
(5) Macht die Gesellschaft von einem Wahlrecht nach § 266 Absatz 1 Satz 3 oder Satz 4 Gebrauch, richtet sich die Gliederung der verkürzten Bilanz nach der Ausübung dieses Wahlrechts. Die Ermittlung der Bilanzposten nach den vorstehenden Absätzen bleibt unberührt.	(5) If the company exercises an option pursuant to § 266 sect. 1 sent. 3 or sent. 4, the structure of the shortened balance sheet shall be based on the exercise of this option. The determination of the balance sheet items according to the preceding sections shall remain unaffected.

§ 264d Kapitalmarktorientierte Kapitalgesellschaft

Eine Kapitalgesellschaft ist kapitalmarktorientiert, wenn sie einen organisierten Markt im Sinn des § 2 Absatz 11 des Wertpapierhandelsgesetzes durch von ihr ausgegebene Wertpapiere im Sinn des § 2 Absatz 1 des Wertpapierhandelsgesetzes in Anspruch nimmt oder die Zulassung solcher Wertpapiere zum Handel an einem organisierten Markt beantragt hat.

§ 264d Capital-market-oriented corporation

A corporation is capital-market oriented if it makes use of an organized market within the meaning of § 2 sect. 11 of the Securities Trading Act (Wertpapierhandelsgesetz) through securities issued by it within the meaning of § 2 sect. 1 of the Securities Trading Act or has applied for the admission of such securities to trading in an organized market.

§ 265 Allgemeine Grundsätze für die Gliederung

(1) Die Form der Darstellung, insbesondere die Gliederung der aufeinanderfolgenden Bilanzen und Gewinn- und Verlustrechnungen, ist beizubehalten, soweit nicht in Ausnahmefällen wegen besonderer Umstände Abweichungen erforderlich sind. Die Abweichungen sind im Anhang anzugeben und zu begründen.

§ 265 General principles for the structure

(1) The form of presentation, in particular the structure of the successive balance sheets and income statements, shall be maintained unless deviations are necessary in exceptional cases due to special circumstances. The deviations shall be stated and justified in the notes.

(2) In der Bilanz sowie in der Gewinn- und Verlustrechnung ist zu jedem Posten der entsprechende Betrag des vorhergehenden Geschäftsjahrs anzugeben. Sind die Beträge nicht vergleichbar, so ist dies im Anhang anzugeben und zu erläutern. Wird der Vorjahresbetrag angepaßt, so ist auch dies im Anhang anzugeben und zu erläutern.

(2) In the balance sheet as well as in the income statement, the corresponding amount of the previous business year shall be stated for each item. If the amounts are not comparable, this shall be stated and explained in the notes. If the previous year's amount is restated, this shall also be stated and explained in the notes.

(continued)

(3) Fällt ein Vermögensgegenstand oder eine Schuld unter mehrere Posten der Bilanz, so ist die Mitzugehörigkeit zu anderen Posten bei dem Posten, unter dem der Ausweis erfolgt ist, zu vermerken oder im Anhang anzugeben, wenn dies zur Aufstellung eines klaren und übersichtlichen Jahresabschlusses erforderlich ist.

(3) Where an asset or liability is attributed to more than one item in the balance sheet, its attribution to other items shall be disclosed in the item under which it is stated or in the notes if necessary for the preparation of clear and transparent financial statements.

(4) Sind mehrere Geschäftszweige vorhanden und bedingt dies die Gliederung des Jahresabschlusses nach verschiedenen Gliederungsvorschriften, so ist der Jahresabschluß nach der für einen Geschäftszweig vorgeschriebenen Gliederung aufzustellen und nach der für die anderen Geschäftszweige vorgeschriebenen Gliederung zu ergänzen. Die Ergänzung ist im Anhang anzugeben und zu begründen.

(4) If there are several lines of business and this requires the financial statements to be structured according to different structuring rules, the financial statements shall be prepared according to the stucturing prescribed to one line of business and be supplemented in accordance with the structure prescribed for the other lines of business. The supplement shall be stated and justified in the notes.

(5) Eine weitere Untergliederung der Posten ist zulässig; dabei ist jedoch die vorgeschriebene Gliederung zu beachten. Neue Posten und Zwischensummen dürfen hinzugefügt werden, wenn ihr Inhalt nicht von einem vorgeschriebenen Posten gedeckt wird.

(5) A further subdivision of the items is permitted; however, the prescribed structure must be observed. New items and subtotals may be added if their content is not covered by a prescribed item.

(6) Gliederung und Bezeichnung der mit arabischen Zahlen versehenen Posten der Bilanz und der Gewinn- und Verlustrechnung sind zu ändern, wenn dies wegen Besonderheiten der Kapitalgesellschaft zur Aufstellung eines klaren und übersichtlichen Jahresabschlusses erforderlich ist.

(6) The structure and designation of the items of the balance sheet and the income statement marked with Arabic numerals shall be changed if this is necessary for the preparation of clear and transparent financial statements due to special features of the corporation.

(7) Die mit arabischen Zahlen versehenen Posten der Bilanz und der Gewinn- und Verlustrechnung können, wenn nicht besondere Formblätter vorgeschrieben sind, zusammengefaßt ausgewiesen werden, wenn
1. entsprechenden Bildes im Sinne des § 264 Abs. 2 nicht erheblich ist,

oder

(7) The items of the balance sheet and the income statement marked with Arabic numerals may, unless special forms are prescribed, be aggregated if
1. they contain an amount that is not material for the presentation of a true and fair view within the meaning of § 264 sect. 2,

or

(continued)

2. dadurch die Klarheit der Darstellung vergrößert wird; in diesem Falle müssen die zusammengefaßten sie einen Betrag enthalten, der für die Vermittlung eines den tatsächlichen Verhältnissen Posten jedoch im Anhang gesondert ausgewiesen werden.	2. the clarity of the presentation is thereby increased; in this case, however, the aggregated items must be reported separately in the notes.
(8) Ein Posten der Bilanz oder der Gewinn- und Verlustrechnung, der keinen Betrag ausweist, braucht nicht aufgeführt zu werden, es sei denn, daß im vorhergehenden Geschäftsjahr unter diesem Posten ein Betrag ausgewiesen wurde.	(8) An item in the balance sheet or income statement which does not show an amount need not be reported unless an amount was reported under that item in the preceding business year.

Zweiter Titel Bilanz	Second title Balance sheet

§ 266 Gliederung der Bilanz	**§ 266 Structure of the balance sheet**
(1) Die Bilanz ist in Kontoform aufzustellen. Dabei haben mittelgroße und große Kapitalgesellschaften (§ 267 Absatz 2 und 3) auf der Aktivseite die in Absatz 2 und auf der Passivseite die in Absatz 3 bezeichneten Posten gesondert und in der vorgeschriebenen Reihenfolge auszuweisen. Kleine Kapitalgesellschaften (§ 267 Abs. 1) brauchen nur eine verkürzte Bilanz aufzustellen, in die nur die in den Absätzen 2 und 3 mit Buchstaben und römischen Zahlen bezeichneten Posten gesondert und in der vorgeschriebenen Reihenfolge aufgenommen werden. Kleinstkapitalgesellschaften (§ 267a) brauchen nur eine verkürzte Bilanz aufzustellen, in die nur die in den Absätzen 2 und 3 mit Buchstaben bezeichneten Posten gesondert und in der vorgeschriebenen Reihenfolge aufgenommen werden.	(1) The balance sheet shall be prepared in account form. In doing so, medium-sized and large corporations (§ 267 sect. 2 and 3) shall report separately and in the prescribed order on the assets side the items designated in section 2 and on the liabilities side the items designated in section 3. Small corporations (§ 267 sect. 1) need only prepare a shortened balance sheet in which only the items designated by letters and Roman numerals in sections 2 and 3 are included separately and in the prescribed order. Very small corporations (§ 267a) need only prepare a shortened balance sheet in which only the items designated by letters in sections 2 and 3 are included separately and in the prescribed order.
(2) Aktivseite	(2) Assets side
A. Anlagevermögen:	A. Non-current assets:
I. Immaterielle Vermögensgegenstände:	I. Intangible assets:
1. Selbst geschaffene gewerbliche Schutzrechte und ähnliche Rechte und Werte;	1. Internally generated commercial property rights and similar rights and assets;
2. entgeltlich erworbene Konzessionen, gewerbliche Schutzrechte und ähnliche Rechte und Werte sowie Lizenzen an solchen Rechten und Werten;	2. Concessions, commercial property rights and similar rights and assets as well as licenses to such rights and assets, acquired against remuneration;
3. Geschäfts- oder Firmenwert;	3. Goodwill;
4. geleistete Anzahlungen;	4. Payments made in advance;

(continued)

II. Sachanlagen:	II. Tangible assets:
1. Grundstücke, grundstücksgleiche Rechte und Bauten einschließlich der Bauten auf fremden Grundstücken;	1. Land, rights similar to land and buildings, including buildings on third-party land;
2. technische Anlagen und Maschinen;	2. technical facilities and machines;
3. andere Anlagen, Betriebs- und Geschäftsausstattung;	3. other facilities and office equipment;
4. geleistete Anzahlungen und Anlagen im Bau;	4. payments made in advance and assets under construction;
III. Finanzanlagen:	III. inancial assets:
1. Anteile an verbundenen Unternehmen;	1. Shares in affiliated companies;
2. Ausleihungen an verbundene Unternehmen;	2. loans to affiliated companies;
3. Beteiligungen;	3. participations;
4. Ausleihungen an Unternehmen, mit denen ein Beteiligungsverhältnis besteht;	4. loans to companies in which a participation exists;
5. Wertpapiere des Anlagevermögens;	5. non-current securities;
6. sonstige Ausleihungen.	6. other loans.
B. Umlaufvermögen:	B. Current assets:
I. Vorräte:	I. Inventories:
1. Roh-, Hilfs- und Betriebsstoffe;	1. Raw materials and other materials;
2. unfertige Erzeugnisse, unfertige Leistungen;	2. unfinished goods; unfinished services;
3. fertige Erzeugnisse und Waren;	3. finished goods and merchandise;
4. geleistete Anzahlungen;	4. payments made in advance;
II. Forderungen und sonstige Vermögensgegenstände:	II. Receivables and other assets:
1. Forderungen aus Lieferungen und Leistungen;	1. Trade receivables;
2. Forderungen gegen verbundene Unternehmen;	2. receivables from affiliated companies;
3. Forderungen gegen Unternehmen, mit denen ein Beteiligungsverhältnis besteht;	3. receivables from companies in which a participation exists;
4. sonstige Vermögensgegenstände;	4. other assets;
III. Wertpapiere:	III. Securities:
1. Anteile an verbundenen Unternehmen;	1. Shares in affiliated companies;
2. sonstige Wertpapiere;	2. other securities;
IV. Kassenbestand, Bundesbankguthaben, Guthaben bei Kreditinstituten und Schecks.	IV. Cash on hand, Bundesbank balances, bank balances and checks.
C. Rechnungsabgrenzungsposten.	C. Deferred expenses.
D. Aktive latente Steuern.	D. Deferred tax assets.
E. Aktiver Unterschiedsbetrag aus der Vermögensverrechnung.	E. Asset surplus from netting.
(3) Passivseite	(3) Equity and liabilities side
A. Eigenkapital:	A. Equity:

(continued)

I. Gezeichnetes Kapital;	I. Subscribed capital;
II. Kapitalrücklage;	II. capital reserve;
III. Gewinnrücklagen:	III. revenue reserves:
1. gesetzliche Rücklage;	1. Legal reserve;
2. Rücklage für Anteile an einem herrschenden oder mehrheitlich beteiligten Unternehmen;	2. reserve for shares in a controlling entity or majority shareholder;
3. satzungsmäßige Rücklagen;	3. statutory reserves;
4. andere Gewinnrücklagen;	4. other revenue reserves;
IV. Gewinnvortrag/Verlustvortrag;	IV. profit/loss carry forward;
V. Jahresüberschuß/Jahresfehlbetrag.	V. net profit/loss of the year.
B. Rückstellungen:	B. Provisions:
1. Rückstellungen für Pensionen und ähnliche Verpflichtungen;	1. Provisions for pensions and similar obligations;
2. Steuerrückstellungen;	2. tax provisions;
3. sonstige Rückstellungen.	3. other provisions.
C. Verbindlichkeiten:	C. Debt:
1. Anleihen, davon konvertibel;	1. Bonds, thereof convertible;
2. Verbindlichkeiten gegenüber Kreditinstituten;	2. bank debt;
3. erhaltene Anzahlungen auf Bestellungen;	3. received advance payments on orders;
4. Verbindlichkeiten aus Lieferungen und Leistungen;	4. trade payables;
5. Verbindlichkeiten aus der Annahme gezogener Wechsel und der Ausstellung eigener Wechsel;	5. payables from the acceptance of bills of exchange drawn and the issuance of own bills of exchange;
6. Verbindlichkeiten gegenüber verbundenen Unternehmen;	6. payables to affiliated companies;
7. Verbindlichkeiten gegenüber Unternehmen, mit denen ein Beteiligungsverhältnis besteht;	7. payables to companies in which a participation exists;
8. sonstige Verbindlichkeiten, davon aus Steuern, davon im Rahmen der sozialen Sicherheit.	8. other payables, thereof tax payables, thereof from social security.
D. Rechnungsabgrenzungsposten.	D. Deferred income.
E. Passive latente Steuern.	E. Deferred tax liabilities.

§ 267 Umschreibung der Größenklassen	**§ 267 Circumscription of the size classes**
(1) Kleine Kapitalgesellschaften sind solche, die mindestens zwei der drei nachstehenden Merkmale nicht überschreiten:	(1) Small corporations are those that do not exceed at least two of the following three characteristics:
1. 6 000 000 Euro Bilanzsumme.	1. €6,000,000 balance sheet total.
2. 12 000 000 Euro Umsatzerlöse in den zwölf Monaten vor dem Abschlußstichtag.	2. €12,000,000 sales revenue in the twelve months preceding the balance sheet date.
3. Im Jahresdurchschnitt fünfzig Arbeitnehmer.	3. Fifty employees on average per year.

(continued)

---

(2) Mittelgroße Kapitalgesellschaften sind solche, die mindestens zwei der drei in Absatz 1 bezeichneten Merkmale überschreiten und jeweils mindestens zwei der drei nachstehenden Merkmale nicht überschreiten:
1. 20 000 000 Euro Bilanzsumme.
2. 40 000 000 Euro Umsatzerlöse in den zwölf Monaten vor dem Abschlußstichtag.
3. Im Jahresdurchschnitt zweihundertfünfzig Arbeitnehmer.

(3) Große Kapitalgesellschaften sind solche, die mindestens zwei der drei in Absatz 2 bezeichneten Merkmale überschreiten. Eine Kapitalgesellschaft im Sinn des § 264d gilt stets als große.

(4) Die Rechtsfolgen der Merkmale nach den Absätzen 1 bis 3 Satz 1 treten nur ein, wenn sie an den Abschlußstichtagen von zwei aufeinanderfolgenden Geschäftsjahren über- oder unterschritten werden. Im Falle der Umwandlung oder Neugründung treten die Rechtsfolgen schon ein, wenn die Voraussetzungen des Absatzes 1, 2 oder 3 am ersten Abschlußstichtag nach der Umwandlung oder Neugründung vorliegen. Satz 2 findet im Falle des Formwechsels keine Anwendung, sofern der formwechselnde Rechtsträger eine Kapitalgesellschaft oder eine Personenhandelsgesellschaft im Sinne des § 264a Absatz 1 ist.

(4a) Die Bilanzsumme setzt sich aus den Posten zusammen, die in den Buchstaben A bis E des § 266 Absatz 2 aufgeführt sind. Ein auf der Aktivseite ausgewiesener Fehlbetrag (§ 268 Absatz 3) wird nicht in die Bilanzsumme einbezogen.

(5) Als durchschnittliche Zahl der Arbeitnehmer gilt der vierte Teil der Summe aus den Zahlen der jeweils am 31. März, 30. Juni, 30. September und 31. Dezember beschäftigten Arbeitnehmer einschließlich der im Ausland beschäftigten Arbeitnehmer, jedoch ohne die zu ihrer Berufsausbildung Beschäftigten.

(2) Medium-sized corporations are those which exceed at least two of the three characteristics referred to in section 1 and do not exceed in each case at least two of the three following characteristics:
1. €20,000,000 balance sheet total.
2. €40,00, 000 sales revenue in the twelve months preceding the balance sheet date.
3. Two hundred and fifty employees on average per year.

(3) Large corporations are those that exceed at least two of the three characteristics specified in section 2. A corporation within the meaning of § 264d shall always be deemed to be large.

(4) The legal consequences of the characteristics according to sections 1 to 3 sent. 1 shall only occur if they are exceeded or fallen short of on the balance sheet dates of two consecutive business years. In the case of a conversion or new foundation, the legal consequences shall already occur if the requirements of section 1, 2 or 3 are met on the first balance sheet date after the conversion or new foundation. Sentence 2 shall not apply in the case of a change of legal form if the entity changing its legal form is a corporation or a commercial partnership within the meaning of § 264a sect. 1.

(4a) The balance sheet total consists of the items listed in letters A to E of § 266 sect. 2. A loss reported on the assets side (§ 268 sect. 3) shall not be included in the balance sheet total.

(5) The average number of employees shall be deemed to be the fourth part of the sum of the numbers of employees on the 31 March, 30 June, 30 September and 31 December, including those employed abroad, but excluding those employed for their vocational training.

(continued)

(6) Informations- und Auskunftsrechte der Arbeitnehmervertretungen nach anderen Gesetzen bleiben unberührt.	(6) The rights of employee representatives to information and disclosure under other laws shall remain unaffected.

§ 267a Kleinstkapitalgesellschaften
(1) Kleinstkapitalgesellschaften sind kleine Kapitalgesellschaften, die mindestens zwei der drei nachstehenden Merkmale nicht überschreiten:
1. 350 000 Euro Bilanzsumme;
2. 700 000 Euro Umsatzerlöse in den zwölf Monaten vor dem Abschlussstichtag;
3. im Jahresdurchschnitt zehn Arbeitnehmer.
§ 267 Absatz 4 bis 6 gilt entsprechend.
(2) Die in diesem Gesetz für kleine Kapitalgesellschaften (§ 267 Absatz 1) vorgesehenen besonderen Regelungen gelten für Kleinstkapitalgesellschaften entsprechend, soweit nichts anderes geregelt ist.
(3) Keine Kleinstkapitalgesellschaften sind:
   1. Investmentgesellschaften im Sinne des § 1 Absatz 11 des Kapitalanlagegesetzbuchs,

   2. Unternehmensbeteiligungsgesellschaften im Sinne des § 1a Absatz 1 des Gesetzes über Unternehmensbeteiligungsgesellschaften oder

   3. Unternehmen, deren einziger Zweck darin besteht, Beteiligungen an anderen Unternehmen zu erwerben sowie die Verwaltung und Verwertung dieser Beteiligungen wahrzunehmen, ohne dass sie unmittelbar oder mittelbar in die Verwaltung dieser Unternehmen eingreifen, wobei die Ausübung der ihnen als Aktionär oder Gesellschafter zustehenden Rechte außer Betracht bleibt.

§ 267a Very small corporations
(1) Very small corporations are small corporations that do not exceed at least two of the following three characteristics:
1. €350,000 balance sheet total;
2. €700,000 sales revenue in the twelve months preceding to the balance sheet date;
3. an annual average of ten employees.
§ 267 sect. 4 to 6 shall apply mutatis mutandis.
(2) The special regulations provided for in this Act for small corporations (§ 267 sect. 1) shall apply mutatis mutandis to very small corporations unless otherwise provided.

(3) No very small corporations are:
   1. Investment companies within the meaning of § 1 sect. 11 of the German Investment Code (Kapitalanlagegesetzbuch),

   2. Private equity companies within the meaning of § 1a sect. 1 of the Act on Private Equity Companies (Gesetz über Unternehmensbeteiligungsgesellschaften) or

   3. companies whose sole objective is to acquire participations in other companies and to manage and exploit those participations without interfering directly or indirectly in the management of those companies, while disregarding the exercise of rights to which they are entitled as shareholders or partners.

(continued)

§ 268 Vorschriften zu einzelnen Posten der Bilanz; Bilanzvermerke

(1) Die Bilanz darf auch unter Berücksichtigung der vollständigen oder teilweisen Verwendung des Jahresergebnisses aufgestellt werden. Wird die Bilanz unter Berücksichtigung der teilweisen Verwendung des Jahresergebnisses aufgestellt, so tritt an die Stelle der Posten "Jahresüberschuß/Jahresfehlbetrag" und "Gewinnvortrag/Verlustvortrag" der Posten "Bilanzgewinn/Bilanzverlust"; ein vorhandener Gewinn- oder Verlustvortrag ist in den Posten "Bilanzgewinn/Bilanzverlust" einzubeziehen und in der Bilanz gesondert anzugeben. Die Angabe kann auch im Anhang gemacht werden.

(2) (weggefallen)

(3) Ist das Eigenkapital durch Verluste aufgebraucht und ergibt sich ein Überschuß der Passivposten über die Aktivposten, so ist dieser Betrag am Schluß der Bilanz auf der Aktivseite gesondert unter der Bezeichnung "Nicht durch Eigenkapital gedeckter Fehlbetrag" auszuweisen.

(4) Der Betrag der Forderungen mit einer Restlaufzeit von mehr als einem Jahr ist bei jedem gesondert ausgewiesenen Posten zu vermerken. Werden unter dem Posten "sonstige Vermögensgegenstände" Beträge für Vermögensgegenstände ausgewiesen, die erst nach dem Abschlußstichtag rechtlich entstehen, so müssen Beträge, die einen größeren Umfang haben, im Anhang erläutert werden.

§ 268 Rules relating to specific items of the balance sheet; balance sheet notes

(1) The balance sheet may also be prepared taking into account the full or partial use of the annual result. If the balance sheet is prepared taking into account the partial use of the annual result, the items "net profit/loss of the year" and "profit/loss carry forward" shall be replaced by the item "retained earnings"; any profit or loss carry forward shall be included in the item "retained earnings" and disclosed separately in the balance sheet. The disclosure may also be made in the notes.

(2) (omitted)

(3) If the equity is used up by losses and there is an excess of liabilities over assets, this amount shall be shown separately on the assets side at the end of the balance sheet under the designation "loss not covered by equity".

(4) The amount of receivables with a remaining term of more than one year shall be noted for each item reported separately. If amounts are reported under the item "other assets" for assets which do not legally exist until after the balance sheet date, amounts which are larger in scope must be explained in the notes.

(continued)

(5) Der Betrag der Verbindlichkeiten mit einer Restlaufzeit bis zu einem Jahr und der Betrag der Verbindlichkeiten mit einer Restlaufzeit von mehr als einem Jahr sind bei jedem gesondert ausgewiesenen Posten zu vermerken. Erhaltene Anzahlungen auf Bestellungen sind, soweit Anzahlungen auf Vorräte nicht von dem Posten "Vorräte" offen abgesetzt werden, unter den Verbindlichkeiten gesondert auszuweisen. Sind unter dem Posten "Verbindlichkeiten" Beträge für Verbindlichkeiten ausgewiesen, die erst nach dem Abschlußstichtag rechtlich entstehen, so müssen Beträge, die einen größeren Umfang haben, im Anhang erläutert werden.	(5) The amount of debt with a remaining term of up to one year and the amount of debt with a remaining term of more than one year shall be noted for each item reported separately. Received advance payments on orders shall be shown separately under debt insofar as advance payments on inventories are not openly deducted from the item "inventories". If amounts are reported under the item "debt" for payables that do not legally arise until after the balance sheet date, amounts that are larger in scope must be explained in the notes.
(6) Ein nach § 250 Abs. 3 in den Rechnungsabgrenzungsposten auf der Aktivseite aufgenommener Unterschiedsbetrag ist in der Bilanz gesondert auszuweisen oder im Anhang anzugeben.	(6) Any difference included in the deferred expenses on the assets side in accordance with § 250 sect. 3 shall be reported separately in the balance sheet or disclosed in the notes.
(7) Für die in § 251 bezeichneten Haftungsverhältnisse sind	(7) For the contingent liabilities referred to in § 251, the following shall apply
1. die Angaben zu nicht auf der Passivseite auszuweisenden Verbindlichkeiten und Haftungsverhältnissen im Anhang zu machen,	1. the information on liabilities not to be shown on the liabilities side and contingent liabilities must be provided in the notes,
2. dabei die Haftungsverhältnisse jeweils gesondert unter Angabe der gewährten Pfandrechte und sonstigen Sicherheiten anzugeben und	2. indicating the contingent liabilities separately in each case, stating the liens and other security collaterals, and
3. dabei Verpflichtungen betreffend die Altersversorgung und Verpflichtungen gegenüber verbundenen oder assoziierten Unternehmen jeweils gesondert zu vermerken.	3. reporting obligations relating to pensions and obligations to affiliated or associated companies separately in each case.

(continued)

(8) Werden selbst geschaffene immaterielle Vermögensgegenstände des Anlagevermögens in der Bilanz ausgewiesen, so dürfen Gewinne nur ausgeschüttet werden, wenn die nach der Ausschüttung verbleibenden frei verfügbaren Rücklagen zuzüglich eines Gewinnvortrags und abzüglich eines Verlustvortrags mindestens den insgesamt angesetzten Beträgen abzüglich der hierfür gebildeten passiven latenten Steuern entsprechen. Werden aktive latente Steuern in der Bilanz ausgewiesen, ist Satz 1 auf den Betrag anzuwenden, um den die aktiven latenten Steuern die passiven latenten Steuern übersteigen. Bei Vermögensgegenständen im Sinn des § 246 Abs. 2 Satz 2 ist Satz 1 auf den Betrag abzüglich der hierfür gebildeten passiven latenten Steuern anzuwenden, der die Anschaffungskosten übersteigt.	(8) If internally generated intangible non-current assets are reported in the balance sheet, profits may only be distributed if the freely available reserves remaining after the distribution plus any profit carry forward and less any loss carry forward at least correspond to the total amounts recognized less the deferred tax liabilities created for this purpose. If deferred tax assets are reported in the balance sheet, sentence 1 shall be applied to the amount by which the deferred tax assets exceed the deferred tax liabilities. In the case of assets within the meaning of § 246 sect. 2 sent. 2, sentence 1 shall be applied to the amount exceeding the acquisition costs minus the deferred tax liabilities created for this purpose.
§ 269 (weggefallen)	**§ 269 (omitted)**
§ 270 Bildung bestimmter Posten (1) Einstellungen in die Kapitalrücklage und deren Auflösung sind bereits bei der Aufstellung der Bilanz vorzunehmen. (2) Wird die Bilanz unter Berücksichtigung der vollständigen oder teilweisen Verwendung des Jahresergebnisses aufgestellt, so sind Entnahmen aus Gewinnrücklagen sowie Einstellungen in Gewinnrücklagen, die nach Gesetz, Gesellschaftsvertrag oder Satzung vorzunehmen sind oder auf Grund solcher Vorschriften beschlossen worden sind, bereits bei der Aufstellung der Bilanz zu berücksichtigen.	**§ 270 Creation of certain items** (1) Allocations to the capital reserve and its reversal must already be made when preparing the balance sheet. (2) If the balance sheet is prepared taking into account the full or partial use of the annual result, withdrawals from revenue reserves as well as allocations to revenue reserves which are to be made by law, the articles of association or statutes or which have been resolved on the basis of such regulations shall already be taken into account in the preparation of the balance sheet.

(continued)

§ 271 Beteiligungen. Verbundene Unternehmen

(1) Beteiligungen sind Anteile an anderen Unternehmen, die bestimmt sind, dem eigenen Geschäftsbetrieb durch Herstellung einer dauernden Verbindung zu jenen Unternehmen zu dienen. Dabei ist es unerheblich, ob die Anteile in Wertpapieren verbrieft sind oder nicht. Eine Beteiligung wird vermutet, wenn die Anteile an einem Unternehmen insgesamt den fünften Teil des Nennkapitals dieses Unternehmens oder, falls ein Nennkapital nicht vorhanden ist, den fünften Teil der Summe aller Kapitalanteile an diesem Unternehmen überschreiten. Auf die Berechnung ist § 16 Abs. 2 und 4 des Aktiengesetzes entsprechend anzuwenden. Die Mitgliedschaft in einer eingetragenen Genossenschaft gilt nicht als Beteiligung im Sinne dieses Buches.

(2) Verbundene Unternehmen im Sinne dieses Buches sind solche Unternehmen, die als Mutter- oder Tochterunternehmen (§ 290) in den Konzernabschluß eines Mutterunternehmens nach den Vorschriften über die Vollkonsolidierung einzubeziehen sind, das als oberstes Mutterunternehmen den am weitestgehenden Konzernabschluß nach dem Zweiten Unterabschnitt aufzustellen hat, auch wenn die Aufstellung unterbleibt, oder das einen befreienden Konzernabschluß nach den §§ 291 oder 292 aufstellt oder aufstellen könnte; Tochterunternehmen, die nach § 296 nicht einbezogen werden, sind ebenfalls verbundene Unternehmen.

§ 271 Participations. Affiliated companies

(1) Participations are shares in other companies that are intended to serve the company's own business operations by establishing a permanent connection to those companies. It is irrelevant whether the shares are securitized or not. A participation shall be presumed if the shares in an company exceed in total one fifth of the nominal capital of that company or, if there is no nominal capital, one fifth of the sum of all capital shares in that company. § 16 sect. 2 and 4 of the Stock Corporation Act (Aktiengesetz) shall apply mutatis mutandis to the calculation. Membership in a registered cooperative shall not be deemed to be a participation within the meaning of this Book.

(2) Affiliated companies within the meaning of this Book are those companies which, as parent or subsidiary companies (§ 290), are to be included in the consolidated financial statements of a parent company in accordance with the regulations on full consolidation, which, as ultimate parent company, is required to prepare the most extensive consolidated financial statements in accordance with the second subsection, even if the preparation is omitted, or which prepares or could prepare exempting consolidated financial statements in accordance with §§ 291 or 292; subsidiaries which are not included in accordance with § 296 are also affiliated companies.

§ 272 Eigenkapital

(1) Gezeichnetes Kapital ist mit dem Nennbetrag anzusetzen. Die nicht eingeforderten ausstehenden Einlagen auf das gezeichnete Kapital sind von dem Posten „Gezeichnetes Kapital" offen abzusetzen; der verbleibende Betrag ist als Posten „Eingefordertes Kapital" in der Hauptspalte der Passivseite auszuweisen; der eingeforderte, aber noch nicht eingezahlte Betrag ist unter den Forderungen gesondert auszuweisen und entsprechend zu bezeichnen.

§ 272 Equity

(1) Subscribed capital shall be stated at par value. The uncalled outstanding contributions to the subscribed capital shall be openly deducted from the item "subscribed capital"; the remaining amount shall be shown as an item "called up capital" in the main column of the liabilities side; the amount called up but not yet paid in shall be shown separately under receivables and designated accordingly.

(continued)

(1a) Der Nennbetrag oder, falls ein solcher nicht vorhanden ist, der rechnerische Wert von erworbenen eigenen Anteilen ist in der Vorspalte offen von dem Posten „Gezeichnetes Kapital" abzusetzen. Der Unterschiedsbetrag zwischen dem Nennbetrag oder dem rechnerischen Wert und den Anschaffungskosten der eigenen Anteile ist mit den frei verfügbaren Rücklagen zu verrechnen. Aufwendungen, die Anschaffungsnebenkosten sind, sind Aufwand des Geschäftsjahrs.

(1b) Nach der Veräußerung der eigenen Anteile entfällt der Ausweis nach Absatz 1a Satz 1. Ein den Nennbetrag oder den rechnerischen Wert übersteigender Differenzbetrag aus dem Veräußerungserlös ist bis zur Höhe des mit den frei verfügbaren Rücklagen verrechneten Betrages in die jeweiligen Rücklagen einzustellen. Ein darüber hinausgehender Differenzbetrag ist in die Kapitalrücklage gemäß Absatz 2 Nr. 1 einzustellen. Die Nebenkosten der Veräußerung sind Aufwand des Geschäftsjahrs.

(2) Als Kapitalrücklage sind auszuweisen

1. der Betrag, der bei der Ausgabe von Anteilen einschließlich von Bezugsanteilen über den Nennbetrag oder, falls ein Nennbetrag nicht vorhanden ist, über den rechnerischen Wert hinaus erzielt wird;
2. der Betrag, der bei der Ausgabe von Schuldverschreibungen für Wandlungsrechte und Optionsrechte zum Erwerb von Anteilen erzielt wird;
3. der Betrag von Zuzahlungen, die Gesellschafter gegen Gewährung eines Vorzugs für ihre Anteile leisten;
4. der Betrag von anderen Zuzahlungen, die Gesellschafter in das Eigenkapital leisten.

(1a) The nominal amount or, in the absence of a nominal amount, the imputed par value of own shares acquired shall be deducted openly in the preliminary column from the item "subscribed capital". The difference between the nominal amount or the imputed par value and the acquisition cost of the treasury shares shall be set off against the freely available reserves. Expenses that are incidental to acquisition are expenses of the business year.

(1b) After the sale of treasury shares, the disclosure pursuant to section 1a sentence 1 shall not apply. Any difference from the proceeds of the sale exceeding the nominal amount or the imputed par value shall be transferred to the respective reserves up to the amount offset against the freely available reserves. Any difference exceeding this amount shall be transferred to the capital reserve in accordance with section 2 no. 1. The incidental costs of the sale shall be expenses of the business year.

(2) The following are to be shown as capital reserve

1. the amount realized on the issue of shares, including subscription rights, in excess of the nominal amount or, in the absence of a nominal amount, in excess of the imputed par value;
2. the amount realized on the issue of bonds for conversion rights and option rights to acquire shares;
3. the amount of additional payments made by shareholders in return for the granting of a preference for their shares;
4. the amount of other additional payments that shareholders make into equity.

(continued)

(3) Als Gewinnrücklagen dürfen nur Beträge ausgewiesen werden, die im Geschäftsjahr oder in einem früheren Geschäftsjahr aus dem Ergebnis gebildet worden sind. Dazu gehören aus dem Ergebnis zu bildende gesetzliche oder auf Gesellschaftsvertrag oder Satzung beruhende Rücklagen und andere Gewinnrücklagen.

(3) Only amounts that have been formed from the result in the business year or in a previous business year may be shown as revenue reserves. These include legal reserves or statutory reserves and other revenue reserves to be created from the result.

(4) Für Anteile an einem herrschenden oder mit Mehrheit beteiligten Unternehmen ist eine Rücklage zu bilden. In die Rücklage ist ein Betrag einzustellen, der dem auf der Aktivseite der Bilanz für die Anteile an dem herrschenden oder mit Mehrheit beteiligten Unternehmen angesetzten Betrag entspricht. Die Rücklage, die bereits bei der Aufstellung der Bilanz zu bilden ist, darf aus vorhandenen frei verfügbaren Rücklagen gebildet werden. Die Rücklage ist aufzulösen, soweit die Anteile an dem herrschenden oder mit Mehrheit beteiligten Unternehmen veräußert, ausgegeben oder eingezogen werden oder auf der Aktivseite ein niedrigerer Betrag angesetzt wird.

(4) A reserve shall be created for shares in a controlling entity or a majority-owned shareholder. The amount to be recognized in the reserve shall correspond to the amount recognized on the assets side of the balance sheet for the shares in the controlling entity or the majority shareholder. The reserve, which must already be formed when the balance sheet is prepared, may be formed from existing freely available reserves. The reserve must be reversed if the shares in the controlling entity or majority shareholder are sold, issued or withdrawn or if a lower amount is recognized on the assets side.

(5) Übersteigt der auf eine Beteiligung entfallende Teil des Jahresüberschusses in der Gewinn- und Verlustrechnung die Beträge, die als Dividende oder Gewinnanteil eingegangen sind oder auf deren Zahlung die Kapitalgesellschaft einen Anspruch hat, ist der Unterschiedsbetrag in eine Rücklage einzustellen, die nicht ausgeschüttet werden darf. Die Rücklage ist aufzulösen, soweit die Kapitalgesellschaft die Beträge vereinnahmt oder einen Anspruch auf ihre Zahlung erwirbt.

(5) If the portion of the net profit for the year attributable to a participation in the income statement exceeds the amounts received as dividends or profit shares or to the payment of which the corporation is entitled, the difference shall be allocated in a reserve which may not be distributed. The reserve shall be reversed to the extent that the corporation receives the amounts or acquires a claim to their payment.

(continued)

§ 273 (weggefallen)	§ 273 (omitted)

§ 274 Latente Steuern

(1) Bestehen zwischen den handelsrechtlichen Wertansätzen von Vermögensgegenständen, Schulden und Rechnungsabgrenzungsposten und ihren steuerlichen Wertansätzen Differenzen, die sich in späteren Geschäftsjahren voraussichtlich abbauen, so ist eine sich daraus insgesamt ergebende Steuerbelastung als passive latente Steuern (§ 266 Abs. 3 E.) in der Bilanz anzusetzen. Eine sich daraus insgesamt ergebende Steuerentlastung kann als aktive latente Steuern (§ 266 Abs. 2 D.) in der Bilanz angesetzt werden. Die sich ergebende Steuerbe- und die sich ergebende Steuerentlastung können auch unverrechnet angesetzt werden. Steuerliche Verlustvorträge sind bei der Berechnung aktiver latenter Steuern in Höhe der innerhalb der nächsten fünf Jahre zu erwartenden Verlustverrechnung zu berücksichtigen.

(2) Die Beträge der sich ergebenden Steuerbe- und -entlastung sind mit den unternehmensindividuellen Steuersätzen im Zeitpunkt des Abbaus der Differenzen zu bewerten und nicht abzuzinsen. Die ausgewiesenen Posten sind aufzulösen, sobald die Steuerbe- oder -entlastung eintritt oder mit ihr nicht mehr zu rechnen ist. Der Aufwand oder Ertrag aus der Veränderung bilanzierter latenter Steuern ist in der Gewinn- und Verlustrechnung gesondert unter dem Posten „Steuern vom Einkommen und vom Ertrag" auszuweisen.

§ 274 Deferred taxes

(1) If there are differences between the commercial-law values of assets, liabilities and deferrals and their values for tax purposes, which are expected to reverse in later business years, the resulting overall tax burden shall be recognized in the balance sheet as deferred tax liabilities (§ 266 sect. 3 E.). Any resulting overall tax relief may be recognized in the balance sheet as deferred tax assets (§ 266 sect. 2 D.). The resulting tax burden and the resulting tax relief can also be recognized without offsetting. Tax loss carry forwards are to be taken into account in the calculation of deferred tax assets in the amount of the losses expected to be offset within the next five years.

(2) The amounts of the resulting tax burden and relief are to be measured at the company-specific tax rates at the time of the reversal of the differences and are not to be discounted. The reported items are to be reversed as soon as the tax burden or relief occurs or is no longer expected. The expense or income from the change in recognized deferred taxes must be shown separately in the income statement under the item "income taxes".

§ 274a Größenabhängige Erleichterungen

Kleine Kapitalgesellschaften sind von der Anwendung der folgenden Vorschriften befreit:
1. § 268 Abs. 4 Satz 2 über die Pflicht zur Erläuterung bestimmter Forderungen im Anhang,
2. § 268 Abs. 5 Satz 3 über die Erläuterung bestimmter Verbindlichkeiten im Anhang,
3. § 268 Abs. 6 über den Rechnungsabgrenzungsposten nach § 250 Abs. 3,
4. § 274 über die Abgrenzung latenter Steuern.

§ 274a Size-dependent simplifications

Small corporations are exempt from the application of the following provisions:
1. § 268 sect. 4 sent. 2 on the obligation to explain certain receivables in the notes,
2. § 268 sect. 5 sent. 3 on the explanation of certain liabilities in the notes,
3. § 268 sect. 6 on deferred expenses in accordance with § 250 sect. 3,
4. § 274 on the recognition of deferred taxes.

(continued)

Dritter Titel Gewinn- und Verlustrechnung	Third title Income statement
§ 275 Gliederung	**§ 275 Structure**
(1) Die Gewinn- und Verlustrechnung ist in Staffelform nach dem Gesamtkostenverfahren oder dem Umsatzkostenverfahren aufzustellen. Dabei sind die in Absatz 2 oder 3 bezeichneten Posten in der angegebenen Reihenfolge gesondert auszuweisen.	(1) The income statement shall be prepared in the form of a list according to the total cost method or the cost of sales method. The items referred to in section 2 or 3 shall be shown separately in the order indicated.
(2) Bei Anwendung des Gesamtkostenverfahrens sind auszuweisen:	(2) If the total cost method is used, the following must be reported:
1. Umsatzerlöse	1. sales revenues
2. Erhöhung oder Verminderung des Bestands an fertigen und unfertigen Erzeugnissen	2. increase or decrease in inventories of finished and unfinished goods
3. andere aktivierte Eigenleistungen	3. other own work capitalized
4. sonstige betriebliche Erträge	4. other operating income
5. Materialaufwand:	5. material expenses:
a) Aufwendungen für Roh-, Hilfs- und Betriebsstoffe und für bezogene Waren	a) expenses of raw materials, of other materials and of purchased goods
b) Aufwendungen für bezogene Leistungen	b) expenses for purchased services
6. Personalaufwand:	6. personnel expenses:
a) Löhne und Gehälter	a) Wages and salaries
b) soziale Abgaben und Aufwendungen für Altersversorgung und für Unterstützung, davon für Altersversorgung	b) Social security contributions and expenses for pensions and other employee benefits, thereof for pensions
7. Abschreibungen:	7. depreciation:
a) auf immaterielle Vermögensgegenstände des Anlagevermögens und Sachanlagen	a) of intangible and tangible non-current assets
b) auf Vermögensgegenstände des Umlaufvermögens, soweit diese die in der Kapitalgesellschaft üblichen Abschreibungen überschreiten	b) of current assets, insofar as these exceed the depreciation customary in the corporation
8. sonstige betriebliche Aufwendungen	8. other operating expenses
9. Erträge aus Beteiligungen, davon aus verbundenen Unternehmen	9. income from participations, thereof from affiliated companies
10. Erträge aus anderen Wertpapieren und Ausleihungen des Finanzanlagevermögens, davon aus verbundenen Unternehmen	10. income from other non-current securities and non-current loans,thereof from affiliated companies
11. sonstige Zinsen und ähnliche Erträge, davon aus verbundenen Unternehmen	11. other interest and similar income, thereof from affiliated companies
12. Abschreibungen auf Finanzanlagen und auf Wertpapiere des Umlaufvermögens	12. amortization and impairment of non-current financial assets and on current securities
13. Zinsen und ähnliche Aufwendungen, davon an verbundene Unternehmen	13. interest and similar expenses, thereof to affiliated companies
14. Steuern vom Einkommen und vom Ertrag	14. income taxes
15. Ergebnis nach Steuern	15. result after taxes
16. sonstige Steuern	16. other taxes
17. Jahresüberschuss/Jahresfehlbetrag.	17. net profit/loss of the year.

(continued)

(3) Bei Anwendung des Umsatzkostenverfahrens sind auszuweisen:	(3) If the cost of sales method is used, the following must be reported:
1. Umsatzerlöse	1. sales revenues
2. Herstellungskosten der zur Erzielung der Umsatzerlöse erbrachten Leistungen	2. production costs of the services rendered to generate the sales revenue
3. Bruttoergebnis vom Umsatz	3. gross margin of sales revenue
4. Vertriebskosten	4. distribution costs
5. allgemeine Verwaltungskosten	5. general administrative costs
6. sonstige betriebliche Erträge	6. other operating income
7. sonstige betriebliche Aufwendungen	7. other operating expenses
8. Erträge aus Beteiligungen, davon aus verbundenen Unternehmen	8. income from participations, thereof from affiliated companies
9. Erträge aus anderen Wertpapieren und Ausleihungen des Finanzanlagevermögens, davon aus verbundenen Unternehmen	9. income from other non-current securities and non-current loans, thereof from affiliated companies
10. sonstige Zinsen und ähnliche Erträge, davon aus verbundenen Unternehmen	10. other interest and similar income, thereof from affiliated companies
11. Abschreibungen auf Finanzanlagen und auf Wertpapiere des Umlaufvermögens	11. amortization and impairment of non-current financial assets and on current securities
12. Zinsen und ähnliche Aufwendungen, davon an verbundene Unternehmen	12. interest and similar expenses, thereof to affiliated companies
13. Steuern vom Einkommen und vom Ertrag	13. income taxes
14. Ergebnis nach Steuern	14. result after taxes
15. sonstige Steuern	15. other taxes
16. Jahresüberschuss/Jahresfehlbetrag.	16. net profit/loss of the year.
(4) Veränderungen der Kapital- und Gewinnrücklagen dürfen in der Gewinn- und Verlustrechnung erst nach dem Posten "Jahresüberschuß/Jahresfehlbetrag" ausgewiesen werden.	(4) Changes in capital and revenue reserves may only be reported in the income statement after the item "net profit/loss of the year".
(5) Kleinstkapitalgesellschaften (§ 267a) können anstelle der Staffelungen nach den Absätzen 2 und 3 die Gewinn- und Verlustrechnung wie folgt darstellen:	(5) Very small corporations (§ 267a) may present the income statement as follows instead of the lists in sections 2 and 3:
1. Umsatzerlöse,	1. Sales revenues,
2. sonstige Erträge,	2. other income,
3. Materialaufwand,	3. material expenses,
4. Personalaufwand,	4. personnel expenses,
5. Abschreibungen,	5. depreciation,
6. sonstige Aufwendungen,	6. other expenses,
7. Steuern,	7. taxes,
8. Jahresüberschuss/Jahresfehlbetrag.	8. net profit/loss of the year.

(continued)

§ 276 Größenabhängige Erleichterungen Kleine und mittelgroße Kapitalgesellschaften (§ 267 Abs. 1, 2) dürfen die Posten § 275 Abs. 2 Nr. 1 bis 5 oder Abs. 3 Nr. 1 bis 3 und 6 zu einem Posten unter der Bezeichnung "Rohergebnis" zusammenfassen. Die Erleichterungen nach Satz 1 gelten nicht für Kleinstkapitalgesellschaften (§ 267a), die von der Regelung des § 275 Absatz 5 Gebrauch machen.	**§ 276 Size-dependent simplifications** Small and medium-sized corporations (§ 267, sect. 1, 2) may aggregate the items § 275, sect. 2, nos. 1 to 5 or sect. 3, nos. 1 to 3 and 6 into one item under the designation "gross profit". The simplifications according to sentence 1 shall not apply to very small corporations (§ 267a) which make use of the regulation of § 275 sect. 5.

§ 277 Vorschriften zu einzelnen Posten der Gewinn- und Verlustrechnung (1) Als Umsatzerlöse sind die Erlöse aus dem Verkauf und der Vermietung oder Verpachtung von Produkten sowie aus der Erbringung von Dienstleistungen der Kapitalgesellschaft nach Abzug von Erlösschmälerungen und der Umsatzsteuer sowie sonstiger direkt mit dem Umsatz verbundener Steuern auszuweisen. (2) Als Bestandsveränderungen sind sowohl Änderungen der Menge als auch solche des Wertes zu berücksichtigen; Abschreibungen jedoch nur, soweit diese die in der Kapitalgesellschaft sonst üblichen Abschreibungen nicht überschreiten. (3) Außerplanmäßige Abschreibungen nach § 253 Absatz 3 Satz 5 und 6 sind jeweils gesondert auszuweisen oder im Anhang anzugeben. Erträge und Aufwendungen aus Verlustübernahme und auf Grund einer Gewinngemeinschaft, eines Gewinnabführungs- oder eines Teilgewinnabführungsvertrags erhaltene oder abgeführte Gewinne sind jeweils gesondert unter entsprechender Bezeichnung auszuweisen. (4) (weggefallen)	**§ 277 Regulations on specific items of the income statement** (1) Income from the sale and rental or leasing of products and from the rendering of services by the corporation after deduction of sales reductions and value added tax as well as other taxes directly related to the sales revenue is reported as sales revenue. (2) Both changes in quantity and changes in value are to be taken into account as increase or decrease in inventories; depreciation, however, is to be taken into account only to the extent that it does not exceed the depreciation otherwise customary in the corporation. (3) Impairments pursuant to § 253 sect. 3 sent. 5 and 6 shall be reported separately in each case or disclosed in the notes. Income and expenses from losses transferred and received or transferred profits on the basis of a profit pooling, profit transfer or partial profit transfer agreement shall each be shown separately under the appropriate designation. (4) (omitted)

(continued)

(5) Erträge aus der Abzinsung sind in der Gewinn- und Verlustrechnung gesondert unter dem Posten „Sonstige Zinsen und ähnliche Erträge" und Aufwendungen gesondert unter dem Posten „Zinsen und ähnliche Aufwendungen" auszuweisen. Erträge aus der Währungsumrechnung sind in der Gewinn- und Verlustrechnung gesondert unter dem Posten „Sonstige betriebliche Erträge" und Aufwendungen aus der Währungsumrechnung gesondert unter dem Posten „Sonstige betriebliche Aufwendungen" auszuweisen.

(5) Income from discounting is reported separately in the income statement under the item "other interest and similar income" and expenses are to be reported separately under the item "interest and similar expenses". Income from currency translation shall be reported separately in the income statement under the item "other operating income" and expenses from currency translation shall be reported separately under the item "other operating expenses".

§ 278 (weggefallen)
Vierter Titel (weggefallen)

§ 278 (omitted)
Title Four (omitted)

§§ 279 bis 283 (weggefallen)
Fünfter Titel Anhang

§§ 279 to 283 (omitted)
Title Five Notes

§ 284 Erläuterung der Bilanz und der Gewinn-und Verlustrechnung
(1) In den Anhang sind diejenigen Angaben aufzunehmen, die zu den einzelnen Posten der Bilanz oder der Gewinn- und Verlustrechnung vorgeschrieben sind; sie sind in der Reihenfolge der einzelnen Posten der Bilanz und der Gewinn- und Verlustrechnung darzustellen. Im Anhang sind auch die Angaben zu machen, die in Ausübung eines Wahlrechts nicht in die Bilanz oder in die Gewinn- und Verlustrechnung aufgenommen wurden.
(2) Im Anhang müssen
1. die auf die Posten der Bilanz und der Gewinn-und Verlustrechnung angewandten Bilanzierungs- und Bewertungsmethoden angegeben werden;
2. Abweichungen von Bilanzierungs- und Bewertungsmethoden angegeben und begründet werden; deren Einfluß auf die Vermögens-, Finanz- und Ertragslage ist gesondert darzustellen;

§ 284 Explanation of the balance sheet and income statement
(1) The notes shall contain the information required for the specific items of the balance sheet or the income statement; it shall be presented in the order of the individual items of the balance sheet and the income statement. The notes shall also contain information which, in exercise of an option, has not been included in the balance sheet or in the income statement.

(2) In the notes
1. the recognition and measurement methods applied to the items in the balance sheet and income statement must be disclosed;

2. deviations from recognition and measurement methods must be stated and justified; their influence on the asset, finance and income position shall be presented separately;

(continued)

3. bei Anwendung einer Bewertungsmethode nach § 240 Abs. 4, § 256 Satz 1 die Unterschiedsbeträge pauschal für die jeweilige Gruppe ausgewiesen werden, wenn die Bewertung im Vergleich zu einer Bewertung auf der Grundlage des letzten vor dem Abschlußstichtag bekannten Börsenkurses oder Marktpreises einen erheblichen Unterschied aufweist;

4. Angaben über die Einbeziehung von Zinsen für Fremdkapital in die Herstellungskosten gemacht werden.

(3) Im Anhang ist die Entwicklung der einzelnen Posten des Anlagevermögens in einer gesonderten Aufgliederung darzustellen. Dabei sind, ausgehend von den gesamten Anschaffungs- und Herstellungskosten, die Zugänge, Abgänge, Umbuchungen und Zuschreibungen des Geschäftsjahrs sowie die Abschreibungen gesondert aufzuführen. Zu den Abschreibungen sind gesondert folgende Angaben zu machen:

1. die Abschreibungen in ihrer gesamten Höhe zu Beginn und Ende des Geschäftsjahrs,

2. die im Laufe des Geschäftsjahrs vorgenommenen Abschreibungen und

3. Änderungen in den Abschreibungen in ihrer gesamten Höhe im Zusammenhang mit Zu- und Abgängen sowie Umbuchungen im Laufe des Geschäftsjahrs.

Sind in die Herstellungskosten Zinsen für Fremdkapital einbezogen worden, ist für jeden Posten des Anlagevermögens anzugeben, welcher Betrag an Zinsen im Geschäftsjahr aktiviert worden ist.

§ 285 Sonstige Pflichtangaben
Ferner sind im Anhang anzugeben:

1. zu den in der Bilanz ausgewiesenen Verbindlichkeiten

---

3. if a measurement method pursuant to § 240 sect. 4, § 256 sent. 1 is applied, the differences must be shown as a lump sum for the respective group if the measurement shows a significant difference compared to a measurement based on the last known stock exchange price or market price before the balance sheet date;

4. disclosures on the inclusion of interest on borrowed capital in the cost of production must be made.

(3) In the notes, the development of the individual items of the non-current assets shall be presented in a separate breakdown. In this context, the additions, disposals, transfers and write-ups of the business year as well as the depreciation, amortization and impairments shall be listed separately, starting from the total acquisition and production costs. The following information shall be provided separately on depreciation, amortization and impairments:

1. The total depreciation, amortization and impairment at the beginning and end of the business year,

2. the depreciation, amortization and impairments recognized during the business year and

3. changes in total depreciation, amortization and impairment in connection with additions, disposals and transfers during the business year.

If interest on borrowed capital has been included in the production costs, the amount of interest recognized in the business year must be stated for each item of non-current assets.

§ 285 Other mandatory information
Furthermore, the notes to the financial statements shall disclose:

1. to the debt recognized in the balance sheet

(continued)

a) der Gesamtbetrag der Verbindlichkeiten mit einer Restlaufzeit von mehr als fünf Jahren,	a) the total amount of debt with a remaining term of more than five years,
b) der Gesamtbetrag der Verbindlichkeiten, die durch Pfandrechte oder ähnliche Rechte gesichert sind, unter Angabe von Art und Form der Sicherheiten;	b) the total amount of debt secured by liens or similar collaterals, indicating the nature and form of the collateral;
2. die Aufgliederung der in Nummer 1 verlangten Angaben für jeden Posten der Verbindlichkeiten nach dem vorgeschriebenen Gliederungsschema;	2. the breakdown of the information required in number 1 for each item of the debt according to the prescribed structure;
3. Art und Zweck sowie Risiken, Vorteile und finanzielle Auswirkungen von nicht in der Bilanz enthaltenen Geschäften, soweit die Risiken und Vorteile wesentlich sind und die Offenlegung für die Beurteilung der Finanzlage des Unternehmens erforderlich ist;	3. the nature and purpose of, and the risks, rewards and financial effects of, transactions not included in the balance sheet, to the extent that the risks and rewards are material and the disclosure is necessary for assessing the financial position of the company;
3a. der Gesamtbetrag der sonstigen finanziellen Verpflichtungen, die nicht in der Bilanz enthalten sind und die nicht nach § 268 Absatz 7 oder Nummer 3 anzugeben sind, sofern diese Angabe für die Beurteilung der Finanzlage von Bedeutung ist; davon sind Verpflichtungen betreffend die Altersversorgung und Verpflichtungen gegenüber verbundenen oder assoziierten Unternehmen jeweils gesondert anzugeben;	3a. the total amount of other financial obligations not included in the balance sheet and not required to be disclosed under § 268 sect. 7 or number 3, provided that such disclosure is material for the assessment of the financial position; of these, obligations relating to pensions and obligations to affiliated or associated companies shall be disclosed separately in each case;
4. die Aufgliederung der Umsatzerlöse nach Tätigkeitsbereichen sowie nach geografisch bestimmten Märkten, soweit sich unter Berücksichtigung der Organisation des Verkaufs, der Vermietung oder Verpachtung von Produkten und der Erbringung von Dienstleistungen der Kapitalgesellschaft die Tätigkeitsbereiche und geografisch bestimmten Märkte untereinander erheblich unterscheiden;	4. the breakdown of sales revenue by areas of activity and by geographically determined markets, insofar as, taking into account the organization of the sale, rental or leasing of products and the provision of services of the corporation, the areas of activity and geographically determined markets differ significantly from one another;
5. (weggefallen)	5. (omitted)
6. (weggefallen)	6. (omitted)
7. die durchschnittliche Zahl der während des Geschäftsjahrs beschäftigten Arbeitnehmer getrennt nach Gruppen;	7. the average number of employees employed during the business year, broken down by groups;

(continued)

8. bei Anwendung des Umsatzkostenverfahrens (§ 275 Abs. 3) a) der Materialaufwand des Geschäftsjahrs, gegliedert nach § 275 Abs. 2 Nr. 5, b) der Personalaufwand des Geschäftsjahrs, gegliedert nach § 275 Abs. 2 Nr. 6;	8. when applying the cost of sales method (§ 275 sect. 3) a) the material expenses for the business year, broken down in accordance with § 275 sect. 2 no. 5, b) the personnel expenses for the business year, broken down in accordance with § 275 sect. 2 no. 6;
9. für die Mitglieder des Geschäftsführungsorgans, eines Aufsichtsrats, eines Beirats oder einer ähnlichen Einrichtung jeweils für jede Personengruppe a) die für die Tätigkeit im Geschäftsjahr gewährten Gesamtbezüge (Gehälter, Gewinnbeteiligungen, Bezugsrechte und sonstige aktienbasierte Vergütungen, Aufwandsentschädigungen, Versicherungsentgelte, Provisionen und Nebenleistungen jeder Art). In die Gesamtbezüge sind auch Bezüge einzurechnen, die nicht ausgezahlt, sondern in Ansprüche anderer Art umgewandelt oder zur Erhöhung anderer Ansprüche verwendet werden. Außer den Bezügen für das Geschäftsjahr sind die weiteren Bezüge anzugeben, die im Geschäftsjahr gewährt, bisher aber in keinem Jahresabschluss angegeben worden sind. Bezugsrechte und sonstige aktienbasierte Vergütungen sind mit ihrer Anzahl und dem beizulegenden Zeitwert zum Zeitpunkt ihrer Gewährung anzugeben; spätere Wertveränderungen, die auf einer Änderung der Ausübungsbedingungen beruhen, sind zu berücksichtigen;	9. for the members of the management board, a supervisory board, an advisory board or a similar body, in each case for each group of persons a) the total remuneration granted for the activity in the business year (salaries, profit participation, subscription rights and other share-based remuneration, expense allowances, insurance premiums, commissions and fringe benefits of any kind). Remuneration that is not paid out but converted into entitlements of another kind or used to increase other entitlements shall also be included in the total remuneration. In addition to the remuneration for the business year, other remuneration granted in the business year but not yet disclosed in any financial statements shall be disclosed. Subscription rights and other share-based payments shall be disclosed with their quantity and fair value at the time they are granted; subsequent changes in value based on a change in the exercise conditions must be taken into account;

(continued)

b) die Gesamtbezüge (Abfindungen, Ruhegehälter, Hinterbliebenenbezüge und Leistungen verwandter Art) der früheren Mitglieder der bezeichneten Organe und ihrer Hinterbliebenen. Buchstabe a Satz 2 und 3 ist entsprechend anzuwenden. Ferner ist der Betrag der für diese Personengruppe gebildeten Rückstellungen für laufende Pensionen und Anwartschaften auf Pensionen und der Betrag der für diese Verpflichtungen nicht gebildeten Rückstellungen anzugeben;

c) die gewährten Vorschüsse und Kredite unter Angabe der Zinssätze, der wesentlichen Bedingungen und der gegebenenfalls im Geschäftsjahr zurückgezahlten oder erlassenen Beträge sowie die zugunsten dieser Personen eingegangenen Haftungsverhältnisse;

10. alle Mitglieder des Geschäftsführungsorgans und eines Aufsichtsrats, auch wenn sie im Geschäftsjahr oder später ausgeschieden sind, mit dem Familiennamen und mindestens einem ausgeschriebenen Vornamen, einschließlich des ausgeübten Berufs und bei börsennotierten Gesellschaften auch der Mitgliedschaft in Aufsichtsräten und anderen Kontrollgremien im Sinne des § 125 Abs. 1 Satz 5 des Aktiengesetzes. Der Vorsitzende eines Aufsichtsrats, seine Stellvertreter und ein etwaiger Vorsitzender des Geschäftsführungsorgans sind als solche zu bezeichnen;

11. Name und Sitz anderer Unternehmen, die Höhe des Anteils am Kapital, das Eigenkapital und das Ergebnis des letzten Geschäftsjahrs dieser Unternehmen, für das ein Jahresabschluss vorliegt, soweit es sich um Beteiligungen im Sinne des § 271 Absatz 1 handelt oder ein solcher Anteil von einer Person für Rechnung der Kapitalgesellschaft gehalten wird;

b) the total remuneration (severance payments, pensions, survivors' benefits and benefits of a similar nature) of the former members of the designated bodies and their survivors. Letter a, sentences 2 and 3 shall apply accordingly. Furthermore, the amount of the provisions for current pensions and vested pension rights recognized for this group of persons and the amount of the provisions not recognized for these obligations shall be stated;

c) the advances and loans granted, indicating the interest rates, the substantial terms and conditions and the amounts repaid or waived, if any, during the business year, as well as the contingent liabilities entered into in favor of such persons;

10. all members of the management board and of a supervisory board, even if they have resigned in the business year or later, with their surname and at least one written-out first name, including the profession exercised and, in the case of listed companies, also the membership in supervisory boards and other supervisory bodies within the meaning of § 125 sect. 1 sent. 5 of the Stock Corporation Act (Aktiengesetz). The chairman of a supervisory board, his deputies and any chairman of the management body shall be designated as such;

11. the name and registered office of other companies, the amount of the share in the equity, the equity and the result of the last business year of such companies for which financial statements are available, insofar as they are participations within the meaning of § 271 sect. 1 or such share is held by a person for the account of the corporation;

(continued)

11a. Name, Sitz und Rechtsform der Unternehmen, deren unbeschränkt haftender Gesellschafter die Kapitalgesellschaft ist;	11a. the name, registered office and legal form of the companies of which the corporation is a partner with unlimited liability;
11b. von börsennotierten Kapitalgesellschaften sind alle Beteiligungen an großen Kapitalgesellschaften anzugeben, die 5 Prozent der Stimmrechte überschreiten;	11b. of listed corporations, all shareholdings in large corporations exceeding 5 per cent of the voting rights shall be disclosed;
12. Rückstellungen, die in der Bilanz unter dem Posten "sonstige Rückstellungen" nicht gesondert ausgewiesen werden, sind zu erläutern, wenn sie einen nicht unerheblichen Umfang haben;	12. provisions that are not shown separately in the balance sheet under the item "other provisions" must be explained if they are not insignificant in size;
13. jeweils eine Erläuterung des Zeitraums, über den ein entgeltlich erworbener Geschäfts- oder Firmenwert abgeschrieben wird;	13. in each case, an explanation of the period over which goodwill acquired for remuneration is amortized;
14. Name und Sitz des Mutterunternehmens der Kapitalgesellschaft, das den Konzernabschluss für den größten Kreis von Unternehmen aufstellt, sowie der Ort, wo der von diesem Mutterunternehmen aufgestellte Konzernabschluss erhältlich ist;	14. the name and registered office of the parent company of the corporation that prepares the consolidated financial statements for the largest scope of companies and the place where the consolidated financial statements prepared by this parent company can be obtained;
14a. Name und Sitz des Mutterunternehmens der Kapitalgesellschaft, das den Konzernabschluss für den kleinsten Kreis von Unternehmen aufstellt, sowie der Ort, wo der von diesem Mutterunternehmen aufgestellte Konzernabschluss erhältlich ist;	14a. the name and registered office of the parent company of the corporation that prepares the consolidated financial statements for the smallest scope of companies and the place where the consolidated financial statements prepared by this parent company can be obtained;
15. soweit es sich um den Anhang des Jahresabschlusses einer Personenhandelsgesellschaft im Sinne des § 264a Abs. 1 handelt, Name und Sitz der Gesellschaften, die persönlich haftende Gesellschafter sind, sowie deren gezeichnetes Kapital;	15. insofar as they are the notes to the financial statements of a commercial partnership within the meaning of the § 264a sect. 1, the name and registered office of the companies that are general partners and their subscribed capital;
15a. das Bestehen von Genussscheinen, Genussrechten, Wandelschuldverschreibungen, Optionsscheinen, Optionen, Besserungsscheinen oder vergleichbaren Wertpapieren oder Rechten, unter Angabe der Anzahl und der Rechte, die sie verbriefen;	15a. the existence of profit participation certificates, profit participation rights, convertible bonds, warrants, options, debtor warrants or comparable securities or rights, stating the number and the rights they represent;

(continued)

16. dass die nach § 161 des Aktiengesetzes vorgeschriebene Erklärung abgegeben und wo sie öffentlich zugänglich gemacht worden ist;	16. that the declaration required under § 161 of the Stock Companies Act (Aktiengesetz) has been made and where it has been made publicly available;

17. das von dem Abschlussprüfer für das Geschäftsjahr berechnete Gesamthonorar, aufgeschlüsselt in das Honorar für
   a) die Abschlussprüfungsleistungen,
   b) andere Bestätigungsleistungen,
   c) Steuerberatungsleistungen,
   d) sonstige Leistungen,
soweit die Angaben nicht in einem das Unternehmen einbeziehenden Konzernabschluss enthalten sind;
	17. the total fee charged by the auditor for the business year, broken down into the fee for
	
	   a) the audit services,
	   b) other assurance services,
	   c) tax advisory services,
	   d) other services,
	to the extent that the disclosures are not included in consolidated financial statements that include the company;

18. für zu den Finanzanlagen (§ 266 Abs. 2 A. III.) gehörende Finanzinstrumente, die über ihrem beizulegenden Zeitwert ausgewiesen werden, da eine außerplanmäßige Abschreibung nach § 253 Absatz 3 Satz 6 unterblieben ist,
   a) der Buchwert und der beizulegende Zeitwert der einzelnen Vermögensgegenstände oder angemessener Gruppierungen sowie
   b) die Gründe für das Unterlassen der Abschreibung einschließlich der Anhaltspunkte, die darauf hindeuten, dass die Wertminderung voraussichtlich nicht von Dauer ist;
	18. for financial instruments belonging to non-current financial assets (§ 266 sect. 2 A. III.), which are reported above their fair value, because an impairment according to § 253 sect. 3 sent. 6 was omitted,
	   a) the book value and fair value of the individual assets or appropriate groupings, and
	
	   b) the reasons for the omission of the impairment, including evidence that the impairment is not expected to be permanent;

19. für jede Kategorie nicht zum beizulegenden Zeitwert bilanzierter derivativer Finanzinstrumente
   a) deren Art und Umfang,
   b) deren beizulegender Zeitwert, soweit er sich nach § 255 Abs. 4 verlässlich ermitteln lässt, unter Angabe der angewandten Bewertungsmethode,
   c) deren Buchwert und der Bilanzposten, in welchem der Buchwert, soweit vorhanden, erfasst ist, sowie
   d) die Gründe dafür, warum der beizulegende Zeitwert nicht bestimmt werden kann;
	19. for each category of derivative financial instruments not accounted for at fair value
	
	   a) their nature and quantity,
	   b) their fair value, insofar as it can be reliably determined in accordance with § 255 sect. 4, stating the measurement method applied,
	   c) their book value and the balance sheet item in which the book value, if any, is recognized, and
	   d) the reasons why the fair value cannot be determined;

20. für mit dem beizulegenden Zeitwert bewertete Finanzinstrumente	20. for financial instruments measured at fair value

(continued)

a) die grundlegenden Annahmen, die der Bestimmung des beizulegenden Zeitwertes mit Hilfe allgemein anerkannter Bewertungsmethoden zugrunde gelegt wurden, sowie	a) the underlying assumptions used in determining fair value using generally accepted measurement methods, and
b) Umfang und Art jeder Kategorie derivativer Finanzinstrumente einschließlich der wesentlichen Bedingungen, welche die Höhe, den Zeitpunkt und die Sicherheit künftiger Zahlungsströme beeinflussen können;	b) the quantity and nature of each class of derivative financial instruments, including the substantial terms and conditions that may affect the amount, timing and certainty of future cash flows;
21. zumindest die nicht zu marktüblichen Bedingungen zustande gekommenen Geschäfte, soweit sie wesentlich sind, mit nahe stehenden Unternehmen und Personen, einschließlich Angaben zur Art der Beziehung, zum Wert der Geschäfte sowie weiterer Angaben, die für die Beurteilung der Finanzlage notwendig sind; ausgenommen sind Geschäfte mit und zwischen mittel- oder unmittelbar in 100-prozentigem Anteilsbesitz stehenden in einen Konzernabschluss einbezogenen Unternehmen; Angaben über Geschäfte können nach Geschäftsarten zusammengefasst werden, sofern die getrennte Angabe für die Beurteilung der Auswirkungen auf die Finanzlage nicht notwendig ist;	21. At a minimum, non-arm's length transactions, to the extent they are material, with related parties, including the nature of the relationship, the value of the transactions and other disclosures necessary for an evaluation of the financial position; except for transactions with and between indirectly or directly wholly-owned entities included in consolidated financial statements; disclosures about transactions may be aggregated by type of transaction if separate disclosure is not necessary for an evaluation of the effects on the financial position;
22. im Fall der Aktivierung nach § 248 Abs. 2 der Gesamtbetrag der Forschungs- und Entwicklungskosten des Geschäftsjahrs sowie der davon auf die selbst geschaffenen immateriellen Vermögensgegenstände des Anlagevermögens entfallende Betrag;	22. in the case of recognition according to § 248 sect. 2, the total amount of the research and development costs for the business year and the amount thereof attributable to the internally generated intangible non-current assets;
23. bei Anwendung des § 254,	23. in case of application of § 254,

(continued)

a) mit welchem Betrag jeweils Vermögensgegenstände, Schulden, schwebende Geschäfte und mit hoher Wahrscheinlichkeit erwartete Transaktionen zur Absicherung welcher Risiken in welche Arten von Bewertungseinheiten einbezogen sind sowie die Höhe der mit Bewertungseinheiten abgesicherten Risiken,	a) the amount of assets, liabilities, pending transactions and transactions expected with a high degree of probability to hedge which risks are included in which types of measurement units, as well as the amount of the risks hedged with measurement units,
b) für die jeweils abgesicherten Risiken, warum, in welchem Umfang und für welchen Zeitraum sich die gegenläufigen Wertänderungen oder Zahlungsströme künftig voraussichtlich ausgleichen einschließlich der Methode der Ermittlung,	b) for the respective hedged risks, why, to what extent and for what period of time the opposing changes in value or cash flows are expected to offset each other in the future, including the method of determination,
c) eine Erläuterung der mit hoher Wahrscheinlichkeit erwarteten Transaktionen, die in Bewertungseinheiten einbezogen wurden,	c) an explanation of the transactions expected with a high degree of probability that have been included in measurement units,
soweit die Angaben nicht im Lagebericht gemacht werden;	to the extent that the disclosures are not made in the management report;
24. zu den Rückstellungen für Pensionen und ähnliche Verpflichtungen das angewandte versicherungsmathematische Berechnungsverfahren sowie die grundlegenden Annahmen der Berechnung, wie Zinssatz, erwartete Lohn- und Gehaltssteigerungen und zugrunde gelegte Sterbetafeln;	24. the actuarial calculation method applied to the provisions for pensions and similar obligations as well as the basic assumptions of the calculation, such as interest rate, expected wage and salary increases and mortality tables used;
25. im Fall der Verrechnung von Vermögensgegenständen und Schulden nach § 246 Abs. 2 Satz 2 die Anschaffungskosten und der beizulegende Zeitwert der verrechneten Vermögensgegenstände, der Erfüllungsbetrag der verrechneten Schulden sowie die verrechneten Aufwendungen und Erträge; Nummer 20 Buchstabe a ist entsprechend anzuwenden;	25. in the case of offsetting assets and liabilities in accordance with § 246 sect. 2 sent. 2, the acquisition costs and the fair value of the offset assets, the settlement amount of the offset liabilities and the offset expenses and income; number 20 letter a shall be applied accordingly;

(continued)

26. zu Anteilen an Sondervermögen im Sinn des § 1 Absatz 10 des Kapitalanlagegesetzbuchs oder Anlageaktien an Investmentaktiengesellschaften mit veränderlichem Kapital im Sinn der §§ 108 bis 123 des Kapitalanlagegesetzbuchs oder vergleichbaren EU-Investmentvermögen oder vergleichbaren ausländischen Investmentvermögen von mehr als dem zehnten Teil, aufgegliedert nach Anlagezielen, deren Wert im Sinn der §§ 168, 278 des Kapitalanlagegesetzbuchs oder des § 36 des Investmentgesetzes in der bis zum 21. Juli 2013 geltenden Fassung oder vergleichbarer ausländischer Vorschriften über die Ermittlung des Marktwertes, die Differenz zum Buchwert und die für das Geschäftsjahr erfolgte Ausschüttung sowie Beschränkungen in der Möglichkeit der täglichen Rückgabe; darüber hinaus die Gründe dafür, dass eine Abschreibung gemäß § 253 Absatz 3 Satz 6 unterblieben ist, einschließlich der Anhaltspunkte, die darauf hindeuten, dass die Wertminderung voraussichtlich nicht von Dauer ist; Nummer 18 ist insoweit nicht anzuwenden;

26. for shares in investment funds within the meaning of § 1 sect. 10 of the German Capital Investment Code (Kapitalanlagegesetzbuch) or investment shares in investment stock corporations with variable capital within the meaning of §§ 108 to 123 of the German Capital Investment Code or comparable EU investment funds or comparable foreign investment assets of more than one tenth, broken down by investment objective, the value within the meaning of §§ 168, 278 of the German Capital Investment Code or § 36 of the German Investment Act (Investmentgesetz) in the version applicable until 21 July 2013 or comparable foreign regulations on the determination of the market value, the difference to the book value and the distribution made for the business year as well as restrictions in the possibility of daily return; in addition, the reasons why an impairment pursuant to § 253 sect. 3 sent. 6 has not been made, including indications that the impairment is not expected to be permanent; number 18 is not applicable in this respect;

27. für nach § 268 Abs. 7 im Anhang ausgewiesene Verbindlichkeiten und Haftungsverhältnisse die Gründe der Einschätzung des Risikos der Inanspruchnahme;

27. for liabilities and contingent liabilities disclosed in the notes pursuant to § 268 sect. 7, the reasons for the assessment of the risk of utilization;

28. der Gesamtbetrag der Beträge im Sinn des § 268 Abs. 8, aufgegliedert in Beträge aus der Aktivierung selbst geschaffener immaterieller Vermögensgegenstände des Anlagevermögens, Beträge aus der Aktivierung latenter Steuern und aus der Aktivierung von Vermögensgegenständen zum beizulegenden Zeitwert;

28. the total amount of the amounts within the meaning of § 268 sect. 8, broken down into amounts from the recognition of internally generated intangible non-current assets, amounts from the recognition of deferred taxes and from the recognition of assets at fair value;

29. auf welchen Differenzen oder steuerlichen Verlustvorträgen die latenten Steuern beruhen und mit welchen Steuersätzen die Bewertung erfolgt ist;

29. on which differences or tax loss carry forwards the deferred taxes are based and which tax rates were used for the measurement;

(continued)

30. wenn latente Steuerschulden in der Bilanz angesetzt werden, die latenten Steuersalden am Ende des Geschäftsjahrs und die im Laufe des Geschäftsjahrs erfolgten Änderungen dieser Salden;

30. if deferred tax liabilities are recognized in the balance sheet, the deferred tax balances at the end of the business year and the changes in these balances during the business year;

31. jeweils der Betrag und die Art der einzelnen Erträge und Aufwendungen von außergewöhnlicher Größenordnung oder außergewöhnlicher Bedeutung, soweit die Beträge nicht von untergeordneter Bedeutung sind;

31. in each case, the amount and nature of the specific income and expenses of extraordinary magnitude or extraordinary significance, unless the amounts are of minor importance;

32. eine Erläuterung der einzelnen Erträge und Aufwendungen hinsichtlich ihres Betrags und ihrer Art, die einem anderen Geschäftsjahr zuzurechnen sind, soweit die Beträge nicht von untergeordneter Bedeutung sind;

32. an explanation of the specific income and expenses in terms of their amount and nature that are attributable to another business year, unless the amounts are of minor importance;

33. Vorgänge von besonderer Bedeutung, die nach dem Schluss des Geschäftsjahrs eingetreten und weder in der Gewinn- und Verlustrechnung noch in der Bilanz berücksichtigt sind, unter Angabe ihrer Art und ihrer finanziellen Auswirkungen;

33. events of special importance which occurred after the end of the business year and which have not been taken into account either in the income statement or in the balance sheet, stating their nature and their financial impact;

34. der Vorschlag für die Verwendung des Ergebnisses oder der Beschluss über seine Verwendung.

34. the proposal for the use of the result or the resolution on its use.

§ 286 Unterlassen von Angaben
(1) Die Berichterstattung hat insoweit zu unterbleiben, als es für das Wohl der Bundesrepublik Deutschland oder eines ihrer Länder erforderlich ist.
(2) Die Aufgliederung der Umsatzerlöse nach § 285 Nr. 4 kann unterbleiben, soweit die Aufgliederung nach vernünftiger kaufmännischer Beurteilung geeignet ist, der Kapitalgesellschaft einen erheblichen Nachteil zuzufügen; die Anwendung der Ausnahmeregelung ist im Anhang anzugeben.
(3) Die Angaben nach § 285 Nr. 11 und 11b können unterbleiben, soweit sie
1. für die Darstellung der Vermögens-, Finanz- und Ertragslage der Kapitalgesellschaft nach § 264 Abs. 2 von untergeordneter Bedeutung sind oder

§ 286 Omission of information
(1) The reporting shall be omitted insofar as it is necessary for the welfare of the Federal Republic of Germany or one of its states.

(2) The breakdown of sales revenue pursuant to § 285 no. 4 may be omitted if, according to reasonable commercial judgment, the breakdown is likely to cause significant disadvantage to the corporation; the application of the exemption shall be disclosed in the notes.

(3) The information pursuant to § 285 nos. 11 and 11b may be omitted insofar as they
1. are of minor importance for the presentation of the asset, finance and income position of the corporation pursuant to § 264 sect. 2 or

(continued)

2. nach vernünftiger kaufmännischer Beurteilung geeignet sind, der Kapitalgesellschaft oder dem anderen Unternehmen einen erheblichen Nachteil zuzufügen.	2. are, according to reasonable commercial judgment, likely to cause a significant disadvantage to the corporation or the other company.
Die Angabe des Eigenkapitals und des Jahresergebnisses kann unterbleiben, wenn das Unternehmen, über das zu berichten ist, seinen Jahresabschluß nicht offenzulegen hat und die berichtende Kapitalgesellschaft keinen beherrschenden Einfluss auf das betreffende Unternehmen ausüben kann. Satz 1 Nr. 2 ist nicht anzuwenden, wenn die Kapitalgesellschaft oder eines ihrer Tochterunternehmen (§ 290 Abs. 1 und 2) am Abschlussstichtag kapitalmarktorientiert im Sinn des § 264d ist. Im Übrigen ist die Anwendung der Ausnahmeregelung nach Satz 1 Nr. 2 im Anhang anzugeben.	The disclosure of the equity and the net result may be omitted if the company to be reported on does not have to disclose its financial statements and the reporting corporation cannot exercise a controlling influence on the company concerned. Sentence 1 No. 2 shall not be applied if the corporation or one of its subsidiaries (§ 290 sect. 1 and 2) is capital-market oriented within the meaning of § 264d on the balance sheet date. Otherwise, the application of the exemption according to sentence 1 no. 2 shall be disclosed in the notes.
4. Bei Gesellschaften, die keine börsennotierten Aktiengesellschaften sind, können die in § 285 Nr. 9 Buchstabe a und b verlangten Angaben über die Gesamtbezüge der dort bezeichneten Personen unterbleiben, wenn sich anhand dieser Angaben die Bezüge eines Mitglieds dieser Organe feststellen lassen.	4. In the case of companies that are not listed stock companies, the information required under § 285 no. 9 letters a and b concerning the total remuneration of the persons referred to therein may be omitted if the remuneration of a member of these bodies can be determined on the basis of this information.

§ 287 (weggefallen)	**§ 287 (omitted)**
§ 288 Größenabhängige Erleichterungen	**§ 288 Size-dependent simplifications**
(1) Kleine Kapitalgesellschaften (§ 267 Absatz 1) brauchen nicht	(1) Small corporations (§ 267 sect. 1) need not
1. die Angaben nach § 264c Absatz 2 Satz 9, § 265 Absatz 4 Satz 2, § 284 Absatz 2 Nummer 3, Absatz 3, § 285 Nummer 2, 3, 4, 8, 9 Buchstabe a und b, Nummer 10 bis 12, 14, 15, 15a, 17 bis 19, 21, 22, 24, 26 bis 30, 32 bis 34 zu machen;	1. provide the information pursuant to § 264c sect. 2 sent. 9, § 265 sect. 4 sent. 2, § 284 sect. 2 no. 3, sect. 3, § 285 nos. 2, 3, 4, 8, 9 lit. a and b, nos. 10 to 12, 14, 15, 15a, 17 to 19, 21, 22, 24, 26 to 30, 32 to 34;
2. eine Trennung nach Gruppen bei der Angabe nach § 285 Nummer 7 vorzunehmen;	2. make a separation by groups in the disclosure pursuant to § 285 no. 7;
3. bei der Angabe nach § 285 Nummer 14a den Ort anzugeben, wo der vom Mutterunternehmen aufgestellte Konzernabschluss erhältlich ist.	3. in the disclosure pursuant to § 285 no. 14a, indicate the place where the consolidated financial statements prepared by the parent company can be obtained.

(continued)

(2) Mittelgroße Kapitalgesellschaften (§ 267 Absatz 2) brauchen die Angabe nach § 285 Nummer 4, 29 und 32 nicht zu machen. Wenn sie die Angabe nach § 285 Nummer 17 nicht machen, sind sie verpflichtet, diese der Wirtschaftsprüferkammer auf deren schriftliche Anforderung zu übermitteln. Sie brauchen die Angaben nach § 285 Nummer 21 nur zu machen, sofern die Geschäfte direkt oder indirekt mit einem Gesellschafter, Unternehmen, an denen die Gesellschaft selbst eine Beteiligung hält, oder Mitgliedern des Geschäftsführungs-, Aufsichts- oder Verwaltungsorgans abgeschlossen wurden.	(2) Medium-sized corporations (§ 267 sect. 2) do not need to provide the information pursuant to § 285 nos. 4, 29 and 32. If they do not provide the information pursuant to § 285 no. 17, they are obliged to provide it to the Chamber of Public Accountants (Wirtschaftsprüferkammer) upon its written request. They need only make the disclosures under § 285 no. 21 if the transactions are directly or indirectly with a partner, companies in which the company itself holds a participation, or members of the management, supervisory or administrative body.

Sechster Titel Lagebericht	**Title Six Management report**

§ 289 Inhalt des Lageberichts	**§ 289 Contents of the management report**
(1) Im Lagebericht sind der Geschäftsverlauf einschließlich des Geschäftsergebnisses und die Lage der Kapitalgesellschaft so darzustellen, dass ein den tatsächlichen Verhältnissen entsprechendes Bild vermittelt wird. Er hat eine ausgewogene und umfassende, dem Umfang und der Komplexität der Geschäftstätigkeit entsprechende Analyse des Geschäftsverlaufs und der Lage der Gesellschaft zu enthalten. In die Analyse sind die für die Geschäftstätigkeit bedeutsamsten finanziellen Leistungsindikatoren einzubeziehen und unter Bezugnahme auf die im Jahresabschluss ausgewiesenen Beträge und Angaben zu erläutern. Ferner ist im Lagebericht die voraussichtliche Entwicklung mit ihren wesentlichen Chancen und Risiken zu beurteilen und zu erläutern; zugrunde liegende Annahmen sind anzugeben. Die Mitglieder des vertretungsberechtigten Organs einer Kapitalgesellschaft, die als Inlandsemittent (§ 2 Absatz 14 des Wertpapierhandelsgesetzes) Wertpapiere (§ 2 Absatz 1 des Wertpapierhandelsgesetzes) begibt und keine Kapitalgesellschaft im Sinne des § 327a ist, haben in einer dem Lagebericht beizufügenden schriftlichen Erklärung zu versichern, dass im Lagebericht nach bestem Wissen der Geschäftsverlauf einschließlich des	(1) The management report shall present a true and fair view of the development and performance of the business and the position of the corporation. It shall contain a balanced and comprehensive analysis of the course of business and the position of the company, commensurate with the scope and complexity of the business activity. The analysis shall include the financial performance indicators most relevant to the business and shall be explained by reference to the amounts and disclosures reported in the financial statements. Furthermore, the expected development with its material opportunities and risks shall be assessed and explained in the management report; underlying assumptions shall be stated. The members of the governing body authorized to represent the corporation which issues securities (§ 2 sect. 1 of the Securities Trading Act (Wertpapierhandelsgesetz)) as a domestic issuer (§ 2 sect. 14 of the Securities Trading Act) and which is not a corporation within the meaning of § 327a shall declare in a written statement to be attached to the management report that, to the best of their knowledge, the management report gives a true and fair view of the development and performance of the business and the position of the corporation,

(continued)

Geschäftsergebnisses und die Lage der Kapitalgesellschaft so dargestellt sind, dass ein den tatsächlichen Verhältnissen entsprechendes Bild vermittelt wird und dass die wesentlichen Chancen und Risiken im Sinne des Satzes 4 beschrieben sind.

together with a description of the principal opportunities and risks as defined in sentence 4.

(2) Im Lagebericht ist auch einzugehen auf:

(2) The management report shall also address:

1. a) die Risikomanagementziele und -methoden der Gesellschaft einschließlich ihrer Methoden zur Absicherung aller wichtigen Arten von Transaktionen, die im Rahmen der Bilanzierung von Sicherungsgeschäften erfasst werden, sowie

1. a) the company's risk management objectives and methods, including its methods for hedging all significant types of transactions that are accounted for in hedge accounting; and

b) die Preisänderungs-, Ausfall- und Liquiditätsrisiken sowie die Risiken aus Zahlungsstromschwankungen, denen die Gesellschaft ausgesetzt ist,

b) the price change, default and liquidity risks as well as the risks from cash flow fluctuations to which the company is exposed,

jeweils in Bezug auf die Verwendung von Finanzinstrumenten durch die Gesellschaft und sofern dies für die Beurteilung der Lage oder der voraussichtlichen Entwicklung von Belang ist;

in each case in relation to the use of financial instruments by the company and insofar as this is relevant for the assessment of the situation or the prospective development;

2. den Bereich Forschung und Entwicklung sowie

2. the area of research and development as well as

3. bestehende Zweigniederlassungen der Gesellschaft.

3. existing branches of the company.

Sind im Anhang Angaben nach § 160 Absatz 1 Nummer 2 des Aktiengesetzes zu machen, ist im Lagebericht darauf zu verweisen.

If disclosures are to be made in the notes pursuant to § 160 sect. 1 no. 2 of the Stock Corporation Act (Aktiengesetz), reference shall be made thereto in the management report.

(3) Bei einer großen Kapitalgesellschaft (§ 267 Abs. 3) gilt Absatz 1 Satz 3 entsprechend für nichtfinanzielle Leistungsindikatoren, wie Informationen über Umwelt- und Arbeitnehmerbelange, soweit sie für das Verständnis des Geschäftsverlaufs oder der Lage von Bedeutung sind.

(3) In the case of a large corporation (§ 267 sect. 3), section 1 sentence 3 shall apply mutatis mutandis to non-financial performance indicators, such as information on environmental and employee matters, insofar as they are of importance for understanding the course of business or the position.

(4) Kapitalgesellschaften im Sinn des § 264d haben im Lagebericht die wesentlichen Merkmale des internen Kontroll- und des Risikomanagementsystems im Hinblick auf den Rechnungslegungsprozess zu beschreiben.

(4) Corporations within the meaning of § 264d must describe in the management report the essential features of the internal control and risk management system with regard to the accounting process.

(continued)

§ 289a Ergänzende Vorgaben für bestimmte Aktiengesellschaften und Kommanditgesellschaften auf Aktien	§ 289a Supplementary requirements for certain stock corporations and partnerships limited by shares

§ 289a Ergänzende Vorgaben für bestimmte Aktiengesellschaften und Kommanditgesellschaften auf Aktien

Aktiengesellschaften und Kommanditgesellschaften auf Aktien, die einen organisierten Markt im Sinne des § 2 Absatz 7 des Wertpapiererwerbs- und Übernahmegesetzes durch von ihnen ausgegebene stimmberechtigte Aktien in Anspruch nehmen, haben im Lagebericht außerdem anzugeben:

1. die Zusammensetzung des gezeichneten Kapitals unter gesondertem Ausweis der mit jeder Gattung verbundenen Rechte und Pflichten und des Anteils am Gesellschaftskapital;

2. Beschränkungen, die Stimmrechte oder die Übertragung von Aktien betreffen, auch wenn sie sich aus Vereinbarungen zwischen Gesellschaftern ergeben können, soweit sie dem Vorstand der Gesellschaft bekannt sind;

3. direkte oder indirekte Beteiligungen am Kapital, die 10 Prozent der Stimmrechte überschreiten;

4. die Inhaber von Aktien mit Sonderrechten, die Kontrollbefugnisse verleihen, und eine Beschreibung dieser Sonderrechte;

5. die Art der Stimmrechtskontrolle, wenn Arbeitnehmer am Kapital beteiligt sind und ihre Kontrollrechte nicht unmittelbar ausüben;

6. die gesetzlichen Vorschriften und Bestimmungen der Satzung über die Ernennung und Abberufung der Mitglieder des Vorstands und über die Änderung der Satzung;

7. die Befugnisse des Vorstands insbesondere hinsichtlich der Möglichkeit, Aktien auszugeben oder zurückzukaufen;

8. wesentliche Vereinbarungen der Gesellschaft, die unter der Bedingung eines Kontrollwechsels infolge eines Übernahmeangebots stehen, und die hieraus folgenden Wirkungen;

---

§ 289a Supplementary requirements for certain stock corporations and partnerships limited by shares

Stock companies and partnerships limited by shares which make use of an organized market within the meaning of § 2 sect. 7 of the Securities Acquisition and Takeover Act (Wertpapiererwerbs- und Übernahmegesetz) by means of shares with voting rights issued by them shall also disclose in the management report:

1. the composition of the subscribed capital, showing separately the rights and obligations attached to each class and the proportion of the capital of the company;

2. restrictions affecting voting rights or the transfer of shares, even if they may arise from agreements between shareholders, to the extent that they are known to the executive board of the company;

3. direct or indirect shareholdings in the capital exceeding 10 per cent of the voting rights;

4. the holders of shares with special rights conferring powers of control and a description of such special rights;

5. the nature of voting right control where employees have an interest in the capital and do not exercise their control rights directly;

6. the legal and statutory regulations for the appointment and dismissal of members of the executive board and on amendments to the Articles of Association;

7. the powers of the executive board, in particular with regard to the possibility of issuing or buying back shares;

8. material agreements of the company that are subject to a change of control as a result of a takeover bid and the effects resulting therefrom;

(continued)

9. Entschädigungsvereinbarungen der Gesellschaft, die für den Fall eines Übernahmeangebots mit den Mitgliedern des Vorstands oder mit Arbeitnehmern getroffen sind.	9. compensation agreements of the company entered into with the members of the executive board or with employees in the event of a takeover bid.
Die Angaben nach Satz 1 Nummer 1, 3 und 9 können unterbleiben, soweit sie im Anhang zu machen sind. Sind Angaben nach Satz 1 im Anhang zu machen, ist im Lagebericht darauf zu verweisen. Die Angaben nach Satz 1 Nummer 8 können unterbleiben, soweit sie geeignet sind, der Gesellschaft einen erheblichen Nachteil zuzufügen; die Angabepflicht nach anderen gesetzlichen Vorschriften bleibt unberührt.	The information pursuant to sentence 1 nos. 1, 3 and 9 may be omitted if it is to be provided in the notes. If information pursuant to sentence 1 is to be provided in the notes, reference shall be made thereto in the management report. The information pursuant to sentence 1 no. 8 may be omitted insofar as it is likely to cause significant disadvantage to the company; the disclosure obligation pursuant to other legal regulations shall remain unaffected.

§ 289b Pflicht zur nichtfinanziellen Erklärung; Befreiungen

(1) Eine Kapitalgesellschaft hat ihren Lagebericht um eine nichtfinanzielle Erklärung zu erweitern, wenn sie die folgenden Merkmale erfüllt:

1. die Kapitalgesellschaft erfüllt die Voraussetzungen des § 267 Absatz 3 Satz 1,
2. die Kapitalgesellschaft ist kapitalmarktorientiert im Sinne des § 264d und
3. die Kapitalgesellschaft hat im Jahresdurchschnitt mehr als 500 Arbeitnehmer beschäftigt.

§ 267 Absatz 4 bis 5 ist entsprechend anzuwenden. Wenn die nichtfinanzielle Erklärung einen besonderen Abschnitt des Lageberichts bildet, darf die Kapitalgesellschaft auf die an anderer Stelle im Lagebericht enthaltenen nichtfinanziellen Angaben verweisen.

(2) Eine Kapitalgesellschaft im Sinne des Absatzes 1 ist unbeschadet anderer Befreiungsvorschriften von der Pflicht zur Erweiterung des Lageberichts um eine nichtfinanzielle Erklärung befreit, wenn

1. die Kapitalgesellschaft in den Konzernlagebericht eines Mutterunternehmens einbezogen ist und

§ 289b Obligation to make a non-financial statement; exemptions

(1) A corporation shall add a non-financial statement to its management report if it meets the following characteristics:

1. the corporation meets the requirements of § 267 sect. 3 sent. 1,
2. the corporation is capital-market oriented within the meaning of § 264d and
3. the corporation has employed more than 500 employees as an annual average.

§ 267 sect. 4 to 5 shall apply accordingly. If the non-financial statement forms a special section of the management report, the corporation may refer to the non-financial information contained elsewhere in the management report.

(2) A corporation within the meaning of section 1 shall, without prejudice to other exemption regulations, be exempt from the obligation to add a non-financial statement to the management report if

1. the corporation is included in the group management report of a parent company and

(continued)

2. der Konzernlagebericht nach Nummer 1 nach Maßgabe des nationalen Rechts eines Mitgliedstaats der Europäischen Union oder eines anderen Vertragsstaats des Abkommens über den Europäischen Wirtschaftsraum im Einklang mit der Richtlinie 2013/34/EU aufgestellt wird und eine nichtfinanzielle Konzernerklärung enthält.

Satz 1 gilt entsprechend, wenn das Mutterunternehmen im Sinne von Satz 1 einen gesonderten nichtfinanziellen Konzernbericht nach § 315b Absatz 3 oder nach Maßgabe des nationalen Rechts eines Mitgliedstaats der Europäischen Union oder eines anderen Vertragsstaats des Abkommens über den Europäischen Wirtschaftsraum im Einklang mit der Richtlinie 2013/34/EU erstellt und öffentlich zugänglich macht. Ist eine Kapitalgesellschaft nach Satz 1 oder 2 von der Pflicht zur Erstellung einer nichtfinanziellen Erklärung befreit, hat sie dies in ihrem Lagebericht mit einer Erläuterung anzugeben, welches Mutterunternehmen den Konzernlagebericht oder den gesonderten nichtfinanziellen Konzernbericht öffentlich zugänglich macht und wo der Bericht in deutscher oder englischer Sprache offengelegt oder veröffentlicht ist.

(3) Eine Kapitalgesellschaft im Sinne des Absatzes 1 ist auch dann von der Pflicht zur Erweiterung des Lageberichts um eine nichtfinanzielle Erklärung befreit, wenn die Kapitalgesellschaft für dasselbe Geschäftsjahr einen gesonderten nichtfinanziellen Bericht außerhalb des Lageberichts erstellt und folgende Voraussetzungen erfüllt sind:

1. der gesonderte nichtfinanzielle Bericht erfüllt zumindest die inhaltlichen Vorgaben nach § 289c und

2. die Kapitalgesellschaft macht den gesonderten nichtfinanziellen Bericht öffentlich zugänglich durch
a) Offenlegung zusammen mit dem Lagebericht nach § 325 oder

---

2. the group management report referred to in point 1 is prepared in accordance with the national law of a member state of the European Union or of another contracting state to the Agreement on the European Economic Area in accordance with Directive 2013/34/EU and includes a non-financial group statement.

Sentence 1 shall apply mutatis mutandis if the parent company within the meaning of sentence 1 prepares and makes publicly available a separate non-financial group report in accordance with § 315b sect. 3 or in accordance with the national law of a member state of the European Union or of another contracting state to the Agreement on the European Economic Area in accordance with Directive 2013/34/EU. If a corporation is exempt from the obligation to prepare a non-financial statement pursuant to sentence 1 or 2, it shall state this in its management report with an explanation of which parent company makes the group management report or the separate non-financial group report publicly available and where the report is disclosed or published in German or English.

(3) A corporation within the meaning of section 1 shall also be exempt from the obligation to add a non-financial statement to the management report if the corporation prepares a separate non-financial report outside the management report for the same business year and the following conditions are met:

1. the separate non-financial report fulfils at least the content requirements according to § 289c and

2. the corporation makes the separate non-financial report publicly available through

a) disclosure together with the management report pursuant to § 325 or

(continued)

b) Veröffentlichung auf der Internetseite der Kapitalgesellschaft spätestens vier Monate nach dem Abschlussstichtag und mindestens für zehn Jahre, sofern der Lagebericht auf diese Veröffentlichung unter Angabe der Internetseite Bezug nimmt.

Absatz 1 Satz 3 und die §§ 289d und 289e sind auf den gesonderten nichtfinanziellen Bericht entsprechend anzuwenden.

(4) Ist die nichtfinanzielle Erklärung oder der gesonderte nichtfinanzielle Bericht inhaltlich überprüft worden, ist auch die Beurteilung des Prüfungsergebnisses in gleicher Weise wie die nichtfinanzielle Erklärung oder der gesonderte nichtfinanzielle Bericht öffentlich zugänglich zu machen.

b) publication on the website of the corporation no later than four months after the balance sheet date and for at least ten years, provided that the management report refers to this publication by stating the website.

Section 1 sentence 3 and §§ 289d and 289e shall apply accordingly to the separate non-financial report.

(4) If the content of the non-financial statement or the separate non-financial report has been audited, the assessment of the audit result shall also be made publicly available in the same way as the non-financial statement or the separate non-financial report.

§ 289c Inhalt der nichtfinanziellen Erklärung

(1) In der nichtfinanziellen Erklärung im Sinne des § 289b ist das Geschäftsmodell der Kapitalgesellschaft kurz zu beschreiben.

(2) Die nichtfinanzielle Erklärung bezieht sich darüber hinaus zumindest auf folgende Aspekte:

1. Umweltbelange, wobei sich die Angaben beispielsweise auf Treibhausgasemissionen, den Wasserverbrauch, die Luftverschmutzung, die Nutzung von erneuerbaren und nicht erneuerbaren Energien oder den Schutz der biologischen Vielfalt beziehen können,

2. Arbeitnehmerbelange, wobei sich die Angaben beispielsweise auf die Maßnahmen, die zur Gewährleistung der Geschlechtergleichstellung ergriffen wurden, die Arbeitsbedingungen, die Umsetzung der grundlegenden Übereinkommen der Internationalen Arbeitsorganisation, die Achtung der Rechte der Arbeitnehmerinnen und Arbeitnehmer, informiert und konsultiert zu werden, den sozialen Dialog, die Achtung der Rechte der Gewerkschaften, den Gesundheitsschutz oder die Sicherheit am Arbeitsplatz beziehen können,

§ 289c Content of the non-financial statement

(1) The non-financial statement within the meaning of § 289b shall briefly describe the business model of the corporation.

(2) The non-financial statement shall also cover at least the following aspects:

1. environmental concerns, which may relate, for example, to greenhouse gas emissions, water consumption, air pollution, the use of renewable and non-renewable energy or the protection of biodiversity,

2. employees' concerns, which may relate, for example, to measures taken to ensure gender equality, working conditions, the implementation of the fundamental conventions of the International Labor Organization, respect for employees' rights to be informed and consulted, social dialogue, respect for trade union rights, health protection or safety at work,

(continued)

---

3. Sozialbelange, wobei sich die Angaben beispielsweise auf den Dialog auf kommunaler oder regionaler Ebene oder auf die zur Sicherstellung des Schutzes und der Entwicklung lokaler Gemeinschaften ergriffenen Maßnahmen beziehen können,

4. die Achtung der Menschenrechte, wobei sich die Angaben beispielsweise auf die Vermeidung von Menschenrechtsverletzungen beziehen können, und

5. die Bekämpfung von Korruption und Bestechung, wobei sich die Angaben beispielsweise auf die bestehenden Instrumente zur Bekämpfung von Korruption und Bestechung beziehen können.

(3) Zu den in Absatz 2 genannten Aspekten sind in der nichtfinanziellen Erklärung jeweils diejenigen Angaben zu machen, die für das Verständnis des Geschäftsverlaufs, des Geschäftsergebnisses, der Lage der Kapitalgesellschaft sowie der Auswirkungen ihrer Tätigkeit auf die in Absatz 2 genannten Aspekte erforderlich sind, einschließlich

1. einer Beschreibung der von der Kapitalgesellschaft verfolgten Konzepte, einschließlich der von der Kapitalgesellschaft angewandten Due-Diligence-Prozesse,

2. der Ergebnisse der Konzepte nach Nummer 1,

3. der wesentlichen Risiken, die mit der eigenen Geschäftstätigkeit der Kapitalgesellschaft verknüpft sind und die sehr wahrscheinlich schwerwiegende negative Auswirkungen auf die in Absatz 2 genannten Aspekte haben oder haben werden, sowie die Handhabung dieser Risiken durch die Kapitalgesellschaft,

---

3. social concerns, which may relate, for example, to dialogue at the local or regional level or to measures taken to ensure the protection and development of local communities,

4. respect for human rights, which may relate, for example, to the avoidance of human rights violations, and

5. the fight against corruption and bribery, which may relate, for example, to the existing anti-corruption and anti-bribery instruments.

(3) For each of the aspects referred to in section 2, the non-financial statement shall contain the information necessary for an understanding of the course of business, the business result, the position of the corporation as well as the impact of its activities on the aspects referred to in section 2, including

1. a description of the concepts pursued by the corporation, including the due diligence processes applied by the corporation,

2. the results of the concepts referred to in number 1,

3. the material risks associated with the corporation's own business activities that are very likely to have or will have a serious adverse effect on the aspects referred to in section 2, and the corporation's management of those risks,

(continued)

---

4. der wesentlichen Risiken, die mit den Geschäftsbeziehungen der Kapitalgesellschaft, ihren Produkten und Dienstleistungen verknüpft sind und die sehr wahrscheinlich schwerwiegende negative Auswirkungen auf die in Absatz 2 genannten Aspekte haben oder haben werden, soweit die Angaben von Bedeutung sind und die Berichterstattung über diese Risiken verhältnismäßig ist, sowie die Handhabung dieser Risiken durch die Kapitalgesellschaft,

5. der bedeutsamsten nichtfinanziellen Leistungsindikatoren, die für die Geschäftstätigkeit der Kapitalgesellschaft von Bedeutung sind,

6. soweit es für das Verständnis erforderlich ist, Hinweisen auf im Jahresabschluss ausgewiesene Beträge und zusätzliche Erläuterungen dazu.

(4) Wenn die Kapitalgesellschaft in Bezug auf einen oder mehrere der in Absatz 2 genannten Aspekte kein Konzept verfolgt, hat sie dies anstelle der auf den jeweiligen Aspekt bezogenen Angaben nach Absatz 3 Nummer 1 und 2 in der nichtfinanziellen Erklärung klar und begründet zu erläutern.

4. the material risks associated with the corporation's business relationships, products and services that are very likely to have or will have a serious adverse effect on the aspects referred to in section 2, to the extent that the information is material and the reporting of those risks is commensurate, and the corporation's management of those risks,

5. the most significant non-financial performance indicators relevant to the business of the corporation,

6. to the extent necessary for comprehension, references to amounts reported in the financial statements and additional explanations thereto.

(4) If the corporation does not pursue a concept with regard to one or more of the aspects referred to in section 2, it shall clearly and justifiably explain this in the non-financial statement instead of the disclosures relating to the respective aspect pursuant to section 3, no. 1 and 2.

---

§ 289d Nutzung von Rahmenwerken

Die Kapitalgesellschaft kann für die Erstellung der nichtfinanziellen Erklärung nationale, europäische oder internationale Rahmenwerke nutzen. In der Erklärung ist anzugeben, ob die Kapitalgesellschaft für die Erstellung der nichtfinanziellen Erklärung ein Rahmenwerk genutzt hat und, wenn dies der Fall ist, welches Rahmenwerk genutzt wurde, sowie andernfalls, warum kein Rahmenwerk genutzt wurde.

§ 289d Use of frameworks

The corporation may use national, European or international frameworks for the preparation of the non-financial statement. The statement shall indicate whether the corporation has used a framework for the preparation of the non-financial statement and, if so, which framework has been used and, if not, why no framework has been used.

---

§ 289e Weglassen nachteiliger Angaben

(1) Die Kapitalgesellschaft muss in die nichtfinanzielle Erklärung ausnahmsweise keine Angaben zu künftigen Entwicklungen oder Belangen, über die Verhandlungen geführt werden, aufnehmen, wenn

§ 289e Omission of disadvantageous information

(1) Exceptionally, the corporation need not include in the non-financial statement information on future developments or matters under negotiation if

---

(continued)

1. die Angaben nach vernünftiger kaufmännischer Beurteilung der Mitglieder des vertretungsberechtigten Organs der Kapitalgesellschaft geeignet sind, der Kapitalgesellschaft einen erheblichen Nachteil zuzufügen, und
2. das Weglassen der Angaben ein den tatsächlichen Verhältnissen entsprechendes und ausgewogenes Verständnis des Geschäftsverlaufs, des Geschäftsergebnisses, der Lage der Kapitalgesellschaft und der Auswirkungen ihrer Tätigkeit nicht verhindert.

(2) Macht eine Kapitalgesellschaft von Absatz 1 Gebrauch und entfallen die Gründe für die Nichtaufnahme der Angaben nach der Veröffentlichung der nichtfinanziellen Erklärung, sind die Angaben in die darauf folgende nichtfinanzielle Erklärung aufzunehmen.

1. the information is, in the reasonable commercial judgment of the members of the corporate body authorized to represent the corporation, likely to cause a material disadvantage to the corporation, and
2. the omission of the information does not prevent a true and fair view of the development of the business, the results of the operations, the position of the corporation and the impact of its activities.

(2) If a corporation makes use of section 1 and the reasons for not including the information cease to exist after the publication of the non-financial statement, the information shall be included in the subsequent non-financial statement.

§ 289f Erklärung zur Unternehmensführung

(1) Börsennotierte Aktiengesellschaften sowie Aktiengesellschaften, die ausschließlich andere Wertpapiere als Aktien zum Handel an einem organisierten Markt im Sinn des § 2 Absatz 11 des Wertpapierhandelsgesetzes ausgegeben haben und deren ausgegebene Aktien auf eigene Veranlassung über ein multilaterales Handelssystem im Sinn des § 2 Absatz 8 Satz 1 Nummer 8 des Wertpapierhandelsgesetzes gehandelt werden, haben eine Erklärung zur Unternehmensführung in ihren Lagebericht aufzunehmen, die dort einen gesonderten Abschnitt bildet. Sie kann auch auf der Internetseite der Gesellschaft öffentlich zugänglich gemacht werden. In diesem Fall ist in den Lagebericht eine Bezugnahme aufzunehmen, welche die Angabe der Internetseite enthält.

(2) In die Erklärung zur Unternehmensführung sind aufzunehmen
1. die Erklärung gemäß § 161 des Aktiengesetzes;

§ 289f Corporate governance statement

(1) Listed stock corporations as well as stock corporations that have exclusively issued securities other than shares for trading on an organized market within the meaning of § 2, section 11 of the Securities Trading Act (Wertpapierhandelsgesetz) and whose issued shares are traded on their own initiative via a multilateral trading system within the meaning of § 2, sect. 8, sent. 1, no. 8 of the Securities Trading Act shall include a corporate governance statement in their management report, which shall form a separate section therein. It may also be made publicly available on the company's website. In this case, a reference shall be included in the management report, which shall include the website.

(2) The corporate governance statement shall include
1. the statement pursuant to § 161 of the Stock Corporation Act (Aktiengesetz);

(continued)

1a. eine Bezugnahme auf die Internetseite der Gesellschaft, auf der der Vergütungsbericht über das letzte Geschäftsjahr und der Vermerk des Abschlussprüfers gemäß § 162 des Aktiengesetzes, das geltende Vergütungssystem gemäß § 87a Absatz 1 und 2 Satz 1 des Aktiengesetzes und der letzte Vergütungsbeschluss gemäß § 113 Absatz 3 des Aktiengesetzes öffentlich zugänglich gemacht werden;	1a. a reference to the company's website on which the remuneration report on the last business year and the auditor's report pursuant to § 162 of the Stock Corporation Act, the applicable remuneration system pursuant to § 87a sect. 1 and 2 sent. 1 of the Stock Corporation Act and the last remuneration resolution pursuant to § 113 sect. 3 of the Stock Corporation Act are made publicly available;
2. relevante Angaben zu Unternehmensführungspraktiken, die über die gesetzlichen Anforderungen hinaus angewandt werden, nebst Hinweis, wo sie öffentlich zugänglich sind;	2. relevant disclosures on corporate governance practices applied beyond the legal requirements, together with an indication of where they are publicly available;
3. eine Beschreibung der Arbeitsweise von Vorstand und Aufsichtsrat sowie der Zusammensetzung und Arbeitsweise von deren Ausschüssen; sind die Informationen auf der Internetseite der Gesellschaft öffentlich zugänglich, kann darauf verwiesen werden;	3. a description of the working methods of the executive board and the supervisory board as well as the composition and working methods of their committees; if the information is publicly available on the company's website, reference may be made to it;
4. bei börsennotierten Aktiengesellschaften die Festlegungen nach § 76 Absatz 4 und § 111 Absatz 5 des Aktiengesetzes und die Angabe, ob die festgelegten Zielgrößen während des Bezugszeitraums erreicht worden sind, und wenn nicht, Angaben zu den Gründen;	4. in the case of listed stock corporations, the determinations pursuant to § 76 sect. 4 and § 111 sect. 5 of the Stock Corporation Act and an indication of whether the determined target figures have been achieved during the reference period and, if not, information on the reasons;
5. die Angabe, ob die Gesellschaft bei der Besetzung des Aufsichtsrats mit Frauen und Männern jeweils Mindestanteile im Bezugszeitraum eingehalten hat, und wenn nicht, Angaben zu den Gründen, sofern es sich um folgende Gesellschaften handelt: a) börsennotierte Aktiengesellschaften, die auf Grund von § 96 Absatz 2 und 3 des Aktiengesetzes Mindestanteile einzuhalten haben oder b) börsennotierte Europäische Gesellschaften (SE), die auf Grund von § 17 Absatz 2 oder § 24 Absatz 3 des SE-Ausführungsgesetzes Mindestanteile einzuhalten haben;	5. the information of whether the company has complied with minimum proportions of women and men on the supervisory board during the reference period and, if not, information on the reasons, in the case of the following companies: a) listed stock corporations that are required to maintain minimum proportions pursuant to § 96 sect. 2 and 3 of the Stock Corporation Act, or b) listed European Companies (SE) that are required to maintain minimum proportions on the basis of § 17 sect. 2 or § 24 sect. 3 of the SE Implementation Act (SE Ausführungsgesetz);

(continued)

6. bei Aktiengesellschaften im Sinne des Absatzes 1, die nach § 267 Absatz 3 Satz 1 und Absatz 4 bis 5 große Kapitalgesellschaften sind, eine Beschreibung des Diversitätskonzepts, das im Hinblick auf die Zusammensetzung des vertretungsberechtigten Organs und des Aufsichtsrats in Bezug auf Aspekte wie beispielsweise Alter, Geschlecht, Bildungs- oder Berufshintergrund verfolgt wird, sowie der Ziele dieses Diversitätskonzepts, der Art und Weise seiner Umsetzung und der im Geschäftsjahr erreichten Ergebnisse.	6. in the case of stock corporations within the meaning of section 1 which are large corporations pursuant to § 267 sect. 3 sent. 1 and sect. 4 to 5, a description of the diversity concept pursued with regard to the composition of the body entitled to representation and of the supervisory board with regard to aspects such as, for example, age, gender, educational or professional background, as well as the objectives of this diversity concept, the manner of its implementation and the results achieved in the business year.
(3) Auf börsennotierte Kommanditgesellschaften auf Aktien sind die Absätze 1 und 2 entsprechend anzuwenden.	(3) Sections 1 and 2 shall apply mutatis mutandis to listed partnerships limited by shares.
(4) Andere Unternehmen, deren Vertretungsorgan und Aufsichtsrat nach § 36 oder § 52 des Gesetzes betreffend die Gesellschaften mit beschränkter Haftung oder nach § 76 Absatz 4 des Aktiengesetzes, auch in Verbindung mit § 188 Absatz 1 Satz 2 des Versicherungsaufsichtsgesetzes, oder nach § 111 Absatz 5 des Aktiengesetzes, auch in Verbindung mit § 189 Absatz 3 Satz 1 des Versicherungsaufsichtsgesetzes, verpflichtet sind, Zielgrößen für den Frauenanteil und Fristen für deren Erreichung festzulegen, haben in ihrem Lagebericht als gesonderten Abschnitt eine Erklärung zur Unternehmensführung mit den Festlegungen und Angaben nach Absatz 2 Nummer 4 aufzunehmen; Absatz 1 Satz 2 und 3 gilt entsprechend. Gesellschaften, die nicht zur Offenlegung eines Lageberichts verpflichtet sind, haben eine Erklärung mit den Festlegungen und Angaben nach Absatz 2 Nummer 4 zu erstellen und gemäß Absatz 1 Satz 2 zu veröffentlichen. Sie können diese Pflicht auch durch Offenlegung eines unter Berücksichtigung von Satz 1 erstellten Lageberichts erfüllen.	(4) Other companies whose representative body and supervisory board are obliged to set targets for the proportion of women and deadlines for achieving them in accordance with § 36 or § 52 of the Act on Limited Liability Companies (Gesetz betreffend die Gesellschaften mit beschränkter Haftung) or § 76, sect. 4 of the Stock Corporation Act, also in conjunction with § 188, sect. 1, sent. 2 of the Insurance Supervision Act (Versicherungsaufsichtsgesetz), or § 111, sect. 5 of the Stock Corporation Act, also in conjunction with § 189, sect. 3, sent. 1 of the Insurance Supervision Act, shall include a corporate governance statement in their management report as a separate section with the stipulations and information in accordance with section 2, number 4; section 1, sentences 2 and 3 shall apply accordingly. Companies which are not obliged to disclose a management report shall prepare a declaration with the stipulations and information pursuant to section 2 number 4 and publish it pursuant to section 1 sentence 2. They may also fulfil this obligation by disclosing a management report prepared taking into account sentence 1.
(5) Wenn eine Gesellschaft nach Absatz 2 Nummer 6, auch in Verbindung mit Absatz 3, kein Diversitätskonzept verfolgt, hat sie dies in der Erklärung zur Unternehmensführung zu erläutern.	(5) If a company pursuant to section 2 number 6, also in conjunction with section 3, does not pursue a diversity concept, it shall explain this in the corporate governance statement.

(continued)

Zweiter Unterabschnitt Konzernabschluc und Konzernlagebericht	Second subsection Consolidated financial statements and group management report
Erster Titel Anwendungsbereich	**First title Scope of application**

§ 290 Pflicht zur Aufstellung	§ 290 Obligation of preparation

§ 290 Pflicht zur Aufstellung
(1) Die gesetzlichen Vertreter einer Kapitalgesellschaft (Mutterunternehmen) mit Sitz im Inland haben in den ersten fünf Monaten des Konzerngeschäftsjahrs für das vergangene Konzerngeschäftsjahr einen Konzernabschluss und einen Konzernlagebericht aufzustellen, wenn diese auf ein anderes Unternehmen (Tochterunternehmen) unmittel- oder mittelbar einen beherrschenden Einfluss ausüben kann. Ist das Mutterunternehmen eine Kapitalgesellschaft im Sinn des § 325 Abs. 4 Satz 1, sind der Konzernabschluss sowie der Konzernlagebericht in den ersten vier Monaten des Konzerngeschäftsjahrs für das vergangene Konzerngeschäftsjahr aufzustellen.
(2) Beherrschender Einfluss eines Mutterunternehmens besteht stets, wenn
1. ihm bei einem anderen Unternehmen die Mehrheit der Stimmrechte der Gesellschafter zusteht;
2. ihm bei einem anderen Unternehmen das Recht zusteht, die Mehrheit der Mitglieder des die Finanz- und Geschäftspolitik bestimmenden Verwaltungs-, Leitungs- oder Aufsichtsorgans zu bestellen oder abzuberufen, und es gleichzeitig Gesellschafter ist;
3. ihm das Recht zusteht, die Finanz- und Geschäftspolitik auf Grund eines mit einem anderen Unternehmen geschlossenen Beherrschungsvertrages oder auf Grund einer Bestimmung in der Satzung des anderen Unternehmens zu bestimmen, oder

§ 290 Obligation of preparation
(1) The legal representatives of a corporation (parent company) with its registered office in Germany shall prepare consolidated financial statements and a group management report for the previous group business year within the first five months of the group business year if it can directly or indirectly exercise a controlling influence on another company (subsidiary company). If the parent company is a corporation within the meaning of § 325 sect. 4 sent. 1, the consolidated financial statements and the group management report shall be prepared in the first four months of the group business year for the previous group business year.
(2) Controlling influence of a parent company always exists if
1. it holds the majority of the shareholders' voting rights in another company;
2. it has the right to appoint or remove the majority of the members of the administrative, management or supervisory body determining the financial and business policy of another company and it is at the same time a shareholder;
3. it has the right to determine the financial and business policies on the basis of a control agreement concluded with another company or on the basis of a regulation in the articles of association of the other company, or

(continued)

4. es bei wirtschaftlicher Betrachtung die Mehrheit der Risiken und Chancen eines Unternehmens trägt, das zur Erreichung eines eng begrenzten und genau definierten Ziels des Mutterunternehmens dient (Zweckgesellschaft). Neben Unternehmen können Zweckgesellschaften auch sonstige juristische Personen des Privatrechts oder unselbständige Sondervermögen des Privatrechts sein, ausgenommen Spezial-Sondervermögen im Sinn des § 2 Absatz 3 des Investmentgesetzes oder vergleichbare ausländische Investmentvermögen oder als Sondervermögen aufgelegte offene inländische Spezial- AIF mit festen Anlagebedingungen im Sinn des § 284 des Kapitalanlagegesetzbuchs oder vergleichbare EU-Investmentvermögen oder ausländische Investmentvermögen, die den als Sondervermögen aufgelegten offenen inländischen Spezial-AIF mit festen Anlagebedingungen im Sinn des § 284 des Kapitalanlagegesetzbuchs vergleichbar sind.	4. from an economic point of view, it bears the majority of the risks and rewards of an company that serves to achieve a narrowly limited and precisely defined objective of the parent company (special purpose entity). In addition to companies, special purpose entities may also be other legal entities under private law or dependent special funds under private law, with the exception of special funds within the meaning of § 2 sect. 3 of the Investment Act (Investmentgesetz) or comparable foreign investment funds or open domestic special AIFs with fixed investment conditions issued as special funds within the meaning of § 284 of the Capital Investment Code (Kapitalanlagegesetzbuch) or comparable EU investment funds or foreign investment funds that are comparable to the open domestic special AIFs with fixed investment conditions issued as special funds within the meaning of § 284 of the Capital Investment Code.
(3) Als Rechte, die einem Mutterunternehmen nach Absatz 2 zustehen, gelten auch die einem anderen Tochterunternehmen zustehenden Rechte und die den für Rechnung des Mutterunternehmens oder von Tochterunternehmen handelnden Personen zustehenden Rechte. Den einem Mutterunternehmen an einem anderen Unternehmen zustehenden Rechten werden die Rechte hinzugerechnet, über die es selbst oder eines seiner Tochterunternehmen auf Grund einer Vereinbarung mit anderen Gesellschaftern dieses Unternehmens verfügen kann. Abzuziehen sind Rechte, die	(3) The rights of a parent company referred to in section 2 shall include the rights of another subsidiary company and the rights of persons acting on account of the parent company or of the subsidiary companies. To the rights of a parent company in another company shall be added the rights which it or any of its subsidiaries has under an agreement with other shareholders of that company. Rights that are to be deducted
1. mit Anteilen verbunden sind, die von dem Mutterunternehmen oder von dessen Tochterunternehmen für Rechnung einer anderen Person gehalten werden, oder	1. are linked to shares held by the parent company or by its subsidiary company for the account of another person, or

(continued)

2. mit Anteilen verbunden sind, die als Sicherheit gehalten werden, sofern diese Rechte nach Weisung des Sicherungsgebers oder, wenn ein Kreditinstitut die Anteile als Sicherheit für ein Darlehen hält, im Interesse des Sicherungsgebers ausgeübt werden.

(4) Welcher Teil der Stimmrechte einem Unternehmen zusteht, bestimmt sich für die Berechnung der Mehrheit nach Absatz 2 Nr. 1 nach dem Verhältnis der Zahl der Stimmrechte, die es aus den ihm gehörenden Anteilen ausüben kann, zur Gesamtzahl aller Stimmrechte. Von der Gesamtzahl aller Stimmrechte sind die Stimmrechte aus eigenen Anteilen abzuziehen, die dem Tochterunternehmen selbst, einem seiner Tochterunternehmen oder einer anderen Person für Rechnung dieser Unternehmen gehören.

(5) Ein Mutterunternehmen ist von der Pflicht, einen Konzernabschluss und einen Konzernlagebericht aufzustellen, befreit, wenn es nur Tochterunternehmen hat, die gemäß § 296 nicht in den Konzernabschluss einbezogen werden brauchen.

2. are linked to shares held as collateral, provided that such rights are exercised in accordance with the instructions of the collateral provider or, if a credit institution holds the shares as collateral for a loan, in the interest of the collateral provider.

(4) For the purpose of calculating the majority pursuant to section 2 no. 1, the portion of the voting rights to which a company is entitled shall be determined by the ratio of the number of voting rights which it can exercise from the shares belonging to it to the total number of all voting rights. The voting rights from own shares belonging to the subsidiary itself, to one of its subsidiaries or to another person for the account of these companies shall be deducted from the total number of all voting rights.

(5) A parent company is exempt from the obligation to prepare consolidated financial statements and a group management report if it only has subsidiaries that do not need to be included in the consolidated financial statements pursuant to § 296.

§ 291 Befreiende Wirkung von EU/EWR-Konzernabschlüssen

(1) Ein Mutterunternehmen, das zugleich Tochterunternehmen eines Mutterunternehmens mit Sitz in einem Mitgliedstaat der Europäischen Union oder in einem anderen Vertragsstaat des Abkommens über den Europäischen Wirtschaftsraum ist, braucht einen Konzernabschluß und einen Konzernlagebericht nicht aufzustellen, wenn ein den Anforderungen des Absatzes 2 entsprechender Konzernabschluß und Konzernlagebericht seines Mutterunternehmens einschließlich des Bestätigungsvermerks oder des Vermerks über dessen Versagung nach den für den

§ 291 Exempting effect of EU/EEA consolidated financial statements

(1) A parent company which is at the same time a subsidiary of a parent company having its registered office in a member state of the European Union or in another contracting state to the Agreement on the European Economic Area need not prepare consolidated financial statements and a group management report, if consolidated financial statements and a group management report meeting the requirements of section 2 are prepared including the auditor's report or the report on the refusal thereof, and shall be disclosed in German or English in accordance with the regulations applicable to

(continued)

entfallenden Konzernabschluß und Konzernlagebericht maßgeblichen Vorschriften in deutscher oder englischer Sprache offengelegt wird. Ein befreiender Konzernabschluß und ein befreiender Konzernlagebericht können von jedem Unternehmen unabhängig von seiner Rechtsform und Größe aufgestellt werden, wenn das Unternehmen als Kapitalgesellschaft mit Sitz in einem Mitgliedstaat der Europäischen Union oder in einem anderen Vertragsstaat des Abkommens über den Europäischen Wirtschaftsraum zur Aufstellung eines Konzernabschlusses unter Einbeziehung des zu befreienden Mutterunternehmens und seiner Tochterunternehmen verpflichtet wäre.

the consolidated financial statements and the group management report that are being dispensed with. Exempting consolidated financial statements and an exempting group management report may be prepared by any company, irrespective of its legal form and size, if the company is a corporation with its registered office in a member state of the European Union or in another contracting state to the Agreement on the European Economic Area and would be obliged to prepare consolidated financial statements including the parent company to be exempted and its subsidiaries.

(2) Der Konzernabschluß und Konzernlagebericht eines Mutterunternehmens mit Sitz in einem Mitgliedstaat der Europäischen Union oder in einem anderen Vertragsstaat des Abkommens über den Europäischen Wirtschaftsraum haben befreiende Wirkung, wenn

(2) The consolidated financial statements and group management report of a parent company with its registered office in a member state of the European Union or in another contracting state to the Agreement on the European Economic Area shall have an exempting effect if

1. das zu befreiende Mutterunternehmen und seine Tochterunternehmen in den befreienden Konzernabschluß unbeschadet des § 296 einbezogen worden sind,

1. the parent company to be exempted and its subsidiaries have been included in the exempting consolidated financial statements without prejudice to § 296,

2. der befreiende Konzernabschluss nach dem auf das Mutterunternehmen anwendbaren Recht im Einklang mit der Richtlinie 2013/34/EU oder im Einklang mit den in § 315e Absatz 1 bezeichneten internationalen Rechnungslegungsstandards aufgestellt und im Einklang mit der Richtlinie 2006/43/EG geprüft worden ist,

2. the exempting consolidated financial statements have been prepared under the law applicable to the parent company in accordance with Directive 2013/34/EU or in accordance with the International Financial Reporting Standards referred to in § 315e sect. 1 and audited in accordance with Directive 2006/43/EC,

3. der befreiende Konzernlagebericht nach dem auf das Mutterunternehmen anwendbaren Recht im Einklang mit der Richtlinie 2013/34/EU aufgestellt und im Einklang mit der Richtlinie 2006/43/EG geprüft worden ist,

3. the exempting group management report has been prepared in accordance with the law applicable to the parent company in accordance with Directive 2013/34/EU and audited in accordance with Directive 2006/43/EC,

4. der Anhang des Jahresabschlusses des zu befreienden Unternehmens folgende Angaben enthält:

4. the notes to the financial statements of the company to be exempted contain the following information:

(continued)

a) Name und Sitz des Mutterunternehmens, das den befreienden Konzernabschluß und Konzernlagebericht aufstellt,	a) Name and registered office of the parent company preparing the exempting consolidated financial statements and group management report,
b) einen Hinweis auf die Befreiung von der Verpflichtung, einen Konzernabschluß und einen Konzernlagebericht aufzustellen, und	b) an indication of the exemption from the obligation to prepare consolidated financial statements and a consolidated management report, and
c) eine Erläuterung der im befreienden Konzernabschluß vom deutschen Recht abweichend angewandten Bilanzierungs-, Bewertungs- und Konsolidierungsmethoden.	c) an explanation of the recognition, measurement and consolidation methods applied in the exempting consolidated financial statements in deviation from German law.

Satz 1 gilt für Kreditinstitute und Versicherungsunternehmen entsprechend; unbeschadet der übrigen Voraussetzungen in Satz 1 hat die Aufstellung des befreienden Konzernabschlusses und des befreienden Konzernlageberichts bei Kreditinstituten im Einklang mit der Richtlinie 86/635/EWG des Rates vom 8. Dezember 1986 über den Jahresabschluß und den konsolidierten Abschluß von Banken und anderen Finanzinstituten (ABl. EG Nr. L 372 S. 1) und bei Versicherungsunternehmen im Einklang mit der Richtlinie 91/674/EWG des Rates vom 19. Dezember 1991 über den Jahresabschluß und den konsolidierten Jahresabschluß von Versicherungsunternehmen (ABl. EG Nr. L 374 S. 7) in ihren jeweils geltenden Fassungen zu erfolgen.

(3) Die Befreiung nach Absatz 1 kann trotz Vorliegens der Voraussetzungen nach Absatz 2 von einem Mutterunternehmen nicht in Anspruch genommen werden, wenn

1. das zu befreiende Mutterunternehmen einen organisierten Markt im Sinn des § 2 Absatz 11 des Wertpapierhandelsgesetzes durch von ihm ausgegebene Wertpapiere im Sinn des § 2 Absatz 1 des Wertpapierhandelsgesetzes in Anspruch nimmt,

Sentence 1 shall apply mutatis mutandis to credit institutions and insurance companies; notwithstanding the other requirements in sentence 1, the preparation of the exempting consolidated financial statements and the exempting consolidated management report for credit institutions shall be in accordance with Council Directive 86/635/EEC of 8 December 1986 on the financial statements and consolidated financial statements of banks and other financial institutions (OJ EC No. L 372 p. 1) and, in the case of insurance companies, in accordance with Council Directive 91/674/EEC of 19 December 1991 on the financial statements and consolidated financial statements of insurance companies (OJ EC No. L 374 p. 7), as amended.

(3) The exemption under section 1 may not be claimed by a parent company despite the existence of the conditions under section 2 if

1. the parent company to be exempted makes use of an organized market within the meaning of § 2 sect. 11 of the Securities Trading Act (Wertpapierhandelsgesetzes) through securities issued by it within the meaning of § 2 sect. 1 of the Securities Trading Act,

(continued)

2. Gesellschafter, denen bei Aktiengesellschaften und Kommanditgesellschaften auf Aktien mindestens 10 vom Hundert und bei Gesellschaften mit beschränkter Haftung mindestens 20 vom Hundert der Anteile an dem zu befreienden Mutterunternehmen gehören, spätestens sechs Monate vor dem Ablauf des Konzerngeschäftsjahrs die Aufstellung eines Konzernabschlusses und eines Konzernlageberichts beantragt haben.

2. shareholders who own at least 10 per cent of the shares in the parent company to be exempted in the case of stock corporations and partnerships limited by shares and at least 20 per cent of the shares in the parent company to be exempted in the case of limited liability companies, no later than six months before the end of the group business year have applied for preparation of consolidated financial statements and a group management report.

§ 292 Befreiende Wirkung von Konzernabschlüssen aus Drittstaaten
(1) Ein Mutterunternehmen, das zugleich Tochterunternehmen eines Mutterunternehmens mit Sitz in einem Staat, der nicht Mitglied der Europäischen Union und auch nicht Vertragsstaat des Abkommens über den Europäischen Wirtschaftsraum ist, braucht einen Konzernabschluss und einen Konzernlagebericht nicht aufzustellen, wenn dieses andere Mutterunternehmen einen dem § 291 Absatz 2 Nummer 1 entsprechenden Konzernabschluss (befreiender Konzernabschluss) und Konzernlagebericht (befreiender Konzernlagebericht) aufstellt sowie außerdem alle folgenden Voraussetzungen erfüllt sind:
1. der befreiende Konzernabschluss wird wie folgt aufgestellt:
   a) nach Maßgabe des Rechts eines Mitgliedstaats der Europäischen Union oder eines anderen Vertragsstaats des Abkommens über den Europäischen Wirtschaftsraum im Einklang mit der Richtlinie 2013/34/EU,
   b) im Einklang mit den in § 315e Absatz 1 bezeichneten internationalen Rechnungslegungsstandards,
   c) derart, dass er einem nach den in Buchstabe a bezeichneten Vorgaben erstellten Konzernabschluss gleichwertig ist, oder

§ 292 Exempting effect of consolidated financial statements from third countries
(1) A parent company that is also a subsidiary of a parent company with its registered office in a state that is not a member of the European Union and is also not a contracting state to the Agreement on the European Economic Area need not prepare consolidated financial statements and a group management report if this other parent company prepares consolidated financial statements (exempting consolidated financial statements) and a group management report (exempting group management report) that comply with § 291 sect. 2 no. 1 and if all of the following conditions are also met:
1. the exempting consolidated financial statements are prepared as follows:
   a) in accordance with the law of a member state of the European Union or of another contracting state to the Agreement on the European Economic Area, in accordance with Directive 2013/34/EU,
   b) in accordance with the International Financial Reporting Standards referred to in § 315e sect. 1,
   c) in such a way that it is equivalent to consolidated financial statements prepared in accordance with the requirements referred to in letter a), or

(continued)

d) derart, dass er internationalen Rechnungslegungsstandards entspricht, die gemäß der Verordnung (EG) Nr. 1569/2007 der Kommission vom 21. Dezember 2007 über die Einrichtung eines Mechanismus zur Festlegung der Gleichwertigkeit der von Drittstaatemittenten angewandten Rechnungslegungsgrundsätze gemäß den Richtlinien 2003/71/EG und 2004/109/EG des Europäischen Parlaments und des Rates (ABl. L 340 vom 22.12.2007, S. 66), die durch die Delegierte Verordnung (EU) Nr. 310/2012 (ABl. L 103 vom 13.4.2012, S. 11) geändert worden ist, in ihrer jeweils geltenden Fassung festgelegt wurden;	d) in such a way that it complies with International Financial Reporting Standards adopted pursuant to Commission Regulation (EC) No. 1569/2007 of 21 December 2007 on the establishment of a mechanism for determining equivalence of accounting standards applied by third-country issuers under Directives 2003/71/EC and 2004/109/EC of the European Parliament and of the Council (OJ L 340, 22.12.2007, p. 66), as amended by Delegated Regulation (EU) No. 310/2012 (OJ L 103, 13.4.2012, p. 11), as amended;
2. der befreiende Konzernlagebericht wird nach Maßgabe der in Nummer 1 Buchstabe a genannten Vorgaben aufgestellt oder ist einem nach diesen Vorgaben aufgestellten Konzernlagebericht gleichwertig;	2. the exempting group management report is prepared in accordance with the requirements set out in number 1 letter a) or is equivalent to a group management report prepared in accordance with those requirements;
3. der befreiende Konzernabschluss ist von einem oder mehreren Abschlussprüfern oder einer oder mehreren Prüfungsgesellschaften geprüft worden, die auf Grund der einzelstaatlichen Rechtsvorschriften, denen das Unternehmen unterliegt, das diesen Abschluss aufgestellt hat, zur Prüfung von Jahresabschlüssen zugelassen sind;	3. the exempting consolidated financial statements have been audited by one or more statutory auditors or by one or more audit firms which, in accordance with the national law applicable to the company that prepared these financial statements are licensed to audit financial statements;
4. der befreiende Konzernabschluss, der befreiende Konzernlagebericht und der Bestätigungsvermerk sind nach den für den entfallenden Konzernabschluss und Konzernlagebericht maßgeblichen Vorschriften in deutscher oder englischer Sprache offengelegt worden.	4. the exempting consolidated financial statements, the exempting group management report and the auditor's report have been disclosed in German or English in accordance with the regulations applicable to the dispensed consolidated financial statements and group management report.

(continued)

---

(2) Die befreiende Wirkung tritt nur ein, wenn im Anhang des Jahresabschlusses des zu befreienden Unternehmens die in § 291 Absatz 2 Satz 1 Nummer 4 genannten Angaben gemacht werden und zusätzlich angegeben wird, nach welchen der in Absatz 1 Nummer 1 genannten Vorgaben sowie gegebenenfalls nach dem Recht welchen Staates der befreiende Konzernabschluss und der befreiende Konzernlagebericht aufgestellt worden sind. Im Übrigen ist § 291 Absatz 2 Satz 2 und Absatz 3 entsprechend anzuwenden.

(3) Ist ein nach Absatz 1 zugelassener Konzernabschluß nicht von einem in Übereinstimmung mit den Vorschriften der Richtlinie 2006/43/EG zugelassenen Abschlußprüfer geprüft worden, so kommt ihm befreiende Wirkung nur zu, wenn der Abschlußprüfer eine den Anforderungen dieser Richtlinie gleichwertige Befähigung hat und der Konzernabschluß in einer den Anforderungen des Dritten Unterabschnitts entsprechenden Weise geprüft worden ist. Nicht in Übereinstimmung mit den Vorschriften der Richtlinie 2006/43/EG zugelassene Abschlussprüfer von Unternehmen mit Sitz in einem Drittstaat im Sinn des § 3 Abs. 1 Satz 1 der Wirtschaftsprüferordnung, deren Wertpapiere im Sinn des § 2 Absatz 1 des Wertpapierhandelsgesetzes an einer inländischen Börse zum Handel am regulierten Markt zugelassen sind, haben nur dann eine den Anforderungen der Richtlinie gleichwertige Befähigung, wenn sie bei der Wirtschaftsprüferkammer gemäß § 134 Abs. 1 der Wirtschaftsprüferordnung eingetragen sind oder die Gleichwertigkeit gemäß § 134 Abs. 4 der Wirtschaftsprüferordnung anerkannt ist. Satz 2 ist nicht anzuwenden, soweit ausschließlich Schuldtitel im Sinne des § 2 Absatz 1 Nummer 3 des Wertpapierhandelsgesetzes

(2) The exempting effect shall only come into effect if the notes to the financial statements of the company to be exempted contain the information specified in § 291 sect. 2 sent. 1 no. 4 and additionally state according to which of the requirements specified in section 1 number 1 and, if applicable, according to the law of which state the exempting consolidated financial statements and the exempting group management report have been prepared. In all other respects, § 291 sect. 2 sent. 2 and sect. 3 shall apply mutatis mutandis.

(3) Where consolidated financial statements approved under section 1 have not been audited by an auditor approved in accordance with the requirements of Directive 2006/43/EC, they shall have an exempting effect only if the auditor has qualifications equivalent to the requirements of that Directive and the consolidated financial statements are audited in a manner consistent with the requirements of Subsection Three. Statutory auditors of companies with their registered office in a third country within the meaning of § 3 sect. 1 sent. 1 of the Auditors' Act (Wirtschaftsprüferordnung), whose securities within the meaning of § 2 sect. 1 of the Securities Trading Act (Wertpapierhandelsgesetz)are admitted to trading on the regulated market of a domestic stock exchange, who are not licensed in accordance with the provisions of Directive 2006/43/EC, shall only have a qualification equivalent to the requirements of the Directive if they are registered with the Chamber of Auditors (Wirtschaftsprüferkammer) pursuant to § 134 sect. 1 of the Auditors' Act or if they have demonstrated equivalence pursuant to § 134 sect. 4 of the Auditors' Act. Sentence 2 shall not apply insofar as exclusively debt instruments within the meaning of § 2 sect. 1 no. 3 of the Securities Trading Act

---

(continued)

1. mit einer Mindeststückelung zu je 100 000 Euro oder einem entsprechenden Betrag anderer Währung an einer inländischen Börse zum Handel am regulierten Markt zugelassen sind oder	1. are admitted to trading on the regulated market of a domestic stock exchange with a minimum denomination of €100,000 each or an equivalent amount of other currency, or
2. mit einer Mindeststückelung zu je 50 000 Euro oder einem entsprechenden Betrag anderer Währung an einer inländischen Börse zum Handel am regulierten Markt zugelassen sind und diese Schuldtitel vor dem 31. Dezember 2010 begeben worden sind. Im Falle des Satzes 2 ist mit dem Bestätigungsvermerk nach Absatz 1 Nummer 4 auch eine Bescheinigung der Wirtschaftsprüferkammer gemäß § 134 Absatz 2a der Wirtschaftsprüferordnung über die Eintragung des Abschlussprüfers oder eine Bestätigung der Wirtschaftsprüferkammer gemäß § 134 Absatz 4 Satz 8 der Wirtschaftsprüferordnung über die Befreiung von der Eintragungsverpflichtung offenzulegen.	2. with a minimum denomination of €50,000 each or an equivalent amount of other currency are admitted to trading on a domestic stock exchange on the regulated market and these debt instruments were issued before the 31 December 2010. In the case of sentence 2, a certificate of the Chamber of Auditors pursuant to § 134 sect. 2a of the Auditors' Act on the registration of the auditor or a confirmation of the Chamber of Accountants pursuant to § 134 sect. 4 sent. 8 of the Auditors' Act on the exemption from the obligation to register shall also be disclosed with the auditor's report pursuant to section 1 number 4.

§ 292a (weggefallen)	**§ 292a (omitted)**

§ 293 Größenabhängige Befreiungen (1) Ein Mutterunternehmen ist von der Pflicht, einen Konzernabschluß und einen Konzernlagebericht aufzustellen, befreit, wenn 1. am Abschlußstichtag seines Jahresabschlusses und am vorhergehenden Abschlußstichtag mindestens zwei der drei nachstehenden Merkmale zutreffen: a) Die Bilanzsummen in den Bilanzen des Mutterunternehmens und der Tochterunternehmen, die in den Konzernabschluß einzubeziehen wären, übersteigen insgesamt nicht 24 000 000 Euro. b) Die Umsatzerlöse des Mutterunternehmens und der Tochterunternehmen, die in den Konzernabschluß einzubeziehen wären, übersteigen in den zwölf Monaten vor dem Abschlußstichtag insgesamt nicht 48 000 000 Euro.	**§ 293 Size-dependent exemptions** (1) A parent company shall be exempt from the obligation to prepare consolidated financial statements and a group management report if 1. at least two of the following three characteristics apply on the balance sheet date of its financial statements and on the preceding balance sheet date: a) The balance sheet totals in the balance sheets of the parent company and the subsidiaries to be included in the consolidated financial statements do not exceed €24,000,000 in total. b) The total sales revenue of the parent company and the subsidiaries to be included in the consolidated financial statements does not exceed€48,000,000 in the twelve months preceding the balance sheet date.

(continued)

c) Das Mutterunternehmen und die Tochterunternehmen, die in den Konzernabschluß einzubeziehen wären, haben in den zwölf Monaten vor dem Abschlußstichtag im Jahresdurchschnitt nicht mehr als 250 Arbeitnehmer beschäftigt;
oder

2. am Abschlußstichtag eines von ihm aufzustellenden Konzernabschlusses und am vorhergehenden Abschlußstichtag mindestens zwei der drei nachstehenden Merkmale zutreffen:
a) Die Bilanzsumme übersteigt nicht 20 000 000 Euro.
b) Die Umsatzerlöse in den zwölf Monaten vor dem Abschlußstichtag übersteigen nicht 40 000 000 Euro.
c) Das Mutterunternehmen und die in den Konzernabschluß einbezogenen Tochterunternehmen haben in den zwölf Monaten vor dem Abschlußstichtag im Jahresdurchschnitt nicht mehr als 250 Arbeitnehmer beschäftigt.

Auf die Ermittlung der durchschnittlichen Zahl der Arbeitnehmer ist § 267 Abs. 5 anzuwenden.
(2) Auf die Ermittlung der Bilanzsumme ist § 267 Absatz 4a entsprechend anzuwenden.
(3) (weggefallen)
(4) Außer in den Fällen des Absatzes 1 ist ein Mutterunternehmen von der Pflicht zur Aufstellung des Konzernabschlusses und des Konzernlageberichts befreit, wenn die Voraussetzungen des Absatzes 1 nur am Abschlußstichtag oder nur am vorhergehenden Abschlußstichtag erfüllt sind und das Mutterunternehmen am vorhergehenden Abschlußstichtag von der Pflicht zur Aufstellung des Konzernabschlusses und des Konzernlageberichts befreit war. § 267 Abs. 4 Satz 2 und 3 ist entsprechend anzuwenden.

c) The parent company and the subsidiaries to be included in the consolidated financial statements have not employed more than 250 employees on an annual average in the twelve months prior to the balance sheet date;

or

2. at least two of the following three characteristics apply on the balance sheet date of a consolidated financial statement to be prepared by it and on the preceding balance sheet date:
a) The balance sheet total does not exceed €20,000,000.
b) Sales revenue in the twelve months preceding the balance sheet date does not exceed €40,000,000.
c) The parent company and the subsidiaries included in the consolidated financial statements have not employed more than 250 employees on an annual average in the twelve months prior to the balance sheet date.

§ 267 sect. 5 shall apply to the determination of the average number of employees.
(2) § 267 sect. 4a shall apply mutatis mutandis to the determination of the balance sheet total.
(3) (omitted)
(4) Except in the cases set out in section 1, a parent company shall be exempt from the obligation to prepare the consolidated financial statements and the group management report if the requirements set out in section 1 are met only on the balance sheet date or only on the preceding balance sheet date and the parent company was exempt from the obligation to prepare the consolidated financial statements and the group management report on the preceding balance sheet date. § 267 sect. 4 sent. 2 and 3 shall apply accordingly.

(continued)

(5) Die Absätze 1 und 4 sind nicht anzuwenden, wenn das Mutterunternehmen oder ein in dessen Konzernabschluss einbezogenes Tochterunternehmen am Abschlussstichtag kapitalmarktorientiert im Sinn des § 264d ist oder es den Vorschriften des Ersten oder Zweiten Unterabschnitts des Vierten Abschnitts unterworfen ist.	(5) Sections 1 and 4 do not apply if the parent company or a subsidiary included in its consolidated financial statements is capital-market oriented within the meaning of § 264d at balance sheet date or it is subject to the regulations of the first or second subsection of the fourth section.

Zweiter Titel Konsolidierungskreis	**Title Two Consolidation scope**

§ 294 Einzubeziehende Unternehmen; Vorlage- und Auskunftspflichten	**§ 294 Companies to be included; obligations to submit documents and provide information**
(1) In den Konzernabschluß sind das Mutterunternehmen und alle Tochterunternehmen ohne Rücksicht auf den Sitz und die Rechtsform der Tochterunternehmen einzubeziehen, sofern die Einbeziehung nicht nach § 296 unterbleibt.	(1) The consolidated financial statements shall include the parent company and all subsidiaries irrespective of the registered office and legal form of the subsidiaries, unless the inclusion is omitted pursuant to § 296.
(2) Hat sich die Zusammensetzung der in den Konzernabschluß einbezogenen Unternehmen im Laufe des Geschäftsjahrs wesentlich geändert, so sind in den Konzernabschluß Angaben aufzunehmen, die es ermöglichen, die aufeinanderfolgenden Konzernabschlüsse sinnvoll zu vergleichen.	(2) If the composition of the companies included in the consolidated financial statements has changed significantly during the business year, information shall be included in the consolidated financial statements to enable a meaningful comparison of successive consolidated financial statements.
(3) Die Tochterunternehmen haben dem Mutterunternehmen ihre Jahresabschlüsse, Einzelabschlüsse nach § 325 Abs. 2a, Lageberichte, gesonderten nichtfinanziellen Berichte, Konzernabschlüsse, Konzernlageberichte, gesonderten nichtfinanziellen Konzernberichte und, wenn eine Abschlussprüfung stattgefunden hat, die Prüfungsberichte sowie, wenn ein Zwischenabschluß aufzustellen ist, einen auf den Stichtag des Konzernabschlusses aufgestellten Abschluß unverzüglich einzureichen. Das Mutterunternehmen kann von jedem Tochterunternehmen alle Aufklärungen und Nachweise verlangen, welche die Aufstellung des Konzernabschlusses, des Konzernlageberichts und des gesonderten nichtfinanziellen Konzernberichts erfordert.	(3) The subsidiaries shall submit to the parent company their financial statements, individual financial statements pursuant to § 325 sect. 2a, management reports, separate non-financial reports, consolidated financial statements, group management reports, separate non-financial group reports and, if an audit has taken place, the audit reports and, if interim financial statements are required to be prepared, financial statements prepared to the date of the consolidated financial statements, without undue delay. The parent company may require any subsidiary to provide any information and evidence necessary for the preparation of the consolidated financial statements, the group management report and the separate non-financial group report.

(continued)

§ 295 (weggefallen)	§ 295 (omitted)

§ 296 Verzicht auf die Einbeziehung
(1) Ein Tochterunternehmen braucht in den Konzernabschluß nicht einbezogen zu werden, wenn
1. erhebliche und andauernde Beschränkungen die Ausübung der Rechte des Mutterunternehmens in bezug auf das Vermögen oder die Geschäftsführung dieses Unternehmens nachhaltig beeinträchtigen,
2. die für die Aufstellung des Konzernabschlusses erforderlichen Angaben nicht ohne unverhältnismäßig hohe Kosten oder unangemessene Verzögerungen zu erhalten sind oder
3. die Anteile des Tochterunternehmens ausschließlich zum Zwecke ihrer Weiterveräußerung gehalten werden.
(2) Ein Tochterunternehmen braucht in den Konzernabschluß nicht einbezogen zu werden, wenn es für die Verpflichtung, ein den tatsächlichen Verhältnissen entsprechendes Bild der Vermögens-, Finanz- und Ertragslage des Konzerns zu vermitteln, von untergeordneter Bedeutung ist. Entsprechen mehrere Tochterunternehmen der Voraussetzung des Satzes 1, so sind diese Unternehmen in den Konzernabschluß einzubeziehen, wenn sie zusammen nicht von untergeordneter Bedeutung sind.
(3) Die Anwendung der Absätze 1 und 2 ist im Konzernanhang zu begründen.

§ 296 Waiver of inclusion
(1) A subsidiary need not be included in the consolidated financial statements if
1. significant and continuing restrictions substantially impair the exercise of the parent's rights over the assets or management of that company,
2. the information required for the preparation of the consolidated financial statements cannot be obtained without unreasonable cost or delay, or
3. the shares of the subsidiary are held exclusively for the purpose of their resale.

(2) A subsidiary need not be included in the consolidated financial statements if it is of minor importance to the obligation to give a true and fair view of the asset, finance and income position of the group. If several subsidiaries correspond to the requirement of sentence 1, these companies shall be included in the consolidated financial statements if together they are not of minor importance.

(3) The application of sections 1 and 2 shall be justified in the notes to the consolidated financial statements.

Dritter Titel Inhalt und Form des Konzernabschlusses

Third title Content and form of the consolidated financial statements

§ 297 Inhalt
(1) Der Konzernabschluss besteht aus der Konzernbilanz, der Konzern-Gewinn- und Verlustrechnung, dem Konzernanhang, der Kapitalflussrechnung und dem Eigenkapitalspiegel. Er kann um eine Segmentberichterstattung erweitert werden.

§ 297 Contents
(1) The consolidated financial statements consist of the consolidated balance sheet, the consolidated income statement, the notes to the consolidated financial statements, the cash flow statement and the statement of changes in equity. It can be expanded to include a segment reporting.

(continued)

(1a) Im Konzernabschluss sind die Firma, der Sitz, das Registergericht und die Nummer, unter der das Mutterunternehmen in das Handelsregister eingetragen ist, anzugeben. Befindet sich das Mutterunternehmen in Liquidation oder Abwicklung, ist auch diese Tatsache anzugeben.

(2) Der Konzernabschluß ist klar und übersichtlich aufzustellen. Er hat unter Beachtung der Grundsätze ordnungsmäßiger Buchführung ein den tatsächlichen Verhältnissen entsprechendes Bild der Vermögens-, Finanz- und Ertragslage des Konzerns zu vermitteln. Führen besondere Umstände dazu, daß der Konzernabschluß ein den tatsächlichen Verhältnissen entsprechendes Bild im Sinne des Satzes 2 nicht vermittelt, so sind im Konzernanhang zusätzliche Angaben zu machen. Die Mitglieder des vertretungsberechtigten Organs eines Mutterunternehmens, das als Inlandsemittent (§ 2 Absatz 14 des Wertpapierhandelsgesetzes) Wertpapiere (§ 2 Absatz 1 des Wertpapierhandelsgesetzes) begibt und keine Kapitalgesellschaft im Sinne des § 327a ist, haben in einer dem Konzernabschluss beizufügenden schriftlichen Erklärung zu versichern, dass der Konzernabschluss nach bestem Wissen ein den tatsächlichen Verhältnissen entsprechendes Bild im Sinne des Satzes 2 vermittelt oder der Konzernanhang Angaben nach Satz 3 enthält.

(3) Im Konzernabschluß ist die Vermögens-, Finanz- und Ertragslage der einbezogenen Unternehmen so darzustellen, als ob diese Unternehmen insgesamt ein einziges Unternehmen wären. Die auf den vorhergehenden Konzernabschluß angewandten Konsolidierungsmethoden sind beizubehalten. Abweichungen von Satz 2 sind in Ausnahmefällen zulässig. Sie sind im Konzernanhang anzugeben und zu begründen. Ihr Einfluß auf die Vermögens-, Finanz- und Ertragslage des Konzerns ist anzugeben.

(1a) The consolidated financial statements shall disclose the name, registered office, commercial register and the number under which the parent company is entered in the commercial register. If the parent company is in liquidation or being wound up, this fact shall also be disclosed.

(2) The consolidated financial statements shall be prepared clearly and transparently. They shall give a true and fair view of the asset, finance and income position of the group in accordance with generally accepted accounting principles. If special circumstances lead to the consolidated financial statements not giving a true and fair view within the meaning of sentence 2, additional disclosures shall be made in the notes to the consolidated financial statements. The members of the governing body of a parent company that issues securities (§ 2 section 1 of the Securities Trading Act (Wertpapierhandelsgesetz)) as a domestic issuer (§ 2 sect. 14 of the Securities Trading Act) and is not a corporation within the meaning of § 327a shall declare in a written statement to be attached to the consolidated financial statements that, to the best of their knowledge, the consolidated financial statements give a true and fair view within the meaning of sentence 2 or that the notes to the consolidated financial statements contain information pursuant to sentence 3.

(3) In the consolidated financial statements, the asset, finance and income position of the companies included shall be presented as if these companies were collectively a single entity. The consolidation methods applied in the previous consolidated financial statements shall be retained. Deviations from sentence 2 are permissible in exceptional cases. They shall be disclosed and justified in the notes to the consolidated financial statements. Their influence on the asset, finance and income position of the group shall be disclosed.

(continued)

---

§ 298 Anzuwendende Vorschriften, Erleichterungen

(1) Auf den Konzernabschluß sind, soweit seine Eigenart keine Abweichung bedingt oder in den folgenden Vorschriften nichts anderes bestimmt ist, die §§ 244 bis 256a, 264c, 265, 266, 268 Absatz 1 bis 7, die §§ 270, 271, 272 Absatz 1 bis 4, die §§ 274, 275 und 277 über den Jahresabschluß und die für die Rechtsform und den Geschäftszweig der in den Konzernabschluß einbezogenen Unternehmen mit Sitz im Geltungsbereich dieses Gesetzes geltenden Vorschriften, soweit sie für große Kapitalgesellschaften gelten, entsprechend anzuwenden.

(2) Der Konzernanhang und der Anhang des Jahresabschlusses des Mutterunternehmens dürfen zusammengefaßt werden. In diesem Falle müssen der Konzernabschluß und der Jahresabschluß des Mutterunternehmens gemeinsam offengelegt werden. Aus dem zusammengefassten Anhang muss hervorgehen, welche Angaben sich auf den Konzern und welche Angaben sich nur auf das Mutterunternehmen beziehen.

§ 298 Applicable regulations, simplifications

(1) §§ 244 to 256a, 264c, 265, 266, 268 sect. 1 to 7, §§ 270, 271, 272 sect. 1 to 4, §§ 274, 275 and 277 on the financial statements and the regulations to the legal form and the business sector of the companies included in the consolidated financial statements and having their registered office within the scope of this Act shall apply mutatis mutandis to the consolidated financial statements, unless their nature requires otherwise or the following regulations provide otherwise.

(2) The notes to the consolidated financial statements and the notes to the parent company's financial statements may be combined. In this case, the consolidated financial statements and the parent company's financial statements must be disclosed together. The combined notes must indicate which disclosures relate to the group and which disclosures relate to the parent company only.

---

§ 299 Stichtag für die Aufstellung

(1) Der Konzernabschluss ist auf den Stichtag des Jahresabschlusses des Mutterunternehmens aufzustellen.

(2) Die Jahresabschlüsse der in den Konzernabschluß einbezogenen Unternehmen sollen auf den Stichtag des Konzernabschlusses aufgestellt werden. Liegt der Abschlußstichtag eines Unternehmens um mehr als drei Monate vor dem Stichtag des Konzernabschlusses, so ist dieses Unternehmen auf Grund eines auf den Stichtag und den Zeitraum des Konzernabschlusses aufgestellten Zwischenabschlusses in den Konzernabschluß einzubeziehen.

§ 299 Closing date for the preparation

(1) The consolidated financial statements shall be prepared as at the balance sheet date of the parent company's financial statements.

(2) The financial statements of the companies included in the consolidated financial statements shall be prepared as at the balance sheet date of the consolidated financial statements. If the balance sheet date of a company is more than three months before the balance sheet date of the consolidated financial statements, this company shall be included in the consolidated financial statements on the basis of interim financial statements prepared as at the balance sheet date and for the period covered by the consolidated financial statements.

(continued)

(3) Wird bei abweichenden Abschlußstichtagen ein Unternehmen nicht auf der Grundlage eines auf den Stichtag und den Zeitraum des Konzernabschlusses aufgestellten Zwischenabschlusses in den Konzernabschluß einbezogen, so sind Vorgänge von besonderer Bedeutung für die Vermögens-, Finanz- und Ertragslage eines in den Konzernabschluß einbezogenen Unternehmens, die zwischen dem Abschlußstichtag dieses Unternehmens und dem Abschlußstichtag des Konzernabschlusses eingetreten sind, in der Konzernbilanz und der Konzern- Gewinn- und Verlustrechnung zu berücksichtigen oder im Konzernanhang anzugeben.	(3) If, in the case of different balance sheet dates, a company is not included in the consolidated financial statements on the basis of interim financial statements prepared for the balance sheet date and the period covered by the consolidated financial statements, events of particular importance for the asset, finance and income position of a company included in the consolidated financial statements which occurred between the balance sheet date of that company and the balance sheet date of the consolidated financial statements shall be taken into account in the consolidated balance sheet and the consolidated income statement or disclosed in the notes to the consolidated financial statements.

Vierter Titel Vollkonsolidierung	**Title Four Full consolidation**
§ 300 Konsolidierungsgrundsätze, Vollständigkeitsgebot (1) In dem Konzernabschluß ist der Jahresabschluß des Mutterunternehmens mit den Jahresabschlüssen der Tochterunternehmen zusammenzufassen. An die Stelle der dem Mutterunternehmen gehörenden Anteile an den einbezogenen Tochterunternehmen treten die Vermögensgegenstände, Schulden, Rechnungsabgrenzungsposten und Sonderposten der Tochterunternehmen, soweit sie nach dem Recht des Mutterunternehmens bilanzierungsfähig sind und die Eigenart des Konzernabschlusses keine Abweichungen bedingt oder in den folgenden Vorschriften nichts anderes bestimmt ist.	**§ 300 Consolidation principles, completeness requirement** (1) The consolidated financial statements shall combine the financial statements of the parent company with the financial statements of the subsidiaries. The parent company's shares in the consolidated subsidiaries shall be replaced by the assets, liabilities, deferred items and special items of the subsidiaries, insofar as they can be accounted for under the law of the parent company and the nature of the consolidated financial statements does not require any deviations or the following regulations do not provide otherwise.

(continued)

(2) Die Vermögensgegenstände, Schulden und Rechnungsabgrenzungsposten sowie die Erträge und Aufwendungen der in den Konzernabschluß einbezogenen Unternehmen sind unabhängig von ihrer Berücksichtigung in den Jahresabschlüssen dieser Unternehmen vollständig aufzunehmen, soweit nach dem Recht des Mutterunternehmens nicht ein Bilanzierungsverbot oder ein Bilanzierungswahlrecht besteht. Nach dem Recht des Mutterunternehmens zulässige Bilanzierungswahlrechte dürfen im Konzernabschluß unabhängig von ihrer Ausübung in den Jahresabschlüssen der in den Konzernabschluß einbezogenen Unternehmen ausgeübt werden. Ansätze, die auf der Anwendung von für Kreditinstitute oder Versicherungsunternehmen wegen der Besonderheiten des Geschäftszweigs geltenden Vorschriften beruhen, dürfen beibehalten werden; auf die Anwendung dieser Ausnahme ist im Konzernanhang hinzuweisen.	(2) The assets, liabilities and deferred items as well as the income and expenses of the companies included in the consolidated financial statements shall be included in full irrespective of their inclusion in the financial statements of those companies, unless the law of the parent company prohibits a recognition or permits an accounting option. Accounting options permitted under the law of the parent company may be exercised in the consolidated financial statements irrespective of their exercise in the financial statements of the companies included in the consolidated financial statements. Recognized items based on the application of rules applicable to credit institutions or insurance companies because of the special nature of the business may be retained; the application of this exception shall be disclosed in the notes to the consolidated financial statements.

§ 301 Kapitalkonsolidierung (1) Der Wertansatz der dem Mutterunternehmen gehörenden Anteile an einem in den Konzernabschluß einbezogenen Tochterunternehmen wird mit dem auf diese Anteile entfallenden Betrag des Eigenkapitals des Tochterunternehmens verrechnet. Das Eigenkapital ist mit dem Betrag anzusetzen, der dem Zeitwert der in den Konzernabschluss aufzunehmenden Vermögensgegenstände, Schulden, Rechnungsabgrenzungsposten und Sonderposten entspricht, der diesen an dem für die Verrechnung nach Absatz 2 maßgeblichen Zeitpunkt beizulegen ist. Rückstellungen sind nach § 253 Abs. 1 Satz 2 und 3, Abs. 2 und latente Steuern nach § 274 Abs. 2 zu bewerten.	**§ 301 Capital consolidation** (1) The value of the shares in a subsidiary included in the consolidated financial statements belonging to the parent company shall be offset against the amount of the subsidiary's equity attributable to these shares. The equity shall be stated at the amount corresponding to the fair value of the assets, liabilities, deferred items and special items to be included in the consolidated financial statements as of the date relevant for offsetting in accordance with section 2. Provisions shall be measured in accordance with § 253 sect. 1 sent. 2 and 3, sect. 2 and deferred taxes in accordance with § 274 sect. 2.

(continued)

(2) Die Verrechnung nach Absatz 1 ist auf Grundlage der Wertansätze zu dem Zeitpunkt durchzuführen, zu dem das Unternehmen Tochterunternehmen geworden ist. Können die Wertansätze zu diesem Zeitpunkt nicht endgültig ermittelt werden, sind sie innerhalb der darauf folgenden zwölf Monate anzupassen. Stellt ein Mutterunternehmen erstmalig einen Konzernabschluss auf, sind die Wertansätze zum Zeitpunkt der Einbeziehung des Tochterunternehmens in den Konzernabschluss zugrunde zu legen, soweit das Tochterunternehmen nicht in dem Jahr Tochterunternehmen geworden ist, für das der Konzernabschluss aufgestellt wird. Das Gleiche gilt für die erstmalige Einbeziehung eines Tochterunternehmens, auf die bisher gemäß § 296 verzichtet wurde. In Ausnahmefällen dürfen die Wertansätze nach Satz 1 auch in den Fällen der Sätze 3 und 4 zugrunde gelegt werden; dies ist im Konzernanhang anzugeben und zu begründen.

(3) Ein nach der Verrechnung verbleibender Unterschiedsbetrag ist in der Konzernbilanz, wenn er auf der Aktivseite entsteht, als Geschäfts- oder Firmenwert und, wenn er auf der Passivseite entsteht, unter dem Posten „Unterschiedsbetrag aus der Kapitalkonsolidierung" nach dem Eigenkapital auszuweisen. Der Posten und wesentliche Änderungen gegenüber dem Vorjahr sind im Konzernanhang zu erläutern.

(4) Anteile an dem Mutterunternehmen, die einem in den Konzernabschluss einbezogenen Tochterunternehmen gehören, sind in der Konzernbilanz als eigene Anteile des Mutterunternehmens mit ihrem Nennwert oder, falls ein solcher nicht vorhanden ist, mit ihrem rechnerischen Wert, in der Vorspalte offen von dem Posten „Gezeichnetes Kapital" abzusetzen.

(2) The offsetting according to section 1 shall be carried out on the basis of the values at the time at which the company became a subsidiary. If the values cannot be finally determined at that time, they shall be adjusted within the following twelve months. If a parent company prepares consolidated financial statements for the first time, values at the time of the subsidiary's inclusion in the consolidated financial statements shall be used as a basis, unless the subsidiary became a subsidiary in the year for which the consolidated financial statements are prepared. The same applies to the first-time inclusion of a subsidiary that was previously waived pursuant to § 296. In exceptional cases, the values according to sentence 1 may also be used in the cases of sentences 3 and 4; this must be stated and justified in the notes to the consolidated financial statements.

(3) Any difference remaining after offsetting is recognized in the consolidated balance sheet as goodwill if it arises on the assets side and under the item "difference from capital consolidation" if it arises on the liabilities side to be shown after equity. The item and significant changes compared to the previous year are to be explained in the notes to the consolidated financial statements.

(4) Shares in the parent company belonging to a subsidiary included in the consolidated financial statements are deducted in the consolidated balance sheet as treasury shares of the parent company, in the pre-column open from the item "subscribed capital" with their nominal value or par value, if such a value does not exist, with its imputed value.

(continued)

§ 302 (weggefallen)	§ 302 (omitted)
§ 303 Schuldenkonsolidierung (1) Ausleihungen und andere Forderungen, Rückstellungen und Verbindlichkeiten zwischen den in den Konzernabschluß einbezogenen Unternehmen sowie entsprechende Rechnungsabgrenzungsposten sind wegzulassen. (2) Absatz 1 braucht nicht angewendet zu werden, wenn die wegzulassenden Beträge für die Vermittlung eines den tatsächlichen Verhältnissen entsprechenden Bildes der Vermögens-, Finanz- und Ertragslage des Konzerns nur von untergeordneter Bedeutung sind.	**§ 303 Liability consolidation** (1) Loans and other receivables, provisions and debt between the companies included in the consolidated financial statements as well as corresponding deferred items shall be omitted. (2) Section 1 need not be applied if the amounts to be omitted are of only minor importance for the presentation of a true and fair view of the asset, finance and income position of the group.
§ 304 Behandlung der Zwischenergebnisse (1) In den Konzernabschluß zu übernehmende Vermögensgegenstände, die ganz oder teilweise auf Lieferungen oder Leistungen zwischen in den Konzernabschluß einbezogenen Unternehmen beruhen, sind in der Konzernbilanz mit einem Betrag anzusetzen, zu dem sie in der auf den Stichtag des Konzernabschlusses aufgestellten Jahresbilanz dieses Unternehmens angesetzt werden könnten, wenn die in den Konzernabschluß einbezogenen Unternehmen auch rechtlich ein einziges Unternehmen bilden würden. (2) Absatz 1 braucht nicht angewendet zu werden, wenn die Behandlung der Zwischenergebnisse nach Absatz 1 für die Vermittlung eines den tatsächlichen Verhältnissen entsprechenden Bildes der Vermögens-, Finanz- und Ertragslage des Konzerns nur von untergeordneter Bedeutung ist.	**§ 304 Treatment of intercompany profits** (1) Assets to be included in the consolidated financial statements which are based wholly or partly on supplies or services between companies included in the consolidated financial statements shall be recognized in the consolidated balance sheet at an amount at which they could be recognized in the balance sheet of that company prepared as at the date of the consolidated financial statements if the companies included in the consolidated financial statements also legally formed a single company. (2) Section 1 need not be applied if the treatment of intercompany profits in accordance with section 1 is of only minor importance for the presentation of a true and fair view of the asset, finance and income position of the group.
§ 305 Aufwands- und Ertragskonsolidierung (1) In der Konzern-Gewinn- und Verlustrechnung sind	**§ 305 Consolidation of expenses and income** (1) In the consolidated income statement,

(continued)

1. bei den Umsatzerlösen die Erlöse aus Lieferungen und Leistungen zwischen den in den Konzernabschluß einbezogenen Unternehmen mit den auf sie entfallenden Aufwendungen zu verrechnen, soweit sie nicht als Erhöhung des Bestands an fertigen und unfertigen Erzeugnissen oder als andere aktivierte Eigenleistungen auszuweisen sind,
2. andere Erträge aus Lieferungen und Leistungen zwischen den in den Konzernabschluß einbezogenen Unternehmen mit den auf sie entfallenden Aufwendungen zu verrechnen, soweit sie nicht als andere aktivierte Eigenleistungen auszuweisen sind.
(2) Aufwendungen und Erträge brauchen nach Absatz 1 nicht weggelassen zu werden, wenn die wegzulassenden Beträge für die Vermittlung eines den tatsächlichen Verhältnissen entsprechenden Bildes der Vermögens-, Finanz- und Ertragslage des Konzerns nur von untergeordneter Bedeutung sind.

1. sales revenues resulting from deliveries and services between the companies included in the consolidated financial statements are to be offset against the expenses attributable to them, insofar as they are not to be shown as an increase in finished or unfinished goods or as other own work capitalized,
2. other income from deliveries and services between the companies included in the consolidated financial statements is to be offset against the expenses attributable to them, insofar as they are not to be shown as other own work capitalized.
(2) Expenses and income need not be omitted pursuant to section 1 if the amounts to be omitted are of only minor importance for the presentation of a true and fair view of the asset, finance and income position of the group.

§ 306 Latente Steuern

Führen Maßnahmen, die nach den Vorschriften dieses Titels durchgeführt worden sind, zu Differenzen zwischen den handelsrechtlichen Wertansätzen der Vermögensgegenstände, Schulden oder Rechnungsabgrenzungsposten und deren steuerlichen Wertansätzen und bauen sich diese Differenzen in späteren Geschäftsjahren voraussichtlich wieder ab, so ist eine sich insgesamt ergebende Steuerbelastung als passive latente Steuern und eine sich insgesamt ergebende Steuerentlastung als aktive latente Steuern in der Konzernbilanz anzusetzen. Die sich ergebende Steuerbe- und die sich ergebende Steuerentlastung können auch unverrechnet angesetzt werden. Differenzen aus dem erstmaligen Ansatz eines nach § 301 Abs. 3 verbleibenden Unterschiedsbetrages bleiben unberücksichtigt. Das Gleiche gilt für Differenzen, die sich zwischen dem steuerlichen Wertansatz einer Beteiligung an einem Tochterunternehmen, assoziierten Unternehmen oder einem

§ 306 Deferred taxes

If measures carried out in accordance with the regulations of this title lead to differences between the commercial-law values of assets, liabilities or deferred items and their values for tax purposes, and if these differences are expected to be reversed in subsequent business years, a total resulting tax burden shall be recognized as a deferred tax liability and a total resulting tax relief as a deferred tax asset in the consolidated balance sheet. The resulting tax burden and the resulting tax relief may also be recognized without being offset. Differences arising from the initial recognition of a remaining difference in accordance with § 301 sect. 3 are not taken into account. The same shall apply to differences arising between the value for tax purposes of a participation in a subsidiary, associated company or joint venture within the meaning of § 310 sect. 1 and the commercial-law value of the net assets recognized in the consolidated financial statements.

(continued)

Gemeinschaftsunternehmen im Sinn des § 310 Abs. 1 und dem handelsrechtlichen Wertansatz des im Konzernabschluss angesetzten Nettovermögens ergeben. § 274 Abs. 2 ist entsprechend anzuwenden. Die Posten dürfen mit den Posten nach § 274 zusammengefasst werden.	§ 274 sect. 2 shall be applied accordingly. The items may be combined with the items under § 274.

§ 307 Anteile anderer Gesellschafter

(1) In der Konzernbilanz ist für nicht dem Mutterunternehmen gehörende Anteile an in den Konzernabschluß einbezogenen Tochterunternehmen ein Ausgleichsposten für die Anteile der anderen Gesellschafter in Höhe ihres Anteils am Eigenkapital unter dem Posten „nicht beherrschende Anteile" innerhalb des Eigenkapitals gesondert auszuweisen.

(2) In der Konzern-Gewinn- und Verlustrechnung ist der im Jahresergebnis enthaltene, anderen Gesellschaftern zustehende Gewinn und der auf sie entfallende Verlust nach dem Posten "Jahresüberschuß/ Jahresfehlbetrag" unter dem Posten „nicht beherrschende Anteile" gesondert auszuweisen.

§ 307 Shares of other shareholders

(1) In the consolidated balance sheet, for shares not belonging to the parent company in a company included in the consolidated financial statement, an adjustment item for the shares of the other shareholders in the amount of their share in the equity is to be shown separately under the item "non-controlling interests" within the equity.

(2) In the consolidated income statement, the profit and loss attributable to other shareholders included in the annual result shall be shown separately under the item "non-controlling interests" after the item "net profit/ loss of the year".

Fünfter Titel Bewertungsvorschriften

Title Five Measurement rules

§ 308 Einheitliche Bewertung

(1) Die in den Konzernabschluß nach § 300 Abs. 2 übernommenen Vermögensgegenstände und Schulden der in den Konzernabschluß einbezogenen Unternehmen sind nach den auf den Jahresabschluß des Mutterunternehmens anwendbaren Bewertungsmethoden einheitlich zu bewerten. Nach dem Recht des Mutterunternehmens zulässige Bewertungswahlrechte können im Konzernabschluß unabhängig von ihrer Ausübung in den Jahresabschlüssen der in den Konzernabschluß einbezogenen Unternehmen ausgeübt werden. Abweichungen von den auf den Jahresabschluß des Mutterunternehmens angewandten Bewertungsmethoden sind im Konzernanhang anzugeben und zu begründen.

§ 308 Uniform measurement

(1) The assets and liabilities of the companies included in the consolidated financial statements which are included in the consolidated financial statements pursuant to § 300 sect. 2 shall be measured uniformly in accordance with the measurement methods applicable to the financial statements of the parent company. Measurement options permitted under the law of the parent company may be applied in the consolidated financial statements irrespective of their exercise in the financial statements of the companies included in the consolidated financial statements. Deviations from the measurement methods applied to the financial statements of the parent company shall be disclosed and justified in the notes to the consolidated financial statements.

(continued)

(2) Sind in den Konzernabschluß aufzunehmende Vermögensgegenstände oder Schulden des Mutterunternehmens oder der Tochterunternehmen in den Jahresabschlüssen dieser Unternehmen nach Methoden bewertet worden, die sich von denen unterscheiden, die auf den Konzernabschluß anzuwenden sind oder die von den gesetzlichen Vertretern des Mutterunternehmens in Ausübung von Bewertungswahlrechten auf den Konzernabschluß angewendet werden, so sind die abweichend bewerteten Vermögensgegenstände oder Schulden nach den auf den Konzernabschluß angewandten Bewertungsmethoden neu zu bewerten und mit den neuen Wertansätzen in den Konzernabschluß zu übernehmen. Wertansätze, die auf der Anwendung von für Kreditinstitute oder Versicherungsunternehmen wegen der Besonderheiten des Geschäftszweigs geltenden Vorschriften beruhen, dürfen beibehalten werden; auf die Anwendung dieser Ausnahme ist im Konzernanhang hinzuweisen. Eine einheitliche Bewertung nach Satz 1 braucht nicht vorgenommen zu werden, wenn ihre Auswirkungen für die Vermittlung eines den tatsächlichen Verhältnissen entsprechenden Bildes der Vermögens-, Finanz- und Ertragslage des Konzerns nur von untergeordneter Bedeutung sind. Darüber hinaus sind Abweichungen in Ausnahmefällen zulässig; sie sind im Konzernanhang anzugeben und zu begründen.	(2) If assets or liabilities of the parent company or of subsidiaries to be included in the consolidated financial statements have been measured in the financial statements of these companies according to methods which differ from those which are to be applied to the consolidated financial statements or which are applied to the consolidated financial statements by the legal representatives of the parent company in the exercise of measurement options, the assets or liabilities measured differently shall be re-measured according to the measurement methods applied to the consolidated financial statements and included in the consolidated financial statements at the new values. Values based on the application of regulations applicable to credit institutions or insurance companies because of the special features of the line of business may be retained; reference must be made to the application of this exception in the notes to the consolidated financial statements. A uniform measurement in accordance with sentence 1 need not be made if its effects are of minor importance for the presentation of a true and fair view of the asset, finance and income position of the group. In addition, deviations are permissible in exceptional cases; they must be disclosed and justified in the notes to the consolidated financial statements.

(continued)

§ 308a Umrechnung von auf fremde Währung lautenden Abschlüssen	**§ 308a Translation of financial statements denominated in foreign currency**

§ 308a Umrechnung von auf fremde Währung lautenden Abschlüssen

Die Aktiv- und Passivposten einer auf fremde Währung lautenden Bilanz sind, mit Ausnahme des Eigenkapitals, das zum historischen Kurs in Euro umzurechnen ist, zum Devisenkassamittelkurs am Abschlussstichtag in Euro umzurechnen. Die Posten der Gewinn- und Verlustrechnung sind zum Durchschnittskurs in Euro umzurechnen. Eine sich ergebende Umrechnungsdifferenz ist innerhalb des Konzerneigenkapitals nach den Rücklagen unter dem Posten „Eigenkapitaldifferenz aus Währungsumrechnung" auszuweisen. Bei teilweisem oder vollständigem Ausscheiden des Tochterunternehmens ist der Posten in entsprechender Höhe erfolgswirksam aufzulösen.

§ 308a Translation of financial statements denominated in foreign currency

The assets and liabilities of a balance sheet denominated in a foreign currency shall, with the exception of equity, which shall be translated into Euros at the historical exchange rate, be translated into Euros at the mean spot exchange rate on the balance sheet date. The items of the income statement shall be translated into Euros at the average exchange rate. Any resulting translation difference shall be reported within the group equity after the reserves under the item "equity difference from currency translation". In the event of partial or complete withdrawal of the subsidiary, the item is to be reversed in the corresponding amount and recognized in profit or loss.

§ 309 Behandlung des Unterschiedsbetrags

(1) Die Abschreibung eines nach § 301 Abs. 3 auszuweisenden Geschäfts- oder Firmenwertes bestimmt sich nach den Vorschriften des Ersten Abschnitts.
(2) Ein nach § 301 Absatz 3 auf der Passivseite auszuweisender Unterschiedsbetrag kann ergebniswirksam aufgelöst werden, soweit ein solches Vorgehen den Grundsätzen der §§ 297 und 298 in Verbindung mit den Vorschriften des Ersten Abschnitts entspricht.

§ 309 Treatment of the difference

(1) The amortization of goodwill to be recognized pursuant § 301 sect. 3 shall be determined in accordance with the regulations of the first section.
(2) A difference to be shown on the liabilities side in accordance with § 301 sect. 3 may be reversed to profit or loss, provided such action is in accordance with the principles of §§ 297 and 298 in conjunction with the regulations of the first section.

Sechster Titel Anteilmto be shown on the l

Sixth title Proportional consolidation

§ 310 Anteilmäßige Konsolidierung

(1) Führt ein in einen Konzernabschluß einbezogenes Mutter- oder Tochterunternehmen ein anderes Unternehmen gemeinsam mit einem oder mehreren nicht in den Konzernabschluß einbezogenen Unternehmen, so darf das andere Unternehmen in den Konzernabschluß entsprechend den Anteilen am Kapital einbezogen werden, die dem Mutterunternehmen gehören.
(2) Auf die anteilmäßige Konsolidierung sind die §§ 297 bis 301, §§ 303 bis 306, 308, 308a, 309 entsprechend anzuwenden.

§ 310 Proportional consolidation

(1) Where a parent company or subsidiary included in consolidated financial statements manages another company jointly with one or more companies not included in the consolidated financial statements, the other company may be included in the consolidated financial statements in proportion to the shares in the capital belonging to the parent company.
(2) §§ 297 to 301, §§ 303 to 306, 308, 308a, and 309 shall apply mutatis mutandis to the proportional consolidation.

(continued)

Siebenter Titel Assoziierte Unternehmen	Title Seven Associated companies
§ 311 Definition. Befreiung (1) Wird von einem in den Konzernabschluß einbezogenen Unternehmen ein maßgeblicher Einfluß auf die Geschäfts- und Finanzpolitik eines nicht einbezogenen Unternehmens, an dem das Unternehmen nach § 271 Abs. 1 beteiligt ist, ausgeübt (assoziiertes Unternehmen), so ist diese Beteiligung in der Konzernbilanz unter einem besonderen Posten mit entsprechender Bezeichnung auszuweisen. Ein maßgeblicher Einfluß wird vermutet, wenn ein Unternehmen bei einem anderen Unternehmen mindestens den fünften Teil der Stimmrechte der Gesellschafter innehat. (2) Auf eine Beteiligung an einem assoziierten Unternehmen brauchen Absatz 1 und § 312 nicht angewendet zu werden, wenn die Beteiligung für die Vermittlung eines den tatsächlichen Verhältnissen entsprechenden Bildes der Vermögens-, Finanz- und Ertragslage des Konzerns von untergeordneter Bedeutung ist.	**§ 311 Definition. Exemption** (1) If a company included in the consolidated financial statements exercises a significant influence on the business and financial policy of a company not included in the consolidated financial statements in which the company has a participation in accordance with § 271 sect. 1 (associated company), this participation shall be reported in the consolidated balance sheet under a special item with an appropriate designation. Significant influence shall be presumed if a company holds at least one fifth of the shareholders' voting rights in another company. (2) Section 1 and § 312 need not be applied to a participation in an associated company if the participation is of minor importance for the presentation of a true and fair view of the asset, finance and income position of the group.
§ 312 Wertansatz der Beteiligung und Behandlung des Unterschiedsbetrags (1) Eine Beteiligung an einem assoziierten Unternehmen ist in der Konzernbilanz mit dem Buchwert anzusetzen. Der Unterschiedsbetrag zwischen dem Buchwert und dem anteiligen Eigenkapital des assoziierten Unternehmens sowie ein darin enthaltener Geschäfts- oder Firmenwert oder passiver Unterschiedsbetrag sind im Konzernanhang anzugeben.	**§ 312 Measurement of the participation and treatment of the difference** (1) A participation in an associated company shall be recognized in the consolidated balance sheet at its book value. The difference between the book value and the proportionate equity of the associated company as well as any goodwill or negative difference included in it must be disclosed in the notes to the consolidated financial statements.

(continued)

---

(2) Der Unterschiedsbetrag nach Absatz 1 Satz 2 ist den Wertansätzen der Vermögensgegenstände, Schulden, Rechnungsabgrenzungsposten und Sonderposten des assoziierten Unternehmens insoweit zuzuordnen, als deren beizulegender Zeitwert höher oder niedriger ist als ihr Buchwert. Der nach Satz 1 zugeordnete Unterschiedsbetrag ist entsprechend der Behandlung der Wertansätze dieser Vermögensgegenstände, Schulden, Rechnungsabgrenzungsposten und Sonderposten im Jahresabschluss des assoziierten Unternehmens im Konzernabschluss fortzuführen, abzuschreiben oder aufzulösen. Auf einen nach Zuordnung nach Satz 1 verbleibenden Geschäfts- oder Firmenwert oder passiven Unterschiedsbetrag ist § 309 entsprechend anzuwenden. § 301 Abs. 1 Satz 3 ist entsprechend anzuwenden.

(3) Der Wertansatz der Beteiligung und der Unterschiedsbetrag sind auf der Grundlage der Wertansätze zu dem Zeitpunkt zu ermitteln, zu dem das Unternehmen assoziiertes Unternehmen geworden ist. Können die Wertansätze zu diesem Zeitpunkt nicht endgültig ermittelt werden, sind sie innerhalb der darauf folgenden zwölf Monate anzupassen. § 301 Absatz 2 Satz 3 bis 5 gilt entsprechend.

(4) Der nach Absatz 1 ermittelte Wertansatz einer Beteiligung ist in den Folgejahren um den Betrag der Eigenkapitalveränderungen, die den dem Mutterunternehmen gehörenden Anteilen am Kapital des assoziierten Unternehmens entsprechen, zu erhöhen oder zu vermindern; auf die Beteiligung entfallende Gewinnausschüttungen sind abzusetzen. In der Konzern-Gewinn- und Verlustrechnung ist das auf assoziierte Beteiligungen entfallende Ergebnis unter einem gesonderten Posten auszuweisen.

(2) The difference according to section 1 sentence 2 shall be allocated to the values of the assets, liabilities, deferred items and special items of the associated company to the extent that their fair value is higher or lower than their book value. The difference allocated in accordance with sentence 1 shall be carried forward, amortized or reversed in the consolidated financial statements in accordance with the treatment of the measurements of these assets, liabilities, deferred items and special items in the financial statements of the associated company. To a remaining goodwill or negative difference after allocation pursuant to sentence 1, § 309 is to be applied accordingly. § 301 sect. 1 sent. 3 shall be applied accordingly.

(3) The values of the participation and the difference shall be determined on the basis of the values at the time the company became an associated company. If the values cannot be finally determined at that time, they shall be adjusted within the following twelve months. § 301 sect. 2 sent. 3 to 5 shall apply mutatis mutandis.

(4) The value of a participation determined in accordance with section 1 shall be increased or decreased in subsequent years by the amount of the changes in equity attributable to the shares in the capital of the associated company belonging to the parent company; profit distributions attributable to the participation shall be deducted. In the consolidated income statement, the result attributable to associated companies shall be reported under a separate item.

(continued)

(5) Wendet das assoziierte Unternehmen in seinem Jahresabschluß vom Konzernabschluß abweichende Bewertungsmethoden an, so können abweichend bewertete Vermögensgegenstände oder Schulden für die Zwecke der Absätze 1 bis 4 nach den auf den Konzernabschluß angewandten Bewertungsmethoden bewertet werden. Wird die Bewertung nicht angepaßt, so ist dies im Konzernanhang anzugeben. Die §§ 304 und 306 sind entsprechend anzuwenden, soweit die für die Beurteilung maßgeblichen Sachverhalte bekannt oder zugänglich sind.

(6) Es ist jeweils der letzte Jahresabschluß des assoziierten Unternehmens zugrunde zu legen. Stellt das assoziierte Unternehmen einen Konzernabschluß auf, so ist von diesem und nicht vom Jahresabschluß des assoziierten Unternehmens auszugehen.

Achter Titel Konzernanhang

§ 313 Erläuterung der Konzernbilanz und der Konzern-Gewinn- und Verlustrechnung. Angaben zum Beteiligungsbesitz.
(1) In den Konzernanhang sind diejenigen Angaben aufzunehmen, die zu einzelnen Posten der Konzernbilanz oder der Konzern-Gewinn- und Verlustrechnung vorgeschrieben sind; diese Angaben sind in der Reihenfolge der einzelnen Posten der Konzernbilanz und der Konzern-Gewinn- und Verlustrechnung darzustellen. Im Konzernanhang sind auch die Angaben zu machen, die in Ausübung eines Wahlrechts nicht in die Konzernbilanz oder in die Konzern-Gewinn- und Verlustrechnung aufgenommen wurden. Im Konzernanhang müssen

1. die auf die Posten der Konzernbilanz und der Konzern-Gewinn- und Verlustrechnung angewandten Bilanzierungs- und Bewertungsmethoden angegeben werden;

(5) If the associated company uses measurement methods in its financial statements which differ from those used in the consolidated financial statements, assets or liabilities valued differently may be valued for the purposes of sections 1 to 4 in accordance with the measurement methods applied to the consolidated financial statements. If the measurement is not adjusted, this shall be disclosed in the notes to the consolidated financial statements. §§ 304 and 306 shall be applied mutatis mutandis insofar as the facts relevant to the assessment are known or accessible.

(6) The last financial statement of the associated company shall be used as a basis. If the associated company prepares consolidated financial statements, these shall be used as a basis and not financial statements of the associated company.

Title Eight Notes to the consolidated financial statements

§ 313 Notes to the consolidated balance sheet and consolidated income statement. Information on shareholdings.
(1) The notes to the consolidated financial statements shall include those disclosures that are required to be made with respect to specific items in the consolidated balance sheet or consolidated income statement; such disclosures shall be presented in the order of the specific items in the consolidated balance sheet and consolidated income statement. The notes to the consolidated financial statements shall also include the information that was not included in the consolidated balance sheet or the consolidated income statement as a result of the exercise of an option. In the notes to the consolidated financial statements,

1. the recognition and measurement methods applied to the items in the consolidated balance sheet and the consolidated income statement are disclosed;

(continued)

2. Abweichungen von Bilanzierungs-, Bewertungs- und Konsolidierungsmethoden angegeben und begründet werden; deren Einfluß auf die Vermögens-, Finanz- und Ertragslage des Konzerns ist gesondert darzustellen.

(2) Im Konzernanhang sind außerdem anzugeben:

1. Name und Sitz der in den Konzernabschluß einbezogenen Unternehmen, der Anteil am Kapital der Tochterunternehmen, der dem Mutterunternehmen und den in den Konzernabschluß einbezogenen Tochterunternehmen gehört oder von einer für Rechnung dieser Unternehmen handelnden Person gehalten wird, sowie der zur Einbeziehung in den Konzernabschluß verpflichtende Sachverhalt, sofern die Einbeziehung nicht auf einer der Kapitalbeteiligung entsprechenden Mehrheit der Stimmrechte beruht. Diese Angaben sind auch für Tochterunternehmen zu machen, die nach § 296 nicht einbezogen worden sind;

2. Name und Sitz der assoziierten Unternehmen, der Anteil am Kapital der assoziierten Unternehmen, der dem Mutterunternehmen und den in den Konzernabschluß einbezogenen Tochterunternehmen gehört oder von einer für Rechnung dieser Unternehmen handelnden Person gehalten wird. Die Anwendung des § 311 Abs. 2 ist jeweils anzugeben und zu begründen;

3. Name und Sitz der Unternehmen, die nach § 310 nur anteilmäßig in den Konzernabschluß einbezogen worden sind, der Tatbestand, aus dem sich die Anwendung dieser Vorschrift ergibt, sowie der Anteil am Kapital dieser Unternehmen, der dem Mutterunternehmen und den in den Konzernabschluß einbezogenen Tochterunternehmen gehört oder von einer für Rechnung dieser Unternehmen handelnden Person gehalten wird;

2. deviations from recognition, measurement and consolidation methods must be stated and justified; their influence on the asset, finance and income position of the group shall be presented separately.

(2) The notes to the consolidated financial statements shall also disclose:

1. name and registered office of the companies included in the consolidated financial statements, the share in the capital of the subsidiaries belonging to the parent company and the companies included in the consolidated financial statements or held by a person acting for the account of these companies, as well as the circumstances requiring inclusion in the consolidated financial statements, unless inclusion is based on a majority of the voting rights corresponding to the shareholding. These disclosures must also be made for subsidiaries that have not been included pursuant to § 296;

2. name and registered office of the associated companies, the share in the capital of the associated companies belonging to the parent company and the subsidiaries included in the consolidated financial statements or held by a person acting for the account of these companies. The application of § 311 sect. 2 shall be stated and justified in each case;

3. name and registered office of the companies included in the consolidated financial statements on a proportionate basis only in accordance with § 310, the facts from which the application of this regulation results, and the share in the capital of these companies belonging to the parent company and the subsidiaries included in the consolidated financial statements or held by a person acting for the account of these companies;

(continued)

4. Name und Sitz anderer Unternehmen, die Höhe des Anteils am Kapital, das Eigenkapital und das Ergebnis des letzten Geschäftsjahrs dieser Unternehmen, für das ein Jahresabschluss vorliegt, soweit es sich um Beteiligungen im Sinne des § 271 Absatz 1 handelt oder ein solcher Anteil von einer Person für Rechnung des Mutterunternehmens oder eines anderen in den Konzernabschluss einbezogenen Unternehmens gehalten wird;	4. name and registered office of other companies, the amount of the share in the capital, the equity and the result of the last business year of these companies for which financial statements are available, insofar as they are participations within the meaning of § 271 sect. 1 or such a share is held by a person for the account of the parent company or another company included in the consolidated financial statements;
5. alle nicht nach den Nummern 1 bis 4 aufzuführenden Beteiligungen an großen Kapitalgesellschaften, die 5 Prozent der Stimmrechte überschreiten, wenn sie von einem börsennotierten Mutterunternehmen, börsennotierten Tochterunternehmen oder von einer für Rechnung eines dieser Unternehmen handelnden Person gehalten werden;	5. all shareholdings in large corporations not to be listed under numbers 1 to 4 that exceed 5 per cent of the voting rights if they are held by a listed parent company, listed subsidiaries or by a person acting for the account of one of these companies;
6. Name, Sitz und Rechtsform der Unternehmen, deren unbeschränkt haftender Gesellschafter das Mutterunternehmen oder ein anderes in den Konzernabschluss einbezogenes Unternehmen ist;	6. name, registered office and legal form of the companies of which the parent company or another company included in the consolidated financial statements is a partner with unlimited liability;
7. Name und Sitz des Unternehmens, das den Konzernabschluss für den größten Kreis von Unternehmen aufstellt, dem das Mutterunternehmen als Tochterunternehmen angehört, und im Falle der Offenlegung des von diesem anderen Mutterunternehmen aufgestellten Konzernabschlusses der Ort, wo dieser erhältlich ist;	7. name and registered office of the company that prepares the consolidated financial statements for the largest scope of companies to which the parent company belongs as a subsidiary and, in the case of disclosure of the consolidated financial statements prepared by that other parent company, the place where they can be obtained;
8. Name und Sitz des Unternehmens, das den Konzernabschluss für den kleinsten Kreis von Unternehmen aufstellt, dem das Mutterunternehmen als Tochterunternehmen angehört, und im Falle der Offenlegung des von diesem anderen Mutterunternehmen aufgestellten Konzernabschlusses der Ort, wo dieser erhältlich ist.	8. name and registered office of the company that prepares the consolidated financial statements for the smallest scope of companies to which the parent company belongs as a subsidiary and, in the case of disclosure of the consolidated financial statements prepared by that other parent company, the place where they can be obtained.

(continued)

---

(3) Die in Absatz 2 verlangten Angaben brauchen insoweit nicht gemacht zu werden, als nach vernünftiger kaufmännischer Beurteilung damit gerechnet werden muß, daß durch die Angaben dem Mutterunternehmen, einem Tochterunternehmen oder einem anderen in Absatz 2 bezeichneten Unternehmen erhebliche Nachteile entstehen können. Die Anwendung der Ausnahmeregelung ist im Konzernanhang anzugeben. Satz 1 gilt nicht, wenn ein Mutterunternehmen oder eines seiner Tochterunternehmen kapitalmarktorientiert im Sinn des § 264d ist. Die Angaben nach Absatz 2 Nummer 4 und 5 brauchen nicht gemacht zu werden, wenn sie für die Vermittlung eines den tatsächlichen Verhältnissen entsprechenden Bilds der Vermögens-, Finanz- und Ertragslage des Konzerns von untergeordneter Bedeutung sind. Die Pflicht zur Angabe von Eigenkapital und Ergebnis nach Absatz 2 Nummer 4 braucht auch dann nicht erfüllt zu werden, wenn das in Anteilsbesitz stehende Unternehmen seinen Jahresabschluss nicht offenlegt.

(4) § 284 Absatz 2 Nummer 4 und Absatz 3 ist entsprechend anzuwenden.

(3) The disclosures required by section 2 need not be made to the extent that, on the basis of reasonable commercial judgment, the disclosures are likely to cause material disadvantage to the parent company, a subsidiary or another company referred to in section 2. The application of the exemption shall be disclosed in the notes to the consolidated financial statements. Sentence 1 shall not apply if a parent company or one of its subsidiaries is capital-market oriented within the meaning of section 264d. The disclosures pursuant to section 2 numbers 4 and 5 need not be made if they are of minor importance for the presentation of a true and fair view of the asset, finance and income position of the group. The obligation to disclose equity and result pursuant to section 2 number 4 need not be fulfilled if the company whose shares are held does not disclose its financial statements.

(4) § 284 sect. 2 no. 4 and sect. 3 shall apply mutatis mutandis.

---

§ 314 Sonstige Pflichtangaben

(1) Im Konzernanhang sind ferner anzugeben:

1. der Gesamtbetrag der in der Konzernbilanz ausgewiesenen Verbindlichkeiten mit einer Restlaufzeit von mehr als fünf Jahren sowie der Gesamtbetrag der in der Konzernbilanz ausgewiesenen Verbindlichkeiten, die von in den Konzernabschluß einbezogenen Unternehmen durch Pfandrechte oder ähnliche Rechte gesichert sind, unter Angabe von Art und Form der Sicherheiten;

§ 314 Other mandatory information

(1) The notes to the consolidated financial statements shall also disclose:

1. the total amount of debt reported in the consolidated balance sheet with a remaining term of more than five years as well as the total amount of debt reported in the consolidated balance sheet which are secured by liens or similar rights from companies included in the consolidated financial statements, stating the type and form of the collateral;

(continued)

2. Art und Zweck sowie Risiken, Vorteile und finanzielle Auswirkungen von nicht in der Konzernbilanz enthaltenen Geschäften des Mutterunternehmens und der in den Konzernabschluss einbezogenen Tochterunternehmen, soweit die Risiken und Vorteile wesentlich sind und die Offenlegung für die Beurteilung der Finanzlage des Konzerns erforderlich ist;

2a. der Gesamtbetrag der sonstigen finanziellen Verpflichtungen, die nicht in der Konzernbilanz enthalten sind und die nicht nach § 298 Absatz 1 in Verbindung mit § 268 Absatz 7 oder nach Nummer 2 anzugeben sind, sofern diese Angabe für die Beurteilung der Finanzlage des Konzerns von Bedeutung ist; davon sind Verpflichtungen betreffend die Altersversorgung sowie Verpflichtungen gegenüber Tochterunternehmen, die nicht in den Konzernabschluss einbezogen werden, oder gegenüber assoziierten Unternehmen jeweils gesondert anzugeben;

3. die Aufgliederung der Umsatzerlöse des Konzerns nach Tätigkeitsbereichen sowie nach geografisch bestimmten Märkten, soweit sich unter Berücksichtigung der Organisation des Verkaufs, der Vermietung oder Verpachtung von Produkten und der Erbringung von Dienstleistungen des Konzerns die Tätigkeitsbereiche und geografisch bestimmten Märkte untereinander erheblich unterscheiden;

4. die durchschnittliche Zahl der Arbeitnehmer der in den Konzernabschluss einbezogenen Unternehmen während des Geschäftsjahrs, getrennt nach Gruppen und gesondert für die nach § 310 nur anteilmäßig konsolidierten Unternehmen, sowie, falls er nicht gesondert in der Konzern-Gewinn- und Verlustrechnung ausgewiesen ist, der in dem Geschäftsjahr entstandene gesamte Personalaufwand, aufgeschlüsselt nach Löhnen und Gehältern, Kosten der sozialen Sicherheit und Kosten der Altersversorgung;

5. (weggefallen)

2. the nature and purpose of, and the risks, rewards and financial effects of, transactions not included in the consolidated balance sheet of the parent company and the companies included in the consolidated financial statements, to the extent that the risks and rewards are material and the disclosure is necessary for assessing the finance position of the group;

2a. the total amount of other financial obligations not included in the consolidated balance sheet and not required to be disclosed under § 298 sect. 1 in conjunction with § 268 sect. 7 or under number 2, provided that such disclosure is relevant to an assessment of the financial position of the group; of these, obligations relating to retirement benefits and obligations to subsidiaries not included in the consolidated financial statements or to associated companies shall be disclosed separately in each case;

3. the breakdown of the group's sales revenue by activity and by geographical market to the extent that, taking into account the organization of the sale, rental or leasing of products and the provision of services of the group, the activities and geographical markets differ significantly from each other;

4. the average number of employees of the companies included in the consolidated financial statements during the business year, broken down by group and separately for the companies consolidated only on a proportionate basis in accordance with § 310, and, if it is not reported separately in the consolidated income statement, the total personnel expenses incurred during the business year, broken down into wages and salaries, social security costs and costs for retirement benefits;

5. (omitted)

(continued)

6. für die Mitglieder des Geschäftsführungsorgans, eines Aufsichtsrats, eines Beirats oder einer ähnlichen Einrichtung des Mutterunternehmens, jeweils für jede Personengruppe:	6. for the members of the management body, a supervisory board, an advisory board or a similar body of the parent company, in each case for each group of persons:
a) die für die Wahrnehmung ihrer Aufgaben im Mutterunternehmen und den Tochterunternehmen im Geschäftsjahr gewährten Gesamtbezüge (Gehälter, Gewinnbeteiligungen, Bezugsrechte und sonstige aktienbasierte Vergütungen, Aufwandsentschädigungen, Versicherungsentgelte, Provisionen und Nebenleistungen jeder Art). In die Gesamtbezüge sind auch Bezüge einzurechnen, die nicht ausgezahlt, sondern in Ansprüche anderer Art umgewandelt oder zur Erhöhung anderer Ansprüche verwendet werden. Außer den Bezügen für das Geschäftsjahr sind die weiteren Bezüge anzugeben, die im Geschäftsjahr gewährt, bisher aber in keinem Konzernabschluss angegeben worden sind. Bezugsrechte und sonstige aktienbasierte Vergütungen sind mit ihrer Anzahl und dem beizulegenden Zeitwert zum Zeitpunkt ihrer Gewährung anzugeben; spätere Wertveränderungen, die auf einer Änderung der Ausübungsbedingungen beruhen, sind zu berücksichtigen;	a) the total remuneration granted for the performance of their duties in the parent company and the subsidiaries in the business year (salaries, profit-sharing, subscription rights and other share-based remuneration, expense allowances, insurance compensation, commissions and fringe benefits of any kind). Remuneration that is not paid out but converted into entitlements of another kind or used to increase other entitlements must also be included in the total remuneration. In addition to remuneration for the business year, other remuneration granted in the business year but not yet reported in any consolidated financial statements shall be disclosed. Subscription rights and other share-based payments shall be disclosed with their number and fair value at the time they were granted; subsequent changes in value based on a change in the exercise conditions shall be taken into account;

(continued)

b) die für die Wahrnehmung ihrer Aufgaben im Mutterunternehmen und den Tochterunternehmen gewährten Gesamtbezüge (Abfindungen, Ruhegehälter, Hinterbliebenenbezüge und Leistungen verwandter Art) der früheren Mitglieder der bezeichneten Organe und ihrer Hinterbliebenen; Buchstabe a Satz 2 und 3 ist entsprechend anzuwenden. Ferner ist der Betrag der für diese Personengruppe gebildeten Rückstellungen für laufende Pensionen und Anwartschaften auf Pensionen und der Betrag der für diese Verpflichtungen nicht gebildeten Rückstellungen anzugeben;

c) die vom Mutterunternehmen und den Tochterunternehmen gewährten Vorschüsse und Kredite unter Angabe der gegebenenfalls im Geschäftsjahr zurückgezahlten oder erlassenen Beträge sowie die zugunsten dieser Personen eingegangenen Haftungsverhältnisse;

7. der Bestand an Anteilen an dem Mutterunternehmen, die das Mutterunternehmen oder ein Tochterunternehmen oder ein anderer für Rechnung eines in den Konzernabschluß einbezogenen Unternehmens erworben oder als Pfand genommen hat; dabei sind die Zahl und der Nennbetrag oder rechnerische Wert dieser Anteile sowie deren Anteil am Kapital anzugeben;

7a. die Zahl der Aktien jeder Gattung der während des Geschäftsjahrs im Rahmen des genehmigten Kapitals gezeichneten Aktien des Mutterunternehmens, wobei zu Nennbetragsaktien der Nennbetrag und zu Stückaktien der rechnerische Wert für jede von ihnen anzugeben ist;

7b. das Bestehen von Genussscheinen, Wandelschuldverschreibungen, Optionsscheinen, Optionen oder vergleichbaren Wertpapieren oder Rechten, aus denen das Mutterunternehmen verpflichtet ist, unter Angabe der Anzahl und der Rechte, die sie verbriefen;

---

b) the total remuneration (severance payments, pensions, survivors' benefits and benefits of a related nature) of the former members of the designated bodies and their survivors granted for the performance of their duties in the parent company and the subsidiaries; letter a sentence 2 and 3 shall be applied accordingly. Furthermore, the amount of the provisions for current pensions and vested pension rights created for this group of persons and the amount of the provisions not created for these obligations shall be disclosed;

c) the advances and loans granted by the parent company and the subsidiaries, indicating any amounts repaid or waived during the business year, as well as contingent liabilities entered into in favor of these persons;

7. the amount of shares in the parent company acquired or pledged by the parent company or by a subsidiary company or by another for the account of a company included in the consolidated financial statements, indicating the number and nominal value or imputed value of those shares and their proportion of the capital;

7a. the number of shares of each class in the parent company subscribed for during the business year under the authorized capital, reporting in respect of par value shares the nominal amount and in respect of no-par value shares the imputed value for each of them;

7b. the existence of participation certificates, convertible bonds, warrants, options or comparable securities or rights from which the parent company is obligated, stating the number and the rights they represent

(continued)

8. für jedes in den Konzernabschluss einbezogene börsennotierte Unternehmen, dass die nach § 161 des Aktiengesetzes vorgeschriebene Erklärung abgegeben und wo sie öffentlich zugänglich gemacht worden ist;	8. for each listed company included in the consolidated financial statements, that the declaration required by § 161 of the Stock Corporation Act (Aktiengesetz) has been made and where it has been made publicly available;
9. das von dem Abschlussprüfer des Konzernabschlusses für das Geschäftsjahr berechnete Gesamthonorar, aufgeschlüsselt in das Honorar für a) die Abschlussprüfungsleistungen, b) andere Bestätigungsleistungen, c) Steuerberatungsleistungen, d) sonstige Leistungen;	9. the total fee charged by the auditor of the consolidated financial statements for the business year, broken down into the fee for a) the audit services, b) other assurance services, c) tax advisory services, d) other services;
10. für zu den Finanzanlagen (§ 266 Abs. 2 A. III.) gehörende Finanzinstrumente, die in der Konzernbilanz über ihrem beizulegenden Zeitwert ausgewiesen werden, da eine außerplanmäßige Abschreibung gemäß § 253 Absatz 3 Satz 6 unterblieben ist, a) der Buchwert und der beizulegende Zeitwert der einzelnen Vermögensgegenstände oder angemessener Gruppierungen sowie b) die Gründe für das Unterlassen der Abschreibung einschließlich der Anhaltspunkte, die darauf hindeuten, dass die Wertminderung voraussichtlich nicht von Dauer ist;	10. for financial instruments belonging to the financial assets (§ 266 sect. 2 A. III.), which are reported in the consolidated balance sheet above their fair value, as an impairment pursuant to § 253 sect. 3 sent. 6 was not carried out, a) the book value and fair value of the individual assets or appropriate groupings, and b) the reasons for the omission of the impairment, including evidence that the decrease in value is not expected to be permanent;
11. für jede Kategorie nicht zum beizulegenden Zeitwert bilanzierter derivativer Finanzinstrumente a) deren Art und Umfang, b) deren beizulegender Zeitwert, soweit er sich nach § 255 Abs. 4 verlässlich ermitteln lässt, unter Angabe der angewandten Bewertungsmethode, c) deren Buchwert und der Bilanzposten, in welchem der Buchwert, soweit vorhanden, erfasst ist, sowie d) die Gründe dafür, warum der beizulegende Zeitwert nicht bestimmt werden kann;	11. for each category of derivative financial instruments not accounted for at fair value a) their nature and scope, b) their fair value, insofar as it can be reliably determined in accordance with § 255 sect. 4, stating the measurement method applied, c) their book value and the balance sheet item in which the book value, if any, is recognized, and d) the reasons why the fair value cannot be determined;
12. für mit dem beizulegenden Zeitwert bewertete Finanzinstrumente	12. for financial instruments measured at fair value

(continued)

a) die grundlegenden Annahmen, die der Bestimmung des beizulegenden Zeitwertes mit Hilfe allgemein anerkannter Bewertungsmethoden zugrunde gelegt wurden, sowie	a) the underlying assumptions used in determining fair value using generally accepted measurement methods, and
b) Umfang und Art jeder Kategorie derivativer Finanzinstrumente einschließlich der wesentlichen Bedingungen, welche die Höhe, den Zeitpunkt und die Sicherheit künftiger Zahlungsströme beeinflussen können;	b) the scope and nature of each class of derivative financial instruments, including the significant terms and conditions that may affect the amount, timing and certainty of future cash flows;
13. zumindest die nicht zu marktüblichen Bedingungen zustande gekommenen Geschäfte des Mutterunternehmens und seiner Tochterunternehmen, soweit sie wesentlich sind, mit nahe stehenden Unternehmen und Personen, einschließlich Angaben zur Art der Beziehung, zum Wert der Geschäfte sowie weiterer Angaben, die für die Beurteilung der Finanzlage des Konzerns notwendig sind; ausgenommen sind Geschäfte zwischen in einen Konzernabschluss einbezogenen nahestehenden Unternehmen, wenn diese Geschäfte bei der Konsolidierung weggelassen werden; Angaben über Geschäfte können nach Geschäftsarten zusammengefasst werden, sofern die getrennte Angabe für die Beurteilung der Auswirkungen auf die Finanzlage des Konzerns nicht notwendig ist;	13. at a minimum, transactions of the parent company and its subsidiaries, if material, with related parties that are not at arm's length, including the nature of the relationship, the value of the transactions and other disclosures necessary for an understanding of the group's financial position; if transactions between related parties included in consolidated financial statements are omitted on consolidation, disclosures about these transactions are exempted; disclosures about these transactions may be aggregated by type of transaction if separate disclosure is not necessary to assess the effect on the group's financial position;
14. im Fall der Aktivierung nach § 248 Abs. 2 der Gesamtbetrag der Forschungs- und Entwicklungskosten des Geschäftsjahres der in den Konzernabschluss einbezogenen Unternehmen sowie der davon auf die selbst geschaffenen immateriellen Vermögensgegenstände des Anlagevermögens entfallende Betrag;	14. in the case of recognition pursuant to § 248 sect. 2, the total amount of the research and development costs of the business year of the companies included in the consolidated financial statements as well as the amount thereof attributable to the internally generated intangible non-current assets;
15. bei Anwendung des § 254 im Konzernabschluss,	15. when applying § 254 in the consolidated financial statements,

(continued)

a) mit welchem Betrag jeweils Vermögensgegenstände, Schulden, schwebende Geschäfte und mit hoher Wahrscheinlichkeit erwartete Transaktionen zur Absicherung welcher Risiken in welche Arten von Bewertungseinheiten einbezogen sind sowie die Höhe der mit Bewertungseinheiten abgesicherten Risiken;

b) für die jeweils abgesicherten Risiken, warum, in welchem Umfang und für welchen Zeitraum sich die gegenläufigen Wertänderungen oder Zahlungsströme künftig voraussichtlich ausgleichen einschließlich der Methode der Ermittlung;

c) eine Erläuterung der mit hoher Wahrscheinlichkeit erwarteten Transaktionen, die in Bewertungseinheiten einbezogen wurden, soweit die Angaben nicht im Konzernlagebericht gemacht werden;

16. zu den in der Konzernbilanz ausgewiesenen Rückstellu006Egen für Pensionen und ähnliche Verpflichtungen das angewandte versicherungsmathematische Berechnungsverfahren sowie die grundlegenden Annahmen der Berechnung, wie Zinssatz, erwartete Lohn- und Gehaltssteigerungen und zugrunde gelegte Sterbetafeln;

17. im Fall der Verrechnung von in der Konzernbilanz ausgewiesenen Vermögensgegenständen und Schulden nach § 246 Abs. 2 Satz 2 die Anschaffungskosten und der beizulegende Zeitwert der verrechneten Vermögensgegenstände, der Erfüllungsbetrag der verrechneten Schulden sowie die verrechneten Aufwendungen und Erträge; Nummer 12 Buchstabe a ist entsprechend anzuwenden;

a) the amount of assets, liabilities, pending transactions and transactions expected with a high degree of probability included to hedge which risks in which types of measurement units, as well as the amount of the risks hedged with measurement units;

b) for the respective hedged risks, why, to what extent and for what period of time the opposing changes in value or cash flows are expected to offset each other in the future, including the method of determination;

c) an explanation of the transactions expected with a high degree of probability that have been included in measurement units,
to the extent that the disclosures are not made in the group management report;

16. the actuarial method used to calculate the provisions for pensions and similar obligations recognized in the consolidated balance sheet, as well as the basic assumptions of the calculation, such as interest rate, expected wage and salary increases and mortality tables used;

17. in the case of offsetting assets and liabilities reported in the consolidated balance sheet in accordance with § 246 sect. 2 sent. 2, the acquisition costs and the fair value of the offset assets, the settlement amount of the offset liabilities and the offset expenses and income; number 12 letter a shall be applied accordingly;

(continued)

---

18. zu den in der Konzernbilanz ausgewiesenen Anteilen an Sondervermögen im Sinn des § 1 Absatz 10 des Kapitalanlagegesetzbuchs oder Anlageaktien an Investmentaktiengesellschaften mit veränderlichem Kapital im Sinn der §§ 108 bis 123 des Kapitalanlagegesetzbuchs oder vergleichbaren EU- Investmentvermögen oder vergleichbaren ausländischen Investmentvermögen von mehr als dem zehnten Teil, aufgegliedert nach Anlagezielen, deren Wert im Sinn der §§ 168, 278 des Kapitalanlagegesetzbuchs oder des § 36 des Investmentgesetzes in der bis zum 21. Juli 2013 geltenden Fassung oder vergleichbarer ausländischer Vorschriften über die Ermittlung des Marktwertes, die Differenz zum Buchwert und die für das Geschäftsjahr erfolgte Ausschüttung sowie Beschränkungen in der Möglichkeit der täglichen Rückgabe; darüber hinaus die Gründe dafür, dass eine Abschreibung gemäß § 253 Absatz 3 Satz 6 unterblieben ist, einschließlich der Anhaltspunkte, die darauf hindeuten, dass die Wertminderung voraussichtlich nicht von Dauer ist; Nummer 10 ist insoweit nicht anzuwenden;

18. as far as they are recognized in the consolidated financial statements, to the shares in investment funds within the meaning of § 1 sect. 10 of the Capital Investment Code (Kapitalanlagegesetzbuch) or investment shares in investment stock corporations with variable capital within the meaning of §§ 108 to 123 of the Capital Investment Code or comparable EU investment funds or comparable foreign investment funds of more than one tenth, broken down by investment objective, whose value within the meaning of §§ 168, 278 of the Capital Investment Code or § 36 of the Investment Act (Investmentgesetz) in the version applicable until 21 July 2013 or comparable foreign regulations on the determination of the market value, the difference from the book value and the distribution made for the business year as well as restrictions on the possibility of daily return; in addition, the reasons why an impairment pursuant to § 253 sect. 3 sent. 6 has not been made, including indications that the decrease in value is not expected to be permanent; number 10 shall not apply in this respect;

19. für nach § 268 Abs. 7 im Konzernanhang ausgewiesene Verbindlichkeiten und Haftungsverhältnisse die Gründe der Einschätzung des Risikos der Inanspruchnahme;

19. for liabilities and contingent liabilities disclosed in the notes to the consolidated financial statements in accordance with § 268 sect. 7, the reasons for the assessment of the risk of utilization;

20. jeweils eine Erläuterung des Zeitraums, über den ein entgeltlich erworbener Geschäfts- oder Firmenwert abgeschrieben wird;

20. an explanation of the period over which goodwill acquired for consideration is amortized;

21. auf welchen Differenzen oder steuerlichen Verlustvorträgen die latenten Steuern beruhen und mit welchen Steuersätzen die Bewertung erfolgt ist;

21. on which differences or tax loss carry forwards the deferred taxes are based and which tax rates were used for the measurement;

22. wenn latente Steuerschulden in der Konzernbilanz angesetzt werden, die latenten Steuersalden am Ende des Geschäftsjahrs und die im Laufe des Geschäftsjahrs erfolgten Änderungen dieser Salden;

22. if deferred tax liabilities are recognized in the consolidated balance sheet, the deferred tax balances at the end of the business year and the changes in these balances during the business year;

(continued)

23. jeweils den Betrag und die Art der einzelnen Erträge und Aufwendungen von außergewöhnlicher Größenordnung oder außergewöhnlicher Bedeutung, soweit die Beträge nicht von untergeordneter Bedeutung sind;	23. in each case, the amount and nature of the specific income and expenses of extraordinary magnitude or extraordinary significance, unless the amounts are of minor importance;
24. eine Erläuterung der einzelnen Erträge und Aufwendungen hinsichtlich ihres Betrages und ihrer Art, die einem anderen Konzerngeschäftsjahr zuzurechnen sind, soweit die Beträge für die Beurteilung der Vermögens-, Finanz- und Ertragslage des Konzerns nicht von untergeordneter Bedeutung sind;	24. an explanation of the specific income and expenses with regard to their amount and nature that are attributable to another group business year, insofar as the amounts are not of minor importance for the assessment of the asset, finance and income position of the group;
25. Vorgänge von besonderer Bedeutung, die nach dem Schluss des Konzerngeschäftsjahrs eingetreten und weder in der Konzern-Gewinn- und Verlustrechnung noch in der Konzernbilanz berücksichtigt sind, unter Angabe ihrer Art und ihrer finanziellen Auswirkungen;	25. events of particular significance that occurred after the end of the consolidated business year and are not reflected in either the consolidated income statement or the consolidated balance sheet, stating their nature and financial impact;
26. der Vorschlag für die Verwendung des Ergebnisses des Mutterunternehmens oder gegebenenfalls der Beschluss über die Verwendung des Ergebnisses des Mutterunternehmens.	26. the proposal for the use of the parent company's profit or, if applicable, the resolution on the use of the parent company's profit.
(2) Mutterunternehmen, die den Konzernabschluss um eine Segmentberichterstattung erweitern (§ 297 Abs. 1 Satz 2), sind von der Angabepflicht gemäß Absatz 1 Nr. 3 befreit.	(2) Parent companies that expand the consolidated financial statements to include segment reporting (§ 297 sect. 1 sent. 2) are exempt from the disclosure requirement pursuant to section 1 no. 3.
(3) Für die Angabepflicht gemäß Absatz 1 Nummer 6 Buchstabe a und b gilt § 286 Absatz 4 entsprechend.	(3) § 286 sect. 4 shall apply mutatis mutandis to the disclosure requirement under section 1 no. 6 letter a and b.

(continued)

Neunter Titel Konzernlagebericht	Title Nine Group management report
§ 315 Inhalt des Konzernlageberichts (1) Im Konzernlagebericht sind der Geschäftsverlauf einschließlich des Geschäftsergebnisses und die Lage des Konzerns so darzustellen, dass ein den tatsächlichen Verhältnissen entsprechendes Bild vermittelt wird. Er hat eine ausgewogene und umfassende, dem Umfang und der Komplexität der Geschäftstätigkeit entsprechende Analyse des Geschäftsverlaufs und der Lage des Konzerns zu enthalten. In die Analyse sind die für die Geschäftstätigkeit bedeutsamsten finanziellen Leistungsindikatoren einzubeziehen und unter Bezugnahme auf die im Konzernabschluss ausgewiesenen Beträge und Angaben zu erläutern. Ferner ist im Konzernlagebericht die voraussichtliche Entwicklung mit ihren wesentlichen Chancen und Risiken zu beurteilen und zu erläutern; zugrunde liegende Annahmen sind anzugeben. Die Mitglieder des vertretungsberechtigten Organs eines Mutterunternehmens, das als Inlandsemittent (§ 2 Absatz 14 des Wertpapierhandelsgesetzes) Wertpapiere (§ 2 Absatz 1 des Wertpapierhandelsgesetzes) begibt und keine Kapitalgesellschaft im Sinne des § 327a ist, haben in einer dem Konzernlagebericht beizufügenden schriftlichen Erklärung zu versichern, dass im Konzernlagebericht nach bestem Wissen der Geschäftsverlauf einschließlich des Geschäftsergebnisses und die Lage des Konzerns so dargestellt sind, dass ein den tatsächlichen Verhältnissen entsprechendes Bild vermittelt wird und dass die wesentlichen Chancen und Risiken im Sinne des Satzes 4 beschrieben sind. (2) Im Konzernlagebericht ist auch einzugehen auf:	**§ 315 Content of the group management report** (1) The group management report shall present the development and performance of the business and the position of the group such that a true and fair view is given. It shall contain a balanced and comprehensive analysis of the development of the business and the position of the group commensurate with the size and complexity of the business. The analysis shall include the financial performance indicators that are most relevant to the business and shall be explained by reference to the amounts and disclosures reported in the consolidated financial statements. Furthermore, the group management report shall assess and explain the expected development with its material opportunities and risks; underlying assumptions shall be stated. The members of the governing body authorized to represent a parent company which issues securities (§ 2 sect. 1 of the Securities Trading Act (Wertpapierhandelsgesetz)) as a domestic issuer (§ 2 sect. 14 of the Securities Trading Act) and which is not a corporation within the meaning of § 327a shall certify in a written statement to be attached to the group management report that to the best of their knowledge the group management report gives a true and fair view of the development and performance of the business and the position of the group, together with a description of the material opportunities and risks associated with the business as set out in sentence 4. (2) The group management report shall also address:

(continued)

1. a) die Risikomanagementziele und -methoden des Konzerns einschließlich seiner Methoden zur Absicherung aller wichtigen Arten von Transaktionen, die im Rahmen der Bilanzierung von Sicherungsgeschäften erfasst werden, sowie	1. a) the group's risk management objectives and methods, including its methods for hedging all significant types of transactions that are recognized according to hedge accounting; and
b) die Preisänderungs-, Ausfall- und Liquiditätsrisiken sowie die Risiken aus Zahlungsstromschwankungen, denen der Konzern ausgesetzt ist, jeweils in Bezug auf die Verwendung von Finanzinstrumenten durch den Konzern und sofern dies für die Beurteilung der Lage oder der voraussichtlichen Entwicklung von Belang ist;	b) the price change, default and liquidity risks as well as the risks from cash flow fluctuations to which the group is exposed, in each case in relation to the use of financial instruments by the group and insofar as this is relevant for the assessment of the situation or the expected development;
2. den Bereich Forschung und Entwicklung des Konzerns und	2. the group's research and development division and
3. für das Verständnis der Lage des Konzerns wesentliche Zweigniederlassungen der insgesamt in den Konzernabschluss einbezogenen Unternehmen.	3. branches of the companies included in the consolidated financial statements that are material to an understanding of the group's position.
Ist das Mutterunternehmen eine Aktiengesellschaft, hat es im Konzernlagebericht auf die nach § 160 Absatz 1 Nummer 2 des Aktiengesetzes im Anhang zu machenden Angaben zu verweisen.	If the parent company is a stock corporation, it shall refer in the group management report to the information to be provided in the notes pursuant to § 160 sect. 1 no. 2 of the Stock Corporation Act (Aktiengesetz).
(3) Absatz 1 Satz 3 gilt entsprechend für nichtfinanzielle Leistungsindikatoren, wie Informationen über Umwelt- und Arbeitnehmerbelange, soweit sie für das Verständnis des Geschäftsverlaufs oder der Lage des Konzerns von Bedeutung sind.	(3) Section 1 sentence 3 shall apply mutatis mutandis to non-financial performance indicators, such as information on environmental and employee matters, insofar as they are of importance for understanding the development of business or the situation of the group.
(4) Ist das Mutterunternehmen oder ein in den Konzernabschluss einbezogenes Tochterunternehmen kapitalmarktorientiert im Sinne des § 264d, ist im Konzernlagebericht auch auf die wesentlichen Merkmale des internen Kontroll- und Risikomanagementsystems im Hinblick auf den Konzernrechnungslegungsprozess einzugehen.	(4) If the parent company or a subsidiary included in the consolidated financial statements is capital-market oriented within the meaning of § 264d, the group management report shall also address the key features of the internal control and risk management system with regard to the accounting process for preparation of the consolidated financial statements.

(continued)

(5) § 298 Absatz 2 über die Zusammenfassung von Konzernanhang und Anhang ist entsprechend anzuwenden.	(5) § 298 sect. 2 on the aggregation of the notes to the consolidated financial statements and the notes to the financial statements shall be applied accordingly.

§ 315a Ergänzende Vorschriften für bestimmte Aktiengesellschaften und Kommanditgesellschaften auf Aktien
Mutterunternehmen (§ 290), die einen organisierten Markt im Sinne des § 2 Absatz 7 des Wertpapiererwerbs- und Übernahmegesetzes durch von ihnen ausgegebene stimmberechtigte Aktien in Anspruch nehmen, haben im Konzernlagebericht außerdem anzugeben:

1. die Zusammensetzung des gezeichneten Kapitals unter gesondertem Ausweis der mit jeder Gattung verbundenen Rechte und Pflichten und des Anteils am Gesellschaftskapital;

2. Beschränkungen, die Stimmrechte oder die Übertragung von Aktien betreffen, auch wenn sie sich aus Vereinbarungen zwischen Gesellschaftern ergeben können, soweit die Beschränkungen dem Vorstand der Gesellschaft bekannt sind;

3. direkte oder indirekte Beteiligungen am Kapital, die 10 Prozent der Stimmrechte überschreiten;

4. die Inhaber von Aktien mit Sonderrechten, die Kontrollbefugnisse verleihen, und eine Beschreibung dieser Sonderrechte;

5. die Art der Stimmrechtskontrolle, wenn Arbeitnehmer am Kapital beteiligt sind und ihre Kontrollrechte nicht unmittelbar ausüben;

6. die gesetzlichen Vorschriften und Bestimmungen der Satzung über die Ernennung und Abberufung der Mitglieder des Vorstands und über die Änderung der Satzung;

7. die Befugnisse des Vorstands insbesondere hinsichtlich der Möglichkeit, Aktien auszugeben oder zurückzukaufen;

§ 315a Supplementary regulations for certain stock corporations and partnerships limited by shares
Parent companies (§ 290) that make use of an organized market within the meaning of § 2 sect. 7 of the Securities Acquisition and Takeover Act (Wertpapiererwerbs- und Übernahmegesetz) by means of shares with voting rights issued by them shall also disclose in the group management report:

1. the composition of the subscribed capital, showing separately the rights and obligations attaching to each class and the proportion of the capital of the company;

2. restrictions affecting voting rights or the transfer of shares, even if they may arise from agreements between shareholders, to the extent that the restrictions are known to the executive board of the company;

3. direct or indirect shareholdings in the capital exceeding 10 per cent of the voting rights;

4. the holders of shares with special rights conferring powers of control and a description of such special rights;

5. the nature of voting control where employees have an interest in the capital and do not exercise their control rights directly;

6. the legal regulations and regulations of the articles of association on the appointment and dismissal of members of the executive board and on amendments to the articles of association;

7. the powers of the executive board, in particular with regard to the possibility of issuing or buying back shares;

(continued)

8. wesentliche Vereinbarungen des Mutterunternehmens, die unter der Bedingung eines Kontrollwechsels infolge eines Übernahmeangebots stehen, und die hieraus folgenden Wirkungen;	8. material agreements of the parent company that are subject to a change of control as a result of a takeover bid and the effects resulting therefrom;
9. Entschädigungsvereinbarungen des Mutterunternehmens, die für den Fall eines Übernahmeangebots mit den Mitgliedern des Vorstands oder mit Arbeitnehmern getroffen sind.	9. compensation agreements of the parent company made with the members of the executive board or with employees in the event of a takeover bid.
Die Angaben nach Satz 1 Nummer 1, 3 und 9 können unterbleiben, soweit sie im Konzernanhang zu machen sind. Sind Angaben nach Satz 1 im Konzernanhang zu machen, ist im Konzernlagebericht darauf zu verweisen. Die Angaben nach Satz 1 Nummer 8 können unterbleiben, soweit sie geeignet sind, dem Mutterunternehmen einen erheblichen Nachteil zuzufügen; die Angabepflicht nach anderen gesetzlichen Vorschriften bleibt unberührt.	The disclosures pursuant to sentence 1 number 1, 3 and 9 may be omitted if they are to be made in the notes to the consolidated financial statements. If disclosures pursuant to sentence 1 are to be made in the notes to the consolidated financial statements, reference shall be made thereto in the group management report. The information pursuant to sentence 1 number 8 may be omitted insofar as it is likely to cause a significant disadvantage to the parent company; the disclosure obligation pursuant to other legal regulations shall remain unaffected.

§ 315b Pflicht zur nichtfinanziellen Konzernerklärung; Befreiungen	**§ 315b Obligation to make a non-financial group statement; exemptions**
(1) Eine Kapitalgesellschaft, die Mutterunternehmen (§ 290) ist, hat ihren Konzernlagebericht um eine nichtfinanzielle Konzernerklärung zu erweitern, wenn die folgenden Merkmale erfüllt sind:	(1) A corporation that is a parent company (§ 290) shall add a non-financial group statement to its group management report if the following characteristics are met:
1. die Kapitalgesellschaft ist kapitalmarktorientiert im Sinne des § 264d,	1. the corporation is capital-market oriented within the meaning of § 264d,
2. für die in den Konzernabschluss einzubeziehenden Unternehmen gilt:	2. to the companies to be included in the consolidated financial statements applies:
a) sie erfüllen die in § 293 Absatz 1 Satz 1 Nummer 1 oder 2 geregelten Voraussetzungen für eine größenabhängige Befreiung nicht und	a) they do not fulfil the conditions for size-dependent exemption set out in § 293 sect. 1 sent. 1 no. 1 or 2, and
b) bei ihnen sind insgesamt im Jahresdurchschnitt mehr als 500 Arbeitnehmer beschäftigt.	b) they employ a total of more than 500 workers on an annual average.

(continued)

§ 267 Absatz 4 bis 5 sowie § 298 Absatz 2 sind entsprechend anzuwenden. Wenn die nichtfinanzielle Konzernerklärung einen besonderen Abschnitt des Konzernlageberichts bildet, darf die Kapitalgesellschaft auf die an anderer Stelle im Konzernlagebericht enthaltenen nichtfinanziellen Angaben verweisen.	§ 267 sect. 4 to 5 and § 298 sect. 2 shall apply accordingly. If the non-financial group statement forms a special section of the group management report, the corporation may refer to the non-financial disclosures contained elsewhere in the group management report.
(2) Ein Mutterunternehmen im Sinne des Absatzes 1 ist unbeschadet anderer Befreiungsvorschriften von der Pflicht zur Erweiterung des Konzernlageberichts um eine nichtfinanzielle Konzernerklärung befreit, wenn	(2) A parent company within the meaning of section 1 shall, without prejudice to other exemption regulations, be exempted from the obligation to add a non-financial group statement to the group management report if
1. das Mutterunternehmen zugleich ein Tochterunternehmen ist, das in den Konzernlagebericht eines anderen Mutterunternehmens einbezogen ist, und	1. the parent company is also a subsidiary that is included in the group management report of another parent company, and
2. der Konzernlagebericht nach Nummer 1 nach Maßgabe des nationalen Rechts eines Mitgliedstaats der Europäischen Union oder eines anderen Vertragsstaats des Abkommens über den Europäischen Wirtschaftsraum im Einklang mit der Richtlinie 2013/34/EU aufgestellt wird und eine nichtfinanzielle Konzernerklärung enthält.	2. the group management report referred to in no. 1 is prepared in accordance with the national law of a member state of the European Union or of another contracting state to the Agreement on the European Economic Area in accordance with Directive 2013/34/EU and includes a non-financial group statement.
Satz 1 gilt entsprechend, wenn das andere Mutterunternehmen im Sinne des Satzes 1 einen gesonderten nichtfinanziellen Konzernbericht nach Absatz 3 oder nach Maßgabe des nationalen Rechts eines Mitgliedstaats der Europäischen Union oder eines anderen Vertragsstaats des Abkommens über den Europäischen Wirtschaftsraum im Einklang mit der Richtlinie 2013/34/EU erstellt und öffentlich zugänglich macht. Ist ein Mutterunternehmen nach Satz 1 oder 2 von der Pflicht zur Erstellung einer nichtfinanziellen Konzernerklärung befreit, hat es dies in seinem Konzernlagebericht mit der Erläuterung anzugeben, welches andere Mutterunternehmen den Konzernlagebericht oder den gesonderten nichtfinanziellen Konzernbericht öffentlich zugänglich macht und wo der Bericht in deutscher oder englischer Sprache offengelegt oder veröffentlicht ist.	Sentence 1 shall apply mutatis mutandis if the other parent company within the meaning of sentence 1 prepares and makes publicly available a separate non-financial group report in accordance with section 3 or in accordance with the national law of a member state of the European Union or of another contracting state to the Agreement on the European Economic Area in accordance with Directive 2013/34/EU. If a parent company is exempt from the obligation to prepare a non-financial group statement pursuant to sentence 1 or 2, it shall state this in its group management report with an explanation of which other parent company makes the group management report or the separate non-financial group report publicly available and where the report is disclosed or published in German or English.

(continued)

(3) Ein Mutterunternehmen im Sinne des Absatzes 1 ist auch dann von der Pflicht zur Erweiterung des Konzernlageberichts um eine nichtfinanzielle Konzernerklärung befreit, wenn das Mutterunternehmen für dasselbe Geschäftsjahr einen gesonderten nichtfinanziellen Konzernbericht außerhalb des Konzernlageberichts erstellt und folgende Voraussetzungen erfüllt:
1. der gesonderte nichtfinanzielle Konzernbericht erfüllt zumindest die inhaltlichen Vorgaben nach § 315c in Verbindung mit § 289c und
2. das Mutterunternehmen macht den gesonderten nichtfinanziellen Konzernbericht öffentlich zugänglich durch
   a) Offenlegung zusammen mit dem Konzernlagebericht nach § 325 oder
   b) Veröffentlichung auf der Internetseite des Mutterunternehmens spätestens vier Monate nach dem Abschlussstichtag und mindestens für zehn Jahre, sofern der Konzernlagebericht auf diese Veröffentlichung unter Angabe der Internetseite Bezug nimmt.

Absatz 1 Satz 3, die §§ 289d und 289e sowie § 298 Absatz 2 sind auf den gesonderten nichtfinanziellen Konzernbericht entsprechend anzuwenden.

(4) Ist die nichtfinanzielle Konzernerklärung oder der gesonderte nichtfinanzielle Konzernbericht inhaltlich überprüft worden, ist auch die Beurteilung des Prüfungsergebnisses in gleicher Weise wie die nichtfinanzielle Konzernerklärung oder der gesonderte nichtfinanzielle Konzernbericht öffentlich zugänglich zu machen.

§ 315c Inhalt der nichtfinanziellen Konzernerklärung

(1) Auf den Inhalt der nichtfinanziellen Konzernerklärung ist § 289c entsprechend anzuwenden.

(3) A parent company within the meaning of section 1 shall also be exempt from the obligation to add a non-financial group statement to the group management report if the parent company prepares a separate non-financial group report apart from the group management report for the same business year and meets the following requirements:
1. the separate non-financial group report fulfils at least the content requirements according to § 315c in conjunction with § 289c and
2. the parent company shall make the separate non-financial group report publicly available by
   a) disclosure together with the group management report pursuant to § 325 or
   b) publication on the parent company's website no later than four months after the balance sheet date and for at least ten years, provided that the group management report refers to this publication by indicating the website.

Section 1 sentence 3, §§ 289d and 289e as well as § 298 sect. 2 shall apply accordingly to the separate non-financial group report.

(4) If the content of the non-financial group statement or the separate non-financial group report has been audited, the assessment of the audit result shall also be made publicly available in the same way as the non-financial group statement or the separate non-financial group report.

§ 315c Content of the non-financial group statement

(1) § 289c shall apply mutatis mutandis to the content of the non-financial group statement.

(continued)

(2) § 289c Absatz 3 gilt mit der Maßgabe, dass diejenigen Angaben zu machen sind, die für das Verständnis des Geschäftsverlaufs, des Geschäftsergebnisses, der Lage des Konzerns sowie der Auswirkungen seiner Tätigkeit auf die in § 289c Absatz 2 genannten Aspekte erforderlich sind.	(2) § 289c sect. 3 shall apply, provided that such information shall be given as is necessary for an understanding of the development of the business, the results of the business, the position of the group and the effects of its activities on the aspects referred to in § 289c sect. 2.
(3) Die §§ 289d und 289e sind entsprechend anzuwenden.	(3) §§ 289d and 289e shall apply mutatis mutandis.
§ 315d Konzernerklärung zur Unternehmensführung	**§ 315d Corporate governance statement**
Ein Mutterunternehmen, das eine Gesellschaft im Sinne des § 289f Absatz 1 oder Absatz 3 ist, hat für den Konzern eine Erklärung zur Unternehmensführung zu erstellen und als gesonderten Abschnitt in den Konzernlagebericht aufzunehmen. § 289f ist entsprechend anzuwenden.	A parent company that is a company within the meaning of § 289f sect. 1 or sect. 3 shall prepare a corporate governance statement for the group and include it as a separate section in the group management report. § 289f shall be applied accordingly.
Zehnter Titel Konzernabschluss nach internationalen Rechnungslegungsstandards	**Tenth title Consolidated financial statements according to international accounting standards**
§ 315e [Konzernabschluss nach internationalen Rechnungslegungsstandards]	**§ 315e [Consolidated financial statements according to international accounting standards]**
(1) Ist ein Mutterunternehmen, das nach den Vorschriften des Ersten Titels einen Konzernabschluss aufzustellen hat, nach Artikel 4 der Verordnung (EG) Nr. 1606/2002 des Europäischen Parlaments und des Rates vom 19. Juli 2002 in der jeweils geltenden Fassung verpflichtet, die nach den Artikeln 2, 3 und 6 der genannten Verordnung übernommenen internationalen Rechnungslegungsstandards anzuwenden, so sind von den Vorschriften des Zweiten bis Achten Titels nur § 294 Abs. 3, § 297 Absatz 1a, 2 Satz 4, § 298 Abs. 1, dieser jedoch nur in Verbindung mit den §§ 244 und 245, ferner § 313 Abs. 2 und 3, § 314 Abs. 1 Nr. 4, 6, 8 und 9, Absatz 3 sowie die Bestimmungen des Neunten Titels und die Vorschriften außerhalb dieses Unterabschnitts, die den Konzernabschluss oder den Konzernlagebericht betreffen, entsprechend anzuwenden.	(1) Where a parent company that shall prepare consolidated financial statements in accordance with the provisions of the First Title is required in accordance with Article 4 of Regulation (EC) No. 1606/2002 of the European Parliament and of the Council of 19 July 2002, as amended, to apply the international accounting standards adopted in accordance with Articles 2, 3 and 6 of the said regulation, only § 294 sect. 3, § 297 sect. 1a, 2 sent. 4, § 298 sect. 1, but this only in conjunction with §§ 244 and 245, as well as § 313 sect. 2 and 3, § 314 sect. 1 nos. 4, 6, 8 and 9, sect. 3, as well as the regulations of the Ninth Title and the regulations outside this subsection concerning the consolidated financial statements or the group management report shall apply accordingly.

(continued)

(2) Mutterunternehmen, die nicht unter Absatz 1 fallen, haben ihren Konzernabschluss nach den dort genannten internationalen Rechnungslegungsstandards und Vorschriften aufzustellen, wenn für sie bis zum jeweiligen Bilanzstichtag die Zulassung eines Wertpapiers im Sinne des § 2 Absatz 1 des Wertpapierhandelsgesetzes zum Handel an einem organisierten Markt im Sinne des § 2 Absatz 11 des Wertpapierhandelsgesetzes im Inland beantragt worden ist.	(2) Parent companies not covered by section 1 shall prepare their consolidated financial statements in accordance with the international accounting standards and regulations referred to therein if an application for the admission of a security within the meaning of § 2 sect. 1 of the Securities Trading Act (Wertpapierhandelsgesetz) to trading on an organized market within the meaning of § 2 sect. 11 of the Securities Trading Act in Germany has been filed for them by the respective balance sheet date.
(3) Mutterunternehmen, die nicht unter Absatz 1 oder 2 fallen, dürfen ihren Konzernabschluss nach den in Absatz 1 genannten internationalen Rechnungslegungsstandards und Vorschriften aufstellen. Ein Unternehmen, das von diesem Wahlrecht Gebrauch macht, hat die in Absatz 1 genannten Standards und Vorschriften vollständig zu befolgen.	(3) Parent companies not covered by sections 1 or 2 may prepare their consolidated financial statements in accordance with the international accounting standards and rules referred to in section 1. A company which exercises this option shall comply fully with the standards and regulations referred to in section 1.

9 Glossary

Account	Summary of similar transactions in a format with two columns; the left side is called the debit side, the right side the credit side.
Acquisition costs	Measure for the initial measurement of acquired assets (§ 255 sect. 1). Acquisition costs are calculated as follows:
	Purchase price or consideration
	− Price reductions
	+ Incidental acquisition costs
	= Initial acquisition costs
	+ Subsequent acquisition costs
	= Total acquisition costs
	All costs must be direct costs. No imputed costs are included. The acquisition process is completed when the asset is ready for operation.
Accruals	Income and expense that have already occurred must be accrued independently of a payment. To do so, in the balance sheet, accrued liabilities and assets are recognized.
Amortization	Depreciation of an intangible or financial asset. See depreciation.
Asset	The abstract recognition criteria are:
	− The asset must provide an economic benefit.
	− The asset must be measurable separately from other assets.
	− The asset must be separately marketable.
	All three criteria must be fulfilled.
	The specific recognition criteria are:
	− Economic ownership: The reporting entity must own the asset economically, i.e. it must be able to use the asset and it must bear the majority of risks and opportunities of using the asset (including possible sales proceeds and changes in value).
	− For proprietorships/partnerships: Distinction between assets of business and private assets of owner.
	− Specific legal rules such as requirements, prohibitions or options for recognition.
Balance sheet	Summary of all assets and liabilities at a specific point in time in a format that uses two columns; on the left side (the debit side) assets are reported, on the right side (the credit side) liabilities and equity. Total assets must always equal total equity and liabilities. For corporations, German GAAP prescribes a detailed structure of the balance sheet (§ 266).
Cash flow	Change in cash and cash equivalents (or: liquid funds); a cash inflow increases cash and cash equivalents, whereas a cash outflow decreases them.

https://doi.org/10.1515/9783110744170-009

Cash flow statement	Presentation of all cash flows in a certain format. According to DRS 21 structured in – cash flow from operating activities, – cash flow from investing activities and – cash flow from financing activities. A cash flow statement is mandatory for consolidated financial statements and for the individual financial statements of capital-market-oriented companies if they do not prepare consolidated financial statements.
Changes-in-equity statement	Presentation of changes in equity in a specific format: The development from opening balance to closing balance must be presented for all line items of equity (DRS 22). The changes-in-equity statement is mandatory for consolidated financial statements.
Completed contract	The only revenue recognition concept that is acceptable according to German GAAP; this means for a typical sale/purchase transaction: – A contract exists, – the goods have been supplied or delivered or the services have been rendered, – the transfer of risks has occurred, in particular of the risk of accidental loss and – any additional condition to request remuneration has been fulfilled.
Consolidated financial statements	Groups that are controlled by a parent company must prepare consolidated financial statements presenting the group as if it were only one entity (§ 290). Small groups are excluded from this obligation (§ 293). Consolidated financial statements consist of (§ 297) – a balance sheet, – an income statement, – notes, – a changes-in-equity statement and – a cash flow statement.
Consolidation procedures	German GAAP provides three ways in which companies can be included the consolidated financial statements: Full consolidation for subsidiaries (that are controlled); this includes capital, liability, income consolidation and consolidation of intercompany profits; Proportional consolidation for joint ventures; At-equity consolidation for participations.
Consolidation scope	The companies that are included in consolidated financial statements (parent company and subsidiaries).

Contingent liabilities	Liabilities that represent a legal obligation but that are currently not probable. Contingent liabilities may not be recognized in the balance sheet but must be reported additionally ("below the balance sheet" (§ 251)); corporations may report them in notes (§ 268 sect. 8 and § 285 no. 27).
Credit/crediting	The right column of an account or a balance sheet is the credit side. Doing an entry on the credit side is called crediting.
Current assets	All assets that are not classified as non-current. Typically, current assets are short term (up to 1 year).
Debit/debiting	The left column of an account or a balance sheet is the debit side. Doing an entry on the debit side is called debiting.
Deferrals	Income and expense that will occur in a defined future time period, but that have been paid or invoiced already, must be recognized as deferred income or expense in the balance sheet (§ 250).
Depreciation	Predictable loss of value of a tangible non-current asset. Because a non-current asset is typically used for several years (i.e. has a definite useful life), its loss of value is reflected by depreciation to the extent it is predictable. A depreciation is an expense but not a cash flow. Depreciation is mandatory under the Commercial Code but may only be based on acquisition or production costs (not on replacement costs or other imputed costs). The Commercial Code requires a depreciation schedule, i.e. a planned and systematic approach, but does not prescribe a specific depreciation method.
Equity	Also called net assets From an accounting perspective it is the residual of assets and liabilities. From a legal perspective it corresponds to the claims of the shareholders of the company.
Expense	A decrease in net assets (or: equity) is called an expense; the recognition of expenses is independent of a past or future payment. Only imputed values that will never lead to a payment may not be included in expenses.
Financial statements	The final result of accounting at the closing date are the financial statements. They consist of a balance sheet and income statement (§ 242). Corporations must add notes (§ 264 sect. 1). Groups must prepare consolidated financial statements (see there, §§ 290).

GAAP	Generally Accepted Accounting Principles In this book, this refers to the underlying principles of accounting, most of which are codified by the Commercial Code, but some are best practice and common understanding. They can be divided into – principles of documentation (focusing on current bookkeeping) and – principles of accounting (focusing on financial statements). If the entirety of legal and other sources that constitute German accounting is referred to, the term *German GAAP* is used in this book.
German GAAP	German generally accepted accounting principles include all laws and other sources that define the accounting for German companies. The central law is the Commercial Code, but there are many other sources such as other laws, court decisions, best practices and underlying principles.
Higher-of-cost-or-market principle	Application of the principle of prudence to the subsequent measurement of liabilities: Compare the initial settlement amount with the current fair value and take the higher one.
Impairment	Decrease in value of an asset that exceeds the regular depreciation/amortization. Depending on the different variants of the lower-of-cost-or-market principle, impairments are mandatory, optional or prohibited.
Imparity principle	Subprinciple of principle of prudence which states that expenses/losses must be recognized when they become probable, even if unrealized (§ 252 sect. 1 no. 4).
Income	An increase in net assets (or: equity) is called income; the recognition of income is independent of a past or future payment. Only imputed values that will never lead to a payment may not be included in income.
Income statement	Presentation of all income and expenses from a reporting period ending with the net result of the period. From an accounting perspective, the income statement is a subledger of equity, and therefore income is recognized as a credit entry, whereas an expense is recognized as a debit entry. Corporations must apply one of two specific formats: total-cost format or cost-of-sales format (§ 275).
Journal entry	The specific form in which a transaction is recorded in the accounting is called a journal entry. It has at least one debit entry and at least one credit entry. A journal entry must always balance; otherwise, the fundamental accounting equation (assets = equity + liabilities) is violated.

Liability	The abstract recognition criteria are as follows: – There must be an obligation (legal or constructive). – It must be an economic burden to fulfil the obligation and the fulfillment must be probable. – The economic burden must be quantifiable. All three criteria must be fulfilled. The one who accepts the obligation must report the liability. Liabilities comprise provisions (uncertain liabilities) and debt or payables (certain liabilities).
Lower-of-cost-or-market principle	Application of the principle of prudence to the subsequent measurement of assets: Compare the initial (amortized) acquisition or production costs with the current fair value and take the lower one (§ 253 sect. 3 and 4). Moderate lower-of-cost-or-market principle: must be applied for non-current assets. Only **permanent** decreases in value are a reason for an impairment. There is an **impairment option** for non-current financial assets in case of a temporary decrease in value (§ 253 sect. 3). Strict lower-of-cost-or-market principle: must be applied for current assets. Any decrease in value must be impaired (§ 253 sect. 4).
Management report	Corporations must prepare a management report in addition to financial statements (§ 264). The management report must provide a verbal description of the business in general, the course of business in the reporting period, the current situation and expected future developments (§ 289; DRS 20).
Measurement	If for a specific transaction it was decided to recognize an asset or liability, the next issue concerns measurement, i.e. at what value will the asset or liability be included in the financial statements. Initial measurement refers to the value of an asset or liability when it is included the first time in the balance sheet. Subsequent measurement refers to the value of an asset or liability at a subsequent closing date.
Non-current assets	All assets that are intended to serve the business continuously (§ 247 sect. 2). Typically, non-current assets are long term (i.e. will be used more than 1 year).
Notes	Corporations must add notes to the financial statements (§ 264). Their purpose is to – make the interpretation of the financial statements easier, – correct the financial statements if necessary, – relieve the information burden in the balance sheet and income statement, – furnish additional information not included in the balance sheet and income statement.

One-entity theory	Fundamental theory for the preparation of consolidated financial statements: The financial statements for the group that is consolidated must be prepared as if the group were a single legal entity (§ 297 sect. 3).
Presentation	Deciding about the way in which specific information is given in the financial statements. Presentation is typically the last decision for a specific transaction (after recognition and measurement).
Present value	Method for initial measurement of an annuity charge, i.e. an obligation to regularly pay a certain amount of money for a certain period of time. It is calculated by discounting future payments.
Principle of prudence	Dominant principle of GAAP; states that all predictable risks and chances must be taken into account (§ 252 sect. 1 no. 4). Derived principles: realization principle and imparity principle.
Production costs	Measure for initial measurement of produced (internally generated) assets (§ 255 sect. 2, 2a and 3). The production costs are calculated as follows: Direct material costs + Direct manufacturing costs + Special direct manufacturing costs + Indirect material costs + Indirect manufacturing costs + Adequate part of depreciation/amortization = Mandatory components of production costs + **Adequate part of general administration** + Adequate part of voluntary social benefits + Adequate part of voluntary pension scheme + Borrowing costs (only if directly related to production process) = **Maximum of production costs** The options can be used only in an identical way for commercial and tax purposes. Any indirect costs must constitute an adequate part related to the specific production process, i.e. without impairment, idle time costs or extraordinary items. Distribution costs, research costs or imputed costs may not be included.
Provisions	Liabilities that are uncertain concerning the reason for the liability or the amount necessary to fulfil the obligation are called provisions. If pending transactions become disadvantageous and will probably result in a loss, a provision for onerous contracts must be recognized. A specific topic in German GAAP are the provisions for omitted maintenance and removal of overburden that must be recognized under certain conditions.
Realization principle	Subprinciple of principle of prudence which states that any income/gain can be recognized only when it is realized (§ 252 sect. 1 no. 4). Realization criteria follow the completed contract method (see there).

Recognition	Including a transaction as an asset or liability in the balance sheet is called recognizing the transaction.
	It is the first step in deciding about the accounting for a specific transaction. The subsequent steps are decisions about the measurement and presentation of the transaction.
Settlement amount	Measure for initial measurement of liabilities. The amount that is required to fulfil the obligation.

10 Vocabulary

Account	Konto
Account system	Kontenrahmen
Accounting	Buchhaltung/Rechnungswesen
Accountability	Rechenschaft
(to be held accountable for something)	(für etwas Rechenschaft ablegen)
(Trade) Accounts receivable	Forderungen (aus Lieferung und Leistung)
(Trade) Accounts payable	Verbindlichkeiten (aus Lieferung und Leistung)
Accrual	Antizipativer Posten (s.u.)
Accrued expenses	Antizipative Rechnungsabgrenzung in den sonstigen Verbindlichkeiten (wörtlich: aufgelaufene Aufwendungen)
Accrued income	Antizipative Rechnungsabgrenzung in den sonstigen Forderungen (wörtlich: aufgelaufene Erträge)
Accumulated profit (-loss) also: retained earnings	Bilanzgewinn (-verlust)
Acquisition costs	Anschaffungskosten
Affiliated company	Verbundenes Unternehmen
Aggregated balance sheet	Summenbilanz
Amortization	Planmäßige Abschreibung von immateriellen oder finanziellen Vermögensgegenständen
Amortized (depreciated) cost	Fortgeführte Anschaffungs- oder Herstellungs-kosten (Anschaffungs- oder Herstellungskosten vermindert um planmäßige Abschreibungen)
Asset	Vermögensgegenstand
Asset and liability accounts	Bestandskonten
Asset ceiling	Obergrenze für die Bewertung von
(acquisition or production cost as asset ceiling)	Vermögensgegenständen (Anschaffungs- oder Herstellungskosten als Obergrenze für Vermögensgegenstände)
Asset or liability account	(aktives oder passives) Bestandskonto
Asset position	Vermögenslage
(asset, financial and income position)	(Vermögens-, Finanz- und Ertragslage)
Advance payment also: down payment	Anzahlung

Balance	Saldo
Balance sheet IFRS: statement of financial position	Bilanz
Balance sheet contraction	Bilanzverkürzung
Balance sheet date also: closing date	Bilanzstichtag, Abschlussstichtag
Balance sheet extension	Bilanzverlängerung
Balance sheet item	Bilanzposten
Bank debt	Bankverbindlichkeiten
Booking journal	Buchungsjournal (Grundbuch)
Bookkeeping double-entry bookkeeping	(laufende) Buchführung doppelte Buchführung

https://doi.org/10.1515/9783110744170-010

Book value	Buchwert
also: carrying amount	Restbuchwert
remaining book value	
Bond	Anleihe
convertible bond	Wandelanleihe
option bond	Optionsanleihe
Borrowing costs (as part of the production costs), also: interest costs	Fremdkapitalkosten (als Teil der Herstellungskosten)

(Not) Called-up capital	(Nicht) Eingefordertes Kapital
To cancel	stornieren
Cancellation	Storno
Capital-market oriented	Kapitalmarktorientiert
Capital reserves	Kapitalrücklagen
Cash and cash equivalents	Zahlungsmittel (Bilanzposten)
Cash flow	Zahlungs(mittel)fluss
Cash inflow	Zahlungs(mittel)zufluss
Cash outflow	Zahlungs(mittel)abfluss
Cash flow statement	Kapitalflussrechnung
Change (increase/decrease) in inventory of finished and unfinished products	Bestandsveränderung (-zunahme/-abnahme) der fertigen und unfertigen Erzeugnisse
Changes-in-equity statement	Eigenkapitalspiegel
Chart of accounts	Kontenplan
To close an account	Ein Konto abschließen
Closing balance	Endbestand
Closing balance sheet	Schlussbilanz
Consolidation	Konsolidierung
at equity	at equity
full	Voll-
proportional (also: proportionate)	Quoten-
capital	Kapital-
liability	Schulden-
income	Ertrags-
of intercompany profits	Zwischengewinneliminierung
Constant-value approach	Festwertansatz
Contingent asset	Eventualforderung
Contingent liability	Eventualverbindlichkeit
Contribution	Einlage
Corporation	Kapitalgesellschaft
Corporation tax	Körperschaftsteuer
Cost formula	Bewertungsvereinfachungen (im Vorratsvermögen)
Cost-of-sales format	Umsatzkostenverfahren
Costs	Kosten
Credit (right side of an account)	Haben (rechte Seite eines Kontos)
Credit balance	Habensaldo
Credit note	Gutschrift (Gutschrift für den Geschäftspartner)
Creditor protection	Gläubigerschutz
Current assets	Umlaufvermögen

Current taxes	Laufende (zu zahlende) Steuern
Current tax assets/liabilities	(Laufende) Steuerforderungen/-verbindlichkeiten
Current tax expense/income	(Laufender) Steueraufwand/-ertrag
Debit (left side of an account)	Soll (linke Seite eines Kontos)
Debit balance	Sollsaldo
Debit note	Lastschrift (Belastung des Geschäftspartners)
Debt	Verbindlichkeit
also: account payable	
Declining balance depreciation	Degressive Abschreibung
Deferral	Transitorischer Posten (s.u.)
Deferred expense	Aktiver Rechungsabgrenzungsposten
also: Prepaid expense	
Deferred income	Passiver Rechnungsabgrenzungsposten
also: prepaid income, unearned revenue (am.)	
Deferred tax asset (liability)	Aktive (passive) latente Steuer
Depreciation	Planmäßige Abschreibung (von Sachanlagen)
Development expenses	Entwicklungsaufwendungen
Direct costs	Einzelkosten
Disclosure	Veröffentlichung
also: publication	
To discount a liability/a provision/a debt	Eine Schuld/eine Rückstellung/eine Verbindlichkeit abzinsen
Dividend	Dividende
Doubtful receivable	Zweifelhafte Forderung
Dunning notice	Mahnbescheid
Dunning process	Mahnwesen/-prozess
Economic ownership	Wirtschaftliches Eigentum
(Accounting/bookkeeping) entry	Buchung
also: posting	
initial entry	Einbuchung
counter-entry	Gegenbuchung
Equity	Eigenkapital
Exchange on asset side	Aktivtausch
also: asset swap	
Exchange on liability side	Passivtausch
also: liability swap	
Excise tax	Verbrauchsteuer
Expenditure	Ausgabe (in der Abgrenzung zu Auszahlung und Aufwand)
Expense	Aufwand
External accounting	Externes Rechnungswesen
also: statutory accounting	
Fair value	Beizulegender Wert ggf. Marktwert
Financial assets	Finanzielle Vermögensgegenstände

Financial position	Finanzlage
(asset, financial and income position)	(Vermögens-, Finanz- und Ertragslage)
Financial result	Finanzergebnis
Financial statements	Jahresabschluss
individual financial statements	Einzelabschluss
consolidated financial statements	Konzernabschluss
Financial year	Geschäftsjahr
also: fiscal year, business year	
short financial year	Rumpfgeschäftsjahr

Gain (a part of income)	Gewinn (als Teil des Ertrags)
General ledger	Hauptbuch
Generally accepted accounting principles	Grundsätze ordnungsmäßiger Buchführung und Bilanzierung
Commercial Code	Handelsgesetzbuch
Goodwill	Geschäfts- oder Firmenwert
Group (of companies)	Konzern
Group assessment	Gruppenbewertung

Hidden reserves	Stille Reserven (Rücklagen)
Higher-of-cost-or-market principle	Höchstwertprinzip

Imputed costs	Kalkulatorische Kosten
Measurement differences	Anderskosten
Additional costs	Zusatzkosten
Impairment (loss)	Außerplanmäßige Abschreibung
Imparity principle	Imparitätsprinzip
Incidental acquisition costs	Anschaffungsnebenkosten
Income	Ertrag
also: revenue (Am.)	
Income and expense accounts	Erfolgskonten
Income position	Ertragslage
(asset, financial and income position)	(Vermögens-, Finanz- und Ertragslage)
Income statement (I/S)	Gewinn- und Verlustrechnung
also: profit and loss statement (P&L, US GAAP)	
Indirect cost	Gemeinkosten
Individual measurement	Einzelbewertung
Input tax	Vorsteuer
also: paid VAT	
Initial measurement	Zugangsbewertung
Intangible asset	Immaterieller Vermögensgegenstand
also: immaterial asset	
Interest expense/income	Zinsaufwand (-ertrag)
Internal accounting	Internes Rechnungswesen
also: managerial accounting	
Internally generated	selbsterstellt
Inventory	Inventar (Verzeichnis aller Vermögensgegenstände)
Inventories	Vorräte

Journal	Journal, Grundbuch
Journal entry	Buchungssatz
also: Posting record, booking record	
To journalize	(Im Grundbuch) verbuchen (journalisieren)

Legal ownership	Rechtliches Eigentum
Lessee	Leasingnehmer
Lessor	Leasinggeber
Liabilities (comprises provisions and debt)	Schulden (umfasst Rückstellungen und Verbindlichkeiten)
Linear depreciation	Lineare Abschreibung
also: straight-line depreciation	
Liquidity	Liquidität
Loan	Kredit (Darlehen)
Loss	Verlust
Loss carry forward	Verlustvortrag
Lower-of-cost-or-market principle	Niederstwertprinzip
Low-value assets	Geringwertige Wirtschaftsgüter

Management report	Lagebericht
Matching principle	Prinzip der periodengerechten Gewinnermittlung
Material	Wesentlich
Materiality	Wesentlichkeit
Materials	Roh-, Hilfs- und Betriebsstoffe
Measurement (of assets and liabilities)	Bewertung (von Vermögensgegenständen und
also: valuation	Schulden)
Measurement of payments	Zahlungsbemessung
Merchant	(Einzel-)Kaufmann

Net assets	Nettovermögen (auch Reinvermögen)
Net financial assets	Nettofinanzvermögen
Net loss	Jahresfehlbetrag/Verlust
Net profit	Jahresüberschuss/Gewinn
also: net result, net income (am.)	
Non-current asset	Anlagevermögen
also: fixed asset	
Non-operating expense	Sachzweckfremder (nicht betriebszielorientierter) Aufwand
Non-operating income	Sachzweckfremder (nicht betriebszielorientierter) Ertrag
Non-period related expense	Periodenfremder Aufwand
also: prior period expense	
Non-period related income	Periodenfremder Ertrag
also: prior period income	
Notes	Anhang

Obligation	Verpflichtung
legal obligation	rechtliche Verpflichtung
constructive obligation	faktische Verpflichtung
continuing obligation	Dauerschuldverhältnis

Onerous contract	Belastender Vertrag
One-entity theory (consolidated financial statements)	Einheitstheorie (Konzernabschluss)
Opening balance	Anfangsbestand
Opening balance sheet	Eröffnungsbilanz
Operating expense	Zweckaufwand (Betriebsaufwand)
Operating result	Betriebsergebnis Betriebsgewinn Betriebsverlust
also: operating profit operating loss	
Other operating expense	Sonstiger betrieblicher Aufwand
Other operating income	Sonstiger betrieblicher Ertrag
(Other) own work capitalized	(Andere) aktivierte Eigenleistung
Outpayment amount	Auszahlungsbetrag
also: disbursement amount	
Output	Leistung (als Gegenstück zu Kosten)
Owner's account	Privatkonto
Own use	Eigenverbrauch

Parent company (of a group)	Mutterunternehmen (eines Konzerns)
Participation	Beteiligung
Partnership	Personengesellschaft
Pending transaction	Schwebendes Geschäft
also: executory contract	
Permanent stock taking	Permanente Inventur
Plan assets	Planvermögen
Post a transaction to accounts	Einen Geschäftsvorfall auf Konten verbuchen
also: record a transaction	
Presentation (of assets and liabilities)	Ausweis (von Vermögensgegenständen und Schulden)
Present value	Barwert
Preparation of financial statements	Erstellung des Jahresabschlusses
Pre- or post-termination stock taking	Vor- oder nachverlagerte Inventur
Principle of congruence	Maßgeblichkeitsprinzip
Principle of prudence	Vorsichtsprinzip
Proceeds	Einnahmen (in der Abgrenzung zu Einzahlung und Ertrag)
Procurement	Beschaffung/Einkauf
Procurement market	Beschaffungsmarkt
Production cost	Herstellungskosten
Profit carry forward	Gewinnvortrag
Profit distribution (to shareholders)	Gewinnverteilung (an Gesellschafter)
Profit use	Gewinnverwendung
(Sole) Proprietorship	Einzelunternehmen
Provision	Rückstellung
Provision for omitted maintenance (removal of overburden)	Rückstellung für unterlassene Instandhaltung (Abraumbeseitigung)
Provision for onerous contracts	Rückstellung für drohende Verluste aus schwebenden Geschäften
Provision for uncertain liabilities	Rückstellung für unsichere Verbindlichkeiten

Raw material	Rohstoffe
Realization principle	Realizationsprinzip
Recognition (of assets and liabilities)	Ansatz (von Vermögensgegenständen und Schulden)
Related party	Nahestehende Person oder Unternehmen
Related-party transaction	Geschäftsvorfall mit nahestehenden Personen oder Unternehmen
Remuneration also: consideration	Entgelt
Repayment amount also: redemption amount	Rückzahlungsbetrag
Reporting	Bericht/Berichtswesen
Reporting entity also: reporting unit	Berichtseinheit
Reporting period	Berichtszeitraum
Research expense	Forschungsaufwendungen
Reserve	Rücklage
Restricted reserves	Gesetzliche Rücklagen
Result from ordinary activities also: earnings before taxes (EBT)	Ergebnis der gewöhnlichen Geschäftstätigkeit Ergebnis vor Steuern
Retained earnings	Bilanzgewinn
Retention period	Aufbewahrungsfrist
Revenue reserves	Gewinnrücklagen
Reversal of an impairment	Zuschreibung
Sales revenue	Umsatzerlöse
Security	Wertpapier
Self-produced also: self-created, internally generated	selbsterstellt
Sequence of consumption	Verbrauchsfolge
Settlement amount	Erfüllungsbetrag
Special direct cost (of production, of sales)	Sondereinzelkosten (der Fertigung, des Vertriebs)
Special ledger	Nebenbuch
(To) split the balance sheet (in accounts)	Die Bilanz auflösen (in Konten)
Statutory reserves	Satzungsmäßige Rücklagen
Stock taking also: keeping physical inventory	Inventur
Subaccount	Unterkonto
Subscribed capital	Gezeichnetes Kapital
Subsequent acquisition costs	Nachträgliche Anschaffungskosten
Subsequent event also: event after reporting period	Nachträgliche Ereignisse (im Sinne von Wertbegründung)
Subsequent measurement	Folgebewertung
Subsequent production costs	Nachträgliche Herstellungskosten
Subsidiary (of a group)	Tochterunternehmen (eines Konzerns)
Subsidiary ledger	Nebenbuch
System of accounts	Kontenrahmen

Tangible assets also: property, plant and equipment	Sachanlagen
Tax deductible	Steuerlich abzugsfähig
Tax loss carry forward	Steuerlicher Verlustvortrag
Taxable profit/loss	Steuerlicher Gewinn / Verlust
Tax payable	Steuerverbindlichkeit, Zahllast
Temporary difference (as basis for deferred taxes)	Temporäre Differenz (als Grundlage für latente Steuern)
Total-cost format	Gesamtkostenverfahren
Trade payable	Verbindlichkeit aus Lieferung und Leistung
Trade receivable	Forderung aus Lieferung und Leistung
Trade tax	Gewerbesteuer
Trial balance	Vorläufige Bilanz (ohne Abschlussbuchungen)
"True and fair view"	"Ein den tatsächlichen Verhältnissen entsprechendes Bild"
Useful life (of an asset) also: economic life	Nutzungsdauer (eines Vermögensgegenstands)

Valuation allowance
  specific valuation allowance
  general valuation allowance
	Wertberichtigung (auf Forderungen)
	  Einzelwertberichtigung
	  Pauschalwertberichtigung

Value-added tax (VAT)	Umsatzsteuer (USt.), auch Mehrwertsteuer
Value clarification	Wertaufhellung
Voucher	Buchungsbeleg

Voucher principle
  (no posting without voucher)
	Belegprinzip
	  (keine Buchung ohne Beleg)

Withdrawal	Entnahme

Literature

Legal sources

Handelsgesetzbuch, last change from 3 June 2021

Aktiengesetz, last change from 3 June 2021

BMF-Schreiben as of 19.04.1971, IV B/2-S2170-31/71

BMF-Schreiben as of 22.12.1975, IV B/2-S2170-161/75

BMF-Schreiben as of 23.12.1991, IV B/2-S2170-115/91

Einkommensteuergesetz, last change from 20 August 2021

Gesetz betreffend die Gesellschaften mit beschränkter Haftung, last change from 3 June 2021

Umsatzsteuergesetz, last change from 3 June 2021

Gesetz zur Stärkung der nichtfinanziellen Berichterstattung der Unternehmen in ihren Lage- und Konzernlageberichten (CSR-Richtlinie-Umsetzungsgesetz) as of 11 April 2017, Bundesgesetzblatt Teil I no. 20, p. 802

All IAS and IFRS as enacted in June 2021

Directive 2014/95/EU of the European parliament and of the council of 22 October 2014

Incoterms 2010, International Chamber of Commerce, 2010

Commentaries and textbooks

Bacher, Urban: *Bilanzierung, Investition und Finanzierung: Gesamtdarstellung mit praxisnahen Übungsfällen: Jahresabschluss, Investitionsplanung, Finanzierung und Finanzanalyse*, 10th ed., NWB-Verlag, 2019

Beisheim, Carsten: CSR-Compliance: Neue Herausforderungen im Reporting, in: Schulz et al., *Compliance Management im Unternehmen*, dfv Mediengruppe, 2016

Beck'scher Bilanzkommentar, 12th ed., Verlag C. H. Beck, 2020

Coenenberg/Haller/Schultze: *Jahresabschluss und Jahresabschlussanalyse*, 26th ed., Schäffer Poeschel Verlag, 2021 referred to as: Coenenberg et al., 2021 (1)

Coenenberg/Haller/Mattner/Schultze: *Einführung in das Rechnungswesen*, 8th ed., Schäffer Poeschel Verlag, 2021 referred to as: Coenenberg et al., 2021 (2)

Hayn/Waldersee: *IFRS und HGB im Vergleich*, 8th ed., Schäffer Poeschel Verlag, 2014

IDW, *IDW Verlautbarungen*, IDW-Verlag, Stand August 2021

Jung, Hans: *Allgemeine Betriebswirtschaftslehre*, 13th ed. DeGruyter Oldenburg, 2016

Muykanovic, Robin: *Leasing in Handels- und Steuerbilanz*, nwb Datenbank (DokID AAAAE-68318), 2014

Nothhelfer/Bacher/Rade/Scholz: *Klausurtraining für Bilanzierung und Finanzwirtschaft*, DeGruyter Oldenbourg, 2015

Weygandt/Kimmel/Kieso: *Financial accounting – IFRS edition*, 3rd ed., Wiley, 2015

Wöhe/Döring: *Einführung in die allgemeine Betriebswirtschaftslehre*, 27th ed. Vahlen, 2020

https://doi.org/10.1515/9783110744170-011

About the author

Prof. Dr. Robert Nothhelfer holds a degree in economics from the University of Freiburg, Germany. His doctoral thesis involved the development of models for learning in organizations. After working many years for Lidl in the retail industry and for the Schwarz-Group, he has taught business administration at the University of Applied Sciences in Pforzheim since 2014. He focuses on finance and accounting as well as compliance and sustainability management. On a part-time basis, he provides consulting services as a monitoring trustee in a partnership with his brother Dr. Wolfgang Nothhelfer (www.noconpartners.com).

https://doi.org/10.1515/9783110744170-012

Index

https://doi.org/10.1515/9783110744170-013

www.ingramcontent.com/pod-product-compliance
Lightning Source LLC
Chambersburg PA
CBHW061742210326
41599CB00034B/6766